10/11

RED–SPOTTED OX
a Pokot Life

As collected, translated and edited by
Pat Robbins

IWGIA Document 124
Copenhagen 2010

RED-SPOTTED OX
A Pokot Life

Author: Pat Robbins
Copyright: The author and IWGIA — 2010 — All Rights Reserved
Editorial Production: Marianne Wiben Jensen
Cover and layout: Jorge Monrás
Proofreading: Diana Vinding
Prepress and Print: Eks-Skolens Trykkeri, Copenhagen, Denmark
ISBN: 978-87-91563-70-6
ISSN: 0105-4503

HURIDOCS CIP DATA

Title: Red-Spotted Ox — A Pokot Life
Editor: Robbins, Pat
Corporate editor: IWGIA
Place of publication: Copenhagen, Denmark
Publisher: IWGIA
Distributors:
Europe: IWGIA, Classensgade 11E, DK Copenhagen 2100—www.iwgia.org
North America: Transaction Publishers, 390 Campus Drive, Somerset,
New Jersey 08873—www.transactionpub.com
Date of Publication: 2010
Pages: 396 p. — ill. — map
Reference to series: IWGIA Document Series, no. 124
Note: Autobiography of a Pokot pastoralist
ISBN: 978-87-91563-70-6
ISSN: 0105-4503
Language: English
Bibliography: Yes
Index terms: Indigenous peoples/Pastoralists/Pokot/traditions/changes
Geographical area: East Africa (Kenya and Uganda)
Geographical code: 5200

**INTERNATIONAL WORK GROUP
FOR INDIGENOUS AFFAIRS**
Classensgade 11 E, DK 2100 - Copenhagen, Denmark
Tel: (45) 35 27 05 00 - Fax: (45) 35 27 05 07
E-mail: iwgia@iwgia.org - Web: www.iwgia.org

IWGIA

In memory of my beloved mother, Martha, who believed in me.
For Larry, my cherished companion in Africa and in life.

CONTENTS

DIAGRAMS, MAPS, CHARTS

SONGS

Languages: Pokot (P), Karamojong (K), Turkana (T), Swahili (S)
The context and use of each song is indicated.

FOREWORD

FOREWORD

*R*ed-Spotted Ox—A Pokot Life is in many respects a remarkable publication.
First of all, it is the autobiography of an indigenous Pokot man, Domonguria, whose life was spent near the Kenya-Uganda border in East Africa. From one
individual's perspective, Domonguria's, as told to Pat Robbins in the early 1970s,
this book deals with the Pokot and their ways of life. Today, oral histories of indigenous peoples are being gathered all over the world, including Africa, and are
used as important tools in indigenous land claims.[1] This, however, was far from
being the case forty years ago, when testimonies by indigenous peoples at best
were used as quotes in anthropological works. Recording Domonguria's words
with the ultimate view of publishing them as a book was thus an unusual approach and—as it turned out—a great endeavour.

When Pat Robbins began working with Domonguria, she was a young woman in her early twenties, freshly arrived from the USA and accompanying her
husband and an archaeological team in their investigation of Stone Age sites in
the Rift Valley of Kenya and in the Kadam area of Karamoja District in north
eastern Uganda. Here, in the harsh environment of Lake Turkana and later of
Kadam, she immediately took a keen interest in the life and ways of the local
people coming to their camp, and soon her attention was drawn to Domonguria,
whom she realized was not only "an excellent guide ... but a natural storyteller as
well." They struck up a friendship and it was with his approval that Pat Robbins
began recording his stories.

Domonguria's purpose, as Pat Robbins explains, was to describe a world that
already then was under rapid change, and he realized full well that by allowing
her to record and write up his stories, he could help to preserve an account of a
unique Pokot way of life for future generations. As he said: "It is time for our
Pokot traditions and history to be written down as well, so that our school children can read about their own heritage and others can understand and appreciate our culture. That is why I recorded this story."

His purpose was thus in no way linked to the indigenous rights movement,
which, at the time, was barely emerging in the Americas and was completely
unknown in Africa. It was to take another 20 years before the concept of indigenousness started being used in an African context by ethnic groups such as the

---

1   One example is that of the #Khomani San of South Africa who used it in their land claim. In some
    cases, such testimonies have been documented and published; see, for example Teemashane
    Trust, *The Khwe of the Okavango Panhandle: The Past Life, Part One: Origin, Land, Leaders, and Tradi-
    tions of the Bugakhwe People* (Shakawe, Botswana: Teemashane Trust, 2002).

Pokot, and yet another decade before it was recognized by the African Commission for Human and Peoples' Rights (ACHPR).[2]

This makes it a book that very much differs from what IWGIA generally publishes. Most IWGIA publications deal with indigenous rights and focus on contemporary issues related to land tenure, access and management of natural resources, self-organization and cultural rights. We were eager to publish *Red Spotted Ox*, because the book presents a unique and vivid picture of an indigenous community and its worldviews at a time when changes were beginning to challenge traditional lifestyles. We also believe that Pat Robbins has succeeded admirably in giving Domonguria an English voice without losing or compromising his Pokot identity.

Domonguria's discussions address a wide variety of subjects, ranging from the adaptations, belief systems, and resiliency of the Pokot people to the impacts of other groups, government policies, cycles of peace and conflict, and the importance of livestock. It thus gives us insight in the very fundamentals from which modern Pokot society has evolved and helps us understand the present situation of the Pokot, what modern development has done to them socially and culturally, the losses they have suffered and the values they still cherish. As Domonguria hoped, such a book could help preserve Pokot cultural heritage for future generations. It will also, hopefully and as experiences from elsewhere have shown, contribute to the strengthening of the Pokot's self-esteem and identity in a world where discrimination and oppression of the weakest still are widespread. The publication of *Red-Spotted Ox* should therefore be seen as an integrated part of IWGIA's commitment to the indigenous pastoralist peoples of Kenya and as a contribution to the work of their organizations.

The Pokot are Kalenjin-speaking peoples who reside in western Kenya and north eastern Uganda. Estimated to number between 250,000 and 350,000, the Pokot see themselves as indigenous to the countries in which they live. The majority of Pokot are found today in Kenya; smaller numbers of Pokot reside in north eastern Uganda.[3] In both countries, they constitute a small minority.

The world as Domonguria knew it has almost disappeared today. National politics, economic developments and socio-cultural policies have deeply affected the Pokot as they have many other indigenous pastoral communities of Kenya and Uganda. For the past decade, the Pokot areas have been experiencing rapid population growth for both humans and livestock; at the same time, pastoralism as a livelihood option is facing an increased number of challenges.

In the past, the Pokot crossed with ease between the two countries, but in recent years that movement has been restricted by national borders. On both sides of the border, they have seen their grazing areas being reduced as a result of land schemes favouring agricultural activities and the establishment of protected areas. In many

---

2   See *Report of the African Commission's Working Group of Experts on Indigenous Populations/Communities* (Banjul, The Gambia: ACHPR and Copenhagen, Denmark: IWGIA, 2005).
3   According to *The World Factbook*, (2009), Kenya is 580,367 sq km in size and has a population estimated at 39,002,772. Uganda covers 241,038 sq km and has a population of 32,369,558.

cases, pastoral communities have been forced out of their ancestral lands. The intro-
duction of so-called group ranches and the privatization of pastoral lands have furthermore exacerbated the pressure on range land with overgrazing and land degra-
dation as a result. Both in Uganda and Kenya, the areas inhabited by the Pokot generally remain poorly developed when it comes to modern physical infrastructure, such
as roads, commercial townships, water supply, schools and hospitals.

As a consequence of all these factors, combined with prolonged drought periods, the precarious food security of the Pokot pastoral households has been
exacerbated,[4] and, according to recent assessments, the greatest challenge today
is endemic poverty.[5] This, in turn, means that insecurity remains a major issue
with frequent clashes over grazing areas and theft of livestock. The massive increase in the availability of guns in the region poses a huge threat to local people
and their livestock. So far, several efforts at conflict resolution between the Pokot,
the Turkana and the Karamajong of Uganda seem to have had little success.

But there have also been more positive developments. Access to primary health
care has improved and is reflected in somewhat lower rates of infant and maternal
mortality. More boys and girls get a school education, although illiteracy is still
widespread. Like other pastoralist groups in Kenya, the Pokot are increasingly taking responsibility for their own development. Many of them have organized at the
community level with the goal of improving their members' well-being through
various activities related to, for instance, infrastructural improvements and ecot-
ourism. Many Pokot women, too, have organized, some with the purpose of doing
away with traditional harmful practices, such as female circumcision, improving
their general condition, e.g. in relation to water supply, etc. Others groups' objectives are aimed at reviving healthy traditional cultures and practices.

However, the Pokot—like other indigenous groups—continue to face a
number of problems, many of them related to the lack of recognition of their
rights as indigenous peoples.

Indigenous peoples like the Pokot generally possess ethnic, religious, or linguistic characteristics that are different from the dominant or numerically supe-
rior groups in the countries of which they are a part. They tend to have a sense of
cultural identity or social solidarity that many indigenous groups attempt to
maintain. In some cases, members of indigenous communities may attempt to
hide their identity, so as not to suffer racial prejudice or poor treatment at the
hands of others. In a number of cases, however, they proclaim their ethnic affili-
ation proudly and openly. Indeed, an important criterion for "indigenousness" is
the identification by people themselves of their distinct cultural identity. Most
indigenous people prefer to reserve for themselves the right to determine who is
and is not a member of their group.

---

4   See, e.g., "West Pokot District Long Rains Assessment Report 20th-25th July 2009" available at
     http://www.kenyafoodsecurity.org/longrains09/district_reports/west_pokot.pdf
5   See "West Pokot District Vision and Strategy: 2005-2015", available at: http://www.aridland.
     go.ke/NRM_Strategy/west_pokot.pdf

Particular problems arise in defining people as indigenous in Africa.[6] In many areas, it is difficult to determine antecedence since a variety of populations have moved in and out of local areas over time. The majority of Africans would identify themselves as belonging to specific ethnic groups even if the governments of the countries in which they live prefer to downplay ethnic differences. The Kenya government, like many African governments, opposes the use of the term indigenous peoples.[7] Kenya initially had a negative position on the adoption of the United Nations Declaration on the Rights of Indigenous Peoples (UNDRIP) and ended up being one of the few African countries that abstained from voting for its adoption by the UN General Assembly in September, 2007. The Kenya government also reacted somewhat negatively to the visit and report of the UN Special Rapporteur on the rights and fundamental freedoms of indigenous peoples that took place in 2007. However, recent developments such as the adoption of a new land policy and the drafting of a new constitution on which indigenous peoples were consulted, have raised hopes for more inclusiveness and understanding of the specific needs of indigenous peoples in the future.

Uganda has a similar position to Kenya on the issue of indigenous peoples, saying in its Constitution that "All Africans are indigenous to Africa." Schedule 3 of the Ugandan Constitution, however, does refer to 56 indigenous communities, including the Pokot, the Batwa, and the Karamojong.[8] Government ministries in Uganda, such as the Ministry of Gender, Labour, and Social Development work on indigenous issues, and the Uganda Human Rights Commission (UHRC) considers indigenous peoples' issues as part of its portfolio. Uganda also voted in favour of the UNDRIP. But, as is the case in Kenya, there is little understanding of the special needs of indigenous pastoralists when it comes to range land management policies, even if Pastoralist Parliamentary Groups (PPG) have been formed in both countries. These parliamentarians are supposed to be concerned with pastoralist development, but have up to now had little political impact.[9]

6   For discussions of the issue of indigenousness in Africa, see Sidsel Saugestad, "Contested Images: Indigenous Peoples in Africa", *Indigenous Affairs* 2/99, pp. 6-9; Alan Barnard and Justin Kenrick (eds.), *Africa's Indigenous Peoples: 'First Peoples' or 'Marginalized Minorities'?* (Edinburgh: Center of African Studies, University of Edinburgh, 2001); African Commission on Human and Peoples' Rights, *Indigenous Peoples in Africa: The Forgotten Peoples? The African Commission's Work on Indigenous Peoples in Africa* (Banjul, the Gambia: ACHPR and Copenhagen, Denmark: IWGIA, 2005).

7   See African Group of States, *Draft Aide Memoire, African Group: United Nations Declaration on the Rights of Indigenous Peoples* (New York: African Group, United Nations, 9 November 2006). In response to this statement, the African Commission on Human and Peoples' Rights (ACPHR) published an *Advisory Opinion of the African Commission on Human and Peoples' Rights on the United Nations Declaration on the Rights of Indigenous Peoples* (ACPHR, 2007); see also Maurice Odhiambo Makoloo, *Kenya: Minorities, Indigenous Peoples, and Ethnic Diversity* (London: Minority Rights Group, 2005).

8   See the Ugandan Constitution of 1995 and the African Commission on Human and Peoples' Rights, *Report of the African Commission's Working Group on Indigenous Populations/Communities. Research and Information Visit to the Republic of Uganda, 14-17, 24-29 July, 2006* (Banjul, The Gambia: ACHPR, and Copenhagen, Denmark: IWGIA, 2009). See also Wairama G. Baker, *Uganda: The Marginalization of Minorities* (London: Minority Rights Group, 2001).

9   See John Morton, *Legislators and Livestock: A Comparative Analysis of Pastoralists Parliamentary Groups in Ethiopia, Kenya and Uganda.* Final Report of the NRI/PENHA Research Project on Pasto-

The claims of indigenous peoples in Kenya and Uganda and other parts of the world are relatively similar: they wish to have their human rights respected; they want ownership and control over their own land and natural resources; and they want the right to participate through their own institutions in the political process at the nation-state, regional, and international levels. Representatives of African indigenous peoples have taken part in a number of international forums on indigenous peoples held by the United Nations, academic institutions and indigenous peoples' human rights and advocacy organizations. One of the major concerns expressed by representatives of African groups at these meetings is that they feel marginalized politically, socially, and economically in the countries in which they live.

The difficulty facing African indigenous peoples, including the Pokot, is that many of the continent's countries are dealing with serious social, economic, political, and environmental difficulties. Fortunately, African governments, civil society, and the international community are starting to pay greater attention to the needs of indigenous peoples and are attempting to come up with programs, policies, and sustainable development programs that take into consideration their varied needs and objectives. These changes are very much what Domonguria wanted to see for the Pokot and for all the peoples of Africa.

A note on the author

Pat Robbins, also known as Martha E. Robbins, has a BA from the University of Maryland, College Park, in English and a Master's degree focusing on Comparative International Education from Michigan State University in East Lansing. She worked with her husband, Larry Robbins, in Kenya in 1969-70 on archaeological excavations and assisted local people with medical care. She was able to record in Swahili the life story of Domonguria and continued this effort when she and her husband returned to Kenya in 1975-76 with their two small children. Over the next four decades, while teaching school in Michigan, assisting on excavations in Botswana, rehabilitating wildlife and raising her growing family, she managed to translate and weave the stories recorded in Kenya together into an autobiography of a traditional Pokot man, the result of which is this volume.

December 2009   **Robert K. Hitchcock**

---

ralists Parliamentary Groups, (2005) accessible at http://www.research4development.info/PDF/outputs/ZC0256a.pdf; see also Ruto Phalya, Mohamud Adan and Isabella Masinde, *Indigenous Democracy: Traditional Conflict Resolution Mechanisms: Pokot, Turkana, Samburu and Marakwet* (Nairobi: Intermediate Technology Development Group — Eastern Africa, 2004).

PREFACE

PREFACE

Pat Robbins

During the 1970s, I had the extraordinary opportunity to record on tape the fascinating personal stories of a traditional Pokot herder, farmer and trader, who was living near the Kenya-Uganda border. His name is Domonguria. During the many years since then, when I wasn't teaching, raising my family or living overseas, I translated the original Swahili recordings, and, with Domonguria's guidance, arranged the many disjointed memoires, tales, songs and descriptions into the form of an autobiography. At last, I can share his words with you!

Domonguria's wonderful narrative weaves stories of sorcery beginning in the 1890s with his youthful adventures, initiations and celebrations, and the responsibilities and challenges of his later years. The reader can witness Domonguria's intimate reflections and emotions as he fights with lions, first sees a white person, goes on raids, kidnaps a woman, falls in love, practices witchcraft and divining, witnesses atrocities, reveals scandals, dances, celebrates, and sings to his cattle. Through one man's unique perspective, this autobiography also becomes a story of the Pokot people—their rituals, songs, legends and values, and their challenges to survive through droughts, raids and encroaching development. It documents a way of life that has largely disappeared in the wake of recent history.

Domonguria

I met Domonguria in 1970, when I was part of an archaeological team surveying and excavating Stone Age sites in Kenya's parched Great Rift Valley, and an adjacent mountainous region in Uganda. In those days, there were no paved roads, bridges or electricity in the areas where we worked, and our 4WD was loaded with camping gear and provisions. The border region we traversed was the home of spear-carrying pastoralists, equally devoted and dependent on their herds, and clashing for more than a century over cattle and pastureland. In Kenya, we spent several months living with the Turkana and their lean herds of cattle, goats and camels, excavating in the scorched, semi-desert plains. The area above the Rift Valley escarpment was the homeland of their cattle-raiding enemies, the

Pokot. We were hoping to explore some of the hills in that region for interesting archaeological sites.

After climbing the steep escarpment, delighted by the more abundant vegetation and the spectacular views, we crossed the border into Uganda and continued driving through a small town called Amudat, which had a police post, a clinic and a few small shops. We decided to set up a temporary camp just outside the town near a water pump.

Almost immediately, we began to meet the local Pokot inhabitants. First, several women, strikingly adorned with huge, coiled metal earrings, necklaces, and bracelets, and rows of colorful beads, came to fetch water at the pump near our camp, balancing large aluminum pots on their heads. Bare-chested, they wore belts decorated with beads or cowrie shells, short skin or beaded aprons, and long skin back skirts that rustled as they walked. Their hair, shaved at the sides, was coiled into thin braids, some intertwined with beads. Talking and laughing among themselves, the women greeted me in Pokot, asking, *"Takwenya?"* We filled our jerry cans with water at the pump, and carried them back to our tents. I began washing laundry in a large bucket, thereby attracting an audience of five or six men, who kept asking for my clothes, glasses or shillings. Then several elders, loudly intoxicated, passed by our camp on a path to their homes.

Presently I noticed a dignified man standing alone, patiently, on the periphery of our camp clearing. He was dressed in the traditional manner of older Pokot men at that time—naked, except for a large, black sheet of cloth draped over one shoulder. He wore a red-beaded necklace, earrings and metal bracelets, and his shaved head was capped by an intricately painted clay headdress, accented by feathers, chains and pompons. Like most Pokot men, he carried a small wooden stool (also used as a headrest) and an impressive seven-foot spear. As soon as the others left, he greeted me quietly in Swahili, the *lingua franca* of East Africa, and asked for a job. Domonguria, it turned out, was the guide we needed to explore the nearby hills. A week later we moved about 20 miles to an area called Katabok, near Kadam Mountain, and spent the next several days, with his help, surveying and climbing.

Mt. Kadam rises dramatically 10,067 feet from the southern plains of northeastern Uganda's sparsely settled Karamoja District. The area around the mountain is grassy, with some scrub brush and occasional acacia trees, which create beautiful silhouettes against the setting sun. Although Karamoja is considered semi-arid, we were pleased to find it had considerably more vegetation than the hot, sand-swept plains of Turkana below the Rift Valley escarpment, where we had previously worked, as well as plentiful game, including giraffes, antelopes, baboons, lions, and hyenas. There were Pokot settlements around the base of the mountain, but Domonguria told us that another people, the Tepeth (So), lived on the higher elevations of Kadam, as well as on the other mountains in the region, Napak and Moroto. Because he knew the landscape so well, Domonguria was an excellent guide. He led us up the mountain slopes through grass taller than our heads, across boulders, and up rock faces to show us caves which had most likely been in use since people first inhabited the area. Some contained huge grain baskets and pots in storage houses built into the cave walls.

As we excavated the grassy slope below one particularly large cave, looking for artifacts and animal bones, we found that Domonguria was not only a capable worker, but a natural storyteller as well. All of us on the dig—Pokot, Kamba and Americans—exchanged jokes, tall tales, songs, and anecdotes about our lives and traditions, speaking in Swahili and singing in our own languages. Domonguria's stories were, by far, the most dramatic and captivating. His experiences spanned a major period of increasing contact and conflict between Western ideas and Pokot traditions. We were especially intrigued to discover that many of Domonguria's accounts could be verified by historical and personal sources, like the medical records in Amudat documenting Domonguria's treatment after he lost his finger in a lion's mouth. I realized how interesting it would be to record such stories about a lifestyle that was changing before our eyes.

I discussed the idea with Domonguria when the excavation was finished, and discovered that such a plan was meaningful to him as well. For although Domonguria valued a traditional Pokot life, he was keenly aware that the future would not accommodate many of the customs he cherished, and this bothered him greatly. He realized that by recording material to be written later, he could preserve an account of a uniquely Pokot way of life, so that the schooled children of the future, who might not know the ways of their ancestors, could at least glimpse their heritage in a book. Thus he agreed to tape in Swahili the story of his life, which revolves around Pokot traditions, legends, songs and history as he experienced them.

After the dig, Domonguria drove with us to a rented house near Nakuru, where my husband intended to analyze the artifacts. The next morning, I put my tape recorder on a camp table in the main room and sat across from Domonguria with my notebook. I encouraged him to talk not only about the more important Pokot rituals, but also about the personal events of his own life, good and bad, from the time he was a small child to the present. Having said these things, I handed him the microphone, showed him how to turn on the machine, and waited. I had no idea what he was going to say. Presently, he began: *I am glad, Pat, that you want to know about the ways of my people. ...*

About The Pokot

Now I would like to introduce you to the Pokot people of East Africa. This will be only a brief summary, because Domonguria will provide many more details.

The Pokot are an indigenous, cattle-loving people who live in northwestern Kenya and the Uganda border region. Some are primarily farmers, and others only keep cattle, sheep and goats, but many Pokot do both, as they move from one environment to another. Often, members of the same family will farm cooler, wetter highlands and seek pasture for their herds on the hot, dry plains, where cattle diseases may be less prevalent. Like other East African pastoralists, their lives depend on the rain, which is often scarce, averaging 10 to 15 inches a year on the plains. Traditionally, herders live mostly on the milk, blood and occasional meat of their animals, and farmers grow millet, sorghum and corn to supplement the milk from their cows.

Living a traditional Pokot life means tending to the herds or farm chores, performing rituals of passage or protection, protecting or enlarging one's herd, and distributing the animals among family and friends for safe-keeping. You are expected to be generous and friendly, and to honor the traditions laid down by the ancestors and by *Tororut* (God). Even young children help with milking, herding small animals and household chores. Rites of passage to adulthood include *sapana* for boys, symbolized by wearing a clay headdress, and circumcision for both boys and girls. Pregnancy, marriage, childbirth, initiations, death, sickness, natural disasters, murder, and many other events are recognized through prescribed rituals. A wide range of beliefs are expressed through divination, sorcery, witchcraft, ancestral communication, clan totems, traditional deiities and other religious practices.

The society is patrilineal, patriarchal and polygamous. In the areas where I worked, a man and his wives share the same compound, building a separate home for each wife. There may be other families, extended relatives or friends living in the same or nearby homesteads, and the women and children help each other tend to the animals and the gardens. Extensive social and economic networks bond family members, clans and cattle associates. There are no traditional chiefs, but male elders assume social power and control the family's assets, the herds. Councils of elders regularly meet to decide conflicts, oversee rituals and make policy. Egalitarian values encourage generosity and the distribution of wealth.

The profound commitment of pastoralists to their herds has been socially and economically necessary. A family's assets are in the form of livestock. Numbers are more important than animal size and milk production, since rituals, bridewealth and bartering involve prescribed numbers of livestock. Cattle are symbols of wealth, blessings and the male identity. Raiding has been commonplace, as warriors are expected to replenish declining herds or to take vengeance on those who have raided them. Domonguria gives many examples of this warrior ethos.

The Pokot and their cattle-herding neighbors, the Karamojong, Turkana, Maasai, Samburu and Jie, are sometimes referred to as Nilotic peoples. Linguistically, the Pokot are related to the Nandi, Marakwet, Kipsigis, Elgeyo, Tugen, Terik and Sebei, whereas the Turkana, Karamojong, Jie and Dodoth form another cluster. The term Kalenjin was adopted in the 1950s and 1960s by politicians of the "Nandi-speaking" communities in Kenya, including the Pokot, to describe their shared ethnicity for the purpose of gaining political influence. Kalenjin peoples now comprise about 12 percent of Kenya's population.

The Pokot population at the time these stories were recorded probably totaled between 130,000 and 220,000,[1] spread out over a strip of land extending from the Lake Baringo area in northwestern Kenya, across the plains and highlands of West Pokot District, where most Pokot live, to the Karamoja plains in northeastern Uganda. The Kenya highlands include the Cherengeni Hills and the Sekerr and Chemerongit mountain ranges, and Mt. Kadam dominates southern Karamoja in Uganda. The Suam, or Turkwell, Kerio, Morun and Weiwei rivers flow northward to Lake Turkana, and there are many dry riverbeds, where people dig wells. The long and short rains vary greatly, depending on the environment. Temperatures range from less than 10 to more than 30° C (50-122° F). Pokot lands are bordered on the north and east by their raiding rivals and occasional neighbors and trading partners, the Karamojong and the Turkana. To the south, landowners have cut them off from their historic enemy, the Maasai. Many other ethnic groups also reside and interact in the area.

A Brief Pokot History

Pokot were previously called Suk (Sukk, Suku) in the literature and by outsiders during colonial times. Other spellings include Pakot and even Pökoot. The Pokot who live in Uganda have been referred to as Upe or Karapokot, because of their proximity to and shared customs with the Karamojong. A single Pokot individual is called Pochon.

Some people think the Pokot were once part of a larger Nandi-speaking people in the Nile valley region. However, they have evidently lived in eastern Africa for centuries as a much smaller population. Armed with spears and bows with poisonous arrows, they have long fought over cattle with their powerful neighbors, the Turkana, the Karamojong, the Maasai and others. As the more powerful Turkana expanded, the Pokot communities retreated further south to the Cherengeni and adjacent volcanic hills, plateaus and plains in northwestern Kenya, where they began to supplement their diet by farming. To outsiders, they retained a ferocious reputation, and Swahili traders in the 1860s reportedly refused to enter Pokot lands.[2]

Joseph Thomson, in 1884, seems to be the first Westerner to personally encounter and write about the Pokot. In the account of his *Journey of Exploration Among the Snowclad Volcanic Mountains and Strange Tribes of Eastern Equatorial Af-*

rica, Thomson wrote that the Pokot were "strong-boned, ugly-looking fellows ... They went absolutely naked ... A piece of flat brass hung from the lower lip of each and must have been both painful and awkward ... The most remarkable feature of the Wa-suk, however, was the manner in which they dressed their hair [a large, decorated, bag-like chignon] ... The Wa-Suk are described as very war-like, and generally quite a match for the Maasai, in whose country they frequent-ly make raids ... They occupy a magnificent and picturesque range of moun-tains..."[3]

Four years later, explorers Count Samuel Teleki and Ludwig von Höhnel passed through the region after discovering Lake Rudolf (later renamed Lake Turkana). According to his diary of July, 1888,[4] Teleki first encountered some short, weak-looking agricultural people on the mountains, but described the "Sukks" of the Kerio valley as "pleasant looking handsome fellows of average height ..." who, when given presents and promises of good fortune, "told me they like my talking as much as their oiling after a bath or drinking fresh milk after a good night's sleep." His companion, Ludwig von Höhnel, also praised the friendliness of Suk herders, in spite of their fearsome reputation as raiders, not-ing their resemblance to the Maasai. When the Pokot steadfastly refused to sell adequate stock to the desperately hungry Austro-Hungarian expedition, wanting only tobacco, Teleki condoned several "thieving excursions" by his men and, fi-nally, a large-scale cattle raid, during which about 80 to 100 Pokot archers and spearmen were killed, and the many wounded "found out what a gun means." Teleki rationalized, "If I had not robbed the Sukks we would have all starved to death by now."

Renewed Pokot expansion began at the end of the nineteenth century, as a result of natural and health disasters. First, during the 1890s, rinderpest caused widespread losses throughout the eastern and southern African plains. Karamo-jong and Tukana herds were especially decimated. This was followed by a dis-ease of small stock, a locust infestation and a drought. Smallpox swept through East Africa beginning in 1899. All of the pastoralists on the plains were dimin-ished in numbers and stock. However, those Pokot who lived on the mountains managed to survive in greater numbers, and many began to migrate to the plains.

The new colonial government also helped to make Pokot expansion possible. In 1907, British soldiers quashed Maasai raids on the Pokot. Then, between 1913 and 1918, the Kenya government sponsored punitive attacks against the power-ful Turkana, seizing their cattle and weapons. Pokot warriors were glad to assist with this effort! After that, some Pokot families began to move westward, settling on previously dangerous lands. However, before long, the Turkana were attack-ing again, and the affected Pokot tried to move to their traditional southern pas-tures, only to be denied access by the recent white settlers. When some continued further to the west, across the border into Uganda, the land appeared vacant, because the Karamojong, already suffering from an outbreak of East Coast Fever, had moved their cattle temporarily to other pastures. As you can imagine, Pokot settlements in those areas remained a source of contention with the Karamojong for many years. The Pokot who settled and grazed their herds in and around Uganda's Karamoja District, adopted so many Karamojong customs that they were often called Karapokot.

The history of Pokot-government relations has not always been easy. Although the first government station was set up in 1903 in Baringo District, the colonial presence was almost nonexistent throughout the remote, inhospitable Pokot countryside, and those officials who were assigned to the few government outposts rarely stayed long. Taxes were imposed around 1910, and headmen and chiefs were appointed to collect them and to provide forced labor for roads and projects. During the 1930s, efforts were made to introduce agricultural tools and techniques, with little success. The seizure of traditional Pokot land for white settlement greatly restricted grazing land for herders. The Kenya government later declared that arid pastures were being overgrazed and mandated annual quotas of cattle sales for each area. Christian missions were established in Kenya Pokot areas during the 1930s and in Uganda's Karamoja District in the 1950s.

Early colonial officials were frustrated by Pokot resistance to government-sponsored "progress". Semi-nomadic, communal people, whose lives revolved around finding pasture for their cattle, were, of course, not interested in permanent settlement and land ownership to the exclusion of their neighbors. The imposition of chiefs conflicted with Pokot egalitarian values. Westernized medicine and religion were considered supplemental to, not substitutions for, their own herbs and beliefs. Skin clothing, beads and headdresses were symbolically meaningful, whereas Western dress lacked cues of Pokot cultural identity. Children were not sent to school, because they were needed for the more important tasks of herding stock and obtaining more cattle through marriage. Domonguria and others later came to realize that many innovations introduced by outsiders had brought benefits to Pokot society—education, tools, roads, famine relief, utensils, cattle markets and trading goods—but they also noticed that craftsmen were no longer making traditional pots and tools and that people were beginning to forget their customs and the responsibilities laid down by the ancestors.

As Kenya and Uganda were modernized, gaining new schools, hospitals, roads, and, finally, independence, the Pokot were left behind and marginalized. Cattle herders, like the Maasai, Turkana, Karamojong or Pokot, were of a different ethnicity than the dominant Bantu-speaking ruling class. They lived in distant, impoverished areas, resisted cultural change, engaged in raiding and violence, and were considered backward. They became an embarrassment to those in power. From 1913 to 1964, West Pokot was isolated as a "closed district", and investment in the area was minimal.

After Kenya's independence in 1963, there were improvement projects in some areas. During the 1980s, churches were encouraged by the government to build more schools, and private and foreign investments provided additional limited services. Government efforts to confiscate weapons and to control raiding resulted in brief periods of peace and vulnerability to attack, followed by re-armament. Pokot districts have had a small representation in Parliament. Development, however, has remained far behind the rest of the country.

In more recent years, new changes have come to Pokot areas. Droughts, violence, epidemics, and restriction of land for pasture have caused widespread poverty. In Uganda, the murderous dictator Idi Amin personally ordered the slaughter of people who adhered to traditional dress. In Kenya, schools and roads have been built, and scores of humanitarian, political and religious teams offer lifestyle alternatives or spiritual salvation. Various projects promote a sedentary, agricultural way of life, group land ownership and reclaimed pasturelands. Many traditions have been discouraged and, too frequently, spears have been replaced by the new power of the AK47. Increasing numbers of men and women, who were once renowned for their independence and pride in their cultural identity, have been reduced to poverty or working as day laborers, often dependent on government handouts. On the other hand, more children are attending school and choosing lifestyles more attuned to the developed world. Perhaps, as Domonguria wished, they can read about their cultural traditions in books like this one.

From Tapes to Book

Domonguria and I recorded almost every day for three months in 1970. The material was totally unprompted and spontaneous. I rarely knew what he would be recording next. I sat across from him with my notebook, listening and jotting down brief notes. Like most men of his area, Domonguria spoke Swahili comfortably and fluently, using a dialect known loosely as "upcountry Swahili," a version not always grammatically correct and with some inventive vocabulary, but perfectly understood—at least in that region—and, luckily, by me.

Unfortunately, I do not know Pokot, Karamojong or Turkana, and I am aware that some of the rich subtleties and nuances of those languages, perhaps relating to age, gender and metaphor, may have been lost in our use of Swahili. Whenever Domonguria chose to use a Pokot or Karamojong word, name or an unfamiliar phrase, we paused, while I questioned him carefully, until I was able to write the sounds so that I could repeat them correctly. In order to inform my translation, all of the songs were also dictated in their original languages (Pokot, Karamojong or Turkana—sometimes two in one song). Eventually, I decided to include this material, so that the reader could get a general sense of how the language sounds.

Domonguria took the recording most seriously, and would sometimes worry over a detail, like a name, for days before he remembered and thus felt comfortable with the accuracy of the recording. Often, he would stop the tape and explain a subject thoroughly and patiently to me to be sure all was understood. He made it clear that he wanted me to add words or ideas from our discussions that could illuminate the meaning of the taped segment. These additions, it turned out, were minimal.

After returning from East Africa, I began the long process of translating the tapes directly into English. When I met with Domonguria again six years later, in 1976, I had the opportunity to clarify some phrases and ideas from my initial translations, ask additional questions and record more material, including his eye-witness accounts of Ugandan dictator Idi Amin's atrocities towards our friends near Mt. Kadam. The essence of all 85 hours of this taped material has been included in the book (eliminating redundancies) along with the explanations Domonguria had insisted I write in my notebook.

The translations did not fit together as a whole, at first. The work consisted of bits and pieces—a song here, a story, joke or serious explanation there—without any systematic arrangement. Sometimes parts of the same story or subject would appear in many different places, as a warm, first-person reminiscence one time and a detached third-person accounting the next. Translating had been straightforward; now came the challenge of weaving the pieces into a coherent whole. Domonguria trusted me to edit and rearrange the material; he would not have recorded it otherwise. "Throw out the bad words" and put it in good form, he told me.

Domonguria agreed with my decision to combine all the parts in the form of an autobiography. I presented him with an oral list of all the topics we had recorded, and he worked with me to arrange them chronologically. We agreed to a few changes as we worked on this. For instance, he had described a typical Pokot wedding in detail, but later he said only a few words about his own wedding. He said this was because he had already explained the ceremony. He agreed that I could change the description to a first person account, including his personal comments, since most of the other stories were autobiographical. We decided to include the many songs and folktales where Domonguria told me they would have been sung or told. He asked me to eliminate redundancies, which I did. He asked me to include words to help the narrative make sense. The phrases I added were taken from our notes and conversations about when and where events occurred or other comments he made that tied the segments together. Finally, Domonguria helped me change 44 names to protect both the innocent and the guilty.

Those who have suggested that I separate my words or ideas from his could not understand that both the translations and the editing were a joint effort (his ideas that I later incorporated into the text), and that Domonguria insisted that I choose the English words that would best convey the meaning of the stories. He may not have been able to read or write, but he was aware of the power of written language. Domonguria's stories came alive through his rich and extensive use of dialogue, and this set the tone for the entire, very personal narrative. He wanted his account of his life and culture to be grammatically correct, fluid and coherent as a whole.

In the Chronology of Events and in the endnotes, when appropriate, I have included references to historical events (like the eclipse) and other accounts to help put some of the story in a larger perspective. Included are comments from other authors that add specific cultural information on topics mentioned in the text. I purposely kept interpretations of culture or events to a minimum, because I wanted Domonguria to speak for himself.

As I perused published literature about the Pokot, I noted similarities and differences between Domonguria's experiences and the accounts and interpretations of anthropologists, explorers and government officials. Until the 1980s, very few works were published specifically about the Pokot, and almost none were about the Karapokot, like Domonguria. More recently, there have been books and dissertations focusing mainly on the West Pokot or Baringo Districts of Kenya. The details of rituals, customs and songs described vary from one source to another, reflecting whether the study group was agrarian or pastoral, the extent of cultural influence by neighboring ethnic groups, exposure to government or Western influence and the dates of study. The comments of research subjects are always prejudiced by their previous associations, gender, age, lifestyles, contacts with missionaries, skills and education. Domonguria's autobiography is no exception, but it has the unique advantage of presenting his specific comments within the known context of his life experiences.

Domonguria led a life based on traditional Pokot values, even as colonial and Western influences encroached. Unlike some other Africans who have written autobiographies, he was not educated in schools and did not travel outside of East Africa. His account is valuable as a record of traditional Pokot society in the border region at a time of early contact with Westerners, before recent destruction and interventions changed that way of life forever. I have done my best to bring his words and thoughts to you. I hope this book will also be useful to scholars as one man's perspective of his culture, from the point of view of an adult male in the 1970s, influenced, as we all are, by gender, age and individual experiences. I fully realize that the voice of one person cannot speak for a whole ethnicity. Conversely, studies of a whole ethnicity may not represent the voice of an individual within that society. Above all, I hope most readers—scholars and non-scholars alike—will enjoy this narrative as a fascinating story of an interesting and adventurous life.

This book would not have been possible without the initial inspiration and continued support of my husband, Larry, the patience of our four children—Dan, Brian, Michael and Mark—and the persistent encouragement of my parents and friends, who continued to believe in my efforts. To all of them I am genuinely grateful. In particular, I wish to thank Larry, Dan, Michael, Diana Vinding, Mari-anne Wiben Jensen and the IWGIA staff for reviewing the manuscript in detail. They offered many valuable suggestions and comments. I am indebted to Robert K. Hitchcock for reviving my interest in revising and publishing this manuscript after so many years and diversions. During that time, the Pokot way of life along the Kenya-Uganda border has changed drastically. Many customs have been discouraged or outlawed, and more children are attending school and beginning a new way of life. I was truly fortunate to have been able to collect and translate this remarkable story while it was still possible.

Rocks or hills can never meet
Only our peoples can come together.

A Pokot saying

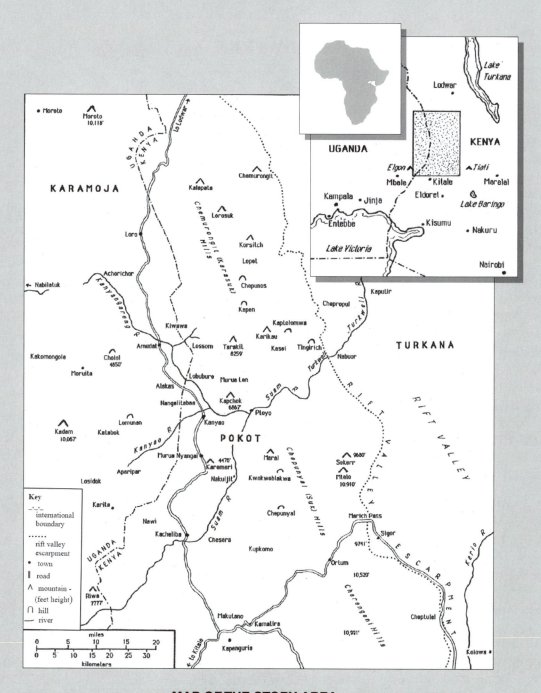

MAP OF THE STORY AREA

FAMILY TREE

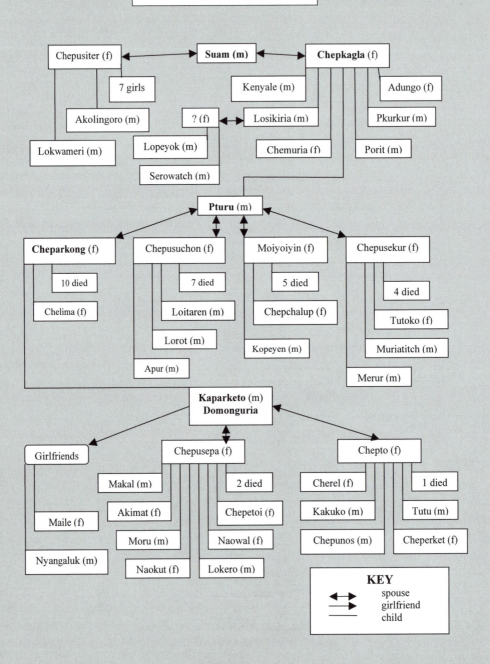

APPROXIMATE CHRONOLOGY OF EVENTS

DATE	HISTORICAL REFERENCE *	STORY
1890-4	Rinderpest epidemic	The Time the Country Became Dark
1896	Drought	The Year the Lizard Cried
1899	Smallpox	Death of Suam
1902	Smallpox	Death of Cheptulel family
1926	Total Solar Eclipse (*14 January 1926*)	The Year the Sun Died
1927-8	Subukia Earthquake (*6 January 1928*)	The Year the Earth Shook
1928	Kitale-Lodwar Road Construction	First move to Lossom
1929	Drought and locust reports	The Year of the Locusts
1930	Reports of generous rainfall	The Year of the Great Rains
1931	Meeting at Lobubure (*December 1931*)	Moving
1932	Tsetse fly infestation	Cattle sickness; return to Lossam
1933	Giacobinid meteor showers (*9 October 1933*)	The Year the Star Went in the Morning
1934	Mention of name in Annual Report	Government work digging wells
1936	Circumcision ceremonies reported	First attempt at circumcision
1939-40	World War II recruitment	*Sapana*; Court case
1946	Circumcision rites near Kacheliba	Circumcision
1950	Battle of Kalowa at Baringo	Marriage
1953	Lorika slain; Kenyatta's trial	Trading
1955	Witch killings	Witch killings
1963	Independence	Sub-chief
1965	Comet	Turkana; Raiding
1970	Personal contact, Comet	Working for Simba
1976	Israeli Entebbe raid	Recording this story

* Details of these references are explained in the endnotes.

PROLOGUE

PROLOGUE

Domonguria

I am glad, Pat, that you want to know about the ways of my people, the Pokot.
I'll try to tell you about the experiences of my life, about our customs and traditions,
and about the old legends as I heard them from the elders.

My father, Pturu, came from the hilly region of Cheptulel, in Kenya, where his family farmed the log-terraced slopes and tended their abundant herds of cattle and goats. When he was still a boy, a terrible epidemic swept through the land, killing thousands of cattle, other livestock, and even wild animals in a matter of weeks. People on the plains, who had no gardens, began to starve, and desperate bands of thieves roamed the hills, looking for food. My grandfather, Suam, moved his family and diminished herd into a cave for protection, but one evening a gang crept up on the old man and left him bound with ropes, while they butchered most of his remaining cattle. The family was forced to depend on their limited stores of grain, as well as the meager bounty from group hunts for survival. Then a severe drought, which lasted two years, killed the crops and caused even more deaths, especially on the plains. Finally, in the wake of these disasters, my people were attacked twice by a murderous new illness called *tetemaji* (smallpox). It claimed the lives of my grandfather Suam, his two wives and most of their 15 children. Only my father and his brother survived.[5]

Weak with hunger, the two young men decided to leave their diseased homestead—the cave on Cheptulel. They journeyed though the mountain pass of Marich with their tiny remaining herd of two cows (one pregnant), a calf and several goats. Eventually, they settled in the region of Kupkomo, where they continued breeding cattle, slowly expanding their herd. There, Pturu met Cheparkong, my mother, and asked her father's permission to marry. He paid only two cows and 15 goats for her, a brideprice that would have been unacceptably low before the epidemic and the drought.

After the wedding, Pturu and Cheparkong worked every day tending their garden and beehives. Soon, they were able to trade extra garden produce and honey for more livestock. When their firstborn, a girl, died, they decided to move with their increasing herd to an area between the Suam River and the hill called Kwokwoblakwa. That is where I was born and given my first name, Kaparketo. Mother was ill for nearly two years after my birth. Only two of her twelve babies survived—my younger sister Chelima and I.

CHILDHOOD

WHEN THE SUN DIED

My memory begins The Year the Sun Died [*1926?*].[6] I was only a small boy when it happened, but old enough to be aware of events around me.

Prayer of Healing

Our neighbor, Chemarkei, lay on a skin in the center of our homestead, surrounded by those who had come to invoke the spirits of *Tororut* (God)[7] on the mountains to cure her. Some of the women sat near her, alternately playing drums they had made out of clay pots, honey gourds or hollow logs: placing thin sticks, feathered like arrow shafts, upright on top of the drums, and rubbing and twirling them up and down against the wet skins to create a rhythmic moan—*kuukuu, kuukuu, voom, voom*—as loud as a lion's roar.[8] In each of the six houses around them, other women, including my mother, were drumming with short sticks on two large poles, suspended by ropes from the ceiling beams, making another cadence—*shay, shay, ka, ka, ka*. Intermittently, the sound of the women's voices blended with the incessant din of their drumming, as they sang a song about our homestead.

Circle of houses, circle of houses	*Kerot korino, kerot korino*
Water in a rock hollow surrounded by many birds	*Chepkolwa nyo koriko terit*
Houses—many, like weaver birds	*Kerot koriko sawach-e*
Circle of houses, birds	*Kerot korino terit-e*

I watched from a distance while the old men who had come to help with the prayers gathered on one side of the homestead to consume a gourd of honey beer and to feast quietly on meat from a black male goat killed by Chemarkei's kinsman. As usual, the elders sat facing towards Mtelo, the greatest mountain of our land, from which all Pokot originated long ago, and where all important decisions are made. Presently, the man who had killed the goat stood up and began to pray in a loud voice, calling upon the spirits of all the mountains of our land, beginning, as always, with Mtelo:

Please Mtelo, help this woman, who is very sick! I pray to you, spirits of Tororut who live at Mtelo and Sekerr, Chepunyal, and Maral. Please, Tingirich, Karikau, Kaptolomwa,

Tarakit ... I cry to the spirits of all the hills of the Pokot. If you hear me, Tororut, if your spirit is there at your hills, show us the good way ... and throw out from us all bad things, for we need your help—you are the greatest of all the country. Now one of us suffers and we cry to you, Tororut: Please help our woman!

When he finished praying, the women began to sing:

> *Wild bee hive, bee hive*
> *There are many on the hill Kaipachora*
> *There are trees with hives, oh aya*
> *They are on Kaipachora*

> *Woe ponut-o, Owe ponut-o*
> *Mipone nyo ka Kaipachora,*
> *Mipone nyo riron-e, oh aya*
> *Mipone nyo ka Kaipachora*

Later the elder prayed once more, and the drums sounded into the night.

The Sun has Died

The next morning, the sun rose brightly. I was in the goat house, as usual, quietly milking the goats before they went to pasture, when all at once I heard singing! At first I wondered if perhaps the neighbor women had returned to give Chemarkei another prayer ceremony, yet this time I could hear men's voices too. Curious, I finished my task, carried the gourd of milk to the door and went out. To my amazement, the countryside was as dark as night! People were singing inside all six houses in the homestead, including our own! Alarmed, I ran to our house and ducked in the door, calling, "Mother! What's happening?"

She was tending the fire in the middle of the floor. "What do you see outside, Kaparketo?" she asked gently.

"It's dark!"

"Yes. The sun has died."

"If it has died, will it get well again if you sing to it?" I asked, remembering Chemarkei.

"I don't know. Our ancestors said so. There is a certain song we are supposed to sing at times like this. Our parents sang it when the huge Taruh comet appeared. And their parents told of how the sun died once before like this, and the elders were able to coax it back with the same song. Your father is telling the others about it now. Listen: the song has begun!"

I watched in the shadows of our round, fire-lit home as my mother hummed one of the prayer ceremony songs from the night before. Soon, my father entered the house and opened his container of ostrich feathers. He withdrew two very long, white plumes and gave one to Mother. Together they began waving the feathers up and down while they sang the song *Chepukopukwa:*[9]

Sun, good, pretty thing	*Chepukopukwa karama karen*
Refrain:	
My father holds a certain bird (feather)	*Kipur papo nyu taret anga*
Ostrich, very good, pretty thing	*Chepsongol karamach kare*
Verses:	
My mother holds another plume	*Kipur yo nyu taret anga*
Ostrich, very good, very pretty thing	*Chepsongol karamach karen kare*
Tell Tororut to bring life	*Lenjina Tororut ipuna sopon*
Tell Tororut, bring the morning	*Lenjina Tororut ipuna yeka*
Tell Tororut to bring white	*Lenjina Tororut ipuna relin*
Tell my Father to come, show us the way	*Lenjina Papo nyu na nyona kumbul or*
Sweet life forever	*Anyen sapon kokai*

They sang, and their voices blended with those of our neighbors. The song wafted skyward from huts throughout the land of the Pokot. Gradually, a dim light made its way through our doorway and grew stronger. I ran out to welcome the sun, as it emerged from the darkness in the sky and shone down upon the cattle in our corral and upon the six houses surrounding our homestead! Already, people were beginning to put away their feathers. The elders consulted with one another, and soon the young men opened the gate and let the cattle out to graze. Then the little children started to play, the older ones herded the goats and sheep to pasture, and the women began tending to the affairs of daily life.

Sex Scandal

Not long after the sun died, a scandal erupted in our homestead when we found out that our neighbors Cheperit and her mother had become pregnant at the same time by the same man, Sangal. All the older boys were snickering about it, having first overheard their parents wondering about the expectant women (neither had a husband), and then discovering the truth (by the women's own admissions!). Soon everyone knew the story. This is how it happened:

Cheperit was in love with Sangal, but her brother found out and threatened to beat her if she saw him again. He told her, "Sangal's father wronged our father, and we should have nothing to do with his family. Even to speak to Sangal is bad luck. Forget him!"

Cheperit, however, found a way around this. She cut a small window in the side of her house right next to her bed, and then told Sangal. That night, he came, put his arm in the window, and found his sweetheart. They made love through the window, and he left undetected.

This went on until one night Cheperit's mother heard the sounds of love-making and be came suspicious. The following evening she called to her daughter, "You, child, come sleep here. I'll sleep there where it's cooler, for I feel very hot." And so the girl and her mother switched places.

Later that night, the mother was awakened by quick and intimate caresses. Sangal was strong and eager, thinking it was his sweetheart Cheperit, and the mother couldn't get away! In fact, she began to enjoy it! She had known no man since the time her husband had died and now Tororut had seen fit to bring her pleasure. She rejoiced! I don't know how many nights after that Sangal made love to Cheperit's mother, but eventually she was quite satisfied and told Cheperit to go back and sleep in her place.

When they both became pregnant and the story was told, the unsuspecting Sangal was honorable enough to go through the pregnancy ceremony with both of them to insure healthy births. But when Cheperit's mother gave birth to twins, Sangal ran away! In his place, her brother-in-law had to come to our homestead to accompany her throughout the *riwoi* ceremony for the birth of twins. Eventually, Sangal did return to marry Cheperit, who had had a healthy son, and they moved away a few months later. They have had a good, long marriage with lots of children.[10]

Eating Like Sakwar

One night, as I was devouring some roast goat, my father walked by and exclaimed, "Look at this boy, Cheparkong! He's eating like Sakwar!"

Mother protested, "Sakwar's not a man—he's a hyena!"

"Or an elephant!" Father added.

"Who is Sakwar?" I asked later, really curious.

"Oh, Sakwar is a giant of a man!" Father exclaimed. "Why, I hear he can eat a whole cow by himself. They say that when he goes to fight the Karamojong or the Turkana, they just take one look at him, give up their cattle and run away! His shield has the strength of a live elephant's hide, his spear blade is enormous, and his arrows have very long shafts.

"He shoots well, too," my uncle joined in. "His arrows sail further than any man's."

Father went on. "I hear that once, on a journey, his party arrived at a stone well called Akeso. They were thirsty and were relieved to find the well filled with water. 'Let my boy drink first,' Sakwar said, and certainly no one was about to argue with *him*. When the boy was finished, Sakwar knelt down to drink. He didn't stop until the well was dry! The others could only moan, 'Oh, what will we do? It's more that 20 miles to the river!'"

"I told you he was a hyena!" Mother said, and everyone laughed.

As a young child, I was also beginning to learn about our many eating customs, especially for ceremonies. I sometimes wondered if our ancestors were fools, because they denied us so much! For instance, if a person eats meat, he cannot drink milk; he must wait until the next day, and then he can't eat meat or even drink broth, because he has drunk the milk![11] We must not taste the milk of a cow that has just calved, nor mix her milk with that of any other cow, until the calf is nearly three weeks old, or the calf will die. Water may be drunk between the meat and soup courses, but not along with food or directly after a meal.

As if those rules were not enough, my family had some eating philosophies of its own. I remember the elders warning my mothers[12] never to wake a sleeping child to give it food, or the stone used for grinding grain into flour will turn to water. Similarly, my father always refused food at night, proclaiming, "Those who eat day and night will die quickly when the rains fail." Nevertheless, I ate heartily.

First Weapons

After I milked the goats each morning, I would take the kids to a pasture where I played with other children my age. One morning, my friend Angela ran to greet me, brimming with excitement. His father had just given him his first set of weapons—a new wooden spear and a set of bow and arrows.

"*Ala!*" I exclaimed. "You're lucky! I wish I had a spear and a bow!"

The rest of that morning and afternoon, Angela and his sister practiced shooting their arrows and throwing their spear, while I looked after the baby goats, watching them jealously. Finally, when I could stand it no longer, I herded the goats home early. I could see my mother on the other side of the corral, by the houses, kneeling to grind millet between two stones. She was rocking back and forth, and my baby sister Chelima was enjoying the ride on her back. I ran across the corral to her, shouting, "Mother! I want a spear! Angela has one, and he has a bow and arrows too! I want mine now! Please find them for me!"

Mother looked up, surprised, and Chelima almost slid off her back. Then she smiled and said, "You are still small, Kaparketo ..." But she must have noticed the disappointment on my face, because she added, "I will find them for you."

Sure enough, the following evening my father presented me with a tiny set of wooden arrows and a bow. Immediately, I stood a stick in the ground and tried to shoot it as I had seen other children do, but the arrows went wild—it was harder than I had imagined! A few mornings later, my father gave me a wooden spear he had carved himself. I left my bow and arrows at home that day and ran to show it to my friends. We practiced spear-throwing all that day and the next. By the third afternoon, the novelty of the spear had worn off a little, and we amused ourselves with other games. It was only after I got home and saw my bow and arrows in my mother's house that I realized I had left my new spear at the pasture! It was too late to go back then, and I didn't want to tell my parents I had forgotten it.

In the days and weeks that followed, I searched and searched for that spear, but I never did find it. However, each morning I practiced archery at home with the other children before taking the goats out, and gradually, my aim improved.

A Stoning

One day towards the end of that year, our neighbors stoned Loweta to death for practicing sorcery. I was upset when I learned the news, because he had always been nice to me, and I played every day with his nephews in their homestead nearby. My uncle Losikiria tried to explain it to me.

"Sorcerers are evil, and it is good to kill them, Kaparketo," he told me. "Many of them, like Loweta, weren't always evil. In fact, Loweta was a fine man until he bought his witchcraft and began to cast spells on people. Many of them died."

When the families of the victims consulted with one another, they realized they had a common enemy, and they marched to Loweta's homestead to accuse him openly. Loweta saw the angry mob coming and knew he was doomed. Several were yelling, "You will not see tomorrow! We will kill you now!"

Loweta did not protest, but only appealed to those in the mob who had been his friends, begging them to give him time enough to make beer so that he could be drunk when they came to kill him. That way, he would not feel as much pain. The crowd agreed, and some of Loweta's old friends even went with him that afternoon to collect honey for the beer. Later, they helped Loweta prepare the mixture in a gourd and hang it from the ceiling beam in his house, above the fire.

The day after the beer was ready, the people came back. Loweta heard them coming and drank the entire gourd, while his neighbors waited patiently outside. Then Loweta walked out into the crowd. One mother, whose child he had killed, grabbed a large stone and threw it at his head.

"No! No!" Loweta cried. "Let the men kill me! Please don't let me die at the hands of a woman!"

Since Loweta had been circumcised in a sowa year,[13] it was decided that a man who was also initiated in one of the *sowa* years should be the first. One man volunteered, claiming Loweta had killed his father. He heaved a large rock at Loweta, and soon seven men—all *sowa*—and two women began stoning him. Then someone in the crowd called out, "Wait! Let's ask him what he knows!"

Loweta was full of blood and could hardly raise his head, but he said, "My witchcraft is far away, and you have no use for it. It is your duty to kill me. I have caused many deaths."

And so they stoned Loweta to death, while his children, Kinang and Lok-wapong, looked on. Later, a song was made up about it, which we still sing today. No harm ever really came to Loweta's children, in spite of the song.

Loweta, Loweta, ah aya
Prepare beer, Loweta
Silently bear the club of the sowa
Loweta, Loweta, oye-o
Even Lokwapong
Even Kinang, Loweta
Silently bear the club of the sowa

Loweta, Loweta ah aya
Ryacha kumun Loweta
Tekanya rungu sowa
Loweta, Loweta, oye-o
Omba Lokwapong
Omba Kinang Loweta
Tekanya na rungu soowa

THUNDER GOD

Moving

About a year after the sun died, Father announced that we would move across the River Suam and settle in the Kayprir region, where he hoped we would find better grass for our cattle. The day before we planned to move, my parents packed all of our good containers, tools and other supplies into *asachai* baskets to hang on the donkeys' backs.[14] Mother told me that before we learned about donkeys from our neighboring tribe, the Karamojong, people carried everything on their own bodies! Then we spread white clay[15] on the faces of all of our animals, and on each other. That night, one of our cows calved, so the move was put off an extra day.

"Remember, Kaparketo," Mother told me as we prepared to leave the next morning, "we must speak to no one during the move, even if we meet others on the same path. We must pass in silence, without even a greeting. It is forbidden to visit with anyone until we have reached our new home site, unpacked our belongings and let out the cattle to graze."

There are many other rules about moving. For instance, one must not settle in places from which people have moved recently, nor must a person settle alone and become an invitation to raiders. I have heard many elders say that if you build your homestead beside a lake the hippos will come to the corral at night to try to mate with the cows, frightening the bulls. At least, no one has claimed it is possible for a cow to become pregnant by such a monster!

We left before dawn, and walked in silence all day until we reached Kapchok hill, near our destination. We camped there, because it is impolite to move into an established homestead on the night of arrival, even if the people are relatives. Sometimes a diviner will read the intestines of a cow or goat to be sure all is well concerning newcomers. If there is some doubt, he might advise them to stay away another four days, while clay is spread on all the children and cattle of the homestead as a precaution.

Evidently, there were no worries about us, because the next morning we moved to an area called Muristit, the site of our new homestead. We herded our cattle into the corral, while mother and the other women found places for their houses and unpacked the donkeys. Then Father let the cattle out to graze, and we were welcomed into our new home.

Ilat and the Flood

While we were living at Kayprir, our cattle grazed at Nakipenet, the site of a deserted Pokot town, where once a large trail crossed the Kanyangareng River. My job was to watch the calves. I would lead them to water one day and to graze the next. Usually, I would take them to a pasture on Kapchok hill, past a large rock face where curious things happened. Some days when I walked by, it would crackle, like a skin that is drying; and I knew it was about to rain. Other times I would hear the cry of a goat coming, it seemed, from under that rock. Once, I saw something like smoke seeping from it. I am sure these things still happen today on Kapchok. But none of them is as mysterious as the vision I saw there when I was bringing the calves home one afternoon.

Just as we reached the bottom of the hill, all of the calves began sniffing the air. They stopped to do this twice, and I wondered what they smelled. Then I saw a man approaching. The calves seemed entranced by his scent, although I was unaware of it. He passed by me to the right without stopping, but I watched him carefully.

He carried two spears and his stool. He wore a yellow belt and a red, beaded necklace, and his arms were abundantly wrapped with beautiful, red copper wire, coiled to perfection. He had a fine, medium build, and his skin had a handsome, red cast, like a Borona or a Somali. Strangely, my eyes were riveted to his body, and I was unable to focus on either his head or his feet. I could not see whether he had shaved his head or put clay in his hair, and, as he passed, I was unable to look into his face. I tried to see what kind of sandals he was wearing, but could not. I gazed after him until he was out of sight. He had been walking on the path that led to our homestead.

"Did you see the wonderful red man who just passed this way?" I asked when I got home. None of my people had seen him, but they questioned me further. "I was unable to see his head or his feet," I explained.

"Oh!" exclaimed my mother and my uncle Losikiria together. "It must have been Ilat! They say it is impossible to focus on Ilat's head or his feet. The boy must have been cursing at the calves! What is to happen now?"

"I didn't say anything bad!" I protested. "The man was one of us!" Yet I began to wonder if, indeed, it had been Ilat, the incarnation of Thunder, and messenger of Tororut.

That evening, I asked my father to tell me about Ilat.

"There are so many matters amongst us which concern Ilat, son," he said. "Thunder has power over the wind, rain, clouds, trees and other natural things of the earth. According to the elders, he punishes those who profane against nature and behave badly. Some people he treats well, and some he punishes. It is said that Ilat is beneath Tororut, yet also *is* Tororut. Everyone believes in Tororut, yet no one has seen him. Why? It must be that Ilat is a visible form of Tororut! No one really knows for sure. He may be supernatural, but we know he is a man, because many people claim to have been taken to his homestead for several days and then returned. Some have disappeared." Then he told me this story:

It is said that once, long before the memory of modern man, the rains failed completely for two years, and our people nearly starved to death. Almost everything Tororut put on the earth perished at the whim of the north wind that drove away the rain clouds. The bodies of cattle, wild animals and humans littered the countryside. Desperate survivors journeyed in vain to the various waterholes and natural wells known to be dwellings of Ilat, only to find them dry.

There was only one well in the entire countryside which still had water. The man who used this well lived on a hill that had more vegetation than on the plains, and eight of his cattle had survived, along with his wife and two children. The rest of his family had starved to death. His cattle had already gone three weeks without sufficient water when, one morning, he went to his well and found only enough water to fill one small gourd. He fell down at the mouth of the well, grieving.

"Dear Tororut!" he cried. "If you are our Father, why do you leave us all to die? This water is my blood! When it is finished, I, too, shall die. Why have you deserted us? What evil have we done? It is *you* who sin, not us; for we are your angels and you have thrown away our children. Ilat, help us!"

He cried like this each morning, and on the fourth day, a man approached him and called out, "You!"

"Yes?" he answered, puzzled. "Who calls me?"

The stranger now stood beside him. "I am Ilat! Why do you grieve and cry to me, saying, 'Ilat has done us wrong'? I have no water! Tapogh[16] is the one who controls the water! Even I cry like you, for Tapogh has wronged us!"

"Then where is Tapogh?"

"I don't know, but I could try to find him."

"Please help me," the man begged. "My people are starving!"

Ilat said, "I will tell him what you have said. Return to this spot in three days, bringing honey-beer,[17] and you shall hear from the one in charge of water."

"How could there be any honey inside my beehive now?" the man protested. "The trees and flowers are dead!"

"You shall find honey," Ilat declared, "for Tororut has helped you."

To his amazement, the man discovered enough honey in his beehive to fill two gourds. He brewed a gourd of beer and carried it to his well before dawn on the third morning. He had been there but two or three minutes, when the stranger appeared.

"Did you follow my instructions?"

"Yes."

"Good. Pour some beer into the gourd-cup for me.

Ilat drank the beer, and then he remarked, "I pleaded with Tapogh on your behalf. I told him, 'If you leave us to die, it must be that you are not our father, but a murderer! Then you deceive the people by claiming you are the Father of the Country! Stop your quarrel with us! Those of us who survive can become the seeds of a new people, until we are many again." Ilat paused, and then instructed the man, "Remain here a few minutes. Something will appear before you and speak to you. Answer respectfully and do not irritate him."

Shortly, the astonished man beheld a cloud forming within his well. It grew little by little until it had enveloped the entire area around the well. Suddenly, a person appeared in the cloud and demanded, "Where is he who cries for water?"

"It is I," said the man, stunned.

"Why do you cry out," the apparition boomed.

"I cry, for I see my death is near."

"Do you know the god of water?"

"I know there is one who is the Father of the Country, and I cry because he has abandoned us."

"The cloud-man roared, "Go tell those of your people who live in the dry riverbeds to abandon their houses and leave at once. If in one week they have not yet gone, it will be futile for them to cry to me!"

While the man gaped, the cloud stood up like a tree before him. It grew until it reached the sky. Then, as he watched in wonder, the spirit went up into the heavens and vanished.

Suddenly, there was a gurgling sound. The man looked down and saw his well gradually filling with water!

"Listen carefully," said the voice of Ilat at his side. "Your termite hill is nearly ready to harvest now, for we have seen the rain-spirit and he has returned to the sky. The rains will come shortly. You must slaughter an ox, save the meat, and use the skin to cover your gourds. Then you will have something to put the termites in after the rains. When you have finished that, go and gather grasses."

"How can I find grass? There is none because of the drought."

"Take the thatch from the roofs of the houses. Put the grasses, firewood, the meat, gourds and all your possessions inside a cave. The rains shall pour for one week; only a cave has the strength to withstand them. On the sixth morning after today, when you see a pillar of cloud rise up again from your well, run to your cave without delay. The rains shall fall with great force, for they have been held back for many days."

The man was watching his well with wonder. It had overflowed and flooded a distance of 100 yards. Then it stopped.

"Finally," Ilat went on sternly, "go and tell all the people who dwell in the houses of Ilat—the dry riverbeds and water basins—to leave their homes! Tell them they are guests in my 'homesteads' where I 'cooked' for many years. Now I am returning to my homes, and everyone should move to higher ground. On the sixth day, if there remains a person at any of my homesteads, his fate is sealed." Ilat abruptly turned and walked away.

The man immediately went to his home, gathered firewood and reeds, and carried them to a cave. Then he slaughtered an ox and prepared his gourds for the white ants (termites), a Pokot delicacy. (When rain follows a prolonged dry period, the insects fly out of their great hills. As they return to the nest, they are trapped and eaten like candy.)[18] Finally, he and his family herded their cattle into the cave and began to eat meals there.

Twice he went to warn the people in the lowlands. "You are strangers in the houses of Ilat," he told them. "You must leave your settlements, for I have seen Ilat, and he is coming soon. Truly, he has already helped me—I have water in my well!"

But the people said, "You are trying to deceive us! What are your motives? How do you expect us to believe there is rain anywhere? We'll stay where we are, and if we die, we die! Ilat has already cast us away."

Only two people left with him, and later four others followed. When they reached his well, the six drank water until one man's stomach burst, and he died.

On the sixth day, they saw a cloud rise up from the well, as Ilat had foretold. The man told his companions, "We must go now!" but they were starving and barely had enough strength to move. They staggered like babies who had just learned to walk. At last, they reached the cave and began devouring the ox their friend had slaughtered.

All this time, they watched the cloud. It rose in a great column, pushing gradually upwards from the well. Finally, it soared, and rains stood in the cloud. Now it spread itself thinly over the entire countryside.

Suddenly, the rains poured. All the rivers flowed again, and all those who were living on the lands by or in the riverbeds, rich and poor, leaders and followers, were swept away by the rushing water and drowned. All of the people of our land perished except those six in the cave (with their families) who had listened to the words of Ilat.

Yes, the rains poured and poured. They poured until the country had once again become good. Even to this day, we cherish the place where Ilat appeared to save our people. A man will not pass by without first ritually entering the water of this sacred well.

My Uncle's Escape

One day a messenger came to our homestead to bring my mother some alarming news about her younger brother's family. Evidently, some people called Europeans had come to their homestead and forcefully seized all the able-bodied men, including my uncle, to work for them. No one knew where they were or when they would come back! Shortly afterwards, my uncle's wife had died, leaving their four-month old infant and three older children destitute.

Mother left immediately to rescue the children. Her brother's family lived in a distant area of the country, and it would take several days for her to cross the mountains and find their homestead. While Mother was gone, Chelima and I moved into the house of our father's second wife, Chepusuchon, who had a small son, Apur. We were eager to meet our new cousins, who would be living with us, but when they finally arrived, we were amazed at how thin and frail they were! Chepusuchon hurried to cook them some food, while they rested with my mother from the long walk.

That evening, Mother told us the real reason for the fate of her brother's household. "My brother's wife died because he put a curse on her!" she exclaimed. "He was enraged because someone had stolen his honey, and he made his wife and older children take an oath, saying, 'If you have eaten the honey, tell me or this oath will kill you!' All of them denied taking the honey, but after my brother was taken away, his wife became seriously ill and confessed. They say she wailed, 'Where is my husband? I thought nothing would happen to me because of the oath! It's true—I was the one who ate the honey! Please find someone who can cure the spell and save me!' Her friends went to get a traditional doctor, but when they returned they found her dead beside her baby."

About a month later, while my friends and I were out with the goats, we saw a gaunt and horrible man approaching us. He had no cape, so we could see from a distance how bony his naked body was—like a shadow! He carried no spear or stool. His clay headdress was old and cracked; the hair had grown through it and extended down his back. We thought he must be an enemy and ran home, leaving the goats to their fate. When we told Father, he grabbed his spear and went back immediately to investigate. He found the man standing there alone with the goats, waiting for him.

We children were certainly surprised when we saw Father and the terrible man bringing the goats home together. "This, children, is your uncle," Father said, and he left to kill a very large black ox to feed the starving man and his children.

It was some time before I began to feel comfortable around this sad uncle who came to live with us. He had a strange story to tell:

"The Europeans took us to work near Moroto, where we cleared land for a road to Lodwar,"[19] he began. "We were treated badly. They never gave us food, and all the men were suffering. Then one day, while no one was watching, I escaped and hid in the bush, but a group of Karamojong men spotted me and took me prisoner. One of them wanted to kill me, but another man felt sorry for me because I was starving. He actually took me to his own home and slaughtered a goat for me to eat! He became my friend, and at night, since I could not sleep inside the homestead, we slept under a single skin blanket just outside the corral gate. He was protecting me from those who wished me dead! Unfortunately, it cost him his life.

"One night, as we lay there, I became aware of some men standing over us. I opened one eye just enough to see four Karamojong, one with a spear poised. I waited for death. One of them whispered, 'There—that's the one!' and I heard the thud of a spear as it entered the body of my friend! He cried out, and the men ran away. I leaped up, sprinted into the corral, grabbed my spear and shield, and ran outside to hide in the bushes nearby. My friend was crying out in agony, and his wife and children ran to him. Then one of them spotted me, and I was seized. I tried to explain how the four men had mistaken their father for me. Luckily, they believed me!

"After my friend died, his oldest son extracted the spear from his body, recognized it as that of a neighbor, and went after him, together with the other men from the homestead. As soon as they left, I ran, traveling as fast as I could without being seen very much. I spent two nights on the road before coming here. I had planned to stay here only a few days before continuing home to my wife and children, but now I find I have no wife—my own curse killed her! And only three of my cattle are left!"

THE YEAR THE EARTH SHOOK

Shortly after my new uncle and his children came to live with us, my family moved to Murua Nyangai, where we lived with a man named Kangaramoi for about a year. That was The Year the Earth Shook, which we call *Koringrin* [*1927-8*].[20]

Childhood Mischief

There were a lot of children in Kangaramoi's village, in addition to all my cousins and siblings who had moved with us. Since the older boys did most of the herding, I usually played with the children who stayed around the houses during the day. There must have been about twenty of us—all eager for adventure and afraid of nothing! As I was bigger than most of them, I became their leader, and, as a result, got into a lot of trouble.

For instance, like all small children, we loved to play imaginary games. Some of us would be cattle, others would be the goats, and the rest, people. Sooner or later, the "people" would decide to eat one of the "cattle." We would get a stick and hit one of the cattle-children, who would fall down and play dead. Then we would pretend to butcher the animal.

One afternoon, as we were playing this, I took out my knife and sharpened it, saying, "Now we will cut the meat of our ox." I took hold of the child's legs and turned him on his back. "One man hold the front legs and another man hold the hind legs," I ordered. I put the point of the knife at the boy's throat, punctured the skin and began to slit down his chest.

"Mother! Mother!" he shrieked, as the blood came. I threw down the knife, and all of us ran to hide. The women came running, but they couldn't find any of us. They searched all that afternoon and evening, then went back home. Gradually, the darkness settled on us, and the smaller children grew afraid. One by one and in small groups, they went home to face their parents' anger. The moment they entered the gate, they were seized for whippings.

"Kaparketo told us to do it!" the little children protested. "He said the boy was our ox and we could get his meat!" Some were whipped and others were spared. I could hear it all from where I hid outside the homestead.

Presently, my mother came outside alone and called for me, but I was quiet. I could imagine the whipping I would get if she ever found me, and I decided to spend the night in the bush. After awhile, Mother gave up and went back inside the gate. I was alone.

The night was quiet—very quiet and very dark. I began thinking about the prowling night creatures which would surely sense that I was there as they passed by. I thought, *What if a hyena sees me? Would he eat me? Of course he would! I would be easy prey, like a young calf.* I decided to climb a tree and sleep in its boughs.

There was a large tree nearby, and I managed to climb half-way up, in spite of the darkness. *If I go just a bit further, I'll be safe from any lunges a hyena might make,* I thought. I groped for a higher branch, and at last my left hand touched one. Then my foot slipped, and I fell. A horrible pain shot through my groin as I hit against a limb below. I grabbed it just in time, and found myself dangling from the tree in total darkness; pain throbbing between my legs. I screamed! Mother came running, found me in the tree and helped me down.

"What's the matter, son?" she asked gently, holding me.

"The tree cut me when I fell!" I sobbed.

When we were inside the corral, near the firelight, Mother saw that my scrotum had been torn open and was bloody. She cried out, and Father came running, asking, "What's wrong?"

"Don't you see where he is hurt?" Mother cried.

Father glanced at the wound and then stormed, "Let it be! What about the boy you tried to slaughter, huh? What about that!" He was furious. He seized me and whipped me until I could no longer tell which pain was coming from my groin. When he was finished, he carried me home, got a thorn needle and sewed me up.

The wound had barely healed, when, once again, things got out of hand. You see, I loved to sit around boasting to the younger children, because they always believed everything I said. One day, we were chatting in front of a hut where a senile old lady always sat. She must have been very old, for her mind didn't work anymore. She didn't know where she was; she merely sat in one place from sunrise until sunset each day.

"Yep," I was telling my friends. "A person as old as that, you know, gets very tough skin. Even if you throw stones or arrows at her, she won't feel it."

"Really?"

"Sure."

So we all decided it would be great fun to shoot arrows at the hapless old woman. (One of the woman's own grandsons was with us, but he was too young to know the difference!) About ten of us stood by the corral fence and aimed at the woman, still sitting in front of her hut. The first arrow missed. Then I tried, but my arrow only bounced off her skin clothing and fell.

"Hey, let's try to hit her clothes off with the arrows," someone said, but I suggested, "No! The clothes just get in the way. I'll undo them so we can see her body and can hit it!"

I went up to the old woman and began to take off her clothes.

"Where are you taking my clothes?" she asked.

"Oh—nowhere. I'll just put them over here." I said, and she seemed satisfied.

"Oh," she nodded.

I went back to the line of children, picked up my bow and an arrow and aimed, just as her older grandson came in the corral and saw us!

"Whaaaa—You fool!" he yelled, suddenly realizing what we were doing. We threw down our weapons and ran. He seized two of the little children roughly and demanded, "Why do you want to hit my grandma?"

"Kaparketo told us that when a person is very old they get such tough skin, you can't even pierce it. It's really tough," they volunteered enthusiastically.

He tore off after me, but I had a head start and was well hidden by the time he burst out of the corral gate. I waited there until that evening, when my mother and some others called for me. I came readily, and they asked me, "Why did you shoot at the old woman?"

"We didn't hit her," I protested. "If we did, she would have felt pain, but she didn't! Those children lied about me. I didn't tell them to do it!"

After hearing this, my mother was really angry with the others. "It's not true!" she yelled. "You accuse my son all the time like this! Why wasn't she hit, if they were all shooting at her? It's a lie against my son!"

She left me alone the rest of that day and the next, and I had time to think about what we had done. I realized how lucky we were that the woman's grandson came along when he did!

More Trouble

In those days, I would eat anything. Once, some little children saw me eating the very large, hard seed of a plant that resembles sisal, and they asked, "How do you eat that?"

"Like this!" I said, and popped another into my mouth.

"We want to eat it too!" they said.

"All right," I shrugged. "Then eat it!"

Two of the children swallowed the large things. Then another, named Arekai came and tried one, but when he swallowed, it got stuck in his throat. It was terrible! He choked and choked. We hit him on the back but it wouldn't come out. Arekai's eyes protruded and he defecated and urinated. We cried a lot and called for help, knowing it was useless.

It was our fantastic luck that a woman happened to be gathering firewood nearby. She ran to us and found the little child nearly dead. She grabbed him and hit him hard on the back. The seed came out, and the child was saved.

Nevertheless, this accident became my fault as well, because the children all said, "Kaparketo showed us this thing and said, 'You should eat it because it is my food!'"

But I wasn't afraid of this accusation. "Why did you eat it if you didn't want to?" I countered angrily. I stalked back to the homestead ahead of the others and told my mother what had happened and how I had not made Arekai eat the fruit. She must have stood up for me, because I heard no more about it after that.

Arekai, by the way, has since become my closest lifelong friend. As adults, we have given one another cattle and goats. He has been like a brother to me.

About five days after Arekai was saved, I was walking with my father to the river, when we came across an eland that had been killed by a lion. That was, I think, the first time I was aware of a lion's real presence.

My father told me, "Go home and tell the people there is meat here."

I was terrified. "No, I don't want to go! What if this animal sees me walking along? Won't he eat me?"

"Well, then, I'll go," Father teased. You stay here."

"*Ala!* What if the lion wants to come back for its food and sees me here? He would eat me too!" I started to cry.

So we both went home to tell the people. A group of us returned to the hill, butchered the meat and carried it home. We feasted on eland that night. Later, we heard the lion roar in the distance, and I was awed. It was the first time I remember hearing a lion. Then it growled, and people remarked that it was coming closer, tracking its meat. I stayed close to my mothers.

The lion caused great havoc that night, circling around the homestead. The cattle were so nervous, everyone was afraid they would bolt outside. Finally, all the adults charged out the gate, lined up against the fence outside the corral and chased him off."

A few weeks after the lion incident, one of the elderly women in our homestead, Kodenyan's wife, died peacefully one night. The next day, we heard some of the older children saying, "They went to put the body out in the bush. I wonder if they are back yet."

Instead of burying her, the family had decided to carry the body into the countryside and place it carefully in a thicket. This is a common enough procedure, but we children were fascinated. The idea of a body intrigued us.

We had no idea it was bad when a person died; we thought they just died like a cow. In fact, I was just wondering about this, when I had an idea. "Do you suppose she is really dead?" I asked my friends. "Maybe she just tried to die but didn't really. Let's go see her!"

We followed the footprints of the man who had carried the body off. We had not gone very far when, suddenly, I saw her there in the bushes!

I exclaimed, "*Ala!* Does a person die like this?" I reached down and grabbed her, calling her by name, but she was silent. Then we all tried calling her, but still she refused to answer.

"Ah, she's just a fool!" I mocked her. "You just stay there, woman! If you don't want to go home, we'll just leave you there! It's your own fault!" Everybody laughed.

Meanwhile, some of the women had discovered our footprints leading towards the spot where the body lay. They told others, and soon the whole force of mothers charged after us. When we saw them, we ran as fast as we could, with the women in hot pursuit. All the smaller children were caught and spanked hard. The rest of us got away.

After awhile, we wandered back home again, trying to act casually. Nothing happened at first, but as soon as we were all well inside the gates, screams came from all around us, as the women rushed us. We were whipped badly, and, as usual, all the children told on me, saying "Kaparketo told us to go see her!"

The next day, my parents sent me out of the homestead, saying, "Go watch the cattle, Kaparketo! Whenever you stay around here you get into trouble!"

Herding with Kilowan

It became my duty to watch the calves all day with an older boy named Kilowan, who was one of Kangaramoi's children. It was exciting being a partner with Kilowan, who treated me as a friend, even though he was more important than I. Kilowan had already pierced his mouth, nose and ears, and wore a small lip plug and beaded earrings. He was skilled with the wooden spear, and practiced each day while the calves grazed. Once, when we were out together, Kilowan stalked a dikdik (a tiny antelope) and killed it with his spear. This pleased his father, Kangaramoi, who took a large male goat to the ironsmith the next day and commissioned a small metal spear to be made for his son.

All the children were envious the morning Kilowan tried out his handsome new spear, with its glistening metal shaft and point. Later, when it was time for us to let the calves out for the day, Kilowan presented me with his old wooden spear, saying, "I want you to have this, Kaparketo. Practice hard with the *korobe* hoops, and one day your father will give you a metal one like mine."

Happily, I set to work tying green sticks into hoops, and I soon had a collection of about twenty. Each morning, before the cattle left, all the boys and girls in our homestead who were old enough would practice together. One would hurl a hoop into the air or roll it along the ground, while another tried to shoot it with an arrow or throw a spear at it. We also practiced shooting at targets, placing

sticks in the ground at varying distances. There was always one child who surpassed the others and some who couldn't hit anything. This was our "school" of
the spear and the bow and arrow.

One afternoon, as we were bringing the calves slowly home, I told Kilowan,
"I'm going on ahead. I'm starved! You bring the calves this time, friend."

I left him and walked on alone. My mind wandered, as I thought about all the
birds, dikdik and rabbits I had tried to spear while watching the calves with Kilowan in recent weeks. I had missed them all, but my aim was slowly improving.
I fantasized about spearing eland and lions one day, relishing in the praise of my
family and friends. I ambled as if in a dream, considering the cattle, people, and
various events in the homestead.

Then, all at once, my mind came back to reality, and I realized I was lost! I
wandered on and on, disoriented, until, thankfully, I saw a homestead in the
distance. It was dusk, so I quickened my pace. The path led through thick vegetation, and I was quite close before I saw, to my great disappointment, that the
homestead was deserted. Not knowing what else to do, I continued walking until
it seemed I was nearly in Karamojong country. I was tired and confused. At last,
I came across five cattle and decided to follow them. The sun had set, and it was
getting darker by the minute. When the cattle finally lay down, I did too, and
soon fell asleep. I was lucky that the man who came searching for his cattle found
me there.

"Please show me where my homestead is," I begged.

"Who is your father?" he asked.

"My father is Pturu."

"And with whom does he stay?"

"There is an elder named Kangaramoi. We live with him."

He smiled. "I know them. But you must come home with me for the night.
Tomorrow I'll take you to your homestead."

"Thank you." I was relieved, hungry and exhausted. We walked to his home,
herding the cattle, and he gave me some milk and porridge. My own father, who
had come searching for me, awakened me in the middle of night. We left the next
morning, and on the way home Father stopped at a friend's corral to ask for a goat.
When we reached our homestead, my people took the partially-digested grasses
from the stomach of an ox that had been slaughtered and spread them all over my
body, for I had gone to sleep in the wilderness. Then they gave me the goat to kill,
and they spread the stomach contents of the goat over me as well. This is our custom to help protect a person who has been lost. Sometimes Kilowan, being more
mature, watched the cattle alone, while I tended to the calves with other children.
It was on one of those evenings that Kilowan did not return with the herd. At
sunset a search party was sent out. They found his body in an open, grassy area,
saturated with blood from multiple spear wounds. The cattle were gone. There
must have been other evidence as well, because the men came back to report that

it was the Karamojong who had stolen the cattle and murdered my friend Kil-owan.

I tried to understand why this had happened to my friend, and why they had stolen our cattle—our livelihood. When I asked my mother, she replied bitterly, "The Karamojong are relentless raiders! Their blood runs fierce, Kaparketo. Why, a Karamojong mother will put stiff porridge on separate plates for each of her children. She mixes butter in the porridge of those who have stolen cattle from the Pokot, the Turkana or the Teso. To the others, she chides, 'Eat yours with water! When you fatten our herds like your brothers, then you will deserve fat in your porridge!'

"Sometimes they even use magic on a raid. I have heard it said that when they reach an intended victim's homestead, they toss a shilling, some beans and sorghum inside the corral and this causes all the people inside to go to sleep. When all is quiet, they open the gate and steal the cattle."

There was talk of revenge. A few months later, some of the men from Kanga-ramoi's household disappeared, but no one spoke about them. Three days later they came back, bringing several head of Karamojong cattle.[21]

Those who had been on the raid behaved very strangely toward me. Whenever I came near one of them, he would duck inside a hut or crouch down and beat at me with his stick until I went away. Once a warrior called my mother to come take me away. Finally an older boy explained, "They are trying to protect you, Kaparketo. Until the new moon, they must not let their shadows fall upon any women, girls or small children."

"Why?"

"Because they have killed. They have avenged your friend."

Flash Flood

When the rains came, they poured. Right after the first storm, we went out to prepare our white ant hills. The termite mound nearest our homestead was taller than a man—a red clay tower jutting out of a parched, grassy clearing, like the stump of a large tree cut off by lightning. We worked all day, until late in the evening, digging holes at the base of the mound, lining and covering them with slippery leaves and grasses. After the next rain, the tasty insects would emerge from this clay village for their mating flights and return only to be caught in the false entrances. We would scoop them up by the thousands, eating as much as we could, and carry the rest home for our mothers to fry. It was happy work, and we finished just in time.

When we were halfway home, sheets of rain tumbled from the sky. The water hammered down on us so that we could hardly walk or see. At last, drenched, we reached the thorn fence around our homestead, found the gate, and ran to our houses. Inside, Mother was starting to cook over the house fire, because of the rain. (Usually we cook outside.) She was wet, and I was alarmed to see her crying.

What's wrong, Mother?" I asked.

"The river flooded and swept away two of the cattle! One died! It was terrible! The other one could be dead by morning if a lion finds it."

Because of my mother's fear, we decided to perform the ritual of *rataw*, to protect the cow from the jaws of predators during the night. In the rain, my father got some hair from either the cow's calf or another one of its clan and gathered some dung from the corral gate the cattle passed through that morning (Kangaramoi's homestead had two gates). He bored a hole in a green *kinyuk* stick and put the hair and dung inside the hollow. Then he called all of us into the corral. We stood, huddled in the rain, while Father went to the gateway and ordered, "Be silent! Close your eyes!" Then he intoned, *"Whether my cow is near or far, whether it is in the thicket or in the open, I say to every hyena, leopard, lion, wild dog, and all other wild animals: Your eyes shall close and darken whenever you want to look upon my cow! You will not see my cow!"* He repeated this a few more times, and then said, "Everyone wake up!" We opened our eyes and ran for cover into our houses.

This small ritual, *rataw,* can also be used to bring back a lost wife. For instance, when a woman repeatedly runs away from her husband, and he knows she is about to try again, he will bore a long hole in a particular log with a milky pith. Into this hole, he will stuff a small piece cut from his wife's skin garments and a *kukulwa* (used for extracting teeth). Soon the wife leaves him for another man, but things do not go right for her. She will not get pregnant, or even menstruate, no matter how many years she stays with her lover. Even if she tries several husbands, she will remain barren, until, at last, she returns to the man she rejected. At that time, he will open the log, remove the two articles, and start to sleep with her. She will begin to menstruate again, and soon will be carrying his child. If such a woman is smart, she will come back while her body is still capable of producing many children.[22]

It continued raining most of that night, and even the young men crowded into the huts to sleep. By morning, the clouds had disappeared, and the early sunlight shimmered on moisture suspended briefly in the air. By noon it would be gone.

After the herd was let out, I went with my parents to search for the missing cow. We followed the riverbed quite a distance before Mother spotted it. The frightened, exhausted animal was caught on some branches, where it had been stranded when the flood waters receded. We made a rope, threw it around the cow's struggling body, and pulled her down. Then we went back to the dead ox, skinned it and took the meat home.

The Curse on Kangaramoi's Wife

Later that rainy season, we learned that Kangaramoi's wife had done a terrible thing: She had held other people's food in her hands during her monthly period.

You see, when a Pokot woman menstruates, she is considered tarnished. If she is outside when her period begins, she will knock near the doorway and call, "Please come out so that I may enter the house." The men come outside, she goes in and sits on the ground, and the men come back inside again. This is because it is forbidden amongst us for a menstruating woman to enter a house while men are inside. Similarly, she must not touch any food other than her own. She rests, and another wife tends to her chores. If her husband has no other wife, he does the work himself, whether it is cooking porridge or milking cows. During her period, a woman drinks no cow milk—only goat milk. Then, when it is finished, she goes to the river to bathe. Only after that may she work and eat as usual. These rules are ancient and still widely practiced.

That is why Kangaramoi was concerned when he discovered his wife was menstruating one night when he slept with her.

"It's nothing," she insisted.

Kangaramoi got up and examined the food left over from the evening meal by the light of the fire. (We save some to eat again in the morning.) He saw some red in it.

"I will curse you if you foul me like this!" he threatened.

"No!" she pleaded. "I just noticed it now. It's not every day."

"I have seen it from you three times!"

"No!"

But the next day, Kangaramoi took out one of his cows. He spread white clay on its head and down its back. Then he took some ostrich feathers and showed them to the cow. He called to his wife:

"You! My wife Chepuchepko! If you want to kill me, this cow will kill you first! I gave away its mother in order to marry you!"

Then he addressed the cow: *"Listen, cow. I hold here the ostrich feathers I wore at the time I took your mother away so I could marry Chepuchepko. Yet now I think this wife has done me a great wrong, and therefore she has become your enemy as well. If I am mistaken and she is good, let her live well. But if she is bad, let her meet her end quickly. These words will suffice. Now go and consider what I have told you."*

Three months later, after a rain, Chepuchepko was waterproofing the thatched roof of her house with dung when she slipped and fell onto a sharp stick. It pierced her chest and throat. She cried out, and one of the other women rushed over and removed the stick. It was a bad wound, and Chepuchepko died the following morning. It was the curse of the cow.

MAKING A HOMESTEAD

We left Kangaramoi's homestead about the time the road to Lodwar was being constructed [1928][23] and settled in the region of Kanyangareng. This time we did not move in with a friend, but made our own homestead at a place called Lossom.

Building our Homes

As we began to build our family homes there, none of us suspected that gradually, we would come to think of Lossom, more than any other place, as home. Even though we have found it necessary to move away from time to time, especially when there has been a drought, in order to find pasture for our cattle, we have always eventually returned to Lossom. Here we have grown up, raised our own children, and watched our own parents grow old. Lossom has become our home indeed.

When we reached the site Father had chosen, Mother, his first wife, instructed the other women where to tie their donkeys and where to build their homes. We were told not to cut the tree where the donkeys were first tied, which we call The Mother of Goat Tree, for firewood or for building any part of the homestead that first day. Then a fire was made, and each woman took some of the fire to her appointed place. (Mother said it was essential for these first fires to be tended well, for if any were allowed to go out, the family would have to move to a new site, even if it was night.) At last, the women began to cook food for us children, and the cattle were allowed to wander. The affairs of the homestead were underway.

In the morning, the building began. The Mother of Goat Tree was cut into support poles and roof beams for our house, and mounds of sticks were collected and lashed together to form the walls. We children were sent to gather loads of grasses for the thatching. Later, our mothers would cover the thatch with dung for waterproofing. After each rain, the roof would be checked and patched with more dung where necessary, and when too much dung accumulated on the roof, it would be removed and burned in a pit, and new dung would be applied.

Larger Pokot homes accommodate goats, as well as people, and include a separate door for the goats. They are sometimes built with a loft, where guests can sleep after a celebration or beer-drinking party. Even cows can be brought inside for milking when it is raining, if there is enough room.

My family's houses have usually been much smaller. There are the two beds, made of sticks and draped with skins: the father's is long enough for him to lie flat,

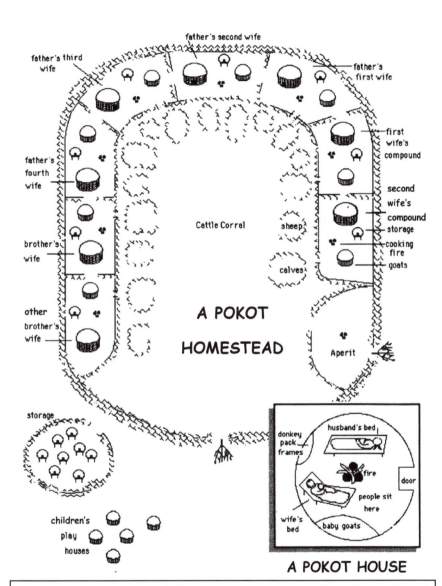

A POKOT HOMESTEAD

father's second wife

father's third wife

father's first wife

first wife's compound

second wife's compound

storage

cooking fire

goats

father's fourth wife

brother's wife

other brother's wife

Cattle Corral

sheep

calves

Aperit

storage

children's play houses

A POKOT HOUSE

donkey pack frames

husband's bed

fire

door

people sit here

wife's bed

baby goats

This diagram of Domonguria's homestead in 1970 shows the relationship between architectural features. The actual corral was much wider and longer, so that the houses were located mostly around the side opposite the door. The shade tree marking the *kurket* was outside the perimeter of this condensed diagram.

with his head propped up on a small wooden stool, while the mother's is elevated so that she can sleep with her back slightly raised, surrounded by her small children. Older girls often sleep with their grandmothers, and older boys sleep outside.[24] The father, of course, must take turns sleeping with each of his wives. The central fireplace consists of three stones, with the firewood between them. There is a small pen for baby goats, and a place to hang the *asachai* (donkey panniers) on the wall. Other things are stored above the low doorway. Outside each house is a cooking fire, the storage hut, which is built on stilts, and a covered goat house (see Diagram).

The wives' compounds surround one side of the cattle corral, the center of any Pokot homestead, like the lyrics of our song: *"Houses in a circle, like many birds around a bowl-shaped rock ..."* There is a brush fence separating the houses and the corral, and a thorn bush fence around the entire homestead. In front of each wife's compound is a small opening in the corral fence, leading to her two enclosures for sheep and calves just inside the corral. On one side of the corral, not directly in front of the houses, is another open enclosure, the *aperit,* where old men talk around the fire, and where young men and older boys sleep on the ground. The *aperit* has its own gates, one leading to the outside, and the other leading into the corral. Finally, just outside every homestead is the *kurket,* the shade of a tree where men gather to talk, eat meat and to pray, always facing towards Mtelo Mountain.[25]

At Lossom, we built extra storage huts for our food near the homestead. A short distance away, Chelima and the other little girls made their play village, a miniature replica of our homestead.

We usually dig wells in the dry riverbeds, but at Lossom this was not necessary. Not far from our homestead was a huge, ancient well called Kanasat, entirely hewn out of rock and as deep as a *walaiya* tree. Twenty people could fit inside this one well to hoist the water up, person to person, until it reached the top. (Women traditionally work at the bottom of a well and the men at the top.) In the darkness of Kanasat, the women usually took off all their clothes to keep from getting soaked. When one needed to urinate, she used a wooden container especially made for that purpose, then passed it to the top of the well to be emptied. I still remember the sound of my mothers' voices at the bottom of that well—small, but strangely magnified. It was the same kind of sound I heard much later coming from a white man's radio!

Our neighbors at Lossom told us Kanasat and other large rock wells were hewn by ancient peoples called Oropom, Murris, Seapaa and Toruk, but no one knows how they managed to bore holes in the midst of solid rock. Even now that we have learned how to strike and lift large stones with European tools, we realize we have yet to master the skills of the ancients! Evidently, the Karamojong encroached on their homelands and exterminated most of those early residents of Kanyangareng. My people absorbed many of the others. I hear occasionally that such-and-such a person is an Oropom[26] or that another is descended from the Seapaa.

We Pokot have a long history of assimilating other people, and the practice has made us numerous and strong. When someone from a different tribe—even an enemy—has wished to settle peacefully among us, we have not questioned his origins. Rather, we have welcomed strangers, saying, "Come. We shall live and work together until you have become one of us. You shall marry and keep adding to your garden until you have a nice farm in our country." Such a person will always be considered a foreigner because he speaks a different language, but his children will be Pokot from birh.

Ostrich Attack

It was right after we had finished building our homestead at Lossom that I first saw an ostrich. In those days, many people in that area raised ostriches for their feathers, which were prized for headdresses and ceremonies. The baby birds were nurtured to adulthood, and then they were herded right along with the family's cattle and goats. Feathers were taken periodically from the live birds, and the owners were able to make a nice profit by trading them for livestock, honey, tobacco, or grain.

Chelima and I were anxious to see such big birds, so when we heard our neighbor's ostrich had wandered home with our cattle one evening, we asked, "Where is it? Can we see it?"

Our mother Chepusuchon pointed to the goat corral. We rushed over to the enclosure and looked in. We couldn't believe our eyes! There it was, a giant heap of plumes with a monstrous, snake-like neck, sitting there asleep with the little goat kids snuggled in its feathers. It was huge!

In the morning when the goats were let out, the ostrich went with them. It was even bigger than I had expected now that it was standing on its enormous legs. Since it was my job to help look after the goats, I was relieved that some adults agreed to go with us!

By midday, I was accustomed to Lingarel's ostrich, though I kept my distance. I played with my friends, and everything went well until a bigger boy and I decided to extract some *maangaa* (hardened sap) from a *panyaret* tree to eat. Little did I know that this was also a favorite food of the ostrich! As soon as the great bird saw us with the *maangaa*, it cocked its head and started coming right towards us with its giant strides.

Everyone yelled, "Run! The ostrich is after you!"

My friend got away, and I tried to run, but the ostrich was too fast. I turned, hoping to climb a tree, but its huge foot slammed into my back and knocked me to the ground. I fell on my face, and the ostrich tread on me and snatched the *maangaa* from my hand. I screamed in terror. Finally, the grownups came running and chased the giant bird away.

The next day I refused to be near the ostrich. I told my mother, "If that thing goes with the goats, I'm not going! It will kill me!" I stayed home until Lingarel came to claim his bird.

Farming, Honey, and Tobacco

Soon after our homestead was established, my family began clearing a field for our crops. We found a suitable place about four miles from our homestead, and each day several people would work there, chopping up the sod with their wooden hoes. (These days, people use axes, machetes and other European tools.) Although each of my mothers had her own garden, the plots were adjacent, and all of us cooperated in any farm work.

Sometimes, Father would talk about the old days, when our ancestors farmed only the steep hillsides, terracing the gardens with logs. As we worked, he told us about growing up on the slopes of Cheptulel, where the rivers continued to flow even when the rains failed, and about the "bridge of water," their irrigation system of carved wooden troughs supported by forked sticks, which radiated to all the area gardens from the mountain streams. After each garden was watered, the farmer would block off his branch of the system with a mound of earth, so that the water could proceed down the troughs and ditches to other fields.[27]

Mountainous regions like Cheptulel, Father explained, were first settled by Pokot after a severe three-year drought decimated most of the herds and peoples of the plains. Men used to have hundreds, or even thousands, of cattle, but these days such wealth is rare. It has always been the responsibility of the hill farmers to help those on the plains in times of famine. If the rains come on time, all is well, and we can live with our herds. But in times of need, people who farm and who store their surplus crops wisely—like us—will have a greater chance of survival.

Of course, farming is meant only to supplement the blood, milk and occasional meat from our herds, not to provide total subsistence. Often a family will split, with some seeking pastures for the herds, and others staying to farm. Sometimes, a family might choose to leave the gardens altogether in order to follow the herds on the plains or to other distant pastures.

The gardens are not always near the homestead, and it is not uncommon for children to be sent up to six miles carrying milk to those in the fields. Shelters are constructed at distant fields, so that farmers can work there several days at a time. When the crops are ripening, women and children take turns sitting on small roofed platforms built on posts, so that they can scare away birds and other destructive animals.[28]

Whenever people return from the garden, they are expected to bathe before entering any houses. Water is brought into the corral, Mother used to explain, "So that everyone sees that we have finished our work, and now we are bathing!" Those who planned to return to the farm the next morning did not have to bathe if they slept in the corral.

When I was young, we usually planted millet and sorghum during the second month, in case the rains began during the third month. Maize is grown these days also, but it is not one of our traditional crops; it came from the Europeans.[29] By the fourth month, the rains had usually come and planting was over. Then, in order to prevent crop failure, Father and certain other elders arranged each year for spirits to walk over all the farms. Afterwards, the spirits would come to one of the home-steads—often ours—to drink beer and eat a stiff porridge. All of us—children and adults—were warned to stay inside the houses during this time. We could hear the noise, but no one could go outside until the spirits left and returned to their own. In fact, they say that if you happen to see one of the ghosts, you will go crazy!

Newborn babies were also capable of influencing the crops. When a baby was born during the sunny, dry season, people would put water and *malot* plants in pots, tie skins over the tops, and turn them upside down. The nursing infant would not be bathed or given water for one week, and during this time it would not rain. Once the baby was bathed and the pots were opened, washed out with water and put away, the rains would come. On the other hand, a baby born when it had been raining too much could be given a covered pot with the request: Please help us shut off the rains! This might work, but we used the procedure mostly for children born during the dry season.

The long rains usually lasted from approximately the sixth through the tenth month, and this was a time for much celebration. The food was harvested, and put into a storage house for about ten months. Afterwards, it would be stored in pots made especially for millet and sorghum. By the eleventh month, our country would become dry, and during the twelfth month we would cut trees, and burn and rake the fields, ready to begin again.

Whenever the harvest was adequate, my father always buried a few large pots of surplus food in a secret cave. He put one or two in each hole, using several caves if necessary, until he had stored enough food to insure the family's survival in time of drought. When I was older, Father showed me the location of his caves, saying, "You, my eldest child, are now the only other person who knows where our stor-age cave is. You must never use this food while people are still healthy."

In addition to herding and farming, my parents established and tended to several beehives in the area around Lossom, so that they would have enough honey for the many celebrations that required honey-beer. Father always traded some of the excess honey for more stock and produce, or for tobacco, which, in turn, could be traded again at a profit, since most adults use tobacco when it is available. For chewing tobacco, we mix the leaves with ashes, spitting on the mix-ture until it holds together in a ball. To make snuff, people put the leaves, soda and a little fat from the stomach of a goat into a skin bag, cover it with a stone, and strike it with a club until it is finely ground. Others prefer to grind the mixture in a horn with a stick. The snuff is then warmed over a fire before use.

LIFE IN LOSSOM

My Lip Plug

There were several other children in our new village besides my sister Chelima and me. As we played together, I noticed that most of the older boys wore earrings, as well as decorative wooden studs under their lower lips. This fashion spread quickly, and it wasn't long before all of our older friends and even some of my age had pierced their ears and were showing off their new carved, wooden lip plugs. *One day I will be like them,* I thought, as I joined a circle of children who were admiring the new ornaments.

"Yes, feast your eyes on us," one boy was bragging. "We know we look great with our pierced mouths!"

"We're certainly more handsome than you *little* children," others added.

A boy next to me stammered, "I-I wish...," but he didn't finish, and there was a long pause. Finally, one of the big boys came over and demanded, "Well, do you want yours pierced or not?"

"Oh, yes! We want it a lot!" a chorus answered.

"Well, in that case, we'll do it for you!" he said triumphantly. "Who is ready to have his pierced first?"

"Me!" the boy next to me shouted. Others nodded their heads.

"Go get thorns and bring them here, if that's what you want," the bigger kids ordered. Three of my friends ran off to get the thorns, while I stood there, trying to decide.

"Pierce my mouth," demanded the first boy, as he produced a thorn.

"Really? Will you be silent, or will you cry?"

"No! I won't cry," he insisted, stiffening.

The bigger boy grasped the lower lip of my friend and pulled it out. He put the thorn inside the mouth between the lower lip and the chin and probed with it, pricking the child and twisting it a little to see if he would cry. "*Ala!* He is brave!" he exclaimed, and shoved the thorn forcefully through the skin. Then he got a small stick, broke it at both ends, and pushed it into the hole.

"Now for your ears," he said, grasping another thorn. He pierced both ears, putting in small sticks so that the wounds would heal around them. The other two children were pierced at the same time. When it was over, they were relieved and excited. "Let's go tell our mothers!" they exclaimed. "Come on, Kaparketo!" And so I went with them.

"Look at us! We've pierced our mouths," they shrieked as they ran into the homestead. I stayed back to watch their happiness.

"Oh! Really! Why, look what you've done! Wonderful!" their mothers cheered, laughing. My mother came out too and smiled at me across the corral.

It was several months after my three friends pierced their mouths that I saw it. The man was wearing the most beautiful metal lip ornament I had ever seen. I did not know him or think about manners, when I walked up to him and demanded boldly, "Friend, give it to me! Please—your lip plug."

The man looked at me with surprise, then laughed and laughed. I felt no shame, but just waited, still transfixed by the glistening ornament.

"Ah," he exclaimed, gaining control. "You say 'give me,' but you have no place to put it! Ha, ha!"

"I'll go pierce my mouth!" I said hopefully.

"You little fool," he chuckled. "First you do that, and *then* you can come to me and I'll give it to you."

"You—you *will*?" I gasped.

"Boy, I'm an ironsmith! I know how to make these things."

"*Ala!* You can make metal this beautiful?"

"Iron, copper, quartz, and I can make handsome ornaments out of the new aluminum cooking pots people have bought at distant shops."

"But I need the one you are wearing! If I pierce my mouth, do you really promise to give it to me?"

"Yes." He smiled, then turned and walked away.

It was evening and I went home. Early the next morning, I got up, went outside and found a large thorn. I pulled out my lip and pushed it through, all at once. It was easy! And I had expected so much pain! I found a stick, broke the ends and inserted it in the wound. Then I walked at once to the homestead where the ironsmith was staying. He was there. I strode up to him and said proudly, "Now, give me my decoration."

The ironsmith hardly glanced at me. He just smiled and said, "Now, child, you keep asking for it, but if I give it to you, where will you put it?"

"Look at my mouth!" I said, trying not to laugh.

The surprised man exclaimed, "Oh! You spoke the truth! You went and pierced your mouth!"

"Sure," I said proudly.

Without hesitation, the ironsmith took the beautiful ornament from his own mouth and handed to me, grinning. I ran back and hid it safely in my house.

That afternoon I asked one of the older boys to pierce my ears and nose. It was all over very quickly. Now I was ready. I could picture myself with my beautiful, shining lip plug, the kind of small, beaded earrings men wear, and, on special occasions like my marriage, a handsome metal *aparparat* hanging from my nose.

As it turned out, the piercing was the easiest part. The sores festered and pained for weeks. I cleaned and tended them, changing the sticks five times, inserting increasingly larger ones. When I pulled out the fifth set of sticks, I saw that the sores were finally healed and the holes were large enough. Then I went to my hiding place and inserted the curved metal stud. Wherever I strutted in the next few days, admiration followed me. My parents were proud and my friends were impressed. And the girls! They gushed, "He is *really brave!* Oh, Kaparketo! It really is handsome on you!"

Craftsmen

A few weeks after I began to wear my new lip plug, I heard that the ironsmith was working again. People said he had made a fire in a small clay house with four openings and put special rocks and charcoal inside. A goatskin bag was used as the bellows, which was swollen and compressed, using the hand straps on either side. The angry fire leapt up and, incredibly, changed the rocks into molten iron! It poured out of two of the openings, while slag came out of the others. The ironsmith did not talk, but worked all afternoon and, they told me, into the middle of the night before resting, eating and drinking great quantities of beer. He made machetes, axes, spears, knives and arrowheads.

Ironsmiths all come from the same clan,[30] and it is possible that Tororut himself taught their ancestors the craft. These days, many tools like the ones our ironsmiths used to make are plentiful in the shops, and our smiths have been forced to rest. Similarly, aluminum pots have replaced our traditional cooking and water vessels, which used to be molded, usually by women, out of black clay found only in a certain place in the hill country.

Some of our jewelry styles have changed as well. I hear that, in earlier times, men who did not wear ear and nose ornaments were never really accepted. (Women have never pierced their noses.) Women without earrings were called *chemasas,* a terrible name—the ultimate insult. Because of this, whenever a Pokot man married an outsider, he would make sure his bride's ears were pierced and give her earrings. Before modern cloth and beads were available, everyone wore only the skins of goats or sheep, and people made beads out of wood and seeds. Children and women would wrap a certain kind of pliable stick[31] around and around their necks and rub it with animal fat and red ochre. These beautiful wooden necklaces are still worn by young girls today. Experts have learned to coil iron, brass, copper and aluminium wire in a similar fashion, adorning our arms and legs and women's necks and ears. Men also used to wear metal torcs before it became more fashionable to use store-bought beads.[32]

Men, like my father, have always made and used wooden bows and arrows, even as new weapons were introduced. Long ago, before we learned about spears from the Karamojong, a woman discovered how to make the poison for our arrow tips. She had observed that birds died after eating the fruit of the *kepukwon* tree ("tree of a woman") and that no grass grew beneath it. Now women no longer know how to make the poison, and only specialists will handle it, because of the danger. Unless they are needed for a hunt or for battle, we leave our poisoned arrows at home. However, these days, some Turkana and the Karamojong have modern guns, and we have been forced to rely once again upon our most ancient strength. Whereas the range of our poisoned arrows cannot compare favorably, they are our only defense in the face of guns.

Recently, I met a man named Kekemuh at Kacheliba who was nearly toothless. He told me that a sore on his hand was once contaminated by some poison from his arrows while he was hunting a Grant's gazelle. After he had cooked and eaten the meat with others, he said he felt as if he were drunk. His hand began to swell, and he fell down. His friends cut into the wound, extracted a lot of already-rotten flesh and bandaged the hand. Then they slaughtered a sheep and fed him the stomach contents and blood until he vomited. (That is when he claims his teeth began to fall out.) The blood and medicine helped him, and he eventually recovered.

Many people were known for their craftsmanship when I was a child at Lossom, but one clearly surpassed all others—our neighbor Lokayo. His skill at house building was renowned and in great demand. People would bring him large sacks of millet, begging him to build two or three houses they had planned. He was an expert carver, famous for his wooden dishes and for his honey and beer gourds, and he was also skilled in twisting the long ropes we used for carrying meat. Nothing, except perhaps birds, ate his crops, because he dug ingenious animal traps at both ends of his garden, camouflaging the tops and erecting sharp, pointed sticks in the bottom of each pit. When Lokayo inspected the traps each morning, he sometimes found large animals suspended on the spears. He could always sell the excess meat to hungry people in exchange for a goat. Lokayo sold surplus tobacco as well, because people were delighted to trade some honey, a goat or millet for a little tobacco to chew. Yes, even when Lokayo grew to be very old, we still called him "Craftsman". I wonder if his children inherited his genius.

The White Cannibal

There was a shop about six miles from Lossom that sold sacks of maize and beads. I was there with my parents one day getting some maize, when we heard that people were dancing the *Semna Kengeiwa* at Kiwawa. Since Kiwawa was near our homestead, where we watered our cattle, we decided to go.

We walked along the river until we came to a huge crowd of people, singing and dancing, and we joined in. The *Semna Kengeiwa* is a wonderful dance. Partners join hands and form a long bridge, sometimes twenty or thirty couples long.

One by one, the couples jump under the bridge until they reach the end and become part of the bridge again. Everyone bobs rhythmically and sings

Refrain:

We are ready to play Kengeiwa, Kengeiwa	*Asena Kengeiwa, a Kengeiwa,*
Let's play Kengeiwa (x5)	*Asena Kengeiwa* (x5)

Interludes:

Who doesn't know the night?...	*Ngo nyo mengit nangat?...*
We're ready to play at night. ...	*Asena nangat ...*

According to the ancient legend about this song,[33] there were once very many people who lived together in a huge cave named Teyai. As they were dancing one night, a bird we call *kokai* [white-naped raven] perched at the top of a tree near the cave. "*Caw!*" he cried. "*Caw! You people, leave this cave! Beware on the third day any person who is still here, for the cave will break and cover him! You are warned!*" At first, the people thought a man was calling to them, but they laughed when they realized the sounds were coming from a bird! Only one man, who was very old, heeded the warnings of the raven. He and his family packed their belongings and left the following afternoon. A few days later they heard that the cave had indeed collapsed, killing nearly 100 people. Since it was that elder's good fortune to have followed the advice of the raven, which we call *Kokai Chemerkot*, he adopted that bird as the totem of his family and his clan, *Chemerkot*.

When it was my turn to jump with my partner through the "cave" of outstretched hands, I jumped backward and my partner forward until we reached the end. Then, as we stood up and raised our hands again for the bridge, I noticed my partner's shocked face. I followed her gaze and saw, at the edge of the crowd, a creature that resembled a man, except that his skin was colorless and his clothes, hair and mannerisms were very strange. There was a female with him.[34]

We stood there, staring, forgetting to dance. Other people took our place in the dance, and I moved to one side with a group of boys.

"What kind of thing is this?" I gasped.

"European," a youth near me said.

"Is a European a person, or what?" I asked.

"A person, but not like us. He's white!"

After a pause, someone else said, "We think these are the same kind of people who used to eat other people long ago—you know, the *Kopembich*."[35]

I nodded, and a chill went through me.

"Yep, that's who they are," a big kid said. "They aren't black people like us."

"Yeah, the bad thing about that man there is that I think he *still* eats people," another added. "Do you know that some people actually saw him take his teeth out of his mouth?"

"*Ala!*" I exclaimed.

"That's impossible," another boy said.

"They saw him take out his teeth and hold them in his hand! He got a little brush and scrubbed them, and when he was done, he put them right back into his mouth again!"

"You're kidding."

"No, and when he put them back, they stood right up just like regular teeth!"

"Kopembich. There can be no doubt."

I was stunned. I thought, *"This man is truly a cannibal. Why else would he take out his teeth and put them back again? He is an enemy."* I ran in panic to find my mother and told her what I had heard. "I want to go home, Mother!" I pleaded.

She seemed a little concerned, but she had been having a good time. "We'll just stay a little while longer," she assured me. "There are hundreds of people here. He won't notice us."

'Where does he sleep?" I was already worried about the night.

Mother nodded towards a white, ghostlike blanket draped over some poles. "That's his house," she said.

The dance finished, and we watched while the white man went to his white cloth cave and picked up a box. He smiled cunningly at us and twisted something on the box. Suddenly, strange voices began issuing forth from the box, speaking foreign tongues and singing weird songs.

"*Aiiiii,*" shrieked some women near me. "The ghosts have come! The ghosts of the cannibals!" They ran away.

The rest of us stayed and watched in curious fright. I heard some men talking. One was saying, "He opens the box sometimes when he walks about to find meat of people. The spirits of the box help guide him."

The European stopped the noises in the box. Then he motioned to a group of women, asking them to do the *Semna Kengeiwa* again. They screamed in terror and ran away to their homes. Some people did start dancing again, and we joined them for a while, keeping as far away from the cannibal as we could. I was glad when my parents decided to leave.

That night, everyone was talking about the European. I asked if the Kopembich were white or black.

"Oh, no one really knows," one of my mothers told me. "They say that once, after three of their elders died, the Pokot killed all the adults and took their small children. They raised them as Pokot, so the children ate our food and forgot cannibalism. But that happened ages ago."

"Remember the story about the Kopembich who lived in the cave in the rock cliff?" my uncle asked.

"Tell us," we begged.

"Well, those people were very hot-tempered and not very smart. They used to get to the cave by climbing an extremely tall tree, which grew below the rock face and extended past the cave. One night, a group of them came back from eating people and just couldn't climb the tree. Maybe they were drunk. Anyway, they were so mad, do you know what they did?"

"What?" we asked.

"They got an axe and chopped the tree down! The next morning the ones who had been sleeping inside the cave awoke to find their "ladder" missing. 'What shall we do?' they moaned. 'If we stay here we shall die!' Then one of them had an idea. He suggested that they hold hands and make a human chain to reach the bottom of the cliff. So they all joined hands and closed their eyes. Since their eyes were closed, of course they all fell down from the cave and died!"

Everybody laughed. Then Father added, "Our elders said that one day those cannibals would return, but I don't believe it. I think the ancient people were stupid for not finishing them off in the first place."

"What about the white man?" we children persisted, but our parents herded us off to bed.

I was tormented all night by my fear of the European. I dreamed he was coming to get me, carrying his box of ghosts. I screamed and screamed and couldn't stop. My father came to my bed and grabbed me. I thought he was the cannibal! I shrieked, jumped up, and nearly fell on the fire. Then I was awake, trembling and crying, and Mother comforted me.

I was not the only one who had been concerned about the European. The next day, people spoke of nothing else. Those who had not seen him asked, "What is this European? Is it like a cow or a baboon?"

"No," they were told. "It looks like a human, but it will repel you like a snake."

We heard that many children had run away when they first saw him, thinking it was a ghost, or perhaps even Tororut. There was some talk of killing him, for most people agreed he must be one of the cannibals of the old legends, or, at least, an enemy. No one had really seen him eat human flesh, although he was observed to eat some other strange foods. Probably his magic potions, people reasoned. The elders considered all this evidence, but it never occurred to them that the European would just leave, which is exactly what he did.

TURKANA AND THE
YEAR OF THE LOCUSTS

We had danced the *Semna Kengeiwa* at the beginning of what should have been the rainy season, but the rains came much too late that year, and the land remained parched and dry. "If the cattle lack grass during the rainy season, they will surely die during the hot season," Father declared. And so we left our homestead in Kanyangareng, and traveled slowly with our herds to the plains of Turkana, where Father had heard there was grass. We stayed six months in an area which has very red soil—even the water is red there; hence it is called Chepropul, a Pokot name meaning "red water.

Learning Respect for a Dwarf

One of our neighbors at Chepropul was a dwarf named Pomut. Shortly after we arrived, we heard that an ox had been killed in his honor because of his courage in challenging a European known as Mr. Major,[36] who, without reason, had confiscated a number of local stock and taken them to Nakuijit, some 35 miles distant. Pomut, following his own cattle, had walked to Nakuijit and confronted the astonished Mr. Major. "I have come for my herd," he had demanded. "Why have you taken all my cattle when I have done no wrong?"

Mr. Major, no doubt surprised to see a Pokot man with the frame of a child, had asked, "Have you paid your tax?"

"Yes, I have paid," Pomut had answered.

"What is your name?"

"Pomut."

"Are—um—are you *married?*"

"Yes. I have two wives."

"And these cattle are *all* yours?" he asked incredulously.

"They are all mine," Pomut had answered without hesitation.

"*Really?* These are *your* cattle?"

"Yes."

After a pause, Mr. Major had challenged Pomut, "What if I were to take your shoes? What could you do about it?"

"If you want my shoes or my cattle, you must kill me first. Then you may have them," Pomut had said coolly. The European, dumbfounded and speechless, had finally stood aside while Pomut claimed his cattle, as well as those belonging to his neighbors.

The day after Pomut brought the herd home, we went to his homestead to join in the celebration. I saw him there for the first time, and, knowing nothing about dwarfs and thinking he was a child, called out to him: "Friend!"

Pomut frowned at me and then began to laugh. "Ah! What do you think you're doing calling me a friend? Look over there—those are your friends, not me! They are my children, and yet you call their father your friend! Ha ha!"

I countered, "Oh yeah? You're just trying to fool me, I know!"

Later I saw my father mixing clay. Then I watched him take the old clay off Pomut's head and put the new, colorful clay on. It was a beautiful headdress. When it was finished, Pomut went to sit in the sun. Still smiting from his insult, I sauntered over and exclaimed, "Hey friend! I want to see your decoration!"

He roared, "Ah! What's this? How has he been brought up? He will ruin my headdress!"

I tapped him on the head, thinking he was just another child, trying to trick me. My father saw this and sprang at me, seized my arms and hit me again and again with his stick until I was trembling. Then he yelled at me, "How do you presume to strike an adult?"

I was really scared, realizing, finally, what I had done. I should have known he was an adult because of the headdress—the symbol of manhood! A youth is not allowed to wear a clay headdress until he undergoes the ritual of sapana, about six or seven years after puberty. After sapana, he is able to marry and assume the responsibilities of adult life.

"I ...I guess he is really a very big man, but I thought he was a child," I cried.

Father grabbed my shoulders and shoved me before Pomut. "You take a good look, Kaparketo!" he said. "Have you put clay in your hair?"

"No."

"Have you taken a wife?"

"No."

"Then why do you say he is your friend? Wait until you have seen his goats and his cattle and his wives and then see if you still feel like taunting him!"

After awhile, a woman brought out some additional clay to give to my father. She also gave him tobacco. Father turned to me and said, "This is the wife of the man you presume to call 'friend!'"

"This is his wife?" I couldn't believe it. Later, I went up to that woman and asked, "Where is your husband?"

"Oh, he's over there," she said, gesturing towards Pomut. I was ashamed, but before we left, I tried on Pomut's shoes when no one was looking. They weren't big enough!

The next day, as we were watering the cattle at the well, my father showed me Pomut's children, who were also there. Two of his girls were very tall, and their bodies had a beautiful, reddish glow. When I expressed surprise, the other children assured me that Pomut had led a completely normal life, with one exception: He had refused to go out at night ever since a time he was nearly eaten by a hyena on his way to see a girlfriend. He had crouched all night in a tree until the hyena finally went away.

Sometime after this, we were invited to feast on another ox that had been slaughtered at Pomut's house. Pomut, remembering my previous humiliation, took some of the meat reserved for adults and brought it to me himself, saying, "Come eat this meat, my friend, because you have said I was your friend. I have found meat for you now, so be sure to remember your friend another day and find some meat for me!" He grinned at me, then turned and walked into the *kurket*, the shade of the ritual tree just outside the corral, where children were not allowed.

Bow and Arrows

I will always remember the day I first shot a bird, because my father was so happy. "Soon you will be ready for the real thing!" he had exclaimed. We were living in Lossom at the time. Several days later, I brought him a rabbit. Almost immediately, he began to whittle some fine, straight shafts for my new arrows. He made a handsome bow, larger than the one I had. The finished arrows, with their sharp, elongated metal points and perfectly placed feathers, were a work of art. I carried them proudly each day in my quiver and practiced while I watched the goats. My aim was improving, but that little antelope, the dikdik, still eluded me.

It was while we were living in Turkana that I finally shot the skittish dikdik with my bow and arrow! I proudly carried the carcass home, herding the calves ahead of me.

"Look! My son is a man," my mother gushed as I entered the corral. "He has brought us food! He has outwitted the dikdik! Only a true marksman can do that! Kaparketo, I'm proud! Now I can be sure we won't starve—my son is able to provide for us!"

When my father came home, Mother ran to meet him at the gate. "Kaparketo shot a dikdik!" she exclaimed. That evening I helped skin the carcass and butcher the meat. Father never said much, but I knew he was proud.

Later that night I heard the men were talking and laughing among themselves, and the subject was archery. One told an outrageous story about a local elder named Perkess, who got an erection while napping up on the shelf of his grain storage hut: "I don't know whether he was dreaming about his wife or what! Anyway, his grandson came by, saw the penis waving in the air and thought it was a rat! The boy called up to him, 'Grandfather, I think there's a rat on you! I'll get my arrow and shoot it!'

"'Good,' replied Perkess sleepily. 'There are lots of rats around here. You're probably right.' The boy got the arrow and saw that the 'rat' was still there, only a little closer to his grandpa. 'Watch out,' he called and shot.

"'*Cheeeeeeee!*' Perkess screamed. Everyone came running, and, of course, the boy ran away when he saw what he had done."

Locusts

We had been at Chepropul only a few months when our cattle succumbed to a disease carried by flies, and many of them died. So at the beginning of the rainy season, we returned to Lossom and settled once again at Kanasat. Several weeks later, torrential rains came—too late and too heavy, followed, much to everyone's astonishment, by a huge onslaught of locusts. The next week, new ones were born to devour the grass and other vegetation throughout the land. That was *Lokingyaka*, the Year of the Locusts. Even the Europeans rounded up people to help destroy the insects.[37]

Meanwhile, the elders directed other efforts to help save our farms. Every woman whose firstborn was a girl was instructed to find a garment made of *po-run* (gazelle skin) and bring it to the gardens in the morning to perform a ritual for chasing away the locusts. Mother was one of those women. Accordingly, at the gardens the next morning she bit a *chepketo* stem, spit on the skin and waved the garment around the garden, using only her left hand. She continued this work throughout the day until sunset, without eating or drinking. Then she bathed in water, put the *chepketo* stick in her mouth and rubbed the wet plant over her whole body. She was allowed to eat food only at night. The next day, Mother and the other women did the same thing, convincing the locusts to settle elsewhere—perhaps in a neighbor's garden. If there was no woman in a homestead whose firstborn was a girl or if there was no gazelle skin, the locusts would eat the crops.

The Disappearance of Kokwa

Our homestead was large at Kanasat, and there were many to share the work. Several other children and I were usually in charge of herding the calves to water on the top of Kanasat hill, where there were very deep rock wells. Sometimes adults would go along, because when the water level was low, it could take up to four men to draw the water, and the person at the bottom could not get out without climbing a pole. But on normal days, we children could tend to it ourselves.

While our calves were at the well, we would play, as all children do. Sometimes we would do things that our fathers would not approve of, just for the fun of it. For instance, we enjoyed throwing rocks in the deepest well to see the water splash up, and my good friend Kokwa, who was my age, liked to curse just as his stone hit the water. Then we would run back to round up the calves, stay a little while, and be off again.

Kokwa and I would often go together to drink at another, smaller stone well nearby. One afternoon, we climbed into the well and Kokwa saw that the water was red like blood. Four times he started to drink anyway, but couldn't bring himself to do it. "Oh, go ahead!" I urged, and he drank.

We had no sooner returned to the calves, than Kokwa started complaining of chills. We took our calves home early, and the two of us went to the place where we played with other children every day after herding. The rest of us had a fine time, but Kokwa just lay down, wrapped in his cloak. We suggested, "If you are so cold, why don't you go home and sit by the fire?"

He said, "Yes, I'll go home."

The next morning, we heard that Kokwa's father had speared an ox and called everyone together in order to pray for his son, who was very ill. (There are two different prayer ceremonies for the sick: one conducted by women and another by men.) My father, a diviner, was asked to read the intestines. He studied them for bad omens, found no sign of death, and did not think it necessary to kill another animal in order to find an intestine with a better fortune to insure a cure for Kokwa. The stomach contents of the ox were spread on Kokwa's forehead, chest and stomach. The whole carcass was then carried outside the homestead. According to custom, it was placed beneath a tree near the fire on a circle of leaves arranged like a homestead. The meat was encased in leaves, and part of the back was butchered, together with the hind legs and the tail. The meat of the femur of the right hind leg, the *amura*, was cooked and served first. The elders who were going to pray sat in the middle, near the offering, holding their spears, while the other men made a circle around them, leaving a space open for a "door," facing Mt. Mtelo.[38] When the sacred meat was eaten, an elder began praying:[39]

"Everyone hear! We pray to Tororut! We pray to Mtelo and Sekerr, Chepunyal, Maral, Tingirich, Karikau, Kaptolomwa, Tarakit, Korsitch, Chepunos, Pcholia, Lorosuk, Kalapata, Chemurongit, Moroto, Kadam, Elgon, Elgon Riwa, Lelon and Cheptulel. Please save our boy and show him a good path. Throw out all his transgressions.

You are our Father. We hear you created all people, and so we ask your help. Every day we are told, 'You should remember Tororut and pray to everyone on all the mountains.' If your man is on all these hills, we ask you to give us a cure for our boy. He is a child of Tororut, and we pray for you to help him. Please remove all bad words from our hearts and help our boy. We are fools in your country, but we pray to you, for you are our Father. Wherever you are, hear our words, hear our tears, hear us cry for our young man. Help him gain strength, so that he may grow up to watch his cattle and his children. Thank you, Great One. Please help, please help cure the sickness of this boy."

When our people pray in this manner on behalf of a sick person, usually Tororut will help him recover. But on the following day, my friend Kokwa's illness had become critical. His family carried him out of the house and laid him under a shade tree, where his mother sat beside him until mid-afternoon. Then a light rain began to fall, and she left to spread more cow dung on the roof of her house for waterproofing. When she came back to the tree, she saw that her son had disappeared! She ran to her house to tell the others, and was startled to see that skin of the ox Kokwa's father had killed for the prayer ceremony, which she had been drying in the sun, had been slashed twice.

Kokwa has never been heard of since. Some people said it must have been Ilat who took my friend, when a rainbow descended from the sky and shook the tree, but no one really knows. Nor did they ever discover who made the holes in the skin.

Much later, two men who claimed to have her child approached Kokwa's mother. One said, "We took your boy because he cursed and threw a rock at my children inside our house, injuring them. If you want him back, bring a white goat to the hill Kapchok and tie it to a certain large tree. The goat, when it sees your son, will break loose and will find him there. If you don't bring the goat, you won't find him."

The next day, the distraught woman went to her husband, who was living at his other house, and told him about the visitors. He exploded, "Ah! Don't talk to me about rubbish like that! Do you think someone who was lost so long ago will magically reappear? Nonsense! Don't come to me with such talk!"

The two men came back to that woman four times. Each time she went again to her husband and each time he refused. They never came again after that, probably because they realized they'd never get anywhere with someone as ill-tempered as Kokwa's father. I think it was indeed they who took my friend Kokwa, and I think he became theirs. But we never knew.

YOUTH

Towards the end of the Year of the Locusts, around the tenth month, the rains returned again with great force. They poured and poured incessantly through the fourth month of the next year, and so people named it The Year of the Great Rains *(Arupe)*. At that time, we moved to the region of Kaido, where we lived and traveled for a few years before returning to Lossom.

During those years, I became old enough to sleep in the *aperit*, the open, fenced area on one side of the cattle corral. There I listened to the talk of the young men and the elders around the fire, and began to understand more of the pastoral traditions and history of my people. The men talked about the herds, the grass-lands, the farms, and the chance of rain. They discussed local news, threats from the Karamojong and the Turkana, and reports of problems with Europeans and their police. Sometimes they just sat quietly together. Then the married men would go off to sleep in their own houses, while the rest of us lay under our goat-skin blankets and slept there beside the cattle.

SORCERY AND THE FAMILY HERDS

Since the time I was old enough to listen, I had heard my father and uncle grumbling about the troubles they were having with some of our cattle associ-ates, a family named Kitelamoi. Behind their frustrations was a long history of suffering, deception and sorcery which would reach a peak during The Year of the Great Rains. But before I tell you this story, I need to explain our system and rules of cattle exchange,[40] so that you will understand the great trust we must place in our cattle associates and what can happen when that trust is breached.

Cattle Exchange

Our herds are divided freely amongst our families and close friends, so that if disaster strikes one homestead, the family's entire herd may not perish. In addi-tion, there are times when—because of hunger, or for certain rituals—a person will need to request cattle from an outsider's herd, thus setting into motion a se-ries of rules carefully laid down by our ancestors.[41] For instance, when someone gives you a cow, you must give him the heifer of that cow several years later, at his request, and the matter is closed. However, if a man gives you a steer, you are required to *loan* him a heifer, thereby establishing a contract between you. You may eat his steer, but the heifer you loaned him matures and produces many calves and heifers, which also mature and calve, until the offspring of the original heifer are many. Your cattle associate benefits greatly from the milk of these cows, but every one of them still belongs to you, the original owner, no matter how many years have passed. In fact, a woman must be careful not to marry into the family of a cattle associate where any offspring of her family's original heifer remain, for it is forbidden for a married woman to live together with her father's cattle. If any of her family's ancestral cattle remain in the homestead, she or her children may die.

There is a system of protocol cattle associates must follow in order to continually test and confirm the good intentions of the trust they have established. Even the way men greet each other on a path has significance. The man who loaned the heifer makes it a point to visit his associate every six to ten years, always entering by the corral gate; never by the door reserved for people. His host makes honey-beer, and at mealtimes, serves him cow blood and milk in separate bowls (usually it is combined first), so he can mix the two himself. A few days later, when the beer is fermented, a goat is slaughtered, and the two partners eat and drink together. The visitor sleeps on a woman's, rather than a man's bed, and when he leaves, he is given goats to take home, like interest on a loan. (It is proper for him to return one of the goats as he is about to leave.) When the owner of the original heifer returns home with his goats, he slaughters one of them and stews all the meat in a clay pot in the center of his corral over a strong-smelling fire made using *tomut* grass and a *tarokwa* (gum-tree) bough. All of the meat must be consumed within the confines of the corral. This completes the ritual of the visit. (There are two exceptions to this procedure: First, if the original cow has not yet calved, it is returned, with about four goats. Second, if the associate refuses to give him goats or otherwise treats him badly, the original owner will take back his cow, if still alive, and all her descendants.)

It is obvious that, in such a system, people will try to cheat. You could give the cattle away and claim they died, or you could wrongly deny that some of the cattle in your herd are the offspring of your associate's cow. If foul play is suspected, a curse can be placed on the associate's homestead, so that any cattle that remain hidden there will have the power to kill the cheater and all his relatives, until they admit to the deception and return the cattle to their rightful owner. Even without a curse, a cow has ways of finding her owner. Tororut tells the cow, "This is your father!" and so she goes to him. She will follow him persistently and lick him until the man begins to suspect that the cow is his.

My father told me that once, before I was born, my uncle tried to hide some Marakwet cattle from their rightful owner by claiming the cattle had died. The man left, but returned again in a few days carrying the prophetic wooden match sticks the Marakwet have always used to find their hidden cattle. He struck the matches against something which resembled a horn, and some of the sticks burned instantly. Then he announced, "My cattle, which you have, are four: two cows and two calves. You have deceived me! If my cattle had died, as you claimed, the matches would not have lit."

My uncle had to admit, "I have done wrong! I was told the cattle died, but I was not home at the time. What do you intend to do?"

The Marakwet replied, "I will take three and leave one for you."

My uncle was relieved, for he had wronged the man, and was grateful for his understanding and good will. He was also impressed with the Marakwet ability to tell truth from matches.

The Cattle Scandal

Now I will tell you how the family cattle scandal began, as I heard it from my father, Pturu, and his brother, Losikiria:

When my father was young, he and his family enjoyed the many blessings of Pokot life on Cheptulel Mountain. Their log-terraced gardens, irrigated by the carved "bridge of water" leading from the cool mountain streams, always produced enough grain to supplement the milk, blood and meat of their large herd of cattle and goats. But when Father became a youth like me, a great epidemic suddenly destroyed most of the herds, and even wild animals, throughout the land. This was The Time the Country Became Dark.[42] Tororut saved only enough beasts to become the seeds of new herds. Indeed, no one was spared, but those, like my father's family, who lived in the cooler hills, fared better than most. Three of our family's cattle survived.

After the dying stopped, desperate strangers began to roam the land, checking the homes of relatives, friends and cattle associates, where they may have been keeping stock, in the hope that some had survived. Likewise, men sometimes traveled great distances trying to breed the one or two animals they had left. Then, as the threat of starvation increased, bands of thieves began to steal and eat more fortunate men's animals, murdering the owners if necessary.

Because of this danger, Grandfather Suam moved his family and remaining herd into a cave for protection. Father, who was the youngest, and his friend, Nasotei, were cautioned never to travel far from home during those difficult times, except to participate in group hunts, when they were armed with spears and poisoned arrows. Father told me they were so hungry those days that they ate every kind of wild food, except snake, hyena and wild dog!

One day, when Pturu, Nasotei, Losikiria, all their brothers, and most of their neighbors were out hunting, a gang of bandits surrounded my grandfather Suam, bound him with ropes, and slaughtered his small herd, dividing the meat between them. They left only a few goats. The last man to leave with his meat took Suam's arrows and hid them in some brush; then he raised his spear over the old man's body. Suam waited to die, but was surprised when the thief cut his bonds with the spear blade and ran away! My grandfather scrambled for his weapons, which, of course, were gone.

Suam knew there was only one hope left. Although none of the family cattle had survived at the homes of any of their friends, relatives or cattle associates near Cheptulel, there was still a chance some cattle remained at an associate's homestead on the more distant mountain of Maral. Many years before, he had requested an ox from that family for the *sapana* celebration of his eldest son, Akolingoro. In return, according to tradition, he had loaned them a heifer named Cheptaret. Possibly, some of the descendants of Cheptaret had survived the epidemic.

Early the next morning, before the first light, Akolingoro set out for Maral on foot. The journey was rugged and long, but Akolingoro was an exceptionally big man and equally strong. After some questioning, he found the homestead of the cattle associate. It was obvious that, even there, people had suffered, but there were still some cattle in the corral.

He announced, "I come from the homestead of Suam, my father, who requested your steer for me to eat at the time of my celebration of manhood, and who has been to visit you only once since then. Our herd has been destroyed by bandits in the wake of the epidemic. How did you fare? Did any of the offspring of our cow Cheptaret survive?"

The man looked confused. "Surely you already know!" he exclaimed. "Several months ago, a man named Makal came from Baringo saying he was the son of a man who long ago gave me a heifer, and he demanded your cow—the only one which had survived. I gave it to him, along with all of its offspring—except this one heifer—and some goats."

"What?" Akolingoro swelled with anger. "I have no brother or kinsman named Makal! He must have known about our arrangement and claimed our cattle! He has cheated us!"

"*Ala!* It must be so!"

Furious, Akolingoro returned to the cave at Cheptulel with the single cow and news of the thievery. Two days later, the outraged Suam left with Akolingoro and two of his three living sons by his second wife, leaving only young Pturu and the women at home. They held fast to the path until they reached the homestead of Makal, son of Loiyamale, for they knew the family that had cheated them. The family name was Kamaril, and they belonged to the clan of lions, *Sukuh*. The father had died, leaving his wife Chemaril and three sons: Makal, Kasenyan and Tanakut. The corral was full of cattle.

Repeatedly, Suam and his sons questioned the family, but the answer was the same: "We have none of your cattle! The one we brought from Maral was ours, but it died anyway."

"If our cow is here, we will bring misfortune to your family!" Suam threatened.

"Just try it!" they scoffed. "Your cow is not here. For all we know, it's at your home and you're trying to trick us!

Frustrated, the men returned to Cheptulel to think and plan. They hunted, helped plant the garden, and tended the animals. At the end of the third month, it rained for two days, and everyone rejoiced and prepared their termite hills, anticipating the life-saving rainy season. But then the clouds went away and did not return. The gardens showed no sign of green and could not flourish with only the trickle of water provided by an irrigation system shared by so many. How much longer, Suam wondered, could his family live on the meager bounty from the group hunts? The wild animals that had survived the epidemic would surely succumb to a drought. The milk from their goats and one cow was hardly enough to sustain them, and they were already dipping into the hidden store of grains he had saved for emergencies. Young Pturu, especially, was growing increasingly weak from hunger.

The Curse of the Cow

At the beginning of the fifth month, Suam, his sons, and six other male relatives left for Baringo to confront Makal's family once again. They arrived in the evening, and marched through the corral and into the *aperit*. Presently, a fire was made, and Makal came and demanded, "Why have all of you come again? You won't find your cow here—It's dead! I've already told you that."

Suam said quietly, "At the Time the Country Became Dark, Tororut gave us a seed, and now you have made evil come of it. You say the cow has died. Did it die because of Tororut or because of you? Now, I don't know what you did with our cow, but I shall find out!"

"Try if you like," Makal shrugged.

Suam's party refused all food—even milk—from the homestead of Makal, having arranged for a neighbor to bring food for them. Then, later that night, Akolingoro began his deed. He stood in the *aperit* and declared in a loud voice:

"Truly, I am convinced that the cow we seek is here, along with its offspring. I pray to you, our ancestors of old, that if our cow is in this homestead, it will cry out and come to me. I shall hold water in my left hand and grass in my right hand. If our cow is here, let it come and eat those two things. When this comes to pass, beware all of you in the homestead of Makal, son of Loiyamale! I forewarn you that when you hold the milk of this cow in your right hand it will become red like blood and will be poison. It will kill those who drink it!

"I am trying this case before you, spirits of our ancient fathers. Listen to our troubles from your graves! We have seen much distress, for Tororut has chosen to bring hunger to the land until many have perished. Our cattle have died, the wild animals have suffered, and in the night lions, leopards and hyenas have begun to stalk people. Now this man,

Makal, wants us to go home, get sick and die too, thinking our cattle are finished. Yet Tororut has tried to help us, for he has spared us one cow. We have tried to reason with Makal, but to no avail. So I ask you, our elders, if our cow is here, to dig a hole amongst the graves where we have buried you, on behalf of our cow."

Early the next morning, before dawn, Akolingoro approached the cattle. He walked around the herd once, throwing grass into their midst, and then went to the homestead where the people had given him milk the day before to request a vessel of water. He carried the water back to Makal's corral and set it down near the *aperit*. Then he stooped down and called out, *"We beckon to you, our cow, calf of Cheptaret. If you are here, please come greet us!"* He said this four times, and the cattle began to bellow. Akolingoro and his brothers walked amongst the cattle until they had passed by each animal. At last, one cow began to take notice—a milking cow whose calf was in the house for calves. It sauntered around the edge of the corral, stood at one side and mooed. Then another and another came, until six cattle stood together, two of them lowing.

Akolingoro, watching from the *aperit*, answered them, saying, *"Thank you for greeting us, you, the children of Cheptaret! This man wants to cast us to the lions, leopards and hyenas!"* The six cattle heard this, and all of them walked inside the *aperit*. Now Akolingoro took grass in his right hand and water in his left. One cow came to eat the grass and another to drink. Four cows did this, and the two young bulls stood by and mooed loudly. People in the neighboring homestead heard and knew that they had responded to their rightful family.

Akolingoro declared, "Truly, Makal, you have tried to steal my cow! Even yesterday, you claimed it was not here and offered me milk of this very cow! Nevertheless, I will not take this cow today, but will wait until your crime is apparent to you. If you had admitted that the cow was here yesterday, I would have led her, with her family, out by way of the corral gate. But now, since I have no permission for this cow, calf of Cheptaret, to use the corral gate, I will have to let her out by way of the low side of the corral, *the place of death. That will be her gate!*[43] One day, when you drink the milk of this cow and it reaches your stomach, your throat will begin to burst and you will be ill. You will low like this cow and you will die! The nipples on the right breasts of your women who have drunk this milk will produce a red, blood-like poison which will kill you all. *Cheptaret will slay you!"* Akolingoro turned to his brothers and said, "Put your shoes on. Let's go." Then, instead of going out the corral gate, they passed by way of the lowest side of the corral, where we bury our dead. They returned home empty-handed.

Six months later, a man from Makal's homestead came to Suam to request an ox for the sapana initiation of a youth. About 200 people came to join in the festivities. Makal had just danced his ox-dance when, suddenly, he doubled over in pain. "My stomach," he groaned. Shortly, he cried out, "It has seized my throat!" He began making throaty, lowing sounds, and the people near him commented among themselves, "Look! He bellows like a cow." Soon Makal could not speak. He was carried to his house, where he died the next morning.

The neighbors realized what was happening and pleaded with Makal's brother Kasenyan. "Did you not see how the sickness came to your brother? It was just as those men from Cheptulel warned. Why do you keep silent and not go at once to them?" But Kasenyan was deaf to their words. Five days later, Makal's sister succumbed to the sickness and died in just two days. The people of the homestead were about to shave their heads in mourning, when the middle wife of Makal became ill. She died on the third day. Two days later, two sons of Makal— the one who tended the calves and the one who tended the cattle—were both attacked by bandits and killed. The neighbors once again pleaded with Makal's brothers to tell the truth.

Several weeks after that, Kasenyan went to see his girlfriend. As he returned home the next morning, sickness overpowered him. "Where, where, where did this disease come from?" he wailed. Then he was quiet for a few minutes and died. Shortly afterwards, the married sister of Makal died, together with her child. Then, suddenly, Makal's first wife died, and the disease attacked the only remaining matron in the homestead, Chemaril, the mother of Makal. She called her remaining son, Tanakut, and said, "Go at once to the mountain Tiati, where I hear there is a brother of Akolingoro. Tell him we have wronged his family greatly by trying to steal their cow. Now, at last, we are contrite and at their mercy, for all my children but you are dead and our household is finished. Ask him to come take his cattle now!"

Tanakut left immediately for Tiati, where he was able to locate the homestead of Lokwameri, son of Suam. By the time the two men returned to the Kamaril homestead, Chemaril was on her deathbed. She strained to say to Lokwameri, "Sir, we have erred badly against you. There is no one as bad as I and there is no matter more evil than this. If I had known, I certainly would not have stolen your cow. Please go now to find all the children of Suam, especially the one named Akolingoro, so all of you can claim your cattle."

"I would like a gift for the journey," said Lokwameri. "Our place is very far away."

Chemaril lifted her hand feebly and motioned toward the herd in the corral. "Will these gifts suit you?" she said. "There are many cattle here, and not one will remain mine! You and your brothers are to take them all to your corral, for they have become poisonous to us."

The moment Lokwameri departed for Cheptulel, Chemaril died. In the end, she revealed to Tanakut that she herself had been the one responsible for the terrible fate of her family. She had told Makal and his brothers that the cattle in question had originally belonged to their uncle, Kitelamoi, and were now rightfully theirs. Indeed, even Makal had been ignorant of the truth; his own mother had doomed him!

Lokwameri began the long journey to his father's home on Cheptulel, walking across the dusty plains sucked dry by the relentless sun. Everywhere there was talk of death. The people of the plains, who relied solely on the blood, milk and meat of their herds, had been decimated, first by the cattle epidemic, and now by drought. It had not rained since those two days a year ago, when the termites were collected. Now, adding to their torture, the weakened people were succumbing to a horrible new illness, later to be called smallpox.

During the third month, just before Lokwameri reached Cheptulel, it rained. The first water sank deeply into the parched soil and disappeared. Then it rained two more days, and people allowed themselves to hope, but the clouds only withered and blew away, and there was nothing more.

At last, Lokwameri brought his family the welcome news of the family cattle which awaited them. Then he rested at his father's house several more days before beginning the long hike back to Baringo with his brother. During that time, a huge star—a comet—appeared over the family home in Cheptulel. It had two very long arms, one on each side, stretching upwards. One of the elders remarked that it looked like the *taruh* basket we use for carrying our loads, and so the comet became known as Taruh. It would prove to be a bad omen, heralding a time of widespread death from smallpox and drought.

When Lokwameri and Akolingoro finally returned to Baringo to reclaim the family cattle, they found the homestead of Tanakut in mourning. Accordingly, they were asked to wait until the moon had completely waned before taking the cattle out of the corral. (This is because the death ceremony can be held only after the moon is finished, and only thereafter can cattle and other gifts be given.) Thus, Akolingoro and Lokwameri had to stay there seven days. One night, a daughter of Makal went outside to urinate. As she was walking back through the corral, a cow kicked her in the side. She was carried into her house and, shortly thereafter, she died. The next morning, Makal's son, who was staying at another homestead, climbed a tree to get some *mukatcho* fruit, slipped, and died from the fall.

On the seventh day, at the time of the new moon, the brothers solemnly entered the corral, surrounded by the empty houses of those who had died from the curse of the cow Cheptaret. Tanakut brought out 28 descendants of the original cow, and gave the location of three others that were being kept at other homesteads. He went on to explain, "In addition, there are six steers at the homestead of Munyan, son of Kitelamoi. Also, I slaughtered an ox belonging to a man named Moitun recently and gave him one of your heifers in return. I will tell you how to find him, and will let him know that the heifer he keeps is yours. Another man once requested one of your milking cows because he was hungry, but he has already repaid me with the cow's heifer, which is here, so that matter is closed. That accounts for all the cattle."

Akolingoro took a red pigment and mixed it inside his shoe, saying, "Good. If there was a cow of mine that you still claimed, you would be doomed. It is this cow and this color which has condemned your family." He then took a white pigment and mixed it in the bowl of a gourd. He spread the red pigment on Tanakut's right side and the white pigment on his left side.

At last, they let out the cattle. Lokwameri was to take the four that were at other nearby homesteads, while Akolingoro was allotted the 28 from the corral, together with the six from Munyan Kitelamoi's homestead. Akolingoro elected to leave the six with Munyan for the time being, and *this was a big mistake,* for it was those six animals, and their descendants, which were to become a constant source of trouble for the family for another generation!

Akolingoro slowly herded the cattle across the parched, roasted plains, creating a cloud of hot dust which hung, suspended, in the dry air. The rains had failed for two years, and the sun shone fiercely. My father called this time *Charakeka.* Everywhere were signs of starvation. They say a certain large lizard crawled to a house of Ilat, the god of thunder, where he knew there was always water, but, alas, it, too, was dry. And so the lizard climbed to the top of a tall tree and wailed:

The lizard cries, oheee	*Kumonyiru, oheee*
Dried up, like the daughter of man	*Kayam so chepto chi*
I am dried up, to die	*Kayam karepas*

I don't know which god opened its mouth to say words like a human! We call this the Year of Kumonyiuh, The Year the Lizard Cried.

With great relief, Akolingoro led the thirsty herd, which would save his family, to the mountain streams of Cheptulel. However, the homecoming was not a happy one, for during his absence, his father—my grandfather Suam—had died of smallpox and had been buried in the cave, in his still-empty corral. In addition, young Pturu, my father, suffering greatly from hunger, had become listless and emaciated, for he had not yet the strength of a man. Indeed, he would have died of starvation without the blood and milk of Akolingoro's reclaimed herd. Slowly, he revived and finally regained his health, just as the rains came back. But the curse of smallpox returned a second time, sweeping its death throughout the land and destroying the rest of the family. Of Suam's sons, only my father and Losikiria were spared.

Soon the two brothers took their allotment of three cows and some goats and left their home on Cheptulel, which had become a place of death and sorrow. Eventually, they settled in the region of Kupkomo, where they managed, through hard work, to increase their stock, and, finally, to marry, establish their own homesteads, and begin their families.

Because of these circumstances, it was not until after my birth that my father and uncle tried to claim the cattle (the original six and their offspring) that remained at the homestead of Kitelamoi. But, alas, Munyan, Kitelamoi's son, tried to conceal and steal our cattle once again, just as Makal had before him! He told my father that all but two of our cattle had succumbed to a sickness we call *mol-molay*, and that those two had subsequently been stricken with *lookoi* and died. My father and uncle simply did not believe him. They argued with Munyan's family about this from the time I was a small boy until I was a youth, old enough to sleep in the *aperit*.

A Spell Breaks Father's Leg

One evening, just as the cattle were coming into the corral, I heard a cry from my father's hut, and was alarmed to see him lying in the doorway! Evidently, he had been resting on his bed, when he heard the cattle returning and decided to go see his herd. As he tried to duck through the doorway, his leg had suddenly collapsed beneath him! I ran to him, calling to my mother, "Father's leg is broken! Come quick!"

My father was always a brave, strong man, but now, watching him writhing in agony, I began to cry. My mother and my uncle Losikiria, who had just come in with the cattle, were able to lift him, but he screamed with pain.

"How did it happen?" Mother asked.

Father could hardly talk. "It broke by itself! There was no reason," he gasped. Then he added viciously, "I bet it's the sorcery of Kitelamoi's son and maybe Kitelamoi's wife, Chepuchemurian! She's a witch! They're trying to steal our cattle!"

We tried to fix his leg, but it surpassed us. Usually, when we set a person's leg, it begins to recover within a week. My father's leg was still in bad shape after three months! It had swollen, and the pain was excruciating.

One day, when he was in considerable agony, Father tried to kill himself. He unsheathed his spear and tried to cut his own throat. Luckily, my mother was nearby and saw what he was doing. She grabbed the spear and struggled with him until the spear came apart, with the blade end in my mother's hand. She threw it outside, but he was determined. He lunged for the quiver that was near him. Mother grabbed its rope handle, but he managed to take the lid off. She screamed and screamed, and everyone came running. "My husband is trying to kill himself!" she shrieked. The others restrained him, while Mother ordered, "Take everything out of the house—rope, fire, stones—everything, so he can't hurt himself. He's in too much pain! He must be helped!" And then she began crying.

After that, my father's brother, Losikiria, went to a practitioner who knew how to interpret events by studying the particles in milk. The diviner told him, "An old woman has bewitched your brother because of cattle. She wants to kill you and your brother so the cattle will be hers. She has searched for other means but failed, so she is trying sorcery. I see she has used a green water snake and something else to make the spell. Now if you want your brother to recover, you must bring that woman to your house, lock her up, beat her, and—if you want— kill her. There is no other way. Even if your brother dies, she will return again for you!"

Losikiria left before dawn the next morning, and arrived at the homestead of Munyan Kitelamoi while Chepuchemurian was still milking the cows. Instead of entering by way of the corral gate, he crept in through a small door in one side of the homestead fence, and saw Chepuchemurian walking to her house to pour the milk into a gourd. Losikiria threw his spear just as she ducked into the doorway, but it narrowly missed and stuck firmly in the pole. Determined, he dived into the house, grabbing the old woman's leg, and hit her repeatedly. Then he dragged her outside and beat her again and again with his club.

Everyone in the homestead came running. Munyan's wife had seen everything, and old Chepuchemurian herself had seen my uncle throw his spear and realized how lucky she had been that the spear had stuck in the seasoned wood of the pole. Had the wood been green, the spear might have gone through and hit her! She was so scared she began to defecate.

"Don't kill me," she pleaded with my uncle. "If your brother has already died, then come back and kill me, but don't do it now! Don't you see that Tororut has just saved me? Please! Look, I'll come now and try to cure your brother—that's all I can do. It wasn't really my idea to put a spell on him. I was told that when your brother died, the cattle would be mine. I did it, yes, but please don't kill me yet. Let me try to cure your brother!" She moaned and cried.

"All right," Losikiria said, considering. "I won't kill you this time because Tororut chose to save you. Let's go!"

"Ooooh—but how do I know you won't kill me on the way?" Chepuchemurian whimpered.

Late that afternoon, when I was still on the mountain looking after the calves, I heard a noise from our homestead in the valley. I wondered if, perhaps, my uncle had returned with the witch. *Or,* I worried, *could my father have succeeded in killing himself at last? But, no, there was nothing he could have used. It must be the witch!*

When I led the calves home, I saw that the witch was indeed there, tied up in a tree. She had been badly beaten. I picked up a rock and threw it at her, hitting her hard in the middle of the back. I reached for another, but Lopeyok's mother ran to stop me, saying, "No, Kaparketo! Don't do that! Let her try to cure your father. If she fails, we'll all kill her!"

Chepuchemurian tried for two days to cure him, and then we let her go home. "Keep your ears alert," Losikiria warned her when she left. "If you hear Pturu has died, neither you nor your son Munyan will be spared. We'll kill you all!"

"Yes," she said weakly. "If he doesn't get better, that's what you should do."

As it turned out, my father did get well and his leg mended, although he became lame, with one leg shorter than the other. As soon as he was strong enough, Father went to Munyan's homestead to retrieve his cattle. Munyan cooperated, but begged him to leave one cow, since he had a small, sick child who desperately needed the milk. Father agreed, and took the other two cattle from that homestead. He collected the remaining three cattle from another homestead.

Unfortunately, Father would grow to regret his compassion for the sick child, because Munyan, like his ancestors, would later report that the one cow we had left there had died! Indeed, the question of that cow and its offspring would plague us through the years, until even I, like my great uncle Akolingoro, would ask our cattle to cry out to us. But that is a later story.

WANDERING YEARS

The year after the Great Rains, when my father's leg was healed, we continued moving from place to place, following the pasture. We left Murukokoi, and, after a brief stay at Alakas, continued on to Lobubure, then to Aneler and finally to Kiwawa. Father would laugh and say we were just like "The Traveler," a man who walked about constantly in search of stock and who was immortalized in song when my father was still young. (In this song, we don't speak about the animals directly. We call small goats "metal beads" and adult goats "mother-of-goat", which can also mean "useless" in general speech. Our counting units are metal rings—each is worth about 100 animals.)

Traveler, traveler,	*Chorchoro chorchoro*
gathering wealth, gaining wealth	*parmangao parmanga*
There are metal beads,	*Kimi teroi kiye*
mother-of-goats, four metal rings	*chepuchocheno karimoris angwan o*
Refrain:	
Mm oha iloya aya oya (x2)	*Mm oha iloya aya oya* (x2)
I go to Tiati—all is fine there…	*Oweta Tiati apurur walo tokol*
I go to Kapukul—all is fine there…	*Oweta Kapukul perur walo tokol*
I go to Chemurongit—all is fine there…	*Oweta Chemurongit perur walo tokol*
I go to Kamatira—all is fine there…	*Owetai Kamatira perur walo tokol*
I go to Mtelo—all is fine there	*Owetai Mtelo perur walo tokol*

Eight months after we moved to Kiwawa, the cattle were struck by a disease the Karamojong call *longorichinuh*.[44] Forty-two of our cattle died, and that was tragedy enough, but there were some men who ended up with less than ten cattle as a result of the disease. After that, we moved back to Lossam for about two years.

Government Trouble

There was a great deal of border trouble at that time, and we encountered a lot of stray cattle in the area. The police and army were seizing cattle freely, and we knew that any cattle lost along the border would surely never return to their owners, so we took any strays we found. It was a bad situation. Finally, one Pokot man named Marenja Petole murdered a police corporal who had appropriated his cattle, and the matter came to a head. The Pokot and Karamojong government-appointed chiefs took the initiative and went to see the government officials at Lobubure. "If you want peace, open the border," they told the government.

The next week, the chiefs called a huge meeting, which was attended by 1300 Pokot, 1100 Karamojong, and the four white officials, who were told again, "If you comply with our request to open the border, we will live more peacefully together." The Europeans, of course, had no choice, and the District Commissioner announced that cattle would be allowed to move freely across the border again.[45]

In those days, the Europeans were extremely harsh. My family and others were required to walk all the way to Kapenguria to pay a tax to their government. Furthermore, there had been an incident some years before in which two itinerant skilled laborers were murdered at night in their camp. The whites had assumed the Pokot living around Chepropul were responsible, although they could produce no evidence and no arrests were made. Indeed, people forgot about it, until one day, suddenly, in the name of the Government, the Europeans seized the cattle and goats of those people they assumed to be the sons of the murderers and locked them up in Amudat for three months! Then, all at once, they reversed their position, let the Pokot men go, and blamed the killings on foreigners!

Pulling our Donkey Teeth

When we first settled in Kiwawa, we noticed that all the children our ages from the homestead nearest ours already had their two lower incisors pulled, like adults. Soon they started teasing us.

"Look at you! You have many teeth like a donkey!" one boy shouted.

"Yeah!" another joined in eagerly.

"You're all really stupid-looking!" the first one chided, while the others gathered around us, taunting us and bragging.

"You're just babies! *Babies! Babies!*"

"We're bigger and smarter than you! All of us have pulled our teeth."

"Everyone knows the child who hasn't pulled his teeth still sleeps with his mother, 'cause he's so stupid!"

That evening I told my mother, "I don't want people to make fun of me again. Who knows how to pull teeth?" She spoke the name of a man who lived in a nearby homestead. (Certain women also pull teeth for children.) While the food was cooking, I ran off to find my companions. "Come, let's go tomorrow," I suggested.

Early the next morning the six of us awakened the man my mother had recommended. "Please," we begged. "Come take out our teeth! We want to get rid of them right now!" He laughed and agreed drowsily. He gathered his instruments, including the blocked arrow (*tarema*) we use for bleeding our cattle, and then he worked quickly. Soon, it was all over, and my friends and I walked home, relieved. We burst into our homestead, calling to our mothers, "Look at us! We've taken out our teeth!"

"Ah, yes, very good!" they answered.

My mother came over to us, and asked, "Now who made fun of you yesterday?" We told her. "Well, go show them!" she exclaimed.

Stealing Sex

After we moved back to Lossom, I became interested in such things as dancing and girls. I never slept whenever I could hear the songs of a dance in the distance! I also liked the idea of sex, but was not yet mature enough to go to the girls openly. Besides, they never would have accepted us—they called us children! We were forced to figure out ways to steal our pleasures from the unsuspecting girls while they slept at night.

We inherited this practice from our ancestors. Even our elders did this when they were young. This is because people frown on open love affairs before adolescence. If they find out a young boy has tried to romance a girl, they beat him and yell, "Don't tell us you want a girlfriend! No one will accept you yet, so be content with stealing!"

Once I went to "steal" from a girl named Cherito, but I found that her skirt was wrapped tightly between her legs. Luckily, I carried a small, sharp knife for the very purpose of cutting a hole in the skirt just large enough for me to use. The next day, one of the women asked Cherito, "Child, what tore your clothes like that?" She looked around, saw the hole and was furious, but, of course, there was nothing she could do!

Another time, I went with my friend Lowetan to a house where three girls slept. Lowetan stood guard outside, while I went in. I fanned the fire enough to see that Atopun and a little girl named Leyuh were sleeping on one bed, while Kopitira slept alone on the other. Very gently, I spread Kopitira's legs apart and saw that it was very good. I was just about to enter, when Atopun leaped up, yelling a warning, and ran to shut the door! The three girls grabbed me and beat me into human porridge. Two of them were very big girls who had already been circumcised, and I was, by comparison, still a little boy! At last, one of the wives in the homestead came to rescue me, and I got away.

Five days later, we had our revenge. We searched for a certain plant and made a powerful sleeping potion called *matarang*. "I wonder if this stuff really works," I remarked, as we mixed it.

"Sure!" Lowetan boasted. "The girls I've used it on sleep like they're dead. In fact, we usually pick them up and carry them outside so we can enjoy them better! Only problem is the big girls are so heavy it takes two or three of us to move one! They don't even wake up until they get cold. Ha! They sure are surprised to find themselves outside!"

Four of us sneaked into Atopun's house that evening and put some of the potion at the heads of both the beds. When we came back later that night, we found them all sleeping soundly and had no trouble satisfying ourselves completely! To top it off, just as we were leaving, Lowetan slapped Atopun's bottom and called, "Get up! You think you're pretty smart for beating on Kaparketo, don't you! So why did you let *all* of us steal you tonight, huh? You're really stupid!" We darted out the door before she could get us!

Lokeris Wins his Bride

While we were playing with sex like this, one of the older girls from the homestead near ours was being courted seriously by a determined man named Lokeris Riamangar. Even when her father rejected him, Lokeris refused to give up. "Why don't you approve of me? he asked, and the father replied, "There is no particular reason. I just don't like you and I never did!" Poor Lokeris even managed to anger the girl's mother. Then he thought of a plan.

One morning, when no one was home except the small children—some of the adults had gone to water the herds, and others were gardening—Lokeris arrived at the girl's homestead, bringing a gourd of honey and another filled with millet. He put them down by the children, took the tops off, and waited. Soon, some of the smaller children started eating the honey. "Go ahead," he encouraged. "Eat as much as you want!" and he left.

That afternoon, the parents came back to find that their children had been eating all day! "Who brought the food here?" they asked, but the children didn't know.

Four days later, Lokeris returned to the homestead to ask, once again, for his sweetheart's hand in marriage. The father refused even to speak with him. Dejected, Lokeris slept with a nearby friend and came back the next day, saying, "The other day I left my gourds here. Now that I know I cannot marry your daughter, I am going home, and I want to take my honey and my millet with me."

The family was nonplused. They assured him they would refill the gourds and give them back in a few days. However, three days later, Lokeris found that they had been unable to find enough honey and millet to fill the gourds. "Why do you torment me? Give me back my gourds!" he demanded.

The girl's people were exasperated. They were forced to concede, "All right, go bring some beer and we will discuss the brideprice! You are a conniving, bad man!"

Upon hearing these good words, Lokeris rejoiced. The bride's people demanded twenty cattle, but Lokeris claimed to have only twelve cattle and ten goats. The family tried to refuse, but kept remembering the debt of honey and millet they owed him. At last, they agreed to let their daughter go for only the twelve cattle and ten goats, so they could have some peace.

My Spear

I remember when Lowetan announced, "I speared a dikdik yesterday! That makes two dikdik and one Thompson's gazelle just this month. I think my father is planning to take a male goat to the ironsmith tomorrow to order a metal spear for me!"

I was jealous! I had been successful with the bow and arrow, but had found the wooden spear more difficult. Even though I was one of the best at practicing with the *korobes* and was second best in my homestead at the still targets, the wild animals had eluded me. *"I wish Tororut would show me an eland or dikdik today,"* I thought. *"Even a lion or a leopard would be welcome now!"*

By chance—or perhaps not—on my way home I heard a rustling in the brush. I knew a large animal was there, but it was hard to see, since the sun had already set. I crouched down and waited. Suddenly, a big hyena ambled out right in front of me!

My spear was ready. I tensed and hurled the wooden shaft with all my strength. I thought I saw it pierce the animal's neck, but the hyena growled and started to run. *"No!"* I thought. *"I couldn't have missed!"* I chased it into the bushes, but my foot got tangled in the underbrush. I reached down to free it, then looked up, and saw that the hyena was gone. Choking with disappointment, I forged ahead anyway, and nearly tripped over the carcass!

The excitement at home nearly matched my own! "He has saved our calves from death!" my mother proclaimed. "The hyena surely would have attacked the calves. Kaparketo saved them"

Whether or not this was true, the hyena was a beginning. The months after that seemed charmed. Tororut showed me several antelopes—some dikdik and even a small eland. The day I carried home the eland, my father took a large male goat to the ironsmith and ordered a spear for me!

About a month later, some of my cattle wandered away one evening, following someone else's herd. It was raining lightly when I began to search for them, but just as I spotted the cattle, it began pouring. I decided to wait under the branches of a large tree. After awhile, I could see that my cows were starting to head back to where I had begun my search, so I ran after them in the rain, only to slip and fall on my new spear! The blade pierced deeply and painfully into my leg, and when I withdrew it, the blood started gushing. I yelled to the other cowherd and he ran to help me, tying a rope tightly around my leg. Then he rounded up my cattle along with his own and said, "Go on home. I'll bring your cattle."

"No, I can take them if I go slowly," I said. I tried to walk a little, but the pain was sharp and throbbing. When I stopped and untied the bandage a little to relieve the pressure, the blood spurted out alarmingly.

"I'll get you some medicine," the other cowherd called as he ran off. He came back in a minute or two with a stick that contained a milky fluid. He touched it to my wound, and the bleeding stopped, for the most part. I was able to walk home.

At the homestead, we used another treatment for my wound: Milk fat was boiled and applied to the cut each morning and evening. It burned a lot, but the method was effective. There was no smell, and the wound healed in less than two weeks.

DANCE, SONGS AND STORIES

Once in a while, if he has enough oxen, an elder will decide to sponsor for his children the huge dance and feast we call *amumor*. He might have 10 or 15 oxen to slaughter for the occasion, and he will ask 15 or so of his contemporaries to each send one or two oxen to the feast. Everyone comes to the dance.

Dressing for the Dance

When we heard there was to be an *amumur* celebration in Na wi, we rejoiced! Father and all the men busied themselves fixing up their clay headdresses, collecting together all their ostrich feathers, and fastening them into the receptacles in the clay. Each wore necklaces and earrings, his best lip plug and, if he had one, the beautiful metal leaf like ornament—the *aparparat*, which hangs beneath the nose. All of the women and girls twined their hair into intricate braids, some laced with beads, and rubbed their bodies with fat until they glistened. Many sewed beads on their skirts, and tied bells on their ankles.

Father's headdress was covered with so many ostrich feathers that you could hardly see his face! He was surely one of the most handsome of men and would be honored at the dance. You see, those who wear ostrich feathers, like my father, are called *kaoweluk*, while those who have none are the *kakuduk*. Throughout the ceremony, the *kaoweluk* do not socialize with the *kakuduk*. It is the job of the *kakuduk*, in fact, to wait upon the *kaoweluk*, cooking their meat, fetching and carrying items and doing other work. (People say the *kaoweluk* are just like the government ordering people around!) I should think that a man who has no ostrich feathers is apt to be rejected by his own wife; she would prefer to follow the handsome *kaoweluk*!

It is the duty of the *kaoweluk*'s wife to take care of her husband's feathers. If they fall, she picks them up. At night, as her husband sleeps, using his wooden stool as a neck rest, she holds vigil to be sure he does not move in a way which could ruin the headdress. She must get her sleep in the daytime.

Animal Songs

After we arrived in Nawi, we feasted and celebrated from sunrise until sunset for four days. We sang and danced to all the songs:[46]

- About the giraffe, with its long, swaying neck and wagging ears and about the little birds with red beaks that like to sit on its pointed head between the horns:

Refrain:
    Birds (oxpeckers) *perch on its head*

    Mm edokete nyiken nyako, ah mm

Falsetto interludes:
    Oye, giraffe!
    Oh three-horned giraffe
    Giraffe (running) *throws out its feet*
    It knows to look far from side to side
    Giraffe of long legs, long legs
    Giraffe, giraffe

    Oye nyakori
    O nyakori louni mumwar
    Nyakori kejadi jadak ah
    Loepasi nyako kireretai
    Nyakori chereo, chero
    Nyakori, nyakoria

    Galloping gracefully, its ears
    Wag up and down, giraffe
    Its curled tail
    Black-tipped tail, black-tipped tail, mm

    Yea yeoo, arumu nye koilele
    Erokono nyikorio
    Nyi cherasia, hiyo
    Lokirioni alado, lokirioni alado, mm

- About cattle (The part about fighting is also sung on raids when the enemy is spotted, before we unsheathe our spears and begin to fight):

Swishing tail
The way of the cow
Meet its wet nose
Its blood is good
Cattle are good
Swish, swish, swish
Swishing cattle tail
We fight for its good smell
Mother of men
Cattle, ah yeleo oh
Fight, fight, fight …
Mother of men, mmm oh

Wata nyalado
Ekepite kanyaite
Ekiriama nyebala ekume
Ejoka nokot toyai
Ejoka wa pokolem toyai
Wata, wata, wata
Wata nyaite alado
Kimaria kinoi nya ore
Totonyi ngkiliok
Napokolem, ah, yaleo oh
Maria, maria, maria…
Toto ngkilioko, mmm oo

And we sang of the elephant, the lion, the leopard, and the rhinoceros, as well as about our sheep and donkeys, but I have never heard songs about goats.

Song of a Wife's Tears

Some of our songs and stories are very old, like the one about the fickle wife, Chepuchemurim. Her husband, Apayete, had been a very rich man until the epidemic of my father's youth wiped out his entire herd. In order to survive, he was forced to switch to farming and moved with his wife to Ipet, near Sigor, where there was an established irrigation system. But Chepuchemurim could not tolerate their new life style. After only two weeks, she complained, "We used to plant a garden and then forget it until the rains came. I don't like this new farm of water! What I know is the milk and fat and meat of cattle! How can you stand to eat these plants alone, without even milk to go with them?" She refused to eat, singing this song of tears to her husband, which we sing at dances now:

Oye woye ye, Chepuchem, woye

Refrain:
   I don't know these ways
   Chepuchem, Chepuchemgurimi

Verses:
   I don't know the seeds of grasses
   I don't know the akarelmut

Oye woye ye, Chepuchem, woye

Mongutan te nyo no
Chepuchem, Chepuchemgurimi

Akusoyo mongutu oyoye
Akarelmut mongutu

I am the child of the son of Cherupun
I am the daughter of Amawi
Children of the ears (frog clan, that
cuts the ears of their cattle short)
Children of the frog clan
I don't understand the child of Kaiputek (hill)
I only know the churn of milk

> *Kuchepu werro Cherupun*
> *Kuchepu Amawi*
> *Kutipiko tulatit*
> *Kutipiko lukenu*
> *Mongutan chepu Kaiputek*
> *Kupoto akeret*

Chepuchemurim continued to suffer and to wail over her fate like this until she could stand it no longer. One night she awakened her husband from a deep sleep. Apayete thought, "Ah, it is morning and my wife wants to give me food!"

But she asked him, "What do you hear?"

"I hear the hyena crying."

"And the other sound? There are two things crying."

"I don't hear anything," Apayete said sleepily.

"You must!" she insisted.

"Only the neighbor's goats," he said.

"Yes, the goats!" she exclaimed. "Why did you pretend not to hear the goats? Don't you see? The goats are mine and the hyena is yours! Today I am going to the place where those goats cried to me. I will sleep with the goats. You can have the hyena!"

And so Chepuchemurim left her husband and offered herself to the neighbor who owned the goats, but he would have nothing to do with her. His wife threatened her with a machete, screaming, "What do you expect to eat here? How dare you come into my home! Get out!"

Chepuchemurim pleaded, "I'll go if you insist, but please reconsider. Let me be your servant. I'll do any kind of work you wish." The wife relented, and Chepuchemurim began looking after her children and performing other household tasks in exchange for the kind of food she craved.

Meanwhile, her distraught husband announced to his friends, "My wife has left me and my cattle have died! I am returning to my own country of Kaiputek, near Loro, to die there. Let's hope a lion meets me on the way."

When he reached Kaiputek, Apayete's family was astonished at his thinness. They organized frequent group hunts with about sixty other men and women, using poisoned arrows made by Lokumakane, and the meat from those hunts saved Apayete. After he gained enough strength, he joined others on a six-day journey to steal cattle from the Karamojong in order to feed the children. Everyone else in the raiding party was allotted one cow or ox, but they took pity on Apayete and gave him a pregnant cow. Three months later, it calved.

When Chepuchemurim heard the news, she left her job, slept six nights in the bush and returned to her husband. She was very thin. Much to her surprise, she found that Apayete, now somewhat fat, had taken a new bride without paying any cattle, since there were no cattle to bargain with. He would have nothing to do with Chepuchemurim. Even the women ridiculed her.

"Ha!" Apayete sneered. "You told me to go sleep with the hyena! Well, I have slept with the hyena, while you slept with goats. What caused you to leave your husband of goats?"

"Please forgive me!" she begged. "It was hunger that destroyed me! I thought we'd die. I'll never complain again! If I can't be your wife, let me be your servant!" But Apayete refused to feed her and sent her to another house so he could sleep with his new wife. Chepuchemurim searched for honey, made beer and called six of her husband's friends to drink it. She asked them to plead with him on her behalf, begging, "Please don't cast me out!"

Eventually, they convinced Apayete to sleep with her once more, thereby accepting her as a wife. But the Karamojong cattle were given to the girl who had helped him hunt, prepare his food, build his house and bed, fetch his water, and who stood by him in their time of need. The cattle reproduced to 15, before the girl gave one to Chepuchemurim.

The lesson of this story is that if wives are satisfied, there is no problem, but when times are bad, they'll leave you for a more fortunate man and send you to the hyena!

Songs of the Widows

Many other songs we sing at dances are about the old days, when my parents were young and the rains came just right. A few of them were composed by two old widows, Chesupit and her friend, the mother of Chepulton, who were known to dance and sing together all night, while their cattle grazed in coolness on the abundant grasses of Kasei. Because the two friends had inherited all their husbands' wealth, their sons, who were still children, always had plenty of milk to drink. Their cattle were healthy, and their farms always produced fine harvests. They say Chesupit used to laugh with Lothilia, her cowherd, about her red-headed steer named Loreko, who was so fat he no longer needed to graze. Indeed, like Loreko, the women had no worries at all and spent their days and nights rejoicing! Two of Chesupit's ox songs became famous:

Her first song says:

Chesupit plays alone
Ah, the cattle sleep
They are squirrel-colored, oh

Chesupit nyi totine
Ah, kerui aite
Nyi ekunyuk, oh

Here is her second song:

Refrain:
> *Ai oh ioh ha Lothilia! Loreko relaxes!*

Verses:
> *Greetings, mother of Chepulton!*
> *Don't any of you little girls*
> *Go tomorrow to tell the men*
> *That the old women were dancing!*
> *If you want to tell them, tell them!*

> *Ai oh ioh, ha Lothilia! Reputhi Loreko!*
>
> *Kimala, kama Chepulton!*
> *Ekumone tiipen chomungitch*
> *Petei asiech kumgoghe*
> *Kadongo kokun*
> *Ato kamwa, kamwa*

We heard that years later Chesupit's steer, Loreko, became so obese he could not even get up by himself. It took eight men to pry him up, using two strong sticks under the legs, while another hit him on the head to arouse him. When they finally slaughtered Loreko for a boy's *sapana* feast, they found the body white as chalk, laden with fat and without a trace of meat! The stomach was huge, and the kidneys were like jerry cans. That was, indeed, a very good year!

But around the tenth month, after the harvest was safely in storage, the Karamojong came, took cattle from Kasei and killed their cowherds. (The attack had been foretold by a man who had read fortunes from a steer's intestines months earlier.) One beautiful girl named Chepuserketch saw the raid, ran to the top of the hill Kapirioko, and cried out loudly to warn her people. A handsome warrior named Maraitai heard, and ran up the hill, calling, "Where are they now?"

Chepuserketch answered, "Very near! Look!" She pointed to the cattle and the raiders, by then only a mile away.

But Maraitai's eyes were elsewhere, for he saw that the girl was naked! She had tied her skirts around her waist in order to climb the hill faster and had forgotten to let them down! She was most attractive, and her ornaments sparkled brightly there on the hilltop. Maraitai forgot all about the enemy, threw down his shield and spear and grabbed the girl!

"What are you doing?" she protested. "Go reclaim our cattle! Then I'll give you what you want from me!"

"Don't worry, I'll tend to everything," he assured her.

Maraitai made love to Chepuserketch three times there on top of Kapirioko, before he picked up his spear and shield and ran to join the other warriors. They cornered the Karamojong in front of a huge rock outcropping and killed 41 of them—Maraitai himself killed two. And while the warriors were bringing back their cattle, Chepuserketch was telling about her own adventures with Maraitai. The elders laughed heartily, and soon made up a song that we still love to sing at dances. We joke that Maraitai killed three things: the woman's sex and the two Karamojong! Chepuserketch came to be known as Chemalowun, meaning "detour on the way to the enemy."

Refrain:

Yi oye aya ah oyayo	*Yi oye aya ah oyayo*
Ah Kapirioko oye	*Ah Kapirioko oye*

Verses:

Oye Chemalowun Chepuserketch	*Oye Chemalowan Chepuserketch*
He killed a woman's sex	*Chepar nyu kuss*
Place of the tiruk fruits at Kasai	*Cheptiruk Kasei*
He detoured at Kasei, ya	*Chemal a Kasei ya*
He detoured at the Kasei tiruk fruits	*Chemal e Kasei cheptiruk o*
Chemalowun (detour of) *Maraitai*	*Chemalowun nya pu Maratai*

Songs of Warriors

Some of our best old songs honor the prowess and cunning of famous Pokot warriors. For instance, when my father was still a boy in Cheptulel, the great warrior Lowalan led a group of men to Kamumbei, at Chepchaipei, and demanded a summit conference with the leaders of our enemies, the Cheblen Marakwet. When Lowalan proposed a peace settlement, the Cheblen leaders responded, "It is done! You are a great leader amongst your people, and we know they will respect your orders for peace." They agreed to call a meeting of both peoples by the river in two days to make the announcement.

Of course, peace was not what Lowalan had in mind, and he had no trouble rounding up nearly 200 men, anxious to get even with the Cheblen, who had killed many Pokot with poisoned arrows. On the appointed day, Lowalan went with some of his contingent to the meeting place, while more than 100 Pokot warriors waited outside. He announced the peace and then said, "We Pokot, since we use spears, will remove the sheaths from the blades as a symbol of the peace. The Marakwet, in turn, will untie their bows." Everyone followed his instructions, and Lowalan led the meeting onwards, then ended it abruptly by saying, "Yes, everyone—Pokot or Marakwet—we have now proclaimed a settlement, and, therefore, close this meeting." Then he turned to his men and said, "My words are *finished!*"

As he spoke the word "finished," he drove his spear into Muritit, the leader of the Marakwet Cheblen, who was standing beside him. This was also the cue for all the Pokot there to attack the Marakwet, who were defenseless, having untied their bows! Those Pokot who had waited outside eagerly joined in the slaughter.[47]

After the killing was over, and the Pokot had taken all the bounty, it is said that Muritit's sister came to the place where he lay murdered and began to sing a mournful song. Muritit, you see, was the only man left in his clan. He had no brothers, and both of his parents had died. Only his sister remained. They say she mourned for one week, then died of grief beside her brother Muritit. This is her song of tears, but for us it is a song of celebration to sing at festive dances.

Refrain:

Mm oh yalaleye, ah oh yalaleye, aya, aya
Ah oh yalaleye, aya, aya

Verses:

Mm, what kind of people are these
   Ah, these people of Lowalan?
Mm, what kind of people are these
   Ah, these, whose shields have black bases?
Mm, what kind of people are these
   Ah, these whose shields have two "horns?"
Mm, what kind of enemies are these
   Ah, these who make three-part quivers?
Mm, what kind of enemies are these
   Ah, these people of Lowalan, aya
Mmm, bad Lowalan e
   Ah, who killed our man
Mm, bad Lowalan e
   Ah, who doesn't know an orphan
Mm, bad Lowalan e
   Ah, who killed our man
Mmm, he was good, like a metal bracelet
   Ah oh yalaleye
Mmm, bad Lowalan
   Who killed Muritit
Mmm, he moved to Kamumbei
   Ah, he came without asking
Mmm, he moved to Chepchaipei
   Ah, he came, a thief
Mm, oh yalaleye, ah oh yalaleye,
   mmm, mmm

Mm oh yalaleye, ah oh yalaleye, aya, aya
Ah oh yalaleye, aya, aya

Mm emne emone
   Ah, emo Lowalan emone
Mm emne emone
   Ah, ka chepto longe leta, aya, aya
Mm emne emone
   Ah, ka kepsakat longe muta, aya, aya
Mm, pun ne pungu
   Ah, ke kuptapat murongita, aya, aya
Mm, pun ne pungi
   Ah, emo Lowalan emone, aya
Mm, iririt Lowalan e
   Ah, nyo kepar chi tenjaa
Mm, iririt Lowalan e
   Ah, nyo mengit tukirion e
Mm, iririt Lowalan e
   Ah, nyo kepar chi ngo
Karam chi nyo kayu tai
   Ah oh yalaleye
Mm, iririt Lowalan-e
   Nyo kepar Muritit
Mm, kiwujit Kamumbei
   Ah kiwujit mateipei, aya, aya
Kiwujit Chepchapei
   Kiwujit matemai
Mm o yalaleye, Ah o yalaleye
   mmm, mmm

Two other songs date to when my mother was a girl in Kupkomo, and over 300 warriors from that region fought on behalf the Chepukosi, a branch of the Sebei. On their way to Kapchemukut, where they hunted and planned the attacks with the Chepukosi, the warriors met some poor people called Cherengan-Mai. One man cried out to them, but no one seemed to take any notice.

The attacks were successful and well planned. Our men captured hundreds of cattle and two women, Cheptoi and Chepukutot, who spent the rest of their lives with us. While resting on the journey home, one of the warriors asked, "Remember the poor man who cried out to us that day at Kipotch?"

Others remarked, "Yes! The man of Cherengan. They are so poor, they will even eat bees!"

And the first man said, "Well, I have made up a song about him," and he sang:

Aaaah, the poor man cries. Others don't hear.	*Aaaah Kirir mewan. Okochi komalian*
At Kapchemulkut (river) the poor man cries	*Kapchemulkut kirir mewan*
He cries from the Kipotch hillside.	*Kirira Kopoch selel*
Sing energetically!	*Otumuh kooror*
Sing, people of the river's uncut ridge	*Otumuh werpu rorok makuren*
He cries, he with unwashed hands	*Kirir chito meuneul*
He cries, he who eats with dirt	*Kirir chito am ta sim*
The Kapchao man cries	*Kirir Kapchao*
Sing, people of Ngoron (river)	*Otumuh werpu Ngoron*

They say one man came back from a trip to Baringo to find that his other four brothers had gone on the raid at Kapchemukut. His wife ranted at him, "You are too late! Everyone else has gone to bring back cattle, and you will have nothing! I can't stay with you! I'd be too humiliated!"

"Don't worry," he told her. "They will share the bounty with me." Sure enough, each of his brothers gave him one cow, and his wife was happy, so he made up this song:

Refrain:

I met my brothers bringing (cattle)	*Ah, konyoru werinyo kurongu*
I shall go ask	*Owe turata*

Verses:

I met my elder brother	*Konoru kuporet*
I met my younger brother	*Konyoru towonyon*
I met a pregnant cow	*Konyoru tepapot*

These are some of the many, many songs we sang and danced to when I was a youth. Many are still popular today.[48]

CLANS

Origin of the Lion Clan

Not long after we returned from the dance in Nawi, I was herding the cattle, when my dog suddenly ran away, barking. I found her near the carcasses of two mauled hyenas and an eland—obviously a lion kill. She had already eaten some of the fetus which had been dragged from the belly of the pregnant eland and was enjoying herself chasing carrion birds off the hyenas. (These birds don't touch the lion's actual prey, because the lion wards them off magically by burying a piece of the tail.) I told my dog, "You look after the meat. I'll head the cattle home and tell our people."

Everyone was drunk at our homestead—my family and all the neighbors—but they went back with me to the kill. We skinned the eland and divided the meat among the homesteads. (There were four homesteads in the area: three were together, and ours was about a mile distant.)

Late that night, we heard the lion calling—first from the place where we took his meat, then nearer and nearer, as he followed our footprints. Suddenly, there was a thunderous roar, and the cattle nearly stampeded. The lion was just outside the corral. One man yelled to him, "Go! We've already eaten the meat! Why don't you just get some more?" This made the lion furious! He bolted around the corral, making a terrific noise. He was not about to take orders from such a man, whose firstborn had been a boy!

Parents of firstborn girls, on the other hand, have powers to chase away large beasts, such as elephants or lions. For instance, if a band of men encounters an elephant on the path, they will ask each other, "Which of you had a daughter first?" One of them will reply, "I did." He will climb a tree, make a noise like a hyena, and the elephant will run away. If a man whose firstborn was a son tried this, the elephant might attack! The elephant knows.

This is why one of my mothers walked into the corral just then, calling loudly to the lion. Not only was her firstborn a daughter, but she herself belonged to the Clan of the Lion. This is how she addressed her Father, the lion:

"Listen! I am here! Why did you want to come to my home? My child found your meat and told me, 'I see that your "father" has slaughtered his "cow,"' and I said, 'Very good. I will go eat the meat my father left for me yesterday.' Did you not smell my scent and know, 'Alas, my child has come to take this meat'? Now, why do you come to make trouble in my corral? What's all this noise about? Do you want to eat my cattle, knowing Tororut divided all things and gave these to us and the wild animals to you? Go find your

own "cattle" in the wilderness! There is no need to make trouble here. Have you already forgotten that when you ran by our homestead in Kakupao Tuwit, my husband said, 'Truly, I want to give my wife's father a cow to eat'? He let a sick cow outside the corral for you then, and you took it into the wilderness to eat. So why do you choose to create this havoc for us now? Since the time my ancestor extracted the stick from your paw, we have been the children of your clan. Now, if you destroy my corral, I will have to cast a spell on you, and you will die in two days. Just try and do something bad to me!"

During my mother's speech, the lion was very quiet. By the time she finished, he had begun to walk away. We could hear him roar in the distance.

Because of our encounter with the lion, we spent much of that night hearing clan stories, beginning with the Origin of the Lion Clan.

Our old elders told us that long ago, the year most of our cattle died, Chemakenya, the Lion, was out hunting his meat, when a stick wounded his foot and broke off inside. He was in such great pain for several days that he was unable to pursue his prey. "What shall I do?" he wondered. "I will die unless I can think of some way to remove the stick." Then he had an idea.

There was a man who lived in a cave within that lion's territory. As he was resting there one day, he heard Chemakenya roaring nearby. The lion came closer and closer, and then, to his surprise, appeared at the mouth of the cave. The man was terrified, but knew he would have no chance if he tried to run. The lion entered the cave.

In spite of his fear, this man thought, "*Ala!* This animal is limping! He walks on three legs and holds his foreleg up." Slowly, Chemakenya limped right up to him and gently placed his right foreleg on the man's knee. The lion closed his eyes and looked away.

"Ohhh!" exclaimed the man sympathetically. "This must be very painful!" He took out his knife and cut into the paw until he found the stick, lodged deeply inside. He extracted first the stick, and then, very carefully, all of the splinters. When he was finished, he told the lion, "Go now. Your leg is cured." Chemakenya left and, after a short time, he roared.

Three weeks later, Chemakenya returned to that man's homestead and walked right up to him. Then he lay down for a little while, got up again and walked around some more. The lion was playing, just like a dog that sees its master! A few minutes later, Chemakenya turned and walked away. Then he roared. Another man, who had witnessed this strange happening from inside the cave, heard the insistent roaring and said, "This creature must want something. You should follow it."

And so the man followed his friend, the lion. Before long, he came across the carcass of a large eland. The lion had drunk its blood, but had not touched the meat! He realized, then, that Chemakenya had intended the meat for him and had gone to search for his own food!

That is how the man and all his descendants, like my mother, came to belong to the clan of Chemakenya, the Lion. It was Tororut's will.

The Buffalo Clan

The mother who bore me belonged to the Buffalo Clan, who claim all buffalo as their own. She was raised on the milk of cattle said to be descendants of the buffalo.

Mother told us that nearly a thousand years ago, her ancestor climbed onto a platform in a fruit tree to lie in wait for the animals that would come to browse. When a buffalo came with its calf, he killed the cow with a poisoned arrow, captured the newborn calf and carried it home, hoping to raise it amongst his cattle.

"Now, how are we going to convince a cow to accept such a calf?" his wife wondered, and then she suggested, "We will slaughter the calf of that very old cow, skin it, and tie it over the buffalo calf, so that the cow will think it is her own!"[49]

The idea worked! The old cow licked and nursed the disguised buffalo for two weeks, and when the skin dried up and was removed, she continued to accept the foster calf. A bull eventually mated with the buffalo cow, and the strange descendants of this union gave rise to a new clan, which continued to keep the buffalo-blooded cattle. My mother claimed her family used to cut and char the horns of all their cattle due to the inherited fierceness of the breed!

The Sun Clan

The elders told an interesting story about the people named Sotot Kachepkai, who belong to the Clan of the Sun. They said that long ago the rains failed for several years, and because the people of the Sun Clan were able to see very far away, they perceived a cloud-covered mountain in the distance. "Perhaps there is rain in that country," they said to one another. And so all of the Kachepkai moved to the mountain and settled there, never to return. In the olden days they were Pokot, but now they are called Maliri. Nevertheless, we hear they still practice the traditions of our mutual ancestors. Their children are circumcised like ours, their wives wear skin rope marriage bracelets, as ours do, and they practice our old customs and sing our traditional songs.

The Baboon Clan

My clan, and my fathers', the Baboon, originated at Tapasiat, which is now known by its Karamojong name, Moroto. These days, as with all clans, we are greatly dispersed. For example, one day recently I walked to Kirikiripa and came across two women speaking a language strange to me, yet when I greeted one, she responded! Curious, I asked her, "When you used to talk to your father long ago, where did he tell you your people came from?"

She answered, "He said we came from Moroto, at a place called Tapasiat."

"Yes, and what is your clan?"

"We are Baboon," she said.

I replied, "Then you are my sister, for I also am of the Baboon Clan of Tapasiat."

The woman, who was named Chemingyen, rejoiced. She and her husband took me to their home, where she cooked for me and offered me a place to sleep on my journey.

Cattle Brands of the Baboon Clan
Male and female patterns are different, but all have a cross mark on the head.

Clan Customs

Each clan has its own customs about marriage and other rituals, as well as its own insignia. We use a thin piece of iron called *machei* for burning brands on our cattle, usually right after they have been weaned. Some clans also cut the ears of their cattle in certain ways, and others may tie a rope around the middle of each ox. Similarly, when we shave the heads of our little children, we leave strips of hair in the pattern of our clans. For instance, we of the baboon clan leave two concentric circles of hair on top of the head, so that anyone who knows the signs will be able to identify our toddlers. When the children are older, the hair is allowed to grow out.

Certain of these customs are followed not only throughout Pokot country, but sometimes even within enemy territories. Once, while passing through Marakwet country, one of my friends pointed to some cattle and exclaimed, "Look at those cattle: they are ours!"

I objected, "What do you mean? The brands are different."

He said, "But look at the ears! They are notched like mine!" Sure enough, when he spoke with the owner, he discovered that they both belonged to the Elephant Clan!

It is sinful to spill the blood of one's own clansman knowingly. Of course, during a battle, men don't know which enemies are related, and they fight openly. But when a warrior recognizes a clansman among the enemy, he will show his spear and say, "You can pass safely." He might even go so far as to warn his enemy clansman of an impending attack, so that he might escape.

Therefore, when one side is at the point of being massacred by the other, it behooves them to start asking about clans! Once a band of Pokot warriors had killed all but 15 opposing Marakwet, when one compassionate Pokot warrior climbed a hill and began calling, "Amongst you, is there anyone of the Sun Clan here?" Silence. "How about Wild Dog?" asked another. "Yes," came one response. "Frog?" called another Pokot. "Yes, here!" a Marakwet said. The two men of the Wild Dog and Frog clans were ordered to bring tobacco to their counterparts. This they did, and their Pokot kinsmen declared, "You are cured and the battle is over! Go bring your relatives, and we will give you water and food to help you recover."

CALL ME RED-SPOTTED OX

Early one morning, about a year after the dance at Nawi, a giant star streaked across the sky and made the world light.[50] Its head was huge and black, and its tail was very long and white. I remember The Year the Star Went in the Morning as the time the seeds of my body issued forth at last! I became a youth who knew neither past nor future, driven by the desire to prove my manhood.

Let the Children Play

One of the homesteads at Lossom belonged to a man named Lokwanale. His lovely daughter, Arupe, became my girlfriend, and sometimes I would go to see her secretly at night.

Once, as we were sleeping together in her mother's house, Arupe's father came to the door, suspicious. He called to his wife and asked her to light the fire. As soon as the coals glimmered, the mother saw me.

"He's here!" she screeched. "Arupe is with her 'husband'! Get him! I'll take care of the girl!" She grabbed a club, and Arupe bolted into the room for baby goats. The mother pounded me twice with the club, but I fended her off with my stool.

"Grab his feet!" Lokwanale yelled to his wife.

"No! He'll kick me!" she yelled back, whacking me some more with the club.

Lokwanale ducked in the door and seized me. He grabbed one of my arms, and I caught one of his. We wrestled, and I managed to push him off balance towards his wife's bed. He released my arm, and I fled out of the door. He tore through the corral after me, but tripped, banging his head against a log. I could hear a woman calling, "Arupe has run outside with her boyfriend!"

"All right, Arupe," Lokwanale shouted from the corral. "If you sleep outside tonight, a snake will bite you. I've cast a spell on you!"

I did not meet Arupe in the darkness, but two hours later I returned and saw her in the corral. She was afraid to go back into the house, fearing her father would beat her.

"Come, let's go sleep outside," I whispered to her, and we did.

The next morning, I was inside a house in my father's homestead, when Arupe's mother arrived. "Where is your son?" I could hear her asking my father.

"Which one?"

"Domonguria."

"He's here."

"And the child?" she demanded

"What child?"

"My daughter!"

"I haven't seen her."

The mother sounded exasperated. "Tonight I want you to tie that boy up to a tree!" she almost shouted. "I don't want him bothering us at night! Last night my husband cracked his head on a log because of your son! So you tie him up!"

Father was incredulous. "*Ala!* Tie him up? You're crazy! I'm not going to tie anyone to a tree!"

"Last night he came after my girl," she protested.

"And I suppose in the past *you* never had a boyfriend?" Father countered. "Go home! Tell your husband and his other wives that I'm not one to meddle in the affairs of children! If you want to cry about it, that's your problem! If I were you, I'd get a good night's sleep instead! After all, that's what children do—you should know that! Why, just yesterday, when I saw boys and girls in the corral together, I didn't think anything of it. I just figured, 'Ah, let them go about their business; everyone does it!' It's pitiful that an adult like you should go about whining over such a thing. It's not as if she's someone's wife. They are sweethearts—so what?"

My father had ridiculed the poor woman into silence! There was a long pause, then Father called to my mother, "Cheparkong, bring milk and tobacco!"

"Do you use tobacco?" he asked Arupe's mother quietly.

"Yes."

"Then chew some tobacco and drink some milk, then go and be content," he said gently. "Really, it's ridiculous to get upset over something like this. Parents shouldn't pry into the comings and goings of their children. Why, my own daughters sleep alone! I don't go there and my wives don't go there. If your son came here at night, I wouldn't ask him what he was looking for. I would know! Tell your husband I'd like to speak to him here later this afternoon."

Arupe's mother left, and, at last, I came out of the house.

When Lokwanale arrived later that afternoon, Father kidded him unmercifully about the large bump on his head. Father laughed and laughed, saying, "You sure brought us a lot of trouble this morning! Crying over the children, when they're just doing what you used to do—it's downright inconsiderate! Ha, ha! Oh well, let's forget it! Have some beer!" Of course, Father was aware that his old friend did not share his mirth.

That is, of course, because he did have a legitimate concern. A girl who gets pregnant by another man before marriage is called *kamatuyon*, and she is worth very little at the time of her wedding. At the most, the father might receive five or ten cattle, when other daughters are drawing anywhere from 25 to 60 head. It is a real tragedy. How can a father augment his herds if his daughters are ruined? For the same reason, people have been reluctant to send their daughters to school these days. Who knows what kind of brideprice a schoolgirl will bring?

From that day on, Lokwanale policed his daughter relentlessly. He stationed her mother at the doorway of the hut so that I could not enter without stepping on her or some of the children. After four days of this frustration, I cornered Arupe while she was watching the goats with another girl. She would not agree to any of my plans for her escape.

Finally, one night I came and, as usual, found the mother with a nursing infant and a larger child just inside the entrance. Carefully, I straddled the doorway, with one foot on each door post, and hoisted myself up high enough to grab the *taranyoi* beam, which runs across the ceiling of the house. I pulled myself up and crawled on it until I was above my girlfriend. It worked! We enjoyed our reunion, and I left by the same route.

This went on for a few nights, until a child spotted us and tattled to its mother. I escaped, but there was a lot of noise. Lokwanale was furious, and came to see my father, who would hear none of it. "Will you continue to argue with me over the affairs of children?" Father asked him. "It's shameful! You did the same thing when you were young. Let the children play!"

Ox of Ropes

Among our peoples, including the Pokot, Karamojong and Turkana, when a youth finds a calf which is especially pleasing to him, he may choose it as his "ox of ropes," his name-ox. All of the oxen celebrated in this way must have the same coloring. Some men like red best, others prefer white and others black. Some like their oxen spotted like a giraffe, and others prefer theirs bluish-gray. I like those with spotted heads.

Some boys choose their name-oxen before puberty, but I chose my first ox of ropes after I had already gone to see girls. He was a beautiful calf—all white, except for red spots on his head and legs. I proclaimed, "Everyone hear! This is my ox of ropes!" From that day on, in addition to the name my mother gave me, I have been known as Domonguria, which means "ox with red spots around the eyes."

I tied eight ropes around the neck of my ox Domonguria to make a collar and attached four white cows' tails, so that they swayed when he walked. I hung a tortoise-shell bell in the middle. Then I cut the front skin of my ox, below the neck, so that a long strip, called *alangangak*, hung down as a decoration in front of the bell. The wound was washed with salt and tied with rope. It healed within two weeks.

Later, when my ox grew large, I fixed his horns. First I burned them until they became flexible, then I cut each one at the base with a knife. Using a stone, I beat them into a pattern I found pleasing—with both horns facing forwards. Then I tied them in place with a rope. By the time this rope wore thin and broke, the horns remained in position.

Like coloration, each man has his own preference about horns for his name-ox. Some fix the horns so that they come together, and others may cut and fix only one horn, so that one stands up and the other points down or forward.[51]

It is customary for us to notch the ears of our oxen when we kill a lion, elephant or an enemy. Sometimes I have cut the ears of a friend's ox of ropes instead. Then, when he celebrates some feat of bravery, he will notch mine. The ears of my ox Domonguria were notched so many times, they flopped over!

Now, as then, when I go to a dance, I celebrate this ox, along with the others I have decorated since. We sing and dance freely until it is Time for the Bulls, when each man sings his ox song, backed up by a chorus of his friends. All men who have oxen of the same coloring will use the same tune for the chorus. For instance, there is one melody we use for red bulls, another for spotted, another for white. At the Time for the Bulls, the people gather around the warriors and chant the appropriate tunes, as the men, one at a time, sing the praises of their favorite oxen. Each raises his arms to show the configuration of the horns he has fixed, and when his song is finished, he jumps forward as high as he can, along with two friends. Finally, three women slowly jump forward to honor them.

When it is my turn, as the chorus chants, I begin with my song - the one for which people call me Domonguria:[52]

Refrain (1-3x):
Beautiful body
Ee Domonguria, Domonguria
Ee Domonguria, Father

Eroko amina
Ee Domonguria
Ee Domonguria papo

Verses:
Its head pleases Lereyang
My white flower pleases Longolol
Ox of my lame father
Its ox-tail collar pleases Lowoiyangor
The horns, spots of my ox are for Lopeyok
The spotted head of my ox is for Korikwang
My ox is for tall Lemaluk
It is good to go (hunting), *Loiyamale*
We will go to find the arid land of the sun
To kill an elephant with Lowoiyangor
Come, (cut) *the ear of the red-spotted hump*
We struck the horns until they went down
We fixed them at the hill Lomasinik
Very big, they please Lereyang
We fixed them at Lokichoggio (river)

Lowana nyema pa Lereyang
Eturut nyema pa Longolol
Equa naite papo kang chodo
Lomonga nyema Lowoiyangor
Loriongo nguria nye aitie ata Lopeyok
Na domo nye aite ata Koriquang
Aitia ta Lemaluk lowoiyan
Ejok ewathia Loiyamale
Atoronya nyakirep kide nya akolong
Areme nye tom kerukutu Lowoiyangor
Apato tomunyei nyereng erok
Arama akakone pa tarakiwo
Arama kolo Lomasinik
Lukuko nyema pa Lereyang
Arama Lokichoggio

On one of my later steers, Lorengaruk, I tied ropes around the base of his fixed horns and attached two white cow tails, cut short, on either side of the rope, beside the eyes. Then I tied a single white cow's tail on the collar in front of the bell. I sing this song to celebrate my ox Lorengaruk:

I found
The bell you see, ah
Inside the shop
For Lorengaruk -u - yaiyay

Wo ngaiyeya
Ariamu nya ka dongodongut-a
Kidingi lo ducan
Lorengoruk u yaiye

I used to sing these songs when I went to romance girls. They were always impressed and knew the oxen for which I sang. My heart rejoiced on these occasions, knowing they thought of me as a child of wealth. For a man without oxen has nothing; without food, he is no longer a man, but is called "dog."

I kept my ox Domonguria for many years—perhaps nine or ten—until the son of Longorimai asked my father if he could slaughter it for his *sapana* celebration of manhood. I agreed, and in return, as is the custom when one requests another's ox of ropes, I, myself, was given a heifer.

If a man still has an ox of ropes at the time of his marriage, he will give it to the bride's father as part of the marriage payment. On this occasion, the ox of ropes is the first animal let out of the corral; all of the other cattle follow behind.

Working for the Government

It was during the year after The Year the Star Went in the Morning that a headman named Kadaban came to our homestead one day and seized me for government work digging wells.[53] My father objected, saying, "He is still a small child! He can't do hard work!" but Kadaban and his men insisted, paying no heed to Father's words.

We went to Amudat, where approximately forty others had been assembled. Amudat, at that time, had two shops, both run by Somalis. In addition, the government-appointed chief, Losile, had a compound of seven houses, the sub-chief had six, and the soldiers had five. The roofs of all of the structures were thatched with grass, not corrugated iron, like the shops these days. From Amudat, we traveled to Kalowas, where we joined 200 others and began our work.

There was a violent storm one day. We heard that the lightning struck over thirty cattle in Kitelarengan, including several belonging to an elder we knew named Kokilea. The lightning tossed them about like so many sacks of maize meal.

After digging two wells at Kalowas, we dug one at Loro, one at Karemeri, one at Kitulel and one at Wokiss. We received no salaries, but there was maize meal. Three months later, the European in charge finally released us from work.

The Evil Eye

Shortly after my return home, I went to see a girl I liked named Kapkachel, hoping she would let me sleep with her for the first time. That evening Kapkachel lit the fire and we visited for awhile inside the hut. Then she left to get some milk for me, and I went outside to urinate. Later, I sat with her, drinking the milk, and before long we were lying down together. Things were going very well, when, suddenly, I began to feel sickness and pain in my body. I was embarrassed, but Kapkachel just laughed and declared, "Ah, Domonguria! I must have put a spell on you with my eyes!"

"You?"

"Yes. I am a Sowawut!" She spit on me, and the pains vanished.

Everyone knows that people of the clan Sowawut have the power to curse other people with their eyes. With only a gaze, they can cause a person to become deathly ill. They do not mean to harm anyone; indeed, they can't control when the power will come. If someone they have looked at gets very sick, they must spit on the person's head and throat to remove the curse, and the victim will vomit and recover. Sometimes the recovery is instant; sometimes it can take a month. Any man who marries a Sowawut wife has no problems as long as the wife is attentive and nearby.

Other peoples, like the Turkana, the Karamojong and the Sebei also have clans that possess the Evil Eye. Probably the Europeans and others do as well. It is Tororut's plan to choose some of each kind to be like this.

My lifelong friend, Arekai, is a Sowawut. Once I got sick after coming home from a dance with him. Two hours later, my condition was much worse, and Arekai declared, "What is this? Maybe I cursed you with my eyes!"

"I don't know—who knows," I groaned. He wiped his saliva on my head and throat, and, within a few minutes, I vomited and recovered. It must have been him!

The Sowawut have no effect on animals, but there are others, called Ngusurot, who do. They belong to Kazetem, the clan of Ilat. They have the power to kill all kinds of baby animals, but their gaze cannot harm people.

First Lion

One day my father sent me to Tarakit to the homestead of a man named Achule in order to fetch some cattle. On the way, I met a group of herders who were upset, because some of their cattle had been eaten by a lion. I arrived late in the evening and spent the night there. The next morning, we heard that a lion had eaten two cattle at Kaapem, and the owner was asking for help. My mission was immediately forgotten: I went on the lion hunt with the men from Tarakit.

A neighbor was waiting for us on the path. He led us to the site of the hunt, where about thirty others were assembled. "Keep quiet," they whispered. "The lion is very near. We dispersed and spread out silently. My group had about 15 men. Four went into the bushes where the lion had disappeared, and the rest of us stalked or hid around the perimeter.

Then I saw her: the lioness started to come out on our side! She walked halfway to our line of hunters, then sensed the danger and began to retreat. Six spears were thrown, but they all went amiss. This agitated the lioness, and she turned and started to come towards us again, running a little. Her mate was still sleeping, but, of course, the nature of the lioness is different: Whereas the male lion has composure, she does not. After all, she is a wife, and it is the nature of wives to fidget.

There were people everywhere in front of her. She came very close to me. Then she stopped, looked into the brush where we were waiting, and crouched low, preparing to spring. Suddenly, she plunged towards us, attacking a man who was just in front of me, and hurling his body into the bushes behind me. She was right there, and, in a split second, I whirled around and rammed my spear into her body. I pushed, rather than threw it, and the spear went true! It pierced her throat, and she fell.

Then I looked behind me at the mutilated man. His flesh had been gouged by her claws. There were also two teeth wounds, but they were not so bad. The man was in terrible pain, of course, but he managed a smile and said to me, "You, boy! Someday, come to me and I will give you a goat. You saved me! She would have destroyed me!" He told me his name was Muria, which means "black man."

After that, several of us went after the male lion, which had run away during the commotion. We tracked him about an hour, before one of the men suggested, "Let's let him go! When he sees his mate has died, he'll move far away to another country, just as any man would, to search for a new mate." So we let him go.

The next day, Achule gave me the cow, with its calf, that I had come to get, and I returned home. I told my father about the lion at Tarakit, and he listened intently. "You did well, Kaparketo," he said. "Your behavior was that of a man."

"Father," I began, "I see that one spear is not enough for me."

He looked at me, surprised, and agreed enthusiastically, "You are right! Go take this calf to the ironsmith and select your spears!"

I went that very afternoon. I found two very much to my liking. When I returned, I gave my small spear to my brother, Apur.

Blindness

The terrible eye disease we call *tiombamut*, or *ptangtang*, was widespread at that time. Thousands succumbed, and the lucky ones were able to summon quickly one of the women who knew how to diagnose and treat the illness. By studying any blood found during a rectal examination, such a practitioner could specify whether a sheep, an ox or a goat should be slaughtered. Then she would dig up a certain root and cook it in one pot, while the meat cooked in another pot. Finally, she would feed a mixture of soup and animal blood to the patient, causing him to vomit profusely and begin to recover. (Only a few people were allowed to eat the cooked meat. If anyone who had previously been treated for this illness ate it, then later drank beer or blood or slept with his wife, he would get sick again.)[54]

We heard that an Indian woman in Amudat became so ill with this disease that she was unable to go to a hospital or anywhere else. At her husband's request, a very good Pokot doctor named Chepuchepkai, wife of Aremesukiria, came to their house and examined her. She diagnosed the sickness as *ptangtang* and advised the couple to slaughter a goat.

"But for us, killing a goat is a very bad thing," the Indian protested.

Chepuchepkai respected the binding customs of others. She said, "If you see that the goat will be too difficult for you, you must find honey instead. I will try to treat her using that" The Indian husband went out immediately to buy honey, while Chepuchepkai prepared the root medicine. As soon as the sick woman drank the syrup, she vomited. She had diarrhea for a day, then recovered completely. Her grateful husband paid Chepuchepkai sixty shillings.

My first symptoms of *ptangtang* occurred when I was out watching the cattle a few weeks after returning from Tarakit. That morning I noticed that blood came out of my nose when I blew it. (I remember feeling annoyed at the inconvenience of a nosebleed just then.) A little later, at midday, my eyes started smarting. I tried to clear them out, but nothing was in them. The irritation did not stop, and by the time I brought the cattle home that evening, my eyes were aching severely. My mother looked at me and exclaimed, "Ah! It is the head sickness—*ptangtang!*" She inserted her hand into my abdomen and found blood. "By tomorrow, you'll have no eyes!" she said. "We'd better kill an ox fast!"

Father was away, so my mother killed the ox herself. While the others were skinning it as fast as they could, Mother ran into her house to get the root she had been keeping in a bag there. She put it in a pot, and the meat was put in another pot and cooked. I drank the soup, along with the ox's blood, and vomited uncontrollably. Exhausted, I slept until nightfall, then got up to drink some milk. By the next morning, I felt fine, although my eyes have been scarred with white markings ever since.

If my mother had not known the treatment, I would be blind now, like my brother Apur. He was not so lucky. Like hundreds of others, his illness was undetected until it was too late. *Why*, I have wondered again and again, expecting no answer. *Why does Tororut allow such tragedy? Why my brother Apur?*

LOVE, LIONS AND ELEPHANTS

When my eyes had fully recovered, I moved with the steers from our home corral to Longoleke for two weeks, and then on to Lomasinik, where there were many people. There I stayed near the homestead of a man named Loram, who had once been a policeman. He had friends from distant places who would sometimes visit him: people from Jinja, Uganda, as well as several Dodoth and Jie men. I enjoyed my time there immensely.

Homestead of Youths

We youths stayed with our herds in a homestead apart from that of the men and their families. There were four of us. One had two cowherds to help watch after his stock, and another had one boy. My other friend and I had no cowherds, so we would take turns watching our combined herds. Our evenings were frequently spent at the local dances, where I soon discovered an attractive girl named Natei, the daughter of Loram's brother. We flirted a great deal with each other and later became lovers.

Several weeks after my arrival, a man from Loram's homestead, named Lokodos, killed an eland and declared that he would prepare the skin to try to win the affections of a girl from a nearby village. He cleaned and softened the leather, made it into a woman's apron (*atela*), and decorated it beautifully with twenty to thirty iron beads. When the garment was finished, he sent a message to the girl's father: "We are about to deliver a skin for your daughter! Please await us!" (Usually the suitor asks a girl for her own *atela* to decorate, and she gives it to the boy her heart desires, but Lokodos hoped this gift would work to his advantage.) At last, on the appointed day, a great number of men joined Lokodos in the fun of ceremoniously presenting the *atela* to his chosen lady. Everyone helped each other in those days, even in frivolity!

That same morning, two of my companions and I went out to hunt a lion. The night before, one of the cowherds had arrived two hours after the cattle came home with news that a lion had killed two of Lokodos' donkeys—a mother and its foal— at a place called Chemisuk. The young donkey had been large enough to carry a burden. It was quite a loss to Lokodos, and we decided to help, even though he was busy with the *atela* presentation. When we reached Chemisuk, we found the head and feet of the mother donkey and the whole carcass of the young one, dragged into the bushes by the river.

Although we were few, we began tracking the lion. The spoor went back and forth endlessly, and we were still tracking in the same area by mid-afternoon. I had noticed a large tree near the trail, and I suggested to my friends, "You continue tracking, while I climb that tree and watch. The lion just might pass by." They agreed, and continued their pursuit in another direction.

I had not been waiting in the tree long, when I saw a pair of lions approaching, slowly and silently. They came as if in a strange, eerie dance. The female would take four careful steps and then stop, her paw poised in the air, while the male followed stealthily, until he nudged his mate with his nose. Then he would wait, paw in the air, while she began again.

The female passed directly beneath my tree, but I had decided to get the male. I tensed, without making a sound. Then he came under the tree, turning his head to look behind, and I threw my spear. It pierced through his back, near where the ribs end, and came out below the throat. The great male leapt up, roaring wildly, and tried to run. Then he fell onto a large, sharp stick, which tore at the wound and caught on his stomach. Amazingly, he wrenched himself free, but I could see some of the viscera still hanging on the stick. He disappeared into a thicket, heading in the direction of the other youths. *It's their good luck that I dealt that lion a mortal wound,* I thought. In fact, I was feeling awfully proud: It was my second lion, and I had killed both within only six months! I called out the news to my companions. They were worried that the wounded lion might still be dangerous, but I reassured them, "Let him go! He can't possibly recover without the entrails that are hanging there on the stick! He must have died."

As we were returning to our homestead, we met Lokodos, Loram and the others coming back from their holiday over the *atela*. My friends dramatized my feat in killing the lion with great enthusiasm. Loram, already in excellent spirits, laughed with delight and exclaimed, "Wonderful! Your donkeys have had vengeance, Lokodos!"

Lokodos proclaimed loudly, "Let no one say these boys are incompetent! They are expectant and brave, like policemen! We rejoice over your good deed!" Then he chuckled to himself and remarked, "I like the part about the guts coming out! *Ala!* That lion won't eat again! He'll become the dung of another animal! Ha, ha, ha!"

Meanwhile, Natei was being ridiculed by several local bachelors because of her affair with me. Those youths had already gone through *sapana* initiation and they wore the clay headdresses of manhood, while I had to be content with the decorations I attached to my hair. According to Natei, one of them had asked her, "Why have you regressed to lie with an uninitiated boy like that, when there are real men who want you? You, Natei, are very stupid!" But she had answered, "You might insult me, but I'm not stupid—only my heart! I love that boy as if he were my husband. It is only my heart which does wrong by loving him."

When Loram heard this talk sometime later, he called Natei to him and said, "What's this I hear about you? Some have tried to belittle your boyfriend, even though he is rich: his father has cattle! If he gets you pregnant, it's not bad! If you want to go to his father's homestead, go ahead!" Natei could hardly believe her ears! Loram, amused at her surprise, explained, "You see, Natei, I am especially fond of this boy. One who helps the holdings of another man to the extent of revenging lost animals is surely a man. He comes to the aid of his friends, and he is good!"

At the next dance, Natei and I celebrated our good fortune. I still remember how brightly the moon shone that night.

Elephants

There were plenty of elephants in the vicinity of Loram's homestead, and a few of them of them became dangerous. One incident involved Lopedur, who would later become my brother-in-law. Very early one morning, just as dawn was break-ing, Lopedur was on his way home from visiting a girlfriend, when he came upon a dying elephant cow on the path. He speared her, and she trumpeted. Just then, the bull came crashing through the brush towards him. There was no time to run. Lopedur threw his last spear, but the elephant, oblivious to the wound, bore down on him. Lopedur ducked to one side, narrowly escaping the murderous feet, and plunged into the woods beside the path. He leaped into a tree, climbing fast, while the bull raged towards him, trumpeting, smashing the trees and bush-es in his way. Then his massive trunk grabbed the tree Lopedur was in, uprooted it, and hurled it around, crushing it into small pieces. Lopedur clung to his branch as it thudded to the ground, landing in some brush, miraculously hidden from the elephant's eyes and storming mass.

When our neighbors found him, Lopedur was nearly dead. People had heard the elephant trumpet and had guessed that Lopedur was the one in danger, for they knew his habit of visiting girls at night. By the time they reached the site of the attack, the bull elephant was gone. They slashed through the brush with ma-chetes, searching the area of destruction, until at last they came upon Lopedur, mangled and semi-conscious, with his legs wrapped around his neck.

They carried him home, slaughtered a goat and cooked it. Lopedur drank the soup, mixed with a root medicine, and vomited blood. Nevertheless, he was forced to eat all of the goat meat, and they gave him fresh cow's blood to drink. By the end of the week he had recovered.

Two weeks later, Chepusia, the wife of Nameri, went to fetch water at the river near us and was killed by an elephant.

By coincidence, about that time a man from Taposa named Lorika came to Amudat and was directed to Loram's homestead in Kanyao. He had a hunting license and a gun, and wanted Loram to kill four elephants for him so that he could have the tusks. Loram agreed. First he hunted in the area where Chepusia had been crushed to death. He climbed a tree, scanned the countryside, and even-tually spotted the large bull elephant in the distance. Then Loram climbed down and stalked the elephant very, very slowly. When he was within a spear's throw, he cocked the gun and aimed. The bull heard and reeled around, just as Loram pulled the trigger. The elephant charged, as Loram kept shooting. After the sixth shot, the beast crashed down, almost at Loram's feet. The man from Taposa was very pleased.

As the ivory trade increased, the elephants began to disappear from our area. Our elders began to sell the coveted tusks after the arrival of white people and other interested foreigners. One tusk would fetch four cattle; both, eight—an of-fer difficult to refuse. However, the rapid loss of our elephants has saddened us greatly. We found one on a group hunt as late as 1969, but now they are gone, except for a few at Elgon and some at Kidepo, in the northern region of the Kara-mojong.

Stalked by a Lion

A beautiful girl I was seeing at that time, Adungol, lived nearly 18 miles away from Loram's compound, and I would have to walk that distance in the dark each night I wished to see her. One evening I had a particularly unnerving experience. I left as usual, crossed the river Akore, which had a lot of water at the time, due to recent rains, and continued up the bank. Just then, I heard the water rustling behind me.

"Ha! It must be Lodeapa going to his girl on the same path," I thought. All the girls lived in one general area and we youths in another, as it happened. (That is not to say our homesteads were crowded together. Lodeapa's house, for instance, was some two miles distant from mine.)

I walked on for another mile and crossed the second river of my journey. I had gone but 150 yards further, when again I heard the water swishing behind me. A chill passed through me. *"If it's my friend, why doesn't he walk with me?"* I thought. *"Maybe it's a hyena—no, nothing stupid like that! Only one kind of animal would track like that—a leopard or a lion!"*

By the time I had walked another half mile and crossed another very small river, I was scared. My very soul quivered, and my legs began to feel heavy. Finally, I crouched low, unsheathed my two spears and waited. I could hear his heavy breathing. It was a lion; there was no doubt.

I was in a bad position, so I went on ahead until I reached a somewhat larger river. The moon had begun to rise enough so that I could make out the wild thicket of trees lining the far bank. I stood quietly for a moment before entering the river, where I would be exposed. A stick snapped, but I could not judge where. I figured he must have gone on ahead of me. He knew this wilderness and could travel faster than I in the darkness. I kept my spears ready and waded across the river and the little creek that followed it. Then I hid in the thicket and waited.

He was very near and was running straight towards me! I raised my arm and hurled my spear. The lion leaped and fled into the night. I ran after him, throwing stones, until I heard him roar far away. He must have been startled, coming upon me earlier than he expected and seeing my spear arm go up.

The lion did not trouble me again that night, but the terror stayed with me. As I lay sleeping with my girl, I began to dream about the lion. I jumped up in my sleep, stepped on the fire and nearly cracked my head on the house beam! The other people there were lucky not to be burned by the flying coals. I tried to go back to sleep, but the dream still controlled me. "What's the matter?" Adungol kept asking. At last my blood lay still, and I told her about the lion.

"Oh, you have been bad!" she admonished me. "Every day I plead with you not to come like that at night. If you want me, come in the daylight! You know very well there are plenty of dangerous animals around here! Who knows which are man-eaters?"

As I walked home early the next morning by the same route, I mused to myself that it was lucky for the lion that he knew about spears!

BAD LUCK AND WORK

Test for the Knife

Soon after I brought the steers back to Lossom, we heard the news that The Knife had come from its place in Cheptulel. All circumcisions are arranged by a certain elder in Cheptulel, where my father was raised, and his decision, or, as we say, "The Knife," goes straight to the people. The news spread that he had authorized a large group circumcision rite to be held in the vicinity of Nangalita-baa.[55]

My father asked me, "Son, are you ready for circumcision?"

"Yes!"

"Then we would like to test you now."

"Good," I answered. "I am ready."

My people gathered around me, while my father took a burning stick from the fire and carefully placed it directly on my nails. Pain shot through my arms, but I did not flinch. I stiffened my body and my countenance to withstand the piercing flame. The test lasted about one minute, and then he withdrew the coal.

"*Aaaiiiiiii!*" Mother shouted happily, and all her co-wives joined in. Father threw the stick back into the fire and came back smiling. "My first son is ready for circumcision!" he proclaimed.

"Yes!" my mothers exclaimed happily. "If he can withstand the fire, surely he can take the knife of circumcision without feeling pain!"

"Go back to your work now, son," Father said. "When the rains come, we will celebrate your circumcision with a grand feast."

Word of my courage spread quickly, and soon all of my relatives were gathering honey for the beer of my celebration. My father asked permission from the elders, and they agreed. If the rains were plentiful that year, all would be well. (Both boys and girls are tested with fire in this way. If they show fear, the circumcision must be put off until another year. Likewise, if the rains fail, the ceremony must be postponed.)

As it turned out, the rains were good, but luck was not. We traveled to Chelo-poi, the designated place, where I met the other initiates, many of whom had come from great distances. There we constructed a circumcision house large enough to sleep 200. We were just putting the finishing touches on the house, as-suming that the first group of initiates would be circumcised the following day, when somebody sneezed! This was extremely bad luck, and we were forced to abandon our efforts and build another house. Then it happened again! We began to build three times, and each time a sneeze stopped us! After we abandoned the third structure, the circumcision elders left us. We were forced to return home.

We had been back but a month when trouble began with the Karamojong, and the circumcision was canceled altogether. Unfortunately, we've been fighting somewhat ever since. Evidently, the Karamojong believe they can't attain man-hood without spearing another man, and this danger has forced the Pokot to all but abandon the ritual of circumcision in Uganda. Circumcision rituals require people to be away from their homes for a prolonged period, and the elders don't want to risk shutting down even for one year in this area, because of the risk of attack. I would have to wait until I was much older, when the rite could be ar-ranged in another, safer place.

Karamojong Trouble

Until that time, we had been living peacefully with the Karamojong for several years. There had been a few incidents, more in the nature of private feuds, but for the most part we had lived, and our cattle had grazed, side by side. Then a Pokot boy inadvertently let his cattle graze and water in an area the Karamojong had set aside exclusively for calves. Two Karamojong men discovered the cattle there and beat the boy fiercely. Somehow, the frightened, battered child managed to run to the river, where he collapsed near his family. All the Pokot there were furi-ous. They stormed back to the pasture and clobbered the two Karamojong.

The next day, a meeting was held at the Kakuriangok well in the dry river bed. The Karamojong claimed, "You started this trouble!" and the Pokot retorted, "You nearly killed the boy!" Tempers mounted quickly, fighting erupted, and Lousiku, a Pokot, got his spear and killed Pulwan, a very highly regarded and well-known Karamojong leader. Everyone was shocked. The Karamojong ran off, taking Pokot cattle, and the Pokot moved away with some Karamojong cat-tle.

The Karamojong wanted revenge. They decided to kill the two most feared Pokot warriors: Lemukol, son of the former chief, Akasile, and Lokitare, his cous-in. They created an incident to bait the warriors by murdering their cowherd and his dog while they slept in their corral at night. The next day, Lemukol and Loki-tare came, following the tracks and raiding Karamojong cattle along the way.

They had collected several herds of cattle, when the police intercepted them and seized the herds.

This put a new twist in the Karamojong plans. They were not about to let the police get away with their prized victims. They ambushed the policemen, beat them with clubs, speared their prisoners, Lemukol and Lokitare, and took back their cattle.

This led to many other incidents and arguments. Four years later, Lousiku was made to pay a fine of sixty cattle for killing Pulwan, and the matter was finished. [56]

Pasture on Fire

One hot day after the murder of Lemukol and Lokitare, I was watching our cattle graze on the hill Kodulem, when I spotted some dikdik just ahead of them. I ran up the hill, aimed my bow and an arrow and shot. The arrow missed the dikdik, but it scraped against some stones and started a fire. The dry grass caught instantly, and soon the whole hillside was burning. I got the cattle down just ahead of the flames. The fire spread and burned for two days until the pasture was completely destroyed. If someone offered you a cow or an ox for finding a single blade of grass there, you would find the task impossible!

I was seized and beaten mercilessly. They tied my arms behind my back and pushed me into the corral. There they brought before me one of my oxen that was just like my ox of ropes, Domonguria, only smaller. It had large, long, magnificently erect horns. I was forced to kill it, for I was in great trouble. After they ate the meat, the elders instructed my father in the ritual he must perform in order to save me from the wrath of Tororut.

Accordingly, Father brewed six gourds of beer, and Mother took five of them to the elders at Lossom. Father and I took the other gourd, a black sheep, some honey-fat, the milk of a cow that had calved once, some millet and some sorghum to a small place called Sikowa, on top of the hill. There we made a large fire with *tarokwa* and *teretwa* sticks and the scented grass we call *tomut*. While the fire burned and smoked, we sang the ritual songs of circumcision: the two of the *tios* (male initiates) and the two of the *chemerin* (female initiates). Then Father slaughtered the sheep and put the meat in a pot to cook, along with the fat of the tail. He took the contents of the sheep's stomach and scattered them all around the area, calling out, *"Tororut, forgive this child for the burning of the hill! We have beaten him, yet he is still small and ignorant in many ways. Now we beg you to forgive the sins of this small child!"*

When the meat was done, Father cut it into 24 pieces. He threw the pieces of meat all around us and said, *"Please, Tororut, take this meat and eat it. Help us recover from this transgression."* After that, he took a cup of the beer and poured some on the ground, saying, *"Tororut, drink this beer and forgive the sins of the child."*

The matter was finished, and we returned home. That April, when the rains came, the grass grew in abundance once again.

Seized for Work

A month later, a soldier and a headman came to our homestead at night. I had gone to see my girlfriend Chepukenar, who lived nearby, taking only my walking stick, stool and cape. I had left my spear in the *aperit*, where a man was sleeping. The soldier saw the spear and questioned him: "Where is the boy named Domonguria?"

He answered, "I don't know," but the soldier persisted. "Does he have a girlfriend?"

"Yes."

"Does she live nearby?"

"Well, he has three girlfriends, but one lives very far away, another is closer, and the third one lives next to us. I see he left his spear and sleeping skins here, so he must be nearby."

"Who is her father?" the headman asked.

"Loropoiyang."

"How many houses are in Loropoiyang's homestead?"

"Three: one for the girl's mother, one for the second wife, and one for his brother."

"Where is the homestead?"

"Do you hear the cow bells now? That's the one."

I was sleeping with my girlfriend Chepukenar, when a soldier burst into the hut, calling, "Domonguria!"

"Augh," I moaned.

"Oh. Well, all right." He retreated. "Sleep with your friend there tonight. Tomorrow morning meet us at your place."

Whenever we slept with girls, we always left them several hours before daybreak, so that no one at home would know we had been gone. Likewise, if a girl I was visiting wanted to milk a cow for me, she would do it in the dark, so that no one would know I was there. My affair with Chepukenar that evening was certainly no secret now, but I went home early anyway.

I found the soldier and the headman sleeping in our *aperit*. At dawn, they took me, along with Chepukenar's brother, Karochile, to Kanyao, where we met perhaps 200 others who had also been seized for government work. There were no shops or permanent buildings at Kanyao then. One European, named Mr. Pete, was in charge of the government project, and all the rest were Africans. His clerk,

Lokiteo, wrote down our names and explained about the work. He said there were two huge trucks, each loaded with 100 very large cloth sacks of insecticide. We were to carry them into the countryside, where the contents would be spread around to control a large infestation of locusts. We had no salary, but there was plenty of maize meal.

The sacks were very heavy. During the second week, Korochile and I came across a man named Lomolikitei, who had fallen on a steep part of the path. The sack was on top of him, and he was unable to move. We thought he was dead, but we couldn't stop to examine him because the path was dangerous and we, too, carried heavy sacks. There was no way around him, so we managed to jump over his body with the sacks on our heads. When we finally reached camp, we told the clerk that a man had died on the path. The clerk told Mr. Pete, who sent two men: one to carry the man and one for the sack.

When they came back into camp, I saw that Lomolikitei was alive, but he was coughing blood. Mr. Pete questioned him and discovered that the sack had broken his nose.

"But why are you coughing blood?" Mr. Pete asked. "Maybe you cut your teeth on a stick."

He made Lomolikitei rinse his mouth with water repeatedly until he could spit without blood. But then Lomolikitei began coughing again and the blood spewed out. Mr. Pete wrote a letter and told the clerk to give the man his ration of maize meal. He told Lomolikitei to go home slowly. I never heard what happened to him. If he made it home and was still coughing blood, the elders would have given him a mixture of honey and boiling water to sip as a tea. This is our remedy for coughing blood.

Three days later, the European told the clerk Lokiteo, "There are two more places to work. I want 120 to go to Keripo and 120 to go to Kilowas with me and Akai, the foreman."

I was in the second group. We left early the following morning for Amudat, where I bought a large, white sheet to wear for one shilling. While we were walking to Kilowas, I speared a dikdik on the side of the road with a long stick I had carved into a spear. We took the dikdik with us to our camp at Kilowas and ate it that night.

At Kilowas, the European assigned three of us—Murinyangai, Lorot and me—to fetch water for the camp. The water was a mile away, and we carried it in large tins. Four days later, Mr. Pete sent Lorot and Murinyangai to work on the locusts and left me to fetch the water alone. I began to work early each morning and made six trips each day. Then I collected firewood, which was plentiful.

After two weeks at Kilowas, we moved to the other side of Amudat and made camp at Kiwawa, where I continued to fetch water and to assist the cook. When another two weeks had passed, Mr. Pete announced that the work was finished and that everyone could go home. Relieved, I prepared to leave, but Mr. Pete stopped me, saying, "*You* are not to go yet. You are coming with *me*." He gave me 30 shillings and told me to get in the car.

Riding in a motorcar was not so bad! When we reached Amudat, Mr. Pete said, "I am going to Soroti in the other car. You will watch my car until I return. Here is the key. Each night I want you to lock the car like this and sleep inside." He gave me half a sack of maize meal, sugar and tea (In those days, I did not know how to use the tea). He also provided me with trousers, a shirt and a blanket.

While Mr. Pete was away, the women and girls brought me lots of milk, and I would pay them with the maize meal. At night I would lock up the motorcar and attend dances far away, always returning well before dawn to sleep in the car. Four times, my girlfriend Arupe came to sleep in the motorcar with me. The seats were very nice.

It happened that the most popular new song that year was about a motorcar! It was composed after some Karamojong tracked their stolen cattle to Lorewur and were ambushed by club-wielding Pokot raiders. When the Karamojong complained to the police, a Pokot sergeant named Korikwang drove into the wild, remote country of Lorewur in pursuit of the raiders. People were astonished to see a vehicle so far from any road, and they were surprised again to find that the driver was one of their own people! After Sergeant Korikwang took the raiders to jail, the people of Lorewur made up this song. Folks began singing it at the dances we call *laleyo*, and we have been singing it ever since.

Refrain:
> *Woe, Sergeant, ho-e*
> *Who brings a motorcar to my area?*
> *Who brings a motorcar to Lorewur?*
> *Ah, Sergeant, oh!*

> *Woe Sergeant, ho-e*
> *Akepune motorcar koroenyu?*
> *Akepune motorcar Lorewur?*
> *Ah, Sergeant, oh*

Verses:
> *Woe, the son of Rionokodo,*
> *Mm, brings the motorcar*
> *The son of* (mother) *Matai*
> *Mm, brings the motorcar*
> *Ai, the young man Korikwang!*
> *Mm, brings the motorcar*

> *Woe wero Rionokodo*
> *Mm, kepune motorcar*
> *Weriko Matai*
> *Mm, kepune motorcar*
> *Ah werru Korikwang*
> *Mm, kepune motorcar*

Those days, people were talking a lot about the Europeans and their government, because of the locust project. No one thought Europeans were cannibals anymore. In fact, everyone agreed that they had brought some progress to our people. But along with their gadgets, tools, schools and maize meal came gonorrhea, prostitution and deceptive thievery. None of these existed amongst our people before the arrival of the white people. The elders, in particular, talked about the horrible diseases brought by the Europeans. Never before, they said, had the Pokot experienced such frequent epidemics.

One very old man told us, "Long ago, a person's death was cause for widespread grief and lamentation. If a child survived the first two years of life, sustained by his mother's milk, one could be sure he would live well into adulthood—until his blood could no longer hold together—as long as there was rain. Drought, not illness, was Tororut's way of controlling the population. He would let the people reproduce for about ten years, then shut off the water for two, killing all but the strongest. But illnesses were rare and short-lived. Epidemics took their toll quickly and then subsided. We did not know the horrors of large-scale and lingering epidemics until the coming of the white man and the devastation of smallpox. Once people began dying like just so many birds, death itself became commonplace and of little importance."

After two weeks, the European returned and loaded all his baggage in the car. The next morning he told me to get in, and we drove away. I had no idea where we were going! We stopped in Kacheliba for only a few minutes, before he told me to get in again. Off we went to Kapenguria. I really started to worry when we drove on from there! Eventually, we reached Kitale, a larger town by far than I had ever seen. There Mr. Pete bought me food and told his servant to go eat with me, while he went off with his European companions. I could not tell you where we slept that night; I just followed the servant.

Early in the morning we were back in the car. The people and the countryside were strange and alarming to me. We came at last to the town of Eldoret, where we stayed with other servants behind the house of another white man. Mr. Pete's wife was there. I was surprised to see that she was still a girl—she had not yet even had a child!

A few days later, Mr. Pete left by himself in the car. The cook said he was going to Nairobi. After a week, he came back and paid me a salary of thirty shillings. Then we got in the car and he drove me all the way back to Amudat.

As soon as we arrived, Chief Losile walked up to Mr. Pete and said with some anger, "Now this boy is the only son of a man! He is the only one in his homestead capable of watching the herds. Let this boy go! His father has cried to me twice for his release!"

Mr. Pete then came to me and said, "I hear your father is worried about you. How many children in your family can help your father with the cattle?"

I answered, "There are only my sister and I. My brother is blind; the rest are too small."

Mr. Pete seemed surprised. "All right, go tend your herds," he said, and I left immediately.

Two weeks later, while I was out watching the cattle, five men—Chief Lo-sile, his clerk and four others—came to our house carrying their record books. They told my father, "We have registered your son Domonguria to pay tax. Find the money and bring it to us this month." My father, luckily, had a little of the money left. The next day, he gave me five shillings for the tax and I paid it.

COMING OF AGE

INDEPENDENCE

Soon after my homecoming, I moved, together with an older friend and our combined herds, away from Lossom to establish a homestead of my own. Altogether there were five of us: my companion, myself, his herdsman, my herdsman,[57] and a little boy who tended the calves. At first we stayed in Nangalitabaa a week, then moved on to Lokichokia for five more weeks. During that time we heard there was plenty of grass in an area between Koteitei and Kodiaka. We decided to settle in that vicinity at a place called Kodukoi, which had the additional advantage of being near the homestead where my favorite girlfriend, Apeyo, was living with her brother. We constructed our corral beside two other homesteads: the largest one included five families and their herds, and the other was for the unmarried men of the first homestead.

As soon as we arrived, our neighbors complained that they could no longer sleep peacefully at night because of a lion that always stalked around the corrals. When my herdsman, Barabara, heard this, he convinced me to wait at least three more days before going to see my girlfriend, so that we could be sure our cattle would be safe. We worked hard each day cutting branches to reinforce the fence around our homestead, and making the small, window-like gate people use when they go outside after dark. We kept watch each night, but the lion did not come.

My Sweetheart Apeyo

At noon on the third day, I took my spears and went to see my girlfriend. I had intended to be home that evening, but, unfortunately, I did not see Apeyo until well after sunset, when she came back from visiting her relatives at Loperut. I could only greet her and tell her I had to leave because of the lion. Apeyo understood, but seemed worried about something else.

"I must warn you," she said. "Some of the older guys near here have found out about you and me, and they might cause trouble. The day before yesterday, we had a dance here at my homestead. Six of them took me aside and demanded, 'What's this we hear about you? Are you having an affair with that kid Domonguria?' I said, 'What if I am?' and they really got angry about it. They said, 'You mean it's really true? Then don't come to dance with us! Why have you slept with a child who hasn't had *sapana*? You fool! What if he gets you pregnant? What will you do then, huh? His father will beat him up and throw you out! You're the one who will lose!'"

"What did you say?"

"I told them, 'Even if he gets me pregnant, that's not so bad. I'll go to his father and I'll live well! I don't worry! I love him, so what else can I do?' Then one of them said, '*Ala!* You sure talk a lot! Let's leave this stupid girl! She sleeps with a child before she sleeps with men! She'd rather make love with a boy who still sleeps with his mother! Laugh at her!' They left me then, but one of them called back, 'You had better warn your lover not to come to any of our dances. We'll beat him up!' So you see, Domonguria, it's best for you to go, even though I think you're wonderful. They're bringing another dance here tonight, and I'm afraid they'll attack you. They hate you, because I have chosen you over them, even though you're still a youth."

I walked home, somewhat disturbed, and went to sleep. Shortly after midnight, I was awakened by people yelling in the homestead next to ours. I grabbed my spears and shoes and ran out. Cattle from the other homestead had stampeded until they were just outside my own corral, causing my herd to panic and crash through the fence. My companions and I ran to stop them and hold them until the neighbors came to round up their cattle.

All of us knew what had happened to make the cattle bolt. We knew the way of the lion: he comes close to a corral fence and farts. The cattle are startled by the odor and stampede, breaking out of the fence. Then the lion makes his kill. It has been his lot to hunt like this and to roam at night, seeing perfectly well in the darkness, since Tororut placed him in the wilderness.

We humans, on the other hand, find it nearly impossible to spot a lion in the darkness. On that particular night, we could not even see how many cattle had been killed. The sky was overcast and it was exceptionally dark. We went to a spot where someone said he had heard a cry from one of the cattle, and there we found a dead steer. He was one of ours and was very fat. We had cut, shaped and tied his horns at the time we moved from the river, and they were still tied.

While we were standing there, the lion terrorized us with a sudden, deafening roar. We chased after him, but we knew he could not be fooled, since he was aware of our inability to stalk him at night. Barabara suggested that one of us climb a tree and wait for him to return to the kill. I volunteered eagerly, remembering the thrill of my earlier two lion kills. They dragged the steer under the tree and I climbed up. The others then made a lot of noise for the ears of the lion, calling to each other, "Let's all go home now! Leave this meat to the lion who owns it!" Soon we heard his roar.

Presently, I heard his footsteps approaching in the grass, and I was aware of a lighter shadow making its way towards my tree. The steer's carcass below me also appeared ghostly white in the darkness, much lighter than the lion. When the lion was directly beneath me, I threw my spear. The lion grunted once, ran on two legs a short distance and fell heavily.

"What happened?" the others called.

The lion was still quite close, but in the darkness I couldn't tell whether he was dead or just crouching there. I explained to my companions that I thought I had given him quite a blow with the spear, yet I was hesitant to climb down. If he was alive, he'd attack me straight away. The other men advised me to stay where I was until a boy brought a fire.

A torch was lit in the homestead, and as soon as it was brought close enough to give off light, I saw that the lion was indeed quite dead. The spear had hit him in the back at the base of his neck, pierced his throat and broken the breastbone. Relieved, I climbed down. I asked that the lion be left until the next morning, when we could skin it and take out the spear.

Feeling triumphant, I returned to sleep the remaining two hours of the night with my girlfriend. Afterwards, I entered the *aperit* and said to Loduk, a youth about my age, "Go tell the young men in the homestead above this that we got the lion tonight!" He started to go with his spear, and I thought to call after him, "Tell them to bring their spears to see if he's still alive!"

I went back home and let the cattle out to graze. Presently, the men came, including those who had threatened me through Apeyo. I showed them the lion, and they forgot all animosity and heaped gratitude upon me! "It was a terrible lion!" they exclaimed. "It terrorized homesteads from Loperit to Kaido to Lokichogio, not to mention ours! All of us are grateful to you for killing it!" They skinned it and put aside the meat from the ribs and that from the lower half of the breast bone for the men to eat later. Then my former adversaries divided the trophy: one wanted the skin for a cape, one the rope (tail), and so forth. They never bothered me after that.

Things went well for Apeyo and me for a time, and I was quite in love with her. Then one night, when I approached her hut, I heard Apeyo yelling inside: "What are *you* doing here? I told you the last time that I wouldn't give in to you! Why have you come back? You know I already have a lover! What do you expect me to do?"

I rushed in and met him. He was in a much more powerful position than I, for he had already put clay on his head. My hair was still sewn with the rope of a tree. I was still considered a child, in spite of my size.[58] Nevertheless I yelled, "What are you here for? This is my girl!"

"*Yours?*" He was obviously surprised.

"Yes."

"You fool, this girl is mature! She wouldn't have a boy like you for her lover! You wouldn't even be an adequate lover for a circumcised girl like this! Ha! The girl for you is an uncircumcised child—that's what you should be seeking! I'm not about to leave her for *you!*"

"Oh really?" I sniggered. "Watch! I think I'll go lie down now!" He bristled, and I swaggered over and sat on Apeyo's bed. His hand shot out and he slapped me hard! We fought like wild beasts inside the house until all the gourds, milk basins, and utensils came crashing down. One large gourd of fat broke into pieces, and the fat splattered all over the house. A woman who was inside the house with us screamed. Then we were fighting outside the house near the door. I grabbed a staff we use for tending calves and struck him on the head. The blood came instantly. He cut me all over with his wrist knife—I still have the scars on my leg and back. Just then, Apeyo's brother came running, having been awakened by the scream and commotion. He stood over us, thrashing us both with a club, until we separated and ran out of the homestead. I got my spear and shoes, which I had left outside, and went home.

Three nights later I returned to sleep with Apeyo. One of her brother's wives, another man's wife and a young, uncircumcised girl were in the house with us. One wife whispered to me, "Apeyo's brother is out to get you. He is very angry. Sleep well, but you should know that!"

Apeyo and I slept well indeed, but that woman did not; she listened by the door. Later, she returned to her own house, telling another wife, "Go watch that house. If that youth Domonguria comes for Apeyo, come tell me, not our husband." The other wife came in, and all was well until she decided to light the fire. It glimmered, caught, and then she saw me. She turned to go tell her co-wife, but met her husband at the door.

"Is there a man in here?" I heard him ask.

"No, there isn't," his wife replied.

He slapped her. "Oh there isn't, is there!"

That was too much. I stood up and called, "Do you want me? Here I am!"

"Come here!"

"All right" I took off my beads and ostrich feathers, while I said, to stall, "You think I'll run away, but I won't. If you want to strike me, do it! I won't run."

"Come on, then!"

Now he thought I would come and just stand there to take the beating! I could see he was standing close to the door, waiting. Instead, I bent down and shot out of the door like a bullet! He lashed out, but his hand fanned the air. I ran and he ran after me around the cattle. The homestead had a gigantic fence around it because of the lion. I headed for the gate, but he got there first. Then I crouched down and tried to disappear amongst the cattle in the darkness, but I realized he would find me eventually. The fence was very close, so I leaped up and got a shaky foothold on one of the posts. (Luckily, the post I landed on was one which had been cut for reinforcing the top of the fence, and it had no thorns.) Just as I was about to fall, I jumped up again, barely making it over the top of fence. I landed hard outside, right onto a long, sharp stick, which stabbed into my leg and broke off inside. I screamed in agony.

Apeyo's brother thought I had been caught in the thorn fence. He cursed at me and remarked, "Stay there in the thorns until tomorrow! Then I'll come teach you a few things!"

His wife was horrified. "*Ala!* Is the child caught in the fence? Aaaaa, this is awful! How can a person survive if he is caught inside those thorns?"

In spite of the pain, I couldn't resist laughing out loud. I called to that wife, who had been my advocate, "*Ala!* You think I'm in the fence? I jumped outside!"

The woman whooped with joy! She kidded her husband, "Do you expect children to stand there and take a beating until they lie down at your feet like a stone? Yes, then I suppose you would mercifully open the gate for them, saying, 'Now you may go.' Ha, ha! This is wonderful!" She called out to me, "He wanted to beat his sister too, but she ran out of the gate while he was chasing you! Now you both are outside! Go find your wife and take her to your father!"

I did try to find her, but without luck, so I went home.

The next morning, when everyone was gone, I hobbled painfully back to retrieve my stool, feathers and beads. Then I went to have the stick extracted from my leg with a knife. My leg was still swollen and stiff three days later, but I felt a desperate need to see my sweetheart Apeyo. I could think of nothing else. I decided to go in spite of the pain.

I had just arrived and lain down beside her, when Apeyo's brother stalked up to the hut and closed the door! I assumed he knew I was there and had decided to shut me in, so I said to him, "Yes, the other day, I escaped you, but I won't be able to today, for my leg is in pain. If you want to finish me off, do it today." It was inevitable, so I hobbled outside and lay down by the door. He struck me viciously, but I did not even attempt to fight back. I groaned, "Hit me until you're satisfied." Finally a stranger came to intervene, and the beating was over. I got up and started to go back inside the house.

The brother's mouth dropped open. "What do you think you're doing, going back inside my sister's house? Get out!"

"I can't go," I said wearily. "I have a sick leg." I ducked inside the door.

"Idiot! How lame can you be? You walked all the way here tonight, didn't you?"

"Look," I replied, "If you want to beat me again, I'll be glad to come out. The one thing I cannot do right now is to walk home. If you don't want your sister to sleep here, send her to another house."

"Idiot!" he thundered, and walked away.

Apeyo went out, then, to fetch water. She boiled it and poured it into a large wooden basin. "Come, let's wash off the blood," she said. I got in, bathed, and then slept happily beside her for the rest of the night. We were still inside the house when they let the cattle out to graze in the morning. I thought of nothing but the joy of being with Apeyo, whom I loved far beyond any girl I had known.

If her brother wanted to get angry and beat me once more, he would. He had not ruined my body; I was ready. Anything was worth the happiness of being in her presence.

My sweetheart brought me milk, but I said, "Keep that until later." We went outside and sat together in the sun at the place where people light the fire in the morning and in the evening. Apeyo's brother was also there, but there was no confrontation this time. In another hour or so, I went back to my girl's house and ate the food she served me. Then I strolled over to where people were playing the game we call *cuchei*.[59] I lay around there until noon, and then went home.

To my surprise, a man from Lossom was waiting for me. He had come all the way to tell me that my father was sick and needed me. The next morning, in spite of the pain, I left for Lossom.

Father was, indeed, very ill. A woman practitioner had arrived the day before to advise him about treatment. He was to kill an ox by clubbing it on the head, then drink the beef soup, together with a certain medicine. Accordingly, the next day Father instructed me to kill the calf of the cow named Angeletch in this way and to skin it. The woman prepared the soup and medicine, gave it to Father to drink, and he vomited. The next day, we noticed that his health had improved slightly. "Yes, my cow must have helped me," he declared. Four days later, Father was talking about going to see his friends at Koakaa. He gave me permission to go back to tend my cattle.

I collected my things and was about to leave, when Father called me back. "Son," he said, with a worried expression, "It bothers me that you have paid tax when you haven't even celebrated your *sapana*. Anyone who has paid tax must be an adult! It is time for you to put clay on your head and become a bull."

What welcome words these were to me! I assured Father that I was eager for the ceremony, and he promised to summon me when he had made the necessary arrangements. I left with a joyful soul.

The happiness did not last long, for when I reached my homestead, I was informed that my sweetheart Apeyo had been promised to another man! Evidently, while she was staying with her brother, a man from Karita had been to see her father and they had agreed on the number of cattle to be paid for her bride price. Her father had sent one of his other sons to fetch Apeyo from her brother's homestead for the wedding, and they were to leave the next day. I was shocked, and overcome with grief.

The next morning, I was about to let the cattle out, when, to my great surprise, Apeyo herself ran breathlessly into my corral! "I've come back to you!" she panted. "I ran away from my brother on the footpath!"

I was bewildered, for I knew the situation was impossible. I was unable to think clearly. Then Apeyo was asking me earnestly, "What are your plans for me?" and I felt tears in my eyes.

I stammered, "I—I, well, I don't know what to say." She looked desperate, and, to my own amazement, I heard myself say, "Come! Let's go to my father!"

Confused thoughts came whirling into my head: *If we go there ... my father has such a fierce temper ... there is no way! ... Yes, he would beat us both ... he would never allow her to stay after all this.*

Finally, I shook my head in despair. I said, "No, Apeyo, you'll have to go. Maybe you could stay here with me until the others find you". Then I reconsidered, "No, no, it's better for you to go now. Your father has already agreed to the marriage cattle, and there is nothing we can do about it."

Apeyo hung her head and began weeping silently.

"Oh, Apeyo! I want you too," I said truthfully. "More than anything else now, I would like to give him cattle for you. I love you! But there are too many things I have to do first. I haven't even put clay in my hair yet, and there are so many other things. Only if I got you pregnant would I have any power to bargain for you."

"I won't go!" she cried. "I'll stay here with you until they find me."

"Do you want your brothers to beat me without reason? No, go to your brother's house. If they find you here, we'll both be tortured."

Apeyo considered this. She wiped the tears from her eyes, stood up straight and said quietly, "You are right. I'll go."

We slept together for the last time that night, and in the morning Apeyo left for her brother's house. I heard they caned her fiercely, dragged her by the arms, and pushed her roughly along the path until they reached her father's homestead, where she was given away in marriage. Since that sad day, I have left Apeyo alone, but I remember her well. Yes, I remember her well.[60]

Pasture Police

Three months after Apeyo left, we moved to a place called Alakas, near Lokwamur, where there was grass. Our homestead included seven people at that time. As we constructed our corral and huts, we did not know that men in that area policed the pasture during the hot, dry season. They would not let anyone else settle there and use the grass.[61]

We had been at Alakas but three days when the trouble started. I was letting blood from a cow, while one of my companions held the head, another the front legs, and another the basin for collecting the blood.[62] Suddenly, a strange voice called to us, "Friends! What do your cattle smell—a lion, or what?" When we lifted our heads, we saw that our corral was completely surrounded by men!

I left the cow, ran to the *aperit*, grabbed two clubs, my spear and shoes, and tore out of the homestead. Three men ran after me. Two of my friends jumped over the fence at a clear point, and the others didn't make it. Outside the corral, the strangers attacked us. They hit me twice, but I got away, and they gave chase.

I outdistanced them, but they caught the man following me and beat him up. Others whipped the three men trapped in our homestead and the six children who were our cowherds. In the midst of this, a man took one small boy to a steer belonging to one of my associates. "Kill it," he ordered. The boy took the man's spear and obeyed him. When the steer dropped, the strangers declared, "Listen! Stop! A steer has died." (It is our custom that when a steer dies, men should lay down their sticks and stop fighting.)

It was almost dark. After a few minutes, some of our assailants went to get fire-wood. I stalked one of them through the brush, crept up from behind, and hit him three or four times with my club. He cried out, and I disappeared into the shadows close by. His friends came running. "Who hit you?" they demanded, angrily.

"I don't know. He got me from behind," the man replied.

I felt satisfied and went surreptitiously back into my homestead. No one would know that I had beaten a man after an ox had died! Later, when the beef was done, we went outside to eat it with those volatile neighbors, according to custom. Then we slept.

The next morning, they made us tie off the throats of all our cattle with skin straps. "Now move out of here!" they commanded. "If you want to play with this grass, we'll eat your cattle until they are finished! You could destroy this grass by letting your cattle graze here during the dry season, yet this pasture belongs to everyone. When it is time, everyone can come and use it."

We moved that day to Nangalitabaa.

BECOMING A MAN

We had been at Nangalitabaa less than a month, when a stranger greeted us with a message from my father: I was to bring the cattle home again very soon, for an important matter awaited me. Filled with anticipation, I entered my father's gate with the steers four days later.

"I have a question to ask you," Father said. "Do you want to go on as you have been, or do you think you are ready for the matter you discussed earlier with me?"

"Yes! I am ready! I want it very much!" I exclaimed, thankfully.

"Then go to Lotuk's homestead. Tell him I sent you to request a steer for your *sapana*!"

I left immediately. Lotuk agreed, and the following morning I led the steer home to Lossom. After I had milked the cows, Father told me, "Go back to your homestead now. Return on the fifth day. Everything will be ready."

When I came back again, I found that Father and my mothers had been busy with the preparations. He had made nine gourds of beer, and the household had been filling more than 150 gourds with milk. Father sent me to borrow some more of the small bells (*kurkuris*) that parents of the initiate wear on their legs during *sapana*. "Ours won't suffice for your mothers," he explained.

I collected the bells from two other homesteads and announced that the celebration would take place the following day. My mothers agreed to spread the news to all the other neighbors. Happily, I returned home and slept.

My *Sapana* Celebration

On the morning of my *sapana*, I speared the ox and others butchered the meat in the *kurket*, according to tradition. First, the hind legs were put aside for the elders to eat the next day. Then each side of beef was cut, together with the front leg. The *takat* (lower half of the breast bone and attached meat, excluding the ribs) was reserved for the youths to cook; the elders won't eat it. The *atachok* (upper half of the breast bone, the attached ribs and the backbone behind the hump, but not including the hump) was taken into one of the houses, and the hump and liver were also reserved.

While the meat was being prepared, I went to get the clay for my headdress (*munyan*) and brought it to the butchering site. One man mixed it for me, while an elder extracted the stomach contents (*achian*) from the steer and put them on the ground. "Come stand on the *achian*," he instructed, and I did. Several people took off all my beads and other ornaments (I wore very many in those days), as well as my garment, and put them on the *achian*, together with my shoes. Then they took handfuls of the *achian* and spread it all over my naked body, including my eyes, head, feet and hair, and dusted it all off again, leaving only that on my hair. Finally, they scrubbed me well with animal fat until the last trace of *achian* came off. (For this particular ceremony, one must not wash the *achian* off with water.) I was warned not to stand near the fire during this ritual cleansing, or I would succumb to a serious illness in the future.

Now the red clay we call *kapulyat* was spread on my achian-covered hair. (This clay was collected at the place we also call Kapulyat, by the Kerio River in the region called Tirioko, near Mt. Tiati. The white clay used later is from Kamukol, in the forest half-way up Tiati.) Within the *kapulyat* layer, they affixed a tied bundle of ostrich feathers and a rope twined from dried tendons. When this was finished, I carried the stomach of the ox to our hut, tied it at its neck, and hung it from the ceiling beam. Afterwards, I returned to the *kurket* to await all the neighbors and other friends.

They brought me a wonderful celebration! Fully 220 or 240 men and maybe 300 women came to my *sapana*. They streamed into our homestead from mid-morning until mid-afternoon. Whenever groups of women approached our homestead, each bringing one or two gourds of milk strapped to her back, they began to sing the two songs that are sung for every boy's *sapana*. And each time the women in our homestead heard those songs, they ran to their houses to get their ceremonial ox horns, filled with fat. They removed the skin lids and went to the gate, holding the horns in the air to welcome the singing newcomers. These songs are precious to us: one must not sing them freely or without bringing milk, and no one may enter the gate during *sapana*, except by means of these songs. The first song says:

Oh elephant! e ah ho-e, ho-e
Open the gate, elephant! e, ahe
Open the gate for the cattle to come

Oh ya pelion e, ah ho-e, ho-e
Iyata orenyo, pelion e, ahe
Iyata or roto toka

It is sung over and over. Here, "elephant" (a clan name) means the people of the homestead, and "cattle" refers to the milk the women have bought.

The second song honors a great warrior. As I heard it being sung for me, I remembered the legend I had heard many times before and reflected that I, too, was becoming a man who would be expected to be brave like the famous Setim. Here is his story:

It was during the second month, the month of planting, that Setim and his men set out for a distant land to fight and to raid cattle. They say the warriors became so hungry on their long journey that they cooked and ate pieces of their leather shields! Altogether, Setim and his band attacked six homesteads, stealing thousands of cattle, and killing many men, women and children. Because so many of the owners were eliminated, the raiders managed to get half-way home before they were attacked by a large group of warriors pursuing the stolen herds.

The battle took place beneath a mountain which seemed insurmountable, and Setim saw that the cattle were exposed and vulnerable. He quietly left the fray, scouted around the edge of the mountain and, luckily, discovered the only way up the slope. Then, while the others were still fighting, he alone herded all the cattle up the difficult path to the top, where it was very cold. Once the cattle were safe, Setim returned to stand guard on a part of the path that was extremely narrow, like a doorway, framed by rock outcroppings.

When the initial round of fighting was over and the enemy was dispersed, Setim's men came for instructions. "Go slaughter enough cattle to satisfy all of us," he commanded. "Cook the meat, milk the cows and eat until you have enough strength for the next battle. Bring my portion here. I'll stand guard. The enemy will be spreading the news and will have reinforcements soon."

As soon as the warriors departed, the enemy returned to challenge Setim there on the path! Setim saw them coming up the slope and immediately killed ten men, using the arrows from only one of his two quivers. Then he blew his horn loudly.[63] His men ran to find Setim surrounded by dead bodies; the others had run away!

The enemy returned four times. It is said that Setim alone killed 38 men at the pass, after which he ran to the bottom of the hill and killed two more. Two other warriors, who were searching for a way up, retreated before that fearsome man! They went back to inform their people and, according to the story, found that their remaining cattle had strayed. At last, in desperation, the survivors gathered their belongings and moved far away in poverty. Setim himself followed their tracks until he was convinced they had indeed gone and would not return to follow him. Just to be sure, he kept the cattle on top of the mountain from the second through the tenth month of that year.

On the eleventh month, he began his victorious journey home. Cattle travel slowly, however, and he did not arrive until the fifth month of the following year. When he was within one or two miles of his home, he blew his horn. His children were incredulous with joy. "Father is coming back!" they squealed. "And he is bringing food!"

Many had thought Setim had perished, and some had even shaved their heads in mourning. His children had grown thin and weak in his absence. Now they ran to open the gates, singing jubilantly the song I was hearing now:

Our Setim! Open the door!	*Setim tenyo iyat or o*
Aye, aye, aya!	*Aye, aye, aya*
Setim! Open the door!	*Setim iyat or e*

While the groups of women filed in, one after another, bringing milk and singing, the guests at my *sapana* enjoyed drinking the milk, including that which we had poured into two large wooden troughs (*atekerai*) that we use for watering cattle, and mixed with the ox's blood. Some of the elders went inside to drink beer, while others relaxed at the *kurket*. Many danced exuberantly until the cattle came home that evening.

Then the elders went into the corral where the cattle lay, bringing the reserved meat: the *atachok*, the hump, and the liver, and called for me to join them. The chief elder took a small bite of each of the three pieces of meat, spitting afterwards under both his armpits and over both shoulders. I did the same. He gave the *atachok* to me then, and I ate it. (This cut of beef is reserved for the initiate. It cannot be served first to anyone else, nor can the initiate eat any other cut of meat.) According to custom, I left a little meat on the bones for the women to eat, and they used the bones to make soup for the elders. After eating, everyone washed his hands and went home.

Following this ceremony, we brought the stomach out to dry in the sun. Four days later, we spread the news that the stomach meat would be ready in two more days. Meanwhile, my mothers were busy grinding quantities of millet— enough for the estimated 100 guests, who might return for the second occasion.

On the day of the feast, they cooked the chopped stomach, together with the millet and poured the mixture into two large *atekerai* for the men, one for the youths and three small ones for the children, as well as one large *ateker* and a number of gourds for the women. Then they poured fat into all the containers, filling them to the brims. The guests came, ate the gruel and meat, and celebrated throughout the day.[64]

On the morning after the feast, we carried the clay called *muruasikar*[65] to an area outside the homestead, where the men of my father's household mixed it well. They unfastened the rope-and ostrich feather decoration from my *kapulyat-*covered hair, and I took it to the house of the calves, as is the custom. When I returned, the men decorated my head handsomely, spreading the grayish-blue *muruasikar* over the red *kapulyat*, then meticulously adding red, yellow and white clays to create one of the traditional, artistic designs we use for our headdresses. (We use traditional Karamojong patterns, as well as our own.) They made three holes in the top of the clay cap and lined them with metal rings (the Turkana use cow teats) to accommodate the ostrich feathers, anchored with rope, which I would wear on special occasions—a very large black feather in the middle and white ones on either side. Another hole was made near the base of the headdress for holding the black ostrich feather pompom. Dangling chains and a small rope were fastened underneath.

One day soon, I would kill another steer, without ceremony, for the purpose of applying the *atoro* decoration on the small, frontal area on top of my head. (It would be said that I had killed the "steer of *atoro*.") During the feast, an artist would apply the colored clays and insert three more metal feather-holes in the *atoro* so that I could wear a white feather in the middle and a yellow or black one on either side.

Meanwhile, the initial clay cap of *sapana* would signify to all that I was truly a man. No one would dare ridicule me as they had in the past, saying I had cheated men out of a circumcised girl when I was only a child! Now all men were my friends.

The First Pokot *Sapana*

One of our neighbors at Lossom, Kolya Nangeletch, told us stories about the very first Pokot *sapana*, which took place during the time of our grandparents in the Karamojong region of Nakere. Kolya himself was born in Nakere and was named after a well in the bedrock, where the honey-eating animal called *kolya* became trapped and died after climbing in to reach the low water. Kolya Nangeletch told us that it was during the great Pokot-Karamojong peace ceremony at Nakere long ago that the Pokot first learned about *sapana* and many other Karamojong traditions that we now take for granted. [66]

He explained that before we learned about *sapana* from the Karamojong, we knew nothing of putting clay on our heads, yet now it has become our most important celebration—even more important than circumcision, which is no longer necessary for becoming a man.[67] The Karamojong taught our elders where to find the different colored clays for the headdress, how to mix milk and blood in the wooden bowl called *ateker* (we had not used the *ateker* before this), and the significance of the three-boned right hind leg of a ritually slaughtered ox, the *amura*, that is reserved only for those who have had *sapana*. (They warned us that if anyone else—such as a woman—eats this forbidden meat, or if any of it is thrown out, the culprit will surely become ill.)

Kolya told us that the Pokot-Karamojong peace agreement, symbolized by this first joint *sapana*, was celebrated with a huge feast and dance (the *amumor*), and both sides slaughtered oxen. The Karamojong elders, who were directing the peace rituals according to their own customs, declared," Since there are so many oxen, we have decided to use only the *amura* of the first ox slaughtered as the sacred meat. All the rest may be cut up and used." But when they discovered that the first ox had been killed by the Pokot, the Karamojong protested, "What? How could this be? Who gave the Pokot permission to kill the first ox? Fools! We've got to use a *Karamojong* ox for the *amura*!" Nevertheless, there was nothing they could do about it, for their own elders had declared it a sacred violation not to use the meat from the first ox!

"And so," Kolya concluded triumphantly, "the Pokot gained power over the Karamojong by means of their own sacred custom! They shall never again overcome us, because our ox took away their strength!"

Evidently, the Karamojong even taught us how to brand our cattle. Kolya claimed we had known nothing of branding until that day at Nakere, when the Karamojong elders proclaimed, "You will be our brothers," and directed each clan of their people to give their brand symbols to a clan of the Pokot. They taught us how to cut and shape the horns of some of our oxen, and how to tie the ropes with bells around their necks.

They also taught us certain dietary customs. For instance, since long ago we have milked our cattle into containers made from the gourds which grow on the *selangwa* vine. We store certain gourds of milk for a very long time, calling it "milk-of-the-year," to be used during the hot, dry season when our cows are not producing enough milk. At the celebration in Nakere, the Karamojong taught us how to mix this milk-of-the-year with stiff porridge made from maize meal, and how to beat milk. They showed us how to make the gourd of wood (the cattle trough) and how to make bowls, cups, plates and spoons out of wood or gourds.

(Our traditional plates were woven or made out of cow skin.) Now, when we eat porridge with milk, we use both traditions—pouring the milk into a gourd cup and eating the stiff porridge from skin or basket plates. Likewise, our elders used to dip *sosion* (palm leaves)[68] into milk and then suck it—milk drunk this way was sweeter than all other milk. Since the meeting with the Karamojong, many small dietary customs, such as this, have been lost. Only the important ones remain.

The Stolen Child

Kolya Nangeletch then told us a story about Cherotwa, a very old woman I had seen as a child in one of the surrounding villages. When she was just a toddler, Kolya said, Cherotwa was kidnapped by the Karamojong on the day of the original *sapana* celebration at Nakere and was hidden in one of the huge baskets used for storing surplus food in caves. After conducting a desperate and exhaustive search, her parents finally gave up looking for their lost child, although they continued living in Karamoja for many years. Later, when Pokot-Karamojong relations became strained, Cherotwa's parents decided to move back to their own country, but their Karamojong neighbors insisted on keeping their cattle and some of their family in Karamoja. Frustrated, Cherotwa's father decided to ask for Pokot help in retrieving his cattle, but no one wanted to risk his life to go on this stranger's personal mission.

One day, during his travels to ask for help, Cherotwa's father met some people, who, like his family, still had a homestead in Karamoja, and they brought him some unexpected and joyous news: They had heard that his long-missing Pokot daughter was not only alive, but was known to be living at a certain Karamojong homestead! They agreed to investigate this rumor for him upon their return to Karamoja.

Several weeks later, the Pokot wife visited the homestead where Cherotwa, now an attractive young woman, was reported to be living. Pretending to be someone else, just a traveler passing through, she stopped to chat with the women of Cherotwa's homestead, asking casual questions about the children there. Soon she was able to identify Cherotwa, and even managed to draw the girl to one side, asking, "Where is your mother? Do you know her?"

"I do not know my mother," Cherotwa replied.

"And your father?"

"I don't know ... I mean, this is my father," she stammered, looking at an elder coming into the corral.

The woman knew she must hurry now, so as not to arouse suspicion. "These people stole you!" she whispered. "Would you like me to show you your real father?"

Cherotwa looked shocked. "Yes!" she exclaimed, wide-eyed.

"I must go now," the Pokot wife said. "I will come back one day, and when you see me walking by, you will know I am calling you. We must not speak. You can tell the others you are going for a walk. Then follow me at a distance to my house. Your father will be there." Cherotwa nodded, and the Pokot woman left. When she arrived at her own home hours later, she told her husband all that had happened. In the morning he left for Pokot country to notify Cherotwa's parents.

Cherotwa's father and four others returned with him to Karamoja a few days later, traveling secretly in darkness. They hid the next day inside his house, while his wife journeyed once again to the girl's homestead. She loitered in the area until she saw Cherotwa and their eyes met. Then she walked home. Later that afternoon, Cherotwa arrived and was led to the house where the men were hiding. As soon as Cherotwa's father saw her, he leapt up and greeted her happily. Everyone rejoiced, except the shaken girl.

"I don't know you," she said.

"This is your father!" they exclaimed. "Your mother is far away in our own country."

"Before I believe you, I will have to see the woman you say is my mother," Cherotwa protested.

"Yes, yes, I understand," her father said. "I just wanted to see you, to know you are really alive! It would be too dangerous to take you home now anyway. But we'll find a way, for you are our daughter indeed!"

Cherotwa left for her Karamojong home, and her father went back to the land of the Pokot, exclaiming. "We have seen her! She is alive!"

Meanwhile, his Pokot friend in Karamoja managed to persuade his in-laws to help Cherotwa's father reclaim his cattle and the rest of his family from the Karamojong. They traveled to the designated Karamoja homesteads, and, working together, herded the cattle at night from one secret place to another until, at last, they were in Pokot country.

The Karamojong, however, soon discovered where they were and made plans to retrieve the cattle: They would move in with their former friend, pretending they desired to settle with the Pokot. Then one night, they would quietly kill him and his family and take the herds. People would be used to seeing them in the area with the cattle and might not be alarmed until they were safely back in Karamoja.

Five men were sent to make advance arrangements for the "peaceful" move to Pokot country. They arrived in the middle of a Pokot celebration. People demanded, "What are you Karamojong doing here?"

"We have come to see our friend, who has moved to your country."

"Very good," they answered. "We will take you to his home at sunset, after the dance."

It happened that Cherotwa's parents were among those at the dance who escorted the Karamojong to their home. When they reached the corral, they seized the messengers and demanded, "Give us our child, whom you kidnapped when the Pokot and Karamojong were staying together! We will reward you."

The Karamojong men stammered, "We don't know where she is. Let us go ask." Another said, "It's not what you think. Someone found the child, but she died. She's there, but she's dead!"

"All right," Cherotwa's father said coolly. "You will have an opportunity to take an oath on your words tomorrow."

In the morning, an elder approached them, carrying some earth and the knife we use for shaving our heads in one hand, and some ostrich feathers in the other. He told them, "If the child is alive in your country, take the feathers. If not, take the earth and the knife. If she is there and you lie, the child will be yours, but your words will bring bad fortune."

Four of the Karamojong were perplexed, but the fifth was angry. "The child died!" he yelled. "I take the earth and knife!"

"Done!" said the elder. "You may go."

When the Karamojong messengers returned with the news, their elders were alarmed. They declared, "The earth and the knife used for shaving one's head at a funeral—these are symbols of the grave! We are doomed! No one can undo what has been done, but perhaps you can make it better by returning the girl."

They brought Cherotwa, then, to her family, but the Pokot elders refused to annul the oath. Death plagued the clan of the Karamojong man who had chosen the earth and knife until, in the end, there was no one left. Meanwhile, Cherotwa grew old in our country, where she belonged.

NEW DEVELOPMENTS

Thunderstorms

I stayed with the herds at Lossom after my *sapana*. Once, four of us were out tending the cattle, when the rains suddenly poured. Quickly, we rounded up the animals and urged them homewards, but when we were within three miles of the corral, at a place called Cheptokol, we were forced to stop. A flash flood had filled the small, usually dry riverbed, and the waters were raging. I knew that by the next day the river would be calm, or even disappear once again, so, as the oldest, I suggested, "Let's take the cattle back to sleep in that abandoned homestead near here. We'll cross the river tomorrow." Two of us led the way with half the cattle. We herded them into the abandoned corral and waited for the other two, Teuko and Lore, but they never came. Concerned, I walked back to

Cheptokol and found the rest of the cattle lying down in the darkness! There was no sign of Teuko or Lore.

The next day, we summoned the neighbors to help us find our two companions. We studied their footprints, then fanned out in every direction to search for them. Every day for two weeks we continued the search, but we never did find Teuko and Lore. Did they drown in the river? Did Ilat claim them? Many years later, when I was fully grown and trading donkeys, I heard that a woman and her child had disappeared during a rain storm from that same spot. *Was it Ilat?* people had wondered then. Just to be safe, we have avoided that place ever since.

Another amazing thing happened during a thunderstorm that season. Powerful winds blew at the walls of our neighbor Jaikimoi's corral at Kwaiadai, until the sticks of the walls were compressed together and the entire enclosure contracted to become a miniature version of the original! There was no structural damage: even the gate was intact. The only difference was that the corral was now much smaller. The next morning everyone came to see it, and most people thought it was a bad omen. Jaikimoi was wondering if he should enlarge the corral to its original size or build a new one. Finally, one old elder declared, "You should let it stay like this. It is Providence."

Considering this, Jaikimoi slaughtered, cooked and ate a black ox inside the miniature corral. He built a new enclosure, but his cattle continued to sleep in the corral the rain had shrunk. During his next four years there, Jaikimoi became a rich man. His cattle, goats and donkeys became plentiful, and his children grew to adulthood, married and celebrated their *sapana*s in that homestead.

But a year after Jaikimoi moved away to Kusilet, because of Karamojong raids, he died and his herds were lost. His children waited six years—until they heard the fighting with the Karamojong had ceased, and then they returned to build their homesteads by the miniature corral at Kwaiadai, where Tororut had chosen to bless them. One of the sons is still living there today.

The Draft

During those years, the English were busy fighting the Italians about their own problems [World War II], and their soldiers began seizing hundreds of Pokot men for their army.[69] The first time they came to our homestead, I was out herding the cattle. Then one night they returned with the sub-chief and conscripted four of our men as soldiers. They picked me too, but the sub-chief said, "No! He is the only one of his father's sons who can look after the herds," so they released me.

We heard there were six circumcised girls who were so distressed over the drafting of their boyfriends that they cooked a dead donkey and ate it, thinking it might kill them and relieve their grief. This story was passed around, and a year later, at the dance of *laleyo*, it was put into song (the names in the song refer to the order in which the girls were circumcied):

<table>
<tr>
<td>

Woe, circumcised girls eat donkeys!
Ahaha, the cut ones eat in vain
My friend eats in vain
Kaporet eats in vain
Sereto eats in vain
Kalopot eats in vain
Chesortum eats in vain,
ah oh ilaiya

</td>
<td>

Woe, kiam muraren sukire
Ahaha, kacheptul kiamu kule
Kiamu kule kongen nyu
Kiamu kule kaporet
Kiamu kule seretao
Kiamu kule kalopot
Kiamu kule chesortum
Ah oh ilaiya

</td>
</tr>
</table>

Unusual Wells

The next rainy season, my best friend, Arekai, and I moved our fathers' herds again to Alakas, which had been opened for pasture. While our cowherd tended to the calves, one of us watched the cattle, and the other fetched water for the herds.

One day, when we were on our way to buy some maize, we stopped at the dry riverbed named Kapchorwa and asked some people there where we might find water to drink. They explained, "There's a well at the end of the river where the water falls during the rains, but you can only use it if your wife had a daughter first. If a person whose first-born was a son enters that well, all the water in this area will dry up!"

I was amazed. "What if you have not yet fathered any children?" I asked.

"Oh, that's nothing! There's no harm in that. Go ahead and fetch some water."

"Does this apply to both men and women?" I asked, curious.

"Both."

We walked along the river, and, in time, came to the well. Two women, some girls and youths were already using it. We asked a boy to hoist up some water for us, and we quenched our thirst. As we walked on, Arekai and I agreed we would not like to live near a river such as this, which rejects people. Everyone should be allowed to fetch water freely!

Through the years I have encountered several other peculiar wells in our country. For instance, the Kwachilopai River well, named Aposeketak, has always been very temperamental. The well—or perhaps Ilat—refuses to give water for a week at a time. Then people kill a black goat near the well and toss its blood and stomach contents into the dry depths, praying, "Help us! Give us water!" This works for two to three months, and then the trouble starts again.

A well we once used near Puriak hill is also odd. Every once in awhile it steams and the water is filled with insects. The rest of the time it is fine. *"Is some-one inside the well?"* people wonder. Likewise, I remember seeing small snakes with white bellies swimming in the salty water of the well at Kakorialet as a child. They didn't harm people, and the people didn't kill them for fear the well water would be finished. When we put the containers down into the water, the little snakes would run into their holes.

Abducting a Wife

One evening at Alakas, Arekai and I tried to let blood from one of the cattle, but the arrow pierced a main artery and the ox died. We skinned it and ate a little of the meat. The next morning we left the cowherd in the homestead with the meat, while the two of us went out together with the cattle and calves. When we reached the intersection of the Alakas road and the track to Amudat, we noticed an attractive girl resting in the shade. (Of course, most girls were attractive to us at that stage of our lives!) We instinctively drew closer to her like two young lions. It was obvious that she was traveling alone.

She greeted us pleasantly enough and asked, "Are there any homes at Kanyao?"

"Oh there aren't any *there*," Arekai volunteered eagerly. "Come sleep in *our* homestead! Tomorrow morning we'll show you a better way!"

"Oh no, I must be going," she said quickly, probably noticing the gleam in his eye. She hurried off.

We watched her go like two cats watching a rat. Finally I could stand it no longer. I exclaimed to my friend, "We can't just let her go! Walking alone like that with no mother or father—we can't leave food like that!"

I called and ran after her, but she ignored me. It was obvious that talking was not going to get me anywhere, so I pounced upon her, seizing her arms. She struggled violently, screaming, but I got her down and spread myself on top of her writhing body. I had nearly found her, when a car came!

I jumped up and ran into the bushes. She ran to the road, waving her arms. The driver stopped and asked, "What's the matter?" She was starting to tell the driver, when I darted out, grabbed her and pulled her back into the bushes with me. The car drove on.

I wrapped my arms around her and carried her, yelling, back to where Arekai was watching the cattle. Her screaming was irritating me. "Why are you yelling, you dummy?" I shouted at her as I put her down. "No one can hear you! Shut up!"

"Yeah, who can hear her?" Arekai added. "It doesn't matter!"

She started to yell again, but I put my hand firmly over her mouth and threatened, "If you continue to resist me, I'll have to take you to your homestead and thank your parents for sending you to me. I'll tell them you really satisfied my appetite!"

She looked shocked and confused. After that, there was no resistance. I lay her down, caressed her body and satisfied myself completely. When it was over, we walked to the river together to quench our thirst and found Arekai watering the cattle there. We filled our containers, carried the water back to the homestead, and cooked the leftover beef. After Arekai arrived with the cattle, we feasted to-gether and slept well.

The next morning the girl (I still did not know her name) said, "I want to go. Come show me the way."

"Ah! You are really foolish!" I exclaimed. "How can you think of going when food is so plentiful? Who will help us eat all this food? Here you have milk and meat, and I sleep with you at night. What more could you want? On the paths you will find lions, eland and rhino. Where will you pass? The road is the only good way, but it is far away. Look, I'll take you to Koduch in three days, all right?" The girl started to protest, but changed her mind and was silent.

She stayed with me two full days like a wife. Her name was Chepureta. On the third morning, she awakened me and said, "Now come show me the path."

"Ooooh," I moaned in the bed. "I feel sick. I guess Arekai will have to tend the cattle, so you'll have no one to take you."

"Where are you sick?" she asked.

"I have a terrible headache," I lied.

"Oh. Then I don't want you to go." She quietly went outside.

Her concern charmed me so much that I decided to take her after all! I waited a few moments, then got up to tell her I was feeling better already, and that we could leave right after Arekai let the cattle out. Chepureta hurried back inside the house to gather her things.

Just then a man appeared outside the gate, claiming to be Chepureta's brother. Before we could stop him, he charged into the homestead, looked into the house and saw her. He entered the door, yelling at her, and started to drag her out. Ob-viously, he intended to hit her. A lot.

I was overcome with shame for what we had done and pity for that nice, in-nocent girl. I rushed to the house and grabbed the man from behind, wrapping my arms around his middle, pulling him free from Chepureta. "Arekai!" I yelled. "Run with the girl! Show her the way!"

Chepureta ducked out of the house, and I could see that her face was full of fear. Then she ran away with Arekai, crying, "Please hold him until I'm gone! He'll beat me up!"

I struggled to hold the angry brother until I thought they had had enough time, then let him go. He wheeled about, swinging his arms at me furiously. I ducked, and started talking fast: "You have no reason to be fighting me! Your sister was lost. Hopelessly lost! Tired—and thirsty!" (He had wrestled me down, but he was listening.) "We met her on the road at night. We gave her food and water. Maybe we should have left her there!"

He frowned, but let me go. "Where did your friend take her?" he asked.

"I don't know."

"Well, I'll go now. If she comes back, please bring her to Amudat. You'll find me there."

"Go. We'll bring her," I replied.

After he left, I walked to the river, relieved, thinking Chepureta had gone. Arekai was there. He said, "Your girl is hiding near here. She's afraid of her brother and doesn't want to meet him on the path. She asked me to bring her water."

I took Chepureta a gourd of water, and returned with some meat to eat by the river with her. I explained about my encounter with her brother and how I had promised to take her to Amudat. She looked terrified.

"Oh, what can I do now?" she asked pitifully. Then she told me why she had been traveling alone the day I accosted her by the road. A terrible man, whom she had spurned repeatedly, had gone to her father to negotiate a marriage without her consent, and she knew her father would agree, because the man was wealthy. Desperate, she had been running towards the temporary sanctuary of her mother's mother's homestead. If her brother found her now, he would beat her and bring her back for the wedding.

I thought about this awhile and suggested, "Someone is coming from my father's home in two days to watch the cattle, so I can go home. I'll take you with me then and show you the path to your grandmother's house. Can you wait until then?"

"Yes," she agreed. "It's better that way. I'll stay like this with you."

We sat quietly together for a few moments, and then I said, "There's no one at the river," and she went into the water to bathe.

When my brother arrived the following evening, he saw Chepureta and asked, "Where did this girl come from?"

"She is our wife! We found her on the road," we told him.

"Oh! You have good luck!" he laughed.

In the morning Chepureta and I left for Lossom, avoiding the paths to Amudat so that we wouldn't meet her brother. Honestly, I had the best of intentions, but when I saw Father's homestead in the distance, I couldn't resist another prank. I remarked to Chepureta, "Come! Let's go ask for some water there. I know that homestead!" I did not tell her it was my own. If I had, she certainly would not have gone in with me.

My sister Chelima greeted me and asked, "How come you're traveling with this girl?"

"No—it's not what you think," I lied. "We just met right here. She wants to go over to Loro."

"Really?"

Chelima then greeted Chepureta, and the two of them went to stir some milk, butter and millet together. After we had eaten, I suggested, "Let's rest a little. The sun is very hot."

But Chelima, always perceptive, said, "This girl's eyes betray that she knows you very well, brother."

"No, of course not!" I shrugged, avoiding my sister's gaze. I went out to lie in the shade.

Unfortunately, while I slept, Chelima took Chepureta into her house, and Chepureta told her everything. I awakened abruptly to Chelima standing over me, demanding: "Why didn't you tell me this was your wife?"

"What do you mean—wife?" I gasped, trying to get up. "She's someone's daughter!"

"Aha! Then why did you bring her here freely like this?"

"I—I just wanted to show her the way," I tried.

"What do you think Father will say when he finds you kidnapped a man's daughter and tricked her into coming to your house like a free woman?" she continued angrily. "I'll tell you what he'll say! He'll ask you if you intend to marry her!"

There was no point in resisting now. "I—I don't know ... No!" I said.

Soon the sun began to set. All the children came home and found Chepureta in the corral. She was ill at ease and did not know what to do. Then Father entered the gate. He greeted both of us. "Whose daughter is this?" he asked me.

"I don't know. I found her today near here."

He turned to her and asked, "Where are you from?"

"Over near Kacheliba."

"Where are you going?"

"To Loro. I—I was lost," she said nervously.

"Oh. Do you intend to sleep here and go tomorrow?"

"Oh, yes. Good," she said, obviously relieved.

But that evening the word spread quickly from Chelima to all my mothers and to my father. At 8 PM, he stalked into the *aperit* and demanded, "Where did you say this girl came from?"

"She's the one who said she came from Kacheliba," I said truthfully.

"Where is she going?"

"She said she wants to go to Loro."

"No! Tell me the truth!" he stormed.

"But I've just told you ..." This would not do.

"If that's all you can say, you aren't going to sleep here tonight! You leave right now and let the daughter of a man stay here instead!" He paused, and I could see he was furious, trying to control himself. Finally he exploded, "*So! You accosted someone's daughter on the road! Then you come to deceive me! You wretch!*"

"She isn't anyone's wife. She's a girl! I don't see what's so wrong. She doesn't belong to anyone. I found her and lusted greatly. What was I to do?" I tried lamely to defend myself.

"I'll tell you what to do!" Father exclaimed. "Be honorable and make her your wife! Did you want to do that?"

"No! I simply found food on the road when I was very hungry, so I ate."

He sighed. "All right, tomorrow morning when it is still dark, take this daughter to her home."

Just then my mother came. Father asked her, "Did you hear your son wronged a man's child? He captured a daughter and molested her for several days! Be sure to provide that poor girl with enough food."

"*Ala!* What? Molested how? He met with his girlfriend—so what? It's the play of children! Let him alone! Don't listen to your father, Kaparketo! He's a real fool!"

Chepureta came by just then, and Mother took her hand. "Now, my son's friend," she said, "Sleep well. If you want to go tomorrow morning, you can go. If you want your friend, my son, to fetch you water, he will. There is plenty of food and a place for you here, and you can stay as long as you like! The houses of your father aren't going anywhere! You can see your parents in due time."

Father looked exasperated. "OK, Cheparkong," he said patiently. "If you insist on doing this, tomorrow you take out all our cattle and give them to the girl's parents. Then your son can live together with this girl legitimately."

"Yes! I'd like that!" Mother said defiantly. "Just remember you said that! You approved the marriage! Tomorrow morning I'll take out the cattle. Do you hear, girl? You can stay forever!"

Chepureta was mute and completely bewildered. Mother spent the night with one of her co-wives so that Chepureta and I could use her bed. My sister Chelima slept in the other bed in our hut.

At daybreak, Mother called in the door, "OK, you two get up now!"

After I came out, my mother went into the house and told Chepureta to take off all her clothes. "Today you will be married in our corral!" Mother and Chelima exclaimed together.

Chepureta sat on the bed without moving and thought and thought. Finally, she whispered, "Now what am I to do?"

"How long are you going to think?" Chelima asked. "Take your clothes off and we'll make you a wife! You can't leave now, for you have come to our home!"

The girl was dumbfounded.

Father heard all the commotion and called my mother. "Cheparkong! You surely didn't mean all you said yesterday!"

"I sure did!" she answered. "You approved the wedding!"

Now even Father was confused. "How many cattle are there?" he asked.

"I don't know—you know!" she chided him.

"OK, have it your way! The cattle will go!"

Soon Chepureta came out, draped in the skin blanket Chelima had given her. She was dazed. All four of my mothers came and instructed her to spread dung on the backs of seven calves and to open the gate for the cattle. My mother brought a nice unbroken gourd of milk and told Chepureta, "You will be like us. All of us women came from homesteads far away. One man searched for us, found us, and put us together in one place. Now you have come to join us! Don't let it concern you that my son accosted you on the path. A girl doesn't know where her husband will come from—out of the sky or from the ground! We meet him like we meet a wild animal! Only Tororut plans these things. If Tororut arranged for you to meet your husband half-way, then that is how it must be. If you are nice to us, we'll be nice to you. If you shun us, we'll shun you. Hear my words!"

She anointed Chepureta's head with milk and passed the gourd to each of her co-wives, who also anointed the girl. Chepureta anointed each of them and my father in return.

I watched my own marriage as a shocked spectator!

They brought a cow skin and put it in the middle of the corral. Chepureta stood on it. They did everything: gave her eleven goats, tied on her new clothes, tied the skin rope of marriage on her wrist, cut the metal wire for the wedding bracelet and wrapped it beautifully around her arm. Then my mother said to my sister, "Go! Bring the scorpion!" (This is the final part of the marriage ritual of the Baboon Clan.)

"No!" Father exclaimed. "Don't give the child of a man a scorpion without knowing if her father agrees! Who knows? After we have agreed on the bride price, you can go find a scorpion to sting her. Only then will the marriage compact be sealed."

My bride was very happy those next days. She was silent and did very good work. She must have thought, *"Ala!* Surely my husband spoke from his soul after all! I am living well now!"

When one week had passed, Father instructed me, "Go to your homestead now and send your brother back. I will go with him to the girl's father's homestead."

I left. Chepureta stayed at Father's homestead, fetching water for the goats and sheep and helping my mothers cultivate the garden.

Meanwhile, my father and brother approached Chepureta's father and told him everything. He was furious, yelling, *"Ah!* If your son took my daughter without *asking me,* I demand sixty cattle!"

Father said, "Aaaaaaa! No! Sixty aren't there. There are twenty."

"Forget the twenty!"

Father tried, "Twenty-five," but he insisted, "Sixty, no less!"

"Agreed. You win. Thirty!"

But the man continued to refuse any bargaining whatsoever! Finally, Father had had enough. "Done!" he exclaimed. "Come get your daughter then! I eat my herds, not people!"

Chepureta's father came back with my father. When they arrived, he said, "Sir, where is your son—the one who took my daughter?"

"He's over at his place."

"Tell him to come bring the girl home."

"No! Why should he bring her? She was traveling alone!"

The next morning Chepureta was summoned from the fields. Her father told her, "Come, let's go," but she protested, saying, "I won't go!"

This could not be allowed: her father had refused consent and had demanded his daughter back. Our marriage would have to be annulled. "Take off your clothes at once!" my mothers demanded. Chepureta hesitated, and they threatened to beat her for her obstinacy. And so Chepureta took off the clothes of my homestead and put back on the clothes she had worn from her own home. She left sadly with her father.

The next day I met some of my family at the river.

"How did the negotiations go?" I asked them.

"Alas, your wife is gone," they told me. "But we think she'll come back. When her father came to take her away, she cried, 'Why do you want to give me to a bad man? Even though I don't really know Domonguria, as least his parents accept me and I like it here!' They had to take her by force."

Sure enough, Chepureta did come back—to the homestead where I first accosted her. She told me that her father had already married her to that other man, but that she had run away from him after two days to join me.

This was too deep for me. "No!" I said firmly. "I will not return to you again. You must go!"

Chepureta stood there awhile, looking at me, and I felt genuinely sorry for her.

"Go!" I repeated.

She turned and slowly walked away.

I realize now that we were wrong, terribly wrong, to kidnap that innocent girl. We were only youths, but much too naive and irresponsible. My father had been right about the scorpion.

My First Raid

The year after my *sapana*, I moved with another man to Loro and, soon afterwards, went to visit one of my father's friends for a week. I had been there only a few days, when I noticed that all the men were consulting with one another, obviously making plans. I was curious, of course, so I asked my father's friend what was going on.

"They want to raid the Karamojong," he confided.

"When?" I asked.

"Tonight. If you want to go along, watch the house of that elder. Let him know, and he will work it out for you."

I kept silent for the remainder of the afternoon. Later, when everyone else apparently went to sleep, I stayed up, watching the elder's house well into the night. I was a man now, and this would, I hoped, be my first raid. I sat there reflecting on all the stories about raiding I had heard since childhood and was filled with anticipation.

You see, since ancient times, we Pokot have fought with our enemies: Karamojong, Turkana, Marakwet and Maasai, as our fathers have taught us it is our duty to do. Especially when there is starvation, some men are bound to suggest, "Rather than dying in vain, shall we not try to steal some wealth and food from another tribe? Even if we die there in the midst of our enemies, what's the difference? Whether a man dies of starvation or in battle, he is gone forever and cannot return again, for there is no man who can rise from the dead!"

I was told that long ago some of our men went to plunder the Turkana for this reason. When they entered Turkanaland it began to rain, and the rains continued during the attack. Perhaps 300 people died in the raid, including children and their mothers, as well as men. When the Pokot led the captured cattle towards our country, the rains continued falling just behind them, covering their tracks, but when they reached the river, they found it impassable. This was a disastrous turn of events, for the high waters detained them, until the enemy came in force to recapture their stock. The Turkana outnumbered our people and annihilated them, except for a few elders, who were not able to cross the river until a week later.

Now one might think, "Truly, what a tragedy!" but it was not bad, really, even though these were my people, Pokot. These things happen to all peoples! Many men die during a raid because, whereas in fighting all men have strength, Tororut will help only certain men. Whether He will choose to help us or our enemies, we cannot know. It is all according to Tororut's plan. Indeed, it is Providence: if Tororut prohibits a man from having something, he shall not have it!

I thought, then, about one of our old fighting songs, the trademark war song of a Pokot hero named Kamirongo Aritile. They say Kamirongo had such a tremendous lust for fighting that he grew restless after only five months without battle! Once, when he heard enemies were raiding at Kupkomo, he left his home in Cheptulel and traveled there to offer his services as a warrior. But when the enemies did not come for several more months, Kamirongo's frustration increased, and he prepared for his war song by digging two holes in the sand and placing a prickly palm stalk (*sosion*) in each one. Then, using a bunch of ostrich feathers, he pushed away the stalk facing in the direction of the enemy's country, and began to sing:

Dikdik above, dikdik below *Tell* (the enemy, come) *on the Teneyon path* *By way of the Kamatira path*	*Sirran ari kundoko, sirran ari kumboro* *Olenjina Tenayon ongu ru-e* *Kamatira ongu ru*

Even as he sang, they say, the enemies started coming to Kupkomo. He fought them furiously for 16 hours nonstop, killing 26 people altogether. Those who were with him that day claimed no man was ever quicker than he who was named Kamirongo, and he was thereafter known to all as Kamirongo Aritile, meaning Kamirongo the Leader. The elders say he may have killed 100 men in his lifetime.

One day—*perhaps this day*—I hoped to sing his song with honor.

I was alerted from these musings around 3:30 AM, when I saw men silently entering the elder's house. After a few minutes I ducked inside the door quietly and saw all of them there.

One of them noticed me and demanded, "You! What are you looking for?"

"Nothing. I came without reason."

"Look, do you know something about this house?"

I was determined not to betray my father's friend's confidence. "No," I replied. "I just saw people coming in. I figured you were probably drinking beer, so I came in case someone would offer me food too."

"Go!" the man said sternly. "We don't want you here!"

Thankfully, the elder of the house entered into the conversation and saved me. "Whose son is he?" he asked.

"He is a stranger from Lossom," answered the others respectfully.

"Oh, then he is the man who came to my friend's homestead."

"That's right."

"Well, let him come!"

That ended the discussion about my uninvited presence.

Now the elder performed a ritual I had not yet known: He spread clay on the face and stomach of each warrior, saying, "All right, go where you want to go!" Six of us were anointed for the raid. We left that night for the region of Maniman in Karamoja country. At a place called Nakalaa, we came across thirty head of cattle and, amazingly enough, found no one inside the corral with them! We took the cattle and had brought them halfway home when, to our unbelievably good fortune, the rains began to pour! We were drenched all the way home. Our tracks were covered, and no one would know which enemy had raided that country!

Once in Pokot territory, we slept in a recently abandoned homestead. The next morning we divided up the cattle. The five others told me firmly, "You knew nothing of this affair and were not included in our plans. It was just your good luck that the elder insisted on your coming! Now, since you've come, we'll give you three head of cattle. If you don't like it, tough!"

I replied, "Thanks! If you want to give me three, that's great!" My allotment, therefore, was two cows and one steer, until one man spoke up and said, "No! There are many cows. Let's give him three cows instead."

I herded my cows to a friend's homestead near Turkana country, and returned to the homestead of my father's friend. It so happened that a man had just married his daughter and, in honor of the occasion, he presented me with a cow and its calf from the newly-paid bride wealth to take home as a gift to my father!

That is how I happened to return to Lossom with five new cattle.

CHELIMA: BECOMING A WOMAN

Getting Father's Consent

The extra cows were especially appreciated at this time, for my father had finally consented to allow my sister Chelima to be circumcised. Quantities of milk would be needed for the celebrations.

Since long ago, we have circumcised both men and women, but these days it is the women's, rather than the men's, ceremony that remains traditionally universal. Just as *sapana* marks the transition between boyhood and manhood, circumcision is the means by which a girl becomes a woman. Girls are usually circumcised within a few years of puberty, but there is no rule. Even older women may be circumcised together with the girls. This is considered good and proper.

All little girls yearn for the year when they feel they can approach their fathers to ask for circumcision. After the sixth month or so, when the rains begin, they plead, "How long must we wait? We want to be circumcised!" But a girl may not be circumcised without her father's permission, and he will wait until he can amass enough milk and honey for a respectable ceremony.

"Not this year," our Father had retorted to my sister in the past. "Do you want to disgrace my homestead? If you were circumcised, everyone would come here expecting to be fed! Where would I find enough beer to satisfy them? And our few milk cows would hardly suffice! When it is time for your circumcision, I want to be assured I have everything I need. Why, this year it was all I could do to give you the steer you sold in order to buy your beads! You must obey me! Maybe next year. Anyway, don't worry, Chelima. The circumcision knife won't go away! It's not as if this is your last chance!" Even when our mother would plead on her behalf, Father had remained resolute.

But Chelima had known her time was coming, and the previous year she had joined other girls in scarifying their bodies for beauty. Some patterns were cut only on the belly, and others were cut around the body, meeting at the back. The scarring process is very painful, and one can easily tell how a girl will endure circumcision by observing her then. One will jump each time the knife cuts her, and you know she will be afraid at circumcision. Another, like my sister, will be as silent as stone, and you know that her spirit is equally strong.

After Father finally agreed to her initiation, Chelima had to undergo the test of fire, as I had done when I had hoped to be circumcised. When Father placed the burning coals on her nails, she hardly flinched! Only when a girl can withstand this pain with dignity is she ready for the knife.

As soon as all their fathers had consented, the Lossom girls began collecting the things they would need for the ceremony: the skin capes called *kalajis*, a trumpet-horn, and various decorations. Chelima and the other initiates from our area built the circumcision hut on one side of a homestead about a mile away from us. The door of their hut faced the countryside, so that they would be able to enter and leave as quickly and inconspicuously as possible during the next three months.

The Karemba Ritual

Girls' circumcision consists of six rituals: two before the surgery, the circumcision itself, and three celebrations following it.[70]

On the night before the first affair, all of the initiates gather together and sing the traditional circumcision songs. They will be sung again and again during the months to come. Most of these songs are reserved only for circumcision rites, and are not sung freely every day. People say they were made up by Sameiwur, the original mother, who, some claim, lived during the time Tororut was creating the world. Men, like myself, don't know most of the women's circumcision songs since, of course, only the women sing them![71] We do know a few, however, such as *Cheripko*, for it is also the happy song women sing immediately after giving birth to a baby girl to announce the news to the family waiting outside (other songs are sung for a baby boy). The name Chesokai, mentioned in this song, means "naughty woman," such as one who prepares food during her period, making her husband sick.

Female genitals! Everyone (approve) *hear!*	*Cheripkenyo! Chamalim!*
Oye oyayo oyewoye yewoye yewoye	*Oye oyayo oyewoye yewoye yewoye*
Oyewoye, genitals of a girl!	*Oyewoye, cheripko*

Female genitals! Chesokai! Oyewoye ... *Matter of the Ancient Mother Sameiwur,* *Oyewoye* *Genitals of a girl!*	*Cheripko! Chesokai! Oyewoye ...* *Kipu Koku Sameiwur,* *Oyewoye...* *Cheripko!*

A second song, sung after *Cheripko*, mentions *susinion* grasses, which the mothers of the new initiates spread on the ground of the house of circumcision. After the surgery, the girls sleep directly on top of the grasses, rather than on skins, covering themselves with *koliken* (goat skin blankets). They sing:

Ah, palm tree, eoyoiye oye oyayo *Ah, circumcised girl, palm tree*	*Ah takaiwa eoyoiye, oye, oyayo* *Ah chemerionda takaiwa*

Verses following:

Ah, circumcised girl… *Song of our Ancient Mother* *Tell father to come near the door* (Tell him) *I sleep on the grass* *I sleep on the grass without fear* *Palm tree*	*Ah chemerionda...* *Kipu Koku* *Ilenjina nyi papo* *Lenjina papo nyono kumbul or* *Kurowun molu* *Kurowun molu kelalem* *Takaiwa*

A third circumcision song refers to our custom of a new bride refusing to have sex with her husband until he promises her a specific cow. The song mentions *lopotwa*, a tree with red fruit smaller than a tomato, the prized *kamartin*—oxen with one horn pointing up and the other twisted down—and *kamultin*—oxen with nice spots.

Refrain:

Very hot vagina *Lopotwa fruit, penis of Ancient Father* *Large cowbell, vagina of Ancient Mother*	*Kiwerwerin sei* *Lopotwa, perit a Kuka* *Kadongut seio Koku*

Verses:

Its purpose is to get cattle, to get kamartin *Its purpose is to get cattle, to get kamultin*	*Tiomba lowan tich nyo kilowun kamartin* *Tiomba lowan tich nyo kilowun kamultin*

The girls sing these and other songs until the middle of the night. The following morning, when it is still quite dark, they arise. This is the day of *karemba*, the first circumcision ritual, in which the girls pose as men.

First each initiate ties bells on her legs, a giraffe's tail on her arm, and dons her cape (*kalaja*). Then the girls take some red and white clay pigments and hike about five miles into the wilderness, where they remove all their clothing and prance about naked in the early morning, like men who are going out to hunt. They are especially careful not to associate with other women during this time. Afterwards, the girls put their cloaks back on and walk to a river or pool. There they mix the pigments with water and, using a small stick, paint their faces beautifully with tiny alternate red and white markings, like the pretty, speckled guinea fowl. Later that morning, the girls walk back to their homestead to rest before the ceremony.

At mid-afternoon, one of the mothers lights a fire at the place where people dance at night, feeding it with logs of the *lopotwa* tree. The girls come out, then, to dance and sing together until evening, when the men come home. During this day of *karemba* and the following day, the initiates must not associate with other women or flirt with men.

The Laleyo Dance

Two days after *karemba* is the wonderful dance of *laleyo*. The women light the fire as before, and sometimes as many as 150 or 200 men, women and children come to cast their souls into the fervor and joy of the dance! During *laleyo*, the initiates have license to forcefully seize their own partners for the dance. It is all part of the fun!

We have many dances and celebrations, but the one that surpasses them all is *laleyo*. All who enter into this celebration sing and dance from the depths of their very being. Indeed, the joy of the dance often seizes the minds and bodies of the participants until many go into trances of supreme bliss. It must be that *laleyo* is a trap of Tororut, gripping the dancer's soul and charging his blood until he is overpowered! The music, the movement, even the words can control a person's thoughts until he is in total communion with the dance. Its essence surges within him and through him. There is a pain, and then a kind of ecstatic death. We have danced many dances and have observed other people's celebrations, but none is as sweet as *laleyo*!

Every year now we are invited to attend a celebration in Moroto, where we see the Karamojong dance. They have no *laleyo*, yet I have seen the Karamojong and even the Turkana go into trances like us. I wonder, sometimes, if other peoples experience such ecstasy. Do white people succumb? It must be so, I believe, for it is a godly experience.

We dance to all the songs at *laleyo*—songs of fighting, animals, unusual and usual events, heroes, sorcerers, romance and sex. Bards will introduce their recently composed songs at *laleyos*, and some will become famous. It is a time of great merriment.

For example, one of the prettiest songs we have sung at *laleyo* is about a girl named Chesongol, who desired a boy whose name was Paretia Omemoi. She went about exclaiming, "Paretia's penis surpasses all men's! I think it's beautiful!" People were amused to hear her talking like this. They told others, and soon everyone knew about Chesongol's infatuation with Paretia. Inevitably, they made up a song about it:

<table>
<tr>
<td>

Chesongol
Beautiful is the penis of your Paretia!
Chesongol (high pitched trill)

</td>
<td>

Chesongol
Kemulanan peret nyo pu Paretia
Chesongol lililili

</td>
</tr>
</table>

One day after this incident, so the story goes, Paretia stole Chesongol's *cheretai* skirt (the full skirt worn at dances). "Hey, friend!" she yelled after him. "I can't go about like this!"

"Come with me if you want your clothes back," he propositioned her, and went on his way. Three days later Paretia suggested, "Come spend the night with me at my place, and you will get your skirt back."

"I can't do that!" she protested. "I'd like to, really, but my parents forbid it. I don't know what they have against you. Please give me my skirt now."

But Paretia only shrugged and said, "Oh well, in that case, I guess I'll have to keep it for a while."

Now Chesongol cried and moaned so much about this that soon all the neighborhoods for miles around knew of her predicament. Everyone also knew when Chesongol did, at last, succumb to Paretia's entreaties and went to sleep with him for three nights, after which Paretia returned the skirt and walked her home. Her brother was furious, slapping and yelling at her, "Why did you go to Paretia, you bad girl?" but Chesongol only sniffed, "What could I do? I went to get my clothes back, and he locked me up!" The neighbors considered the situation hilarious, and at the next *laleyo* there appeared a second song about Chesongol. (Women sing and dance to these two songs with tremendous glee during *laleyo*s, but it is wrong to sing them at home in front of children.):

<table>
<tr>
<td>

Refrain:
   Paretia! Give me my clothes!
   Paretia, ummmm, Paretia

Verses:
   Give me my dancing skirt
   Give me my full skirt
   Give me my skirt
   Child of Kachepie
   Son of the Kachepie clan
   Paretia Omemoi

</td>
<td>

Paretia, konanun serenyu!
Paretia, ummm, Paretia

Konanun lokitor
Konanun cheretai
Konanun chemunya
Wero kachepie
Wero kachemuma
Paretia Omemoi

</td>
</tr>
</table>

Circumcision

The day after *laleyo* is the day of circumcision. First, the initiates escort the circumciser to their homestead. Then they go to bathe in the river and to find a stone or stones to sit upon during the rite. Finally, they approach the corral resolutely, throw off their clothes, and stand at the gate, boldly awaiting their turns.

When each initiate hears the women rejoicing over the girl ahead of her, she walks into the corral bravely. If she carries one of the stones, she puts it down confidently in the center of the corral, then sits upon it silently, with her legs outstretched and her head high. She gazes into the distance, like someone who is scanning the countryside, and does not look at people or nearby things. Her father stands over her with his spear unsheathed, and the circumciser takes her instrument, which is similar to a horn, and begins to cut.[72]

When it is finished, the initiate's mother comes to raise her from the stone. (Some girls who are exceedingly brave will resist, saying, "It isn't finished yet!", and they will have to be shown the excised parts as proof!) If a girl withstands the surgery with honor, her father will feel great joy. He will sheath his spear and proudly walk away, knowing that everyone saw that his daughter was brave.

However, if a girl disgraces her father by showing obvious fear, he will raise his spear as if to kill her, and others will have to hold him back and take his spear away. He will have experienced great shame, and it will be widely advertised that his daughter did poorly: that she is lacking in spirit. When the girls sing each day in the house of circumcision during their period of seclusion, she will be silent. How could she sing who has so shamed her father? She cannot be allowed, once again, to disgrace her father's ears! "Shut up, stupid!" the other girls will order her. "How dare you sing! You have dishonored your father and brought shame to your whole homestead. Let *us* sing so that our fathers will rejoice over *us*!" Her father will not wear bells on his legs like all the other parents. And from that day forward, she will be known as Cheptuh, which means "cast off." It is quite probable that she will be the last of her circumcision group to be married, because no one will readily want her.

After the mother raises her newly circumcised daughter from the stone, she leads her outside the gate. At that time, any man who wishes to marry the girl may offer his walking stick, saying, "Take this and I will give you such and such a cow." She may accept, or she may refuse by folding her arms. At any rate, she must not speak, even if he asks her questions. During her seclusion, if she converses with other people, she will whisper so that her father won't hear.

Once circumcised, initiates are called *chemerin* during the next three months. (Each girl is called a *chemerion*.) Those who sat on the first stone are hereafter called *kaporet*, the girl who brought the second stone and all who sat upon it are named *sereto*, and those who used the third stone are called *kalopot*. If there are additional girls, they are named *kaporet, sereto and kalopot*, in that order, according to the stones they sat upon, until it is finished.

The mothers give their daughters special sticks, which the *chemerin* (initiates) place in the doorway of the circumcision house.[73] This is to warn strangers visiting the homestead that the house is off-limits. It is extremely bad luck for any adult to enter a house of circumcision during the ensuing weeks. Even if you enter by mistake, the mothers will seize you and keep whipping you, until you agree to kill an ox for absolution.

The Lupol Ceremony

Following the circumcision, there are three other ceremonies.

The first, called *lupol*, occurs about ten days after the circumcision. It is just like the *sapana* celebration, in which all the neighboring women come bringing milk. The mothers wait for each other outside the corral gate and then sing the two songs for opening the door: that of the elephant and that of Setim, the warrior. (They do this each time they bring milk to a celebration.) The *chemerin* come out to eat the food of *lupol*, then retreat into their house for another month. They must not sleep elsewhere until the circumcision rites are over.

During this period, the *chemerin* disguise themselves, by spreading a chalk-like clay all over their faces and legs. Their only garments are their large skin blankets. Shortly after the *lupol* feast, the initiates go into the bush to collect special walking sticks, called *sinditei*, and to gather the tree fibers they twist into ropes for tying their cloaks at the neck and at the waist. Onto the long rope of the belt, each girl ties a bell made from a tortoise shell, with a goat hoof as a clapper. Then, when she walks, one hears those rattling and swishing sounds we call *karikaret*.

Chemerin often sing together as they walk about, waving their *sinditei* up and down in time to the songs. When two *chemerin* meet, they sing and salute each other by standing slightly apart, propping their *sinditei* on the ground, and waving the tops of the long sticks back and forth towards each other in time to the singing. Then one girl holds her cloak out and the other taps it lightly with her *sindit*, making a clicking noise in her mouth, and the salute is reversed.

Although the *chemerin* are allowed to walk about during this time, they must take strict precautions: first and foremost, the initiates must avoid their fathers. "Fathers" include not only their biological fathers and grandfathers, but also their uncles, fathers' close friends and the fathers of their co-initiates. If the girls happen to be in the vicinity of any of these men, they must cover their heads, and if a father comes close enough, the girls may even have to fall to the ground and cover themselves completely. They must never be close enough to any of these men to be recognized or even seen. For this reason, when the *chemerin* return together from an outing, they begin to sing as they approach the homestead as a warning to those inside. If a father is present and hears the singing, he will duck inside a house and call to his wife, "Tell our daughter she may come now, without worry. I am inside." The *chemerin* will enter the circumcision house as quickly as possible. A *chemerion* approaching the homestead alone will warn the others by whistling. After the men have retreated into their houses, one of the women whistles back to let her know that the way is clear.

Feast: Removal of the Grasses

The second post-circumcision ceremony occurs a month or so after *lupol*. The women once again bring gourds of milk and sing at the gate, and the fathers prepare even more beer than on the first occasion—perhaps 20 gourds each. The reason for this celebration is the removal of the *susinion* grass of seclusion from the circumcision hut. After the grass is taken out, everyone drinks milk and beer and dances enthusiastically.

Meanwhile, the *chemerin* fetch water and gather lots of fragrant *tomut* grasses. They wash, spread fat on their bodies, and put the sweet-smelling grasses in the fire. Each girl holds her blanket over the burning grasses long enough for the tomut scent to permeate the leather. Now, even without seeing them, people will be aware of the presence of *chemerin* by their scent, which is reminiscent of Lux soap. And if you sleep with a *chemerion*, everyone will know your secret by your smell alone!

The circumcision hut, you see, is no longer prohibited to outsiders, but all young men who enter must bring gifts of iron beads (*teroi*) to their girlfriends inside. Sometimes young men proposition *chemerin* ahead of time, and the girls who agree say, "Bring some *teroi* when you hear they are taking out the *susinion*." (All girls will want to give men who have brought many *teroi* a place to lie under their skin blankets. One who brings nothing will find no place to rest!) In fact, the *chemerin* now turn aggressive in their pursuit of the iron beads: they go about zealously seizing young men, stripping them of their beads, spears and shoes, and running with their bounty into the circumcision hut to await their ransom: *teroi*!

During the next one or two months, the girls continue to walk about and may even attend dances at night, especially when there is no moon, disguised by the white clay on their faces and legs. They are irrepressible: they continue to rob youths of their beads and gear in exchange for *teroi*, and if they find a young man with no *teroi*, they may keep his possessions! Yet even a man of great strength would never dare to hit a *chemerion*, for she has powers of witchcraft. If she judges a person to be bad, she can strike him with her *sindit*. He will become sick and will have to suffer, until he begs another *chemerion* to cure him with her *sindit*. So you see why most people try to avoid too much contact with these girls!

The Mysterious *Chemerin*

The daughter of Kitonging, the ironsmith, once told me that during her period of seclusion, she and her companions met some unknown *chemerin* singing initiation songs beside a nearby riverbed. Oddly, the new girls were completely covered by their cloaks, except for their *sinditei*, waving up and down in time to the music—even their faces were indiscernible. My friend could not see if the other girls were red, black or white, so carefully were they disguised! *Are they children of Tororut or of man?* they wondered.

Then one of the strange *chemerin* greeted them in the manner of Pokot and explained that they came from a hill named Tingirich, above the river. They asked my friend, "Where are you from?" and she answered, "If we tell you, our fathers might find out and beat us." The two groups talked for several hours, but the Tingirich girls never showed their faces. After agreeing to meet again in two days, all the initiates sang together, as is the custom of *chemerin* before parting.

During their third encounter, the Tingirich girls announced, "We cannot see you again like this, my friends. We told our parents about you and they were furious, saying, 'It's just your luck that we can't beat you now! If you see those girls again, you will not be welcome in our homesteads!' We must hurry home now before our fathers return. But we shall meet you again one day!" My friend never saw them after that.

Several years later, however, eight new initiates from Chotuh were about to ambush youths for *teroi* beads, when they heard other *chemerin* singing. They, too, began singing, and the two groups met as before. The other *chemerin* were completely disguised, and only their *sinditei* and their hands were visible outside the cloaks. The initiates exchanged information about their homesteads, and the strange girls suggested, "Let's meet together again each day, and on the fourth day, you can come to our homestead for a meal." Seven of the Chotuh girls accepted, but one hesitated.

When they told their mothers about their new friends, the mothers exclaimed, "Ah! If they are secretive like that, it's not good! You must not see them!" But the Chotuh girls did not take their mothers' advice. Their disguised friends, angry that they had told their mothers, admonished them, saying, "You did wrong! We did not tell our mothers about *you!*" Then one of them remarked, "Oh, it's nothing! Now come eat with us—today!"

"Would you come to our home, if we invited you?" a Chotuh girl asked, a little concerned.

"Of course! But first come to our home."

One girl still refused, but her companions went off happily with the mysterious *chemerin*. "Wait for us here!" they called back.

The lone girl waited there until nearly sunset, then walked home, singing, hoping the others would answer. But they never did, and they were never seen again. Some say those strange girls must have been the children of Ilat. Perhaps he wanted our initiates for wives or daughters. Who knows?

Lapan

Just before the final circumcision ceremony, the father of each initiate gets a skin and dries it by the fire, after which it is sewn into garments with a large needle we call *seduk*. It is the responsibility of the father of the homestead where the girls are staying to soak all these skin garments in a great quantity of beer until they swell and become pliable. The other fathers, meanwhile, prepare as many gourds of beer as they can—40 for a man with successful beehives, ten for one who could find very little honey.

On the day of *lapan*[74] the women again bring milk, singing, and there ensues the wonderful dance of *laleyo*.

The morning after the dance, the *chemerin* finally take off their capes and the tortoise-shell bells, which the little girls scoop up. They put on their beads and other jewelry they have collected to beautify their necks and ears. Then they don their new skin clothing—the apron, or *atela*, and the back skirt we call *cheptoro*. Once dressed in this way, each girl is no longer a *chemerion*, only a *kaporet*, *sereto* or *kalopot*. All of the families and friends come early that morning to witness the girls coming out of the circumcision house, emerging with their heads still covered in the presence of their fathers. Each father then approaches his daughter and delivers a small sermon.

I watched as my sister Chelima came out of the door, still veiled. Father walked with pride up to his daughter, who, all knew, had honored him with her courage during the circumcision. He said, "If you are good, child, and always obey me, I will continue to rejoice that you are my daughter! The day after tomorrow, I shall award you the calf of my cow. However, if you are bad or disobedient, I will disown you and you shall have none of my cattle!" Chelima removed her veil, then, and father anointed her head with milk. Now she was a woman, prepared to be married when the time came.

My Sister's Sorrow

Right after my sister's circumcision, we heard that there had been a battle between the Pokot and the Karamojong at Katotin, and so I left Lossom with several others, ready to fight. However, when we arrived, we found out that the "battle" had only been a spat between children using clubs, not spears, and that the incident had been exaggerated out of proportion. There would be no fight!

While we were at Katotin, which is on the plains, we became aware that the Karamojong there were making fun of us behind our backs, calling us "baboons" because we live in the hills. This irked us, and finally, a man named Mirei took two poisoned arrows out of his quiver and shot them at a sapling. The tree drooped and died within two hours! The Karamojong present were amazed and frightened, and we overheard one of their elders saying, "Now do you understand what we've been telling you? If you ridicule these baboons, they can kill you instantly with their powerful sticks!"

When I came back from Katotin, I found my father terribly agitated. Chelima, it seems, had been deeply in love with a certain young man and had hoped to marry him shortly after her circumcision. However, when her suitor had asked my father for her hand in marriage, Father had refused adamantly. My sister had been so distraught, she had run away to her lover's homestead.

This would not do! I left immediately to retrieve my sister. Chelima resisted me, screaming, begging and pleading, until I had to hit her to make her obey. She could not be allowed to offer herself freely as a man's wife like this, no matter how much they loved one another! If my father refused, that was that! How could she dishonor him by denying him the cattle she would bring through a properly sanctioned wedding? I spoke to her thus as we walked back to Father's homestead. My sister was crying.

Shortly afterwards, Father arranged for her to be married to a fine man named Lopedur. We rejoiced at her wedding, and the cattle of her bride wealth greatly augmented our herds. My sister became an exemplary wife and mother.

But Chelima's old suitor refused to give her up. "She'll return to me one day!" he would say again and again. Over the years, he would become obsessed with his love for my sister, and, in the end, as you will see, it would destroy her.

CATTLE AND ROMANCE

DECEPTION AND LOVE

Cattle Arguments

While I was staying in the vicinity of Lossom, my father and I had many discussions about our long-standing cattle feud with the family of Munyan. As I have told you, long ago, their relatives, the family of Makal, had tried to steal our cattle during the time of the great drought and famine. My grandfather Suam and great uncle Akolingoro had finally retrieved the cattle from Makal, but six had remained in the corral of Munyan, who later reported, falsely, that those cattle had died. When I was a child, Munyan's mother, Chepuchemurian, admitted she had tried to kill my father by witchcraft, so that he would not return to claim the cattle, and she had succeeded in making him lame. Munyan finally gave my father five of his six cattle, with their offspring, but begged us to leave one to provide milk for a little child who was sick.

Our compassion soon backfired. First, Munyan claimed the cow had died, having produced no calves! We simply did not believe him. Then, at the time the newly-drafted Pokot soldiers were garrisoned in Turkana and fighting for the English, we were astonished to learn that Munyan's people tried to use the English government to make a case against Father to the officials at Kapenguria. He was hoping to retrieve some of the cattle we had rightly claimed years earlier! Tomena, the chief, suggested that Munyan make an oath with my father to settle the issue. He explained, "Pturu will give you one ox, and you will cut it in half and scatter the blood on all parties concerned. Those who are lying about the ownership of the cattle will die. If your plea is correct, you will eventually get all the cattle you dispute."

When Munyan's family agreed, the chief asked my father, who was staying in Kapenguria at the time, if he would agree to the oath. "Question those people carefully," Father advised. "Find out whether they sincerely believe their claim is just, or if they are merely trying to scandalize me into giving them cattle."

Tomena decided to interview Munyan's people once more, in the presence of my father. When they insisted they really did want to make an oath, Tomena said, "All right. If you are sincere in this matter, please write your sign in this police book. If your claim is unjust, you will, of course, have to pay the consequences" They refused to sign.

"Really!" Father remarked bitterly. "If you refuse to put your hand print there and thereby take responsibility for your actions, please go away and don't bother us anymore! Truthfully, I wish you would sign, so that we could settle this matter once and for all!"

Father went back home then, and waited. When nothing happened after three months, we knew that they had decided not to follow through.

It vexed me that this family should repeatedly try to claim cattle that were rightfully ours, and, now that I was grown, I decided to do something about it. Resolutely, I set out alone for the homestead of Munyan, son of Kitelamoi.

When I told Munyan the reason for my visit, he was angry. We argued and insulted one another to the point of fighting, but others intervened, saying, "This is not the kind of argument that can be settled with clubs! Fight with your mouths and tongues!" We agreed, and a few days later a local court was convened to hear the issue.[75] We presented our cases before the elders, but it soon became apparent that the matter could not be resolved without further evidence. Disappointed, I returned home.

Shortly thereafter, my suspicions were verified, when a relative who lived near Munyan came to my homestead to tell me that he had been surprised and concerned to see one of our cattle in the corral of his neighbor—a man called Lokilongiletch. "Munyan killed one of Lokilongiletch's steers, and, in exchange, gave him the heifer of your cow!" he explained. "I knew the heifer belonged to our family, because, since we are all neighbors, I know its sire and dam, which are yours. I went to Munyan and asked him, 'What do you think you're doing? You know that is our cow!' But he denied it."

Five months later I traveled there to explain our predicament to Lokilongiletch, the neighbor, who now had our heifer. I questioned him, "How well do you know Munyan?"

"What do you want?" he asked, irritably.

I explained, "I have heard that you have a heifer that Munyan gave you. The problem is that I think it is my cow."

"*Ala!* But if this cow really is yours, what should I do?"

I replied, "It's up to you to decide what to do about that man! Meanwhile, I am determined to find our cattle! I know there is at least one in your herd, but there could be more. I will have to take your cattle out of the corral for one day, remove the cow in question and cast sand at the rest. If there are any more of my cattle in your herd, the spell will work, and your household will be finished."

He cried out, "Truly, son of Pturu, even I have heard what Munyan has done to your father, and I can't argue with you about injustice! But how do I know that this particular cow is really yours? I need to seal a traditional bond of friendship with you in order to be sure you aren't just trying to take out your vengeance on me!"

"Maybe you are trying to cheat *me!* How do I know?" I answered, paying no attention to his words about the friendship pact.

Lokilongiletch left to discuss the matter with his wife, who was in his mother's house, and I waited a long time. Finally, he came out and challenged me: "If you come without malice, then why do you intend to confiscate my cattle all at once like this? I know how to settle this matter! I will tell Munyan to repay a steer in place of the one he ate; then I will bind your honor by performing the ancient friendship ceremony."

This was not at all what I had had in mind! I was angry, and refused to listen to that man or to discuss the situation further that night.

It was well before dawn when Lokilongiletch's mother awakened me, ranting, "Look, since you made your case with Munyan, we've eaten four milk cows—no more! But they were ours! I don't know what to do with you! You claim we are cheating you! You come here practically a stranger, wanting to wipe out our homestead in one day, and then you would go home satisfied! I am *furious* with you! You refuse to bond yourself to us to prove you have no evil intent! Why, you don't even know these cattle! You don't even know what your own cattle from Munyan's homestead look like! Yet, you have the nerve to be angry at *us*! Now you tell me: How do you expect to find your cattle? Who can describe each one's markings to you?"

I was at a loss to know how to react to this situation. I did not proceed with my plan that day, and in the evening, I was called to that mother's house. There I saw the gourd of beer, which had been prepared and tied to the ceiling beam above the fire. I knew they were going to try to force me into a friendship pact, and I felt terribly uncomfortable.

"Sit on the bed," Lokilongiletch ordered.

This is very serious, I thought. *All I wanted was to get my cattle. I could get angry, refuse food—anything, but this!* But as I stood there, perplexed, Lokilongiletch bodily turned me around and sat me on the bed. The matter was beyond me; I would have to go through with it.

We drank the beer of friendship there until the next morning. The next day, Lokilongiletch entered the goat corral and let out 21 goats. Then he brought three cows: one with a nursing calf and another large one. Together, we led the animals to my father's homestead.

When we arrived, Father told him sternly, "Since you have done this, I order you to get your steer from Munyan. Then I will return your goats and come to get my heifer."

Soon after my new partner left, Father went to see him to explain in detail our long-standing troubles with Munyan and his family. Lokilongiletch was outraged, and left immediately for another homestead where he knew Munyan kept a steer. He claimed the animal and took it home. He has become our friend and cattle associate to this day.

Munyan, we heard, was perplexed when he heard our partner had taken his steer, but he decided it was to his advantage to forget the incident. It would be over a year before I would continue to pursue our claim against him.

Meeting Cheparai

Meanwhile, I established my own homestead in Achorichor with most of the steers from my father's herd. After I had been living there several months, Father summoned me back to Lossom one day and asked me to go to his brother's house at Ptoya to collect some *somongi* containers[76] he needed for his beer, milk and tobacco. I left for Ptoya early the next morning and reached my uncle's house at sunset, just in time to enjoy an evening meal of hot, stiff porridge and milk.

We were still eating, when two girls came into the homestead looking for some calves that had wandered home with my uncle's herd. The oldest one immediately caught my eye. She was especially attractive, with a healthy, tall body, reddish skin, good teeth, large eyes, and a very pleasant manner. She came to greet me, knowing I was a stranger, and went to tether her calves. Intrigued, I beckoned to her little sister and asked, "Where do you live?"

"Oh, our house is very near—just down there!" she replied. They led the calves away, while I watched with interest.

Several hours later I heard some singing coming from another nearby homestead. My aunt's sister called to me, "Domonguria! Come! Let's go to the dance!"

"I'm ready!" I called back, as I went to get my shoes and spear.

The tall, pretty girl was there, along with about sixty others. All of us jumped and sang and started a dance called *ngatian.* The tall girl came to dance with me then, and we played together for the rest of the evening. Afterwards, she and her friends walked part of the way home with us, before the path divided and we went to our separate homesteads.

The next morning, after the cattle and goats were let out, her family called at our gate, and we went together to the neighborhood gardens. I watched the girl there as she tended the crops, and I even found myself gazing at her as she cooked and ate the maize! She seemed charming and industrious, yet one thing bothered me. Whereas she dressed and acted like a circumcised, unmarried girl, her wrist was wrapped with copper wire and tied with the coiled leather bracelet of marriage! It was obvious that she had once been married (a woman cannot remove her wedding bracelet, even if the marriage fails), but I wanted to know more.

That night I asked my aunt, "Mother, that girl has the metal bracelet and rope of marriage on her arm—who tied her with the rope?"

My aunt shook her head and sighed. "I'm telling you the truth, son: three men have married her and she left all of them! The first one paid 15 cattle and 20 goats, the second paid 21 cattle and 25 goats, and the third paid 20 cattle and 12 goats. She rejected them all, and her father had to return all the animals. *Ah!* Now people say, 'Forget about that girl! No one is good enough for her! Let her stay alone!'"

"What do they call her?"

"Cheparai."

"Who is her father?"

"Her father is Ngongeluk and her mother is Cheptei."

I thought this over for a while, trying to accept my aunt's advice, but my desire was too powerful. Finally, I confessed, "Oh mother! Even if she has rejected her husbands, my soul has fallen in love with her! Seducing her would not be enough; I want her forever! If she will have me, I want her to be my wife. What can I do?"

My aunt looked at me with kind, understanding eyes. She did not seem surprised at my outburst.

I asked, hesitantly, "Really, mother, tell me the truth: did she reject *them*, or, indeed, was she so bad that the husbands *made* her go?"

"No! She is a fine girl and knows how to work well," my aunt said emphatically. It was obvious that she liked Cheparai. "But the fact remains that she *did* leave the marriages."

"I know. Maybe it seems unreasonable, but I still want her! But I need to know first whether she will accept *me*."

My aunt laughed. "Oh well, if you want her *that* much, I will ask her for you!"

"Thanks!"

The next morning the neighbors came calling for us once again. After we had been working in the gardens awhile, my aunt beckoned to Cheparai. I saw them talking together, glancing in my direction, and I tried to preoccupy myself with the hoeing.

That evening my aunt told me, "She wanted to know all about your homestead. I told her about your father and all your mothers, and assured her that we know your family well. In fact, I reminded her that we brought two cows from your home just last year. She said she thought it presumptuous of a stranger to come and propose marriage, and I told her, 'What difference does that make? You will be his wife forever, no matter where he comes from! I know the son of Pturu well, and he speaks truly!' Then she said, 'Let me think about this until tomorrow evening. I'll give you my answer then—and I will be honest.'"

I worked next to Cheparai the following day, making conversation, watching her lovely face, and wondering what she was thinking. We returned to the homestead around noon. Late that afternoon, Cheparai came to the corral gate and called to my aunt. They talked together, and Cheparai left. My aunt came back and told me, "She wants to hear the words from your own mouth!"

That night there was another dance. Soon after we arrived, I asked my aunt's sister to tell Cheparai to meet me by a certain large rock nearby. I walked there, and found her waiting for me in the darkness.

"I'm glad to see you," I said.

"I've come," she said quietly. "Now, what do you want?"

"I want *you!*" I exclaimed.

"I have been told so. But—*how* do you want me?" she asked.

"My soul adores you," I said earnestly. "Can you find it in your heart to love me?"

"But I have only just met you! How can you, a stranger, say you want me?"

"I speak with the power of love! There is no rule for finding a wife! If I discover you here, surely I cannot leave you! And if Tororut wants you to meet your husband on the road, then surely it will be so!"

She hesitated. "But ... what do you want me to do now?"

"I want you to be my lover!"

"What sort of lover?"

"A lover who will be my wife forever."

Cheparai looked at me for a long time before casting her eyes down. "I don't know what to do," she said. "I have refused so many men, yet I have heard all about you and your family from your aunt and uncle, and I like what I hear. Did you intend to see my father, or only me?"

"I will not approach your father until I know your desire. I am aware that you rejected others, and that is why I would rather wait until I see that my words please you, and until I find that your words please me. That is all I have to say."

I waited, and in the silence I studied her, while she fidgeted and sighed. Suddenly, she looked up. The worry had vanished from her face, and she was smiling.

"Yes," she said. "It will be as you say. I will not have a *casual* affair with you, but if you want me for your wife, I would love it!"

This was wonderful! We both laughed.

"Done!" I exclaimed. "I admit I want to be your lover now, but I won't leave it at that—I'll take you to my homestead so that my parents and our cattle can see you with their own eyes!"

"Yes, but aren't you going to try to see my father first?"

"No. I'll negotiate with him after I know that the marriage will work out. It's best for both of us that way. Now..."

"Yes?"

"Where can we sleep?"

She smiled. "I don't know. There is one house—a storage house—have you seen the one in the middle?"

"Yes."

"You will find me there tonight."

We went back to the dance and joined in eagerly, then left for our separate homes.

After a few hours, I walked to the village storage house, which was built in the middle of the surrounding homesteads. She was there, waiting for me, and another girl lay near her, asleep. She had spread out the skins well. We embraced, then made love, and it was wonderful. As I lay there afterwards, enjoying the warmth of her beautiful body, I began to worry.

"Cheparai?"

"Hmmm?"

"When I'm talking about something, I don't want ..." This was difficult. Finally, I said, "Cheparai, don't ever contradict me!"

"I won't," she said sweetly, and drew closer.

Tororut's Denial

Very early in the morning, one week later, Cheparai and I left for my home. My aunt had agreed to tell Cheparai's father that she had run away with me, but that she would return. We took gourds of milk, maize, beer and tobacco with us on the donkeys. When we came to the river Suam, we found the water up to my waist. I waded across with the donkeys first, then came back to help Cheparai.

That afternoon we reached Father's homestead. Since it is not considered proper for a person returning home from an extended trip to enter his homestead straightaway, we rested a few minutes nearby. Then Cheparai suggested, "I'll wait outside. You go on in."

I went in the gate and found the mother of Merur. Suddenly, the situation seemed amusing to me, and I called, "Mother! I found a girl near here, but she refused to speak to me! Go ask her where she's from."

"Where is she?"

"Out there under a tree."

Merur's mother went out, questioned Cheparai and then came back. "What's the matter with that child?" she remarked. "She says she comes from Ptoya, but doesn't know where she is going! Can't figure it out! How did you meet her?"

"I don't know."

Just then my sister Chelima came in with her new infant. She had arrived for a visit only the day before. I greeted her fondly, and was admiring the baby, when Merur's mother told her about the girl. Chelima, of course, was not to be fooled. "Something's going on!" she exclaimed. "The girl won't say and neither will he!"

After casting a suspicious glance in my direction, Chelima walked out the gate to greet Cheparai. I could hear their conversation.

"All right, tell me everything!" my sister demanded. "How did you come and with whom?"

"I came from Kenya with a man."

"Who?"

"The man who just came to this house."

"Oh. That's it."

"Yes."

"Yes, now I see! Why didn't you tell the woman just then?"

"I don't know. I just didn't know what to do."

Chelima marched back into the homestead and announced to Merur's mother, "Domonguria has brought a wife! He hasn't yet stopped trying to deceive us! He's brought the daughter of a man!" Soon the news was proclaimed to everyone in the homestead.

My own mother had gone out drinking with my father the day before, and they were expected to arrive later that afternoon. Meanwhile, all the rest of my mothers and uncles got together to prepare for the occasion of letting a new wife into the homestead.

When they were ready, Cheparai was called to stand at the gate of the corral. There, she was presented with an ox which had been won by a spear, a gift that allowed her to enter the corral legitimately as a bride. Once inside, Cheparai was given a male goat, a gesture which "closed" the gate behind her.

"Sit down and rest now," my mothers told her. "Tomorrow we'll find you a scorpion with a long tail, and you will be one of us!" They went to get some milk for her, but Cheparai refused to drink the milk of our cattle until the marriage had been completed. Merur's mother gave her a milk goat, then, so that she could drink from her own animal. After that, all the women hurried off to fetch water so that they could make beer for the marriage ceremony.

When my parents came home that afternoon and found the beer fermenting, Father asked, "What's going on?"

"Domonguria has brought a man's daughter!" volunteered Merur's mother cheerfully.

"Whose daughter?"

"The daughter of a man of Kenya named Ngongeluk."

"Uh...oh....oh..." Father suddenly looked distraught. "The daughter of Ngongeluk?" he repeated.

"Yes. Is something wrong?"

"Ay, ay, aaaaaiiiy," Father moaned. "He is wrong to trouble a man's daughter freely! Now this child—she isn't Cheparai, is she?"

"Why, yes!"

"Ah, then he has troubled her for no reason! No good will come of this! It is beyond me! Hmmm ..., but let it be for now."

All the women protested his concern immediately. "A good wife like this? We don't want to let her go! We want her to stay with us!" they exclaimed, but Father was silent. I had been watching from one of the houses, and I was confused and alarmed by his reaction.

I did not sleep with Cheparai that night, for it is customary not to consummate marriage until the second night after a wife is brought home. The next day passed peacefully, and we lay together that night in preparation for our wedding.

In the morning we welcomed my beautiful Cheparai into our homestead as a wife. All of the ceremonies for that occasion were performed, and I gave her 12 cattle and 18 goats.

It was not until a few days later that my father explained to me the cause of his initial distress over my marriage to Cheparai. He said, "Long ago, my son, the elders of our clan found that if we choose wives from her clan, they will have great difficulty in pregnancy and childbirth. This happened many times in the past and was considered a bad omen. Now we don't marry their daughters, and they don't marry us."

I was concerned, and I spoke to Cheparai about it, but what could we do then? We were very happy together, and determined that nothing would come between us.

But two weeks after that, my father spoke more forcefully. He asked me, "Domonguria, if you get this man's child pregnant, what are you going to do? You have heard the omen: She will be cursed at the time of delivery. I don't like it! The girl should go!"

Cheparai was there, and she exclaimed, "I won't leave! If you want to carry me, go ahead, but I won't go alone!"

I also retorted to my father, "Sir, you are a fool to believe that! You say my wife won't give birth well, but you don't know!"

The following week I took four shillings to the shop to buy beads and brass wire for Cheparai. Joyously, she fastened the rows of beads to form a collar which lay exquisitely over her chest and shoulders. Then I bent the glistening brass carefully to form smooth coils around her neck and arms. It pleased me to be decorating my bride with the colorful jewelry of marriage.

But my Father took Cheparai aside and pleaded, "Child, my child, please listen well to what I have to say! I do not intend to refuse you your husband, and I am not refusing you for my son. But Tororut wronged us all long ago! How can you stay, knowing this?"

Cheparai replied, "I don't understand what you are saying."

"Ah, well," Father sighed, and was silent for a long time after that.

However, three months later, Father came back from drinking beer one day and called, "Daughter-in-law! Come here! Domonguria! Come!"

We obeyed. Then Father called together four little children—two boys and two girls. He told Cheparai to take one boy and one girl and gave me the other two.

Then he asked me, "Who is this," nodding towards Cheparai.

She is my wife," I answered.

He continued, "Daughter-in-law?"

"Yes."

"Who is this?"

"My husband."

"What's this?"

"A child—a girl."

"And this?"

"A boy child."

He asked me the same questions, and then said, "For you two, you husband and wife, what am I to do?"

"We want to have our children," Cheparai said proudly.

"How?"

"We want to have girls and boys."

"Then, my dear, you should go to your father, and you shall find children. You won't find children in this homestead, because Tororut has denied it. Not me! I see you together with children like this and I think, 'Is it not good?'"

"It is good!" we said together.

"Now both of you consider my words. I have thought and thought about this. I have a friend, an elder, who can fix things so that the two of you can live together in good health without children. If you would like me to make arrangements with him, I will do it. You would be childless, but at least you would escape the tragedy and death that a childbirth would bring. Now you must make a decision. Do you want to live without children?"

We thought about Father's words for two weeks. I asked my wife, "What shall we do?" and she answered, "I won't go."

Finally, I traveled to her father's homestead to consult with him. He was not angry about my arrangement with his daughter, but he said, "These words of your father are true. It is like this: we don't marry your children and you don't marry ours. Tororut banned it long ago. Now you go and bring my daughter home."

I went back and told my lovely Cheparai what her father had said. She began to cry.

I said, with difficulty, "Considering what your father and mine have said, what path are we to follow? All of the elders agree. We must end the marriage and return you to your home."

Cheparai cried for a very long time. When she finally regained her composure, she said simply, "You will take me to my father's home."

On the third day, I returned her to her father and left her forever.

My Case Against Munyan

Trying to forget Cheparai, I turned my attention once again to efforts to reclaim our ancestral cattle from Munyan. After I made arrangements for tending the herds, I left for Munyan's homestead, determined to be more aggressive this time. I walked defiantly into his corral, and Munyan bristled. "I know you bring malice!" he yelled. "I don't want anything to do with it!"

"Oh really," I snickered. "Indeed I did come with a purpose—my cattle! I am going to cast sand on your entire herd, and if my cattle are here, they will kill you! If you order me out, I will not leave without bringing misfortune to your family, for you have continuously abused us! Father's leg has been ruined because of your evil mother, yet we took nothing of yours! Now we discover you have been stealing our cattle all along! You repeatedly try to kill us! Why?"

We flew into a rage, ready to lash out at each other. Then Munyan's own brother-in-law reprimanded him, saying, "Really, Munyan, this is despicable! You are about to fight a man who has yet to do anything bad in your homestead!"

Munyan cooled down slightly, and I put on my shoes, took my spear and walked away towards the homestead of my partner Lokilongiletch. Munyan was immediately suspicious and sent a boy to follow me. He questioned Lokilongiletch's wife and announced that Munyan wanted me to return. I said to the boy, "Tell Munyan that if he has already let even one cow of mine out of his corral, I will return peacefully today. Otherwise, I will bring him trouble tomorrow!"

The next morning, I assembled nearly fifty people from the area and made a case against Munyan. The elders agreed with me. They told Munyan, "You have wronged this man, and we see he is a good man. Find the words that will satisfy Pturu's son. He is persistent! Why, he wonders, did you not follow through with the case you tried to make in Kapenguria several years ago?"

"That case is closed," I interrupted, trying not to complicate the matter. "But you have cheated us. Tomorrow I will bring the head of a hyena, and we will see if you are lying! After that, we will leave your cattle alone and let the magic decide." To make this oath, I would place the hyena head at the corral gate, together with an *arenyon*—a red sapling painted with red and white stripes, the white pigment having been mixed with hyena dung. All of the cattle and Munyan's children would have to jump over them when I said, *Jump! If any of my cattle are here, they will kill you!*

"No!" Munyan objected nervously. "I won't do that! If you bring a hyena head to my homestead, I won't cooperate. It is evil! You want to murder us!"

One man remarked, "Now if you refuse that, what do you intend to do? If you want this case finished, tell him you will give him his cattle tomorrow, and he will take them home."

"No," said Munyan. "I want to go to Muru, near Kupkomo to discuss this with the Kamaril (lion clan) part of the family."

I laughed sarcastically. "You want to go there really? Do you honestly think those people will agree? Just who do you expect to find at Muru? My uncle Akolingoro made an oath with those people long ago and they have all perished! You won't find anyone there—two clans in that family died as a result of our dealings with Makal! If there is one man left, he certainly won't want to come see *us!* He'll tell you, 'No! That man is a true wizard! If one goes to see him, he will die when he returns home! He wields a powerful poison!' But we'll set aside the case, and I'll give you permission to go for one month. After that, I'll be ready for you—we won't fart around like this then! Now I'll go home."

I did return in one month, but Munyan was still not home. After five days, I decided to leave to tend to my father's herds and other affairs.

A SON

Chepochesondu's Good News

The next year, I had an opportunity to continue presenting my grievance against Munyan to the elders. However, after only two days of testimony, I was called home again and informed, through a messenger, that an important matter awaited me at the home of my current girlfriend Chepochesondu. Confused, I left immediately for her homestead.

Chepochesondu's father greeted me and asked, "Do you know why I have sent for you?"

I replied honestly, "No. In the past I've come only to play with your daughter."

"Well, you'll find out. Meanwhile, make yourself at home!"

Almost an hour and a half later, a little girl called, "Mother wants you to come to our house!" I followed her and saw that her mother had already prepared food for me. After the meal, the woman asked, "Have you heard the news—the reason we sent for you?"

I told her there had been no explanation.

"Well then ...Why have you come here in the past?" she asked (as if she didn't know!)

"I really don't understand what this is all about," I said, exasperated. "Your daughter and I have been lovers, that's all."

"Well thanks for mentioning *that!*" She looked relieved. "Go talk to your girl-friend now, and then come back to tell us your decision."

Puzzled, I went to Chepochesondu's house and asked her, "What's going on here?"

She smiled. "Well, I think I'm pregnant, and they have found out," she said quietly. "They asked me who made me pregnant, and I told them, 'The son of Pturu has been my lover.' They wanted to know if there have been others, and I assured them there has been no one else." Then she looked up at me seriously and declared, "They wanted you to know, in case you want to marry me. That is why they called you."

"*Ala!* Truly this is great news!" I exclaimed. "How long do you think you've been pregnant?"

Two months now."

"Good! This is wonderful! Thank you very much for carrying my child!"

We sat down together, and I tried to organize my thoughts about this new and complicated revelation. Finally, I explained, "The only problem is my father. He is a very fierce man—no one is more hot-tempered than he! I truly don't know whether he will be willing to give away the cattle for you or not. If he refuses, no man will go against his will. But if he agrees, he will say so at once, and we will follow through."

"But what about *you*—I mean, your *soul?*" Chepochesondu asked earnestly.

"There is no other answer," I assured her. "I want you and, because of that, you say you want me! Tororut has surely blessed us with this pregnancy! It is wonderful! People will certainly be surprised when they hear we are going to have a baby! Everyone will rejoice!"

When Chepochesondu and I had finished talking, I went back to her mother's house. I declared, "Truly you beckoned me to hear happy news! Why didn't you tell me earlier?"

"We wanted to be sure you had indeed been her lover and were responsible for her pregnancy. You see, no one knows whether or not you intend to marry her."

I explained, "The truth is that I have no choice in the matter. It's up to my father. I hope to make her my wife, especially under the circumstances. In any case, I certainly have no intentions of ignoring her or pretending that I have not been her lover. In fact, from today onwards, I will no longer come and go at night surreptitiously as I have in the past. I will come in daylight."

"Thank you," she said. "You are free to go now. I only wanted your words, nothing else. You may come to see my daughter as you wish."

I went out to take a nap under a shade tree.

Later that night, Loriongole called me once again to his wife's house. He asked me the same questions, and I explained my circumstances as I had before. I finished by saying, "I can say no more. Please invite my father to come to your house, so you can ask him all you want to know. I am merely his cowherd—the cattle belong to him! If he agrees to the marriage, there will be no problem. His fortune is sufficient. He could give you twenty to forty cattle without difficulty. The only trouble so far is that we have yet to approach him about this!"

Chepochesondu's father said, "Thank you. Now go sleep with your sweetheart. Tomorrow, go home and ask your father to come here. Return on the day after tomorrow."

I left the next morning for Father's homestead and told him everything.

"Stupid! he exploded. *Idiot!"* He swore loudly and began slapping me repeatedly with such force that I had to retreat. He yelled, "You say they want me to come there? You *fool!* I'm not about to go! I didn't send you to his daughter! This is *your* fault! If you have a fortune, *you* go pay the bride wealth! If you have none, that's your problem!"

I sulked until the next day, when I forced myself to repeat Father's words to Loriongole. He was incensed, but his wife calmed him. "Don't be angry at Domonguria," she said. "Now your child is pregnant and there is nothing you can do!"

I slept with Chepochesondu that night, and left with a heavy soul.

Curse on Munyan

In my distress, I had nearly forgotten about the case with Munyan that awaited me. This time, my father and my brother Lopeyok accompanied me to the house of Lokilongiletch, Munyan's neighbor, who was now bound to us as both friend and cattle associate. Well before dawn the following morning, the three of us walked to Munyan's homestead and made a fire outside the corral. There my father beckoned to his cattle, saying:

If you, my cattle, are here in the homestead of the son of Kitelamoi, open your mouths, because you smell me and know that your father has come to see you. If you are here, cry out! I demand, by the spirits of our ancestors, that you open your mouths! Smell my odor, and if I am not your father, keep quiet. If I am, cry out, so that I might hear! I will tell you what I have in mind, but first I must hear your lowing."

My father sat down, and I stood and repeated the same message to the cattle. My brother followed me. Then my father got up and announced, "We have now said it three times."

At once, the cattle started lowing—crying out!

Father said, *"Thank you. Alas, you are here! I see now that you have indeed swindled me of my cattle, Munyan. You have heard the cattle bellow! We will take them and leave you trouble! Now I call to the hyena: if you are nearby in the countryside, hear the sounds of my cattle, as they cry out from the homestead of Munyan! These are the cattle by which we make an oath upon your head. If you hear me, hyena, cry out now!"* … We waited only a short time before the hyena called out four times, then stopped. *"Thank you!"* Father answered. *"Now I will instruct you: Each night, when it is the time*

Tororut decreed that you should prowl in the darkness, come by the homestead of Munyan and sit in this place to wait for nourishment. I will give you food here every month! You are quiet now, and have heard my orders."

Munyan's neighbors, his wives and his people—all who heard our threat—were very much afraid. One of Munyan's wives ran away that very night, saying, "Who would stay now in this homestead? This family's cattle have killed people in the past! It must be that my husband has stolen this man's cattle and they are here! I will escape this doom!" And so this wife, Chepusokong, left her husband and her children and fled.

One man pleaded to my father, "Don't stay on the low side of the homestead, the place of the dead! Come on the high ground by the cattle gate!"

At first, Father refused, saying, "I will stay here until it is time for me to go. Then I will leave by the gate," but that man begged him so much that he agreed.

Everyone began to question Munyan, who was now obviously afraid: "How long have these people—their cattle—been in your homestead?"

He answered, "I can't say, but I will give him the cow which is mooing—the one whose tail was cut off long ago by an unknown cause. It has a calf of two months."

Father resisted. "We are not satisfied with these cattle! We will go home and return later."

Everyone started yelling at Munyan, then, crying, "How could you steal from another man? Do you want our children to die? You are killing our children and our children's children, and you will die with them, until only our cattle remain!"

The in-laws threatened, "If you steal from Pturu, we want to take back our daughters, since you desire them dead! You heard it—the hyena is waiting for people on the low ground, where Pturu made the fire!"

Finally, Munyan conceded six cattle, saying, "Take these now. There is another cow far away at another homestead. You will eventually get all your cattle."

We took the six cattle home that day.

Five months later we returned, only to find, to our amazement, that Munyan had gone to Kacheliba to challenge us! We followed him there, and each of us presented our case to the chief.

One witness said, "Munyan wrongly concealed this man's cattle, until Pturu came to call them, and they answered him. We all heard—all the neighbors, their wives and small children! His wife ran away! He is a very bad man! Don't listen to him. Don't give in to him. He is our enemy and wants to kill our children."

The chief told Munyan to name all the cattle that belonged to Pturu, even those which might be far away. "Say them all and I will write them in my book", he demanded.

Munyan had no choice.

We took 16 cattle from him at that time. Then we went to round up cattle he had claimed were at seven other homesteads. At one place, the people balked, saying, "We don't even know the cattle of that man! He told you wrongly!" We believed them. Munyan had been right about some cattle, but wrong about others. We took the ones that everyone agreed were ours.

In the end, we believed we had claimed most—but probably not all—of our ancestral cattle. Father was satisfied. Nevertheless, he had left Munyan with the curse, and that man died three years later. His people have not forgotten us. Just the other day, I asked about the children of Munyan, and the elders cried to me, "Let it be! If you try for more cattle, these children will die, for they don't even know whose cattle are whose!"

I have heard the words of the elders, and have now agreed to let the matter rest.

The Birth of My Son

During the time we were dealing with Munyan and bringing our cattle home, I had been unable to visit Chepochesondu, who was pregnant with my child. Restless and upset, I had begun seeing another girl, named Chemukan, but my soul ached for the woman who should have been my wife.

The day we heard the news that Chepochesondu had given birth to a baby boy, Father let out three large steers and commanded me, "Take these to the girl's homestead."

Loriongole accepted the cattle, but demanded, "What will the child eat? I see you have not brought food to support my child."

I reported this to Father, who sent me back again with his message: "This child will become mine. I will feed him until he is grown and supports himself."

Chepochesondu's father was outraged at this suggestion. "No! My child will not go to your homestead! Bring food for him here!" Once again I carried the message home.

"I see that man is rejecting his child," scoffed Father. "Go sell one steer, son. Bring me the money."

I received 258 shillings for the steer. I used four shillings to buy clothes, five for beads and one for tobacco. I handed the rest to Father. He gave me 100 shillings to take to Loriongole, who was now satisfied. "Good," he said. "My child has now found food. You can go home."

And so my infant son, Nyangaluk, stayed with his mother.

Circumcision

At the time of the next rains [1946],[77] I was finally able to be circumcised. Once again, initiates came from far and near to a place in Kenya authorized by the elder of Cheptulel. There we built the circumcision house, where we would live for the next three months. It was very large and had two doors.[78] No fire was allowed in the house. It was off-limits to uncircumcised men, other than the initiates *(tios)*, and, of course, to women. One elder was appointed to tend to the house, and several others had the responsibility of serving us the food our mothers prepared and brought for us.

The *tios* consisted of many age groups. Some were small, some were older boys, and some were adult men like me. Just like the *chemerin*, we *tios* slept on *susinion* grass, rather than on skins. We sang together and urinated on the same nearby tree, which was selected for the exclusive use of the initiates, even before the house was built. (This tree would wither and die after our departure.) Because we were circumcised together, we became like brothers. Hereafter, we could neither seduce nor marry the child of any man we slept with in the circumcision house.

It is said that when the *tios* sing, the sound is so beautiful that women and uncircumcised boys who are very near will swoon! Whenever our mothers brought food to the compound, the men stationed outside called to alert us: "Your mothers come now! Sing!" Our mothers would hear the sweet sound of our voices and begin to wave fat-filled horns up and down, pausing to dip their hands in the fat and spread it on the chests of nearby men who had been circumcised. They were enchanted by the singing and wanted to go to their sons, but if any tried to enter the circumcision house, they were stopped!

We *tios*, in turn, were happy and grateful to our mothers for bringing us food during this time, and, indeed, for our entire upbringing, and so each initiate sang for his mothers' ears to tell her, "Come, mother, with pride, for you have raised me well. You took all the proper precautions during pregnancy and guided me well though childhood. Indeed, all I am and all I have is due to you!"

We sang, then, the same two songs a mother sings to announce that she has just given birth to a baby boy. (A boy whose mother has died will sing to the other mothers who are tending to him, but will not sing those parts which refer to his natural mother.) In these songs, Chepkur is the Original Mother. The mothers of the initiates are referred to by the names of two of the many garments they wear, especially during the circumcision of their sons: the *pemoi*, a skin neckpiece in the shape of an apron, with long, narrow iron bells sewn on each side so that they clang together, and the skin *lukutia* belts, decorated with rows of cowrie shells, which have special significance in child-rearing.[79] The *chepomut* is a bull with very large horns. Its name is *Sangarian*. We begin with the song *Kuparaka*.

A very big occasion! A very big occasion!	*Kuparaka a oye, oo, Kuparaka*
Sons of Nunu! Sons of Chepkur!	*Werpu Nunu! Werpu Chepkur!*
People of shut-in children	*Werpu karmoi*
A big occasion!	*Kuparaka!*

Verses (sung in any order)

Tell Chepkur a oye	Lenjina Chepkur a oye
Go to Marich!	Wiya nyi Marik
Get the pemoi!	Wiya male pemoi!
Take out the ox horns, a oye	Wiya chenga lale, a oye
The horns of a chepomut a oye oo, oo	Lale to chepomut a aye oo, oo
The horns of Sangarian!	Lale to Sangarian
Tell the cowrie-shelled belt	Lenjina sekermu
Put fat inside	Tena nyi mwada
Get ready to annoint us!	Yela ewoo, yela kopach!
Tell her stomach	Lenjina cheptomu
Of the lukutus (beaded belt)	Woke lukutus
Come near the door	Nyono kumbul or
Come, my mother	Nyono nyi yo nyuno
Come to the house (of tios), wave (the horns)!	Nyono nyi ka pkeyass!

The second song can also include all the other verses from the first song

Refrain:

Olileye, oyeoo, olileye	Olileye oyeoo olileye

Verses:

Sons of Nunu, ah olileye	Werpu Nunu a olileye
Boys who are shut in, ah	Werpu karmoi a
Tell the cowrie-shelled belt, ah …	Lenjina sekermu …

The male circumcision rituals are, in many ways, similar to those of girls' circumcision, but the ceremony is on a much larger scale. (I don't know who determined these customs, but I believe it must have been Kupeiyeng, the bald Original Father.) About two weeks after the circumcision, when our wounds were somewhat healed, we went to the beer drinking ceremony called *lupol*, like that of the *chemerin*. Then, half a month later, when we began going outside, each of us wore a mask, consisting of a fringe of bark-fiber ropes, laced together, dyed with red ochre, and tied around the forehead so that the ropes hung down to cover the face. If a *tiosion* sees his mother, he will lower the hood of ropes to cover his eyes and will lie down until his mother goes by, just like a *chemerion* hides from her father. It is very bad for the mother to see his face at this time.

Finally, just as the *chemerin* demand *teroi* from young men, the *tios* demand the same from girls they meet. However, we *tios* made special weapons for this purpose: small rounded objects mounted onto arrow shafts. If we came across a girl who had not yet given us *teroi*, we would shoot her in the leg several times until she limped! Thus, all girls made an effort to find metal beads to give us! We traveled far in search of the decorations, sometimes sleeping two or three nights in the bush on a quest. At night, during these journeys, we would stand at the gate of a homestead to ask for food, singing the traditional song for opening the door:

Oh elephant	*Oh ya pelion e, ah ho-e, ho-e*
Open the door, elephant	*Iyata orenyo, pelion e, ahe*
Open for the cattle to come!	*Iyata or roto toka*

Upon entering, we would sing:

Oye, Ancient Father, hoye	*Oye Kuko, hoye*
Hoyaoo yoa yao oo, oo yoa, yao	*Hoyaoo yoa yao oo, oo yoa, yao*
O Kupeiyeng (bald man) *mm*	*Oh ye Kupeiyeng, mm*
Tell Chepkur	*Lenjina Chepkur*
Prepare to anoint us!	*Yela eoo yela kupach, oya*
Tell the cowrie-shelled belt	*Lenjina sekermu*
Go to Marich	*Wiya Marik*
Go get horns	*Wiya chenga lale*
Horns of chepomut	*Lale to chepomut*
Put fat inside	*Tena nyi mwada*
Come to the house, wave (the horns)	*Nyono nyi ka pkeyass*

Then we would sing the two circumcision songs described above. There were many other songs, as well, but these are the most important. When we sang the songs of *tios*, the women of the homestead we were visiting always supplied our needs, giving us a steer to slaughter and eat.

After our three-month period of seclusion was over, each of us killed a goat or steer to leave at the circumcision site for those who had helped with the rituals. We threw away any projectiles we had left, took off our old clothes and donned any new ones we had, as well as all the new beads people had brought us. As I came out of the house, my mother greeted me and anointed my head with milk, just as my father had done for Chelima at her circumcision. Then she presented me with an ox. My initiation was complete.[80]

All circumcised men are identified by the year in which they are circumcised.[81] I was circumcised in the year *kurongora*. If the elders decide that there are too many initiates for one year, some of them will be circumcised another year, and they might be called by a different name, such as *kupkoimut* or *sowa*. In the past, other names were also used, but they have since been rejected for various reasons. *Sombai* was rejected, for instance, after lions and leopards ate many of the initiates. *Kinou* was thrown out after torrential rains that year brought hardship to the land. People were unable to go out to eat, drink water or collect firewood, and the cattle had nowhere to graze. *Nyongu* was eliminated because its initiates murdered people in excess; they would hike great distances for a month at a time, murder all the inhabitants, eat their cattle, and travel on to kill more people and eat their wealth, like soldiers do today. Many of the circumcision years named *kurongora* have also produced renowned fighters, and I understand some of the elders are concerned about this. Others want to leave the name alone for awhile.

Fighting for Custody

After I returned from Kenya, I found my girlfriend, Chemukan, quite pregnant. I acknowledged responsibility for the pregnancy and spoke to her family, but we did not talk of marriage. Unfortunately, our baby died at birth.

Meanwhile, my rejected "wife" Chepochesondu lived at her father's homestead, while our son grew out of infancy and began to toddle about. When he was ready to be weaned, Father let out two cows and one steer, and we brought them to Chepochesondu's mother. Our purpose was to take the child with these cattle.

Chepochesondu was furious. "I will not give up my child!" she protested.

I murmured, "And I don't want to give up my wife."

Father glared at me. "Well if you have the cattle, give them! Go marry her if you can! But since you have no cattle, I don't see that you have any say in the matter!"

Loriongole also refused to let the boy go, but my father warned him, "Our child does not like the milk of other cows. He won't thrive! It is the way Tororut made things long ago: when a baby lives on the milk of other people's cattle, his body won't thrive! Do you want my grandson to be emaciated? You'd better take care of my boy!"

Worried, Chepochesondu brought the child to stay at our homestead for two months. She lived with me like a wife, and, together with our son Nyangaluk, we were a happy family. Then Chepochesondu's father, uncle and mother arrived, demanding, "We want our cattle if you want our daughter! We want thirty cattle and twenty goats—fifty altogether!"

"I shall not pay even one cow!" Father snapped. "If you want to take your daughter, take her! But I refuse to give up my boy Nyangaluk. I have paid goats for him."

Angrily, Chepochesondu's family left, and Chepochesondu soon followed, taking our son back to her father's house. I was distraught.

At last, in desperation, Father decided to put an end to the matter by arranging a marriage for me. After a two-day visit to one of his acquaintances, Father approached me cheerfully, declaring, "Son, I know you want a wife, and since I rejected the mother of your child, I have found another girl for you! Now you can forget Nyangaluk's mother!"

Totally surprised, I asked, "Where is this girl you want to give me?"

He told me that he had discussed the matter with his friend, telling him, "That boy has exasperated me over a girl he got pregnant! I won't have her! In fact, I would like your child instead. What do you say?"

"Well, I don't know," the man had answered. "No one knows whether he will love my daughter. Maybe he wants to marry the mother of his child."

Father had protested, "No! He won't disobey me."

But the man had declared, "Who knows? Before I make a decision, I must hear whether or not he agrees to my daughter."

"And so I want you to go and see her, son," Father concluded. "Tell me what you think of her."

I had no choice. The next day I walked straight to that man's homestead and saw the girl. She was pitifully short! Downright *incomplete!* I thought: *Aw! Surely, I don't want this! Taking her would be like taking nothing! I can't have her!* But I was in a real spot, then, because the people had seen me come in. Nevertheless, I was determined not to incriminate myself. Her father came to welcome me, asking, "Why have you come?"

"Oh, I was just walking by," I lied, too obviously.

'No, tell me what you want to say," he prodded.

"Say? I don't have anything to say," I stammered ridiculously. "I'm just walking in the area."

"Your father came the other day to talk about my daughter."

Oh no, I thought. "Oh, *really?* He never told me that!"

"Are you sure?"

"Yes."

"I don't believe it! Why did you come here then? You don't usually come this way."

"Oh, well, I was—just looking at the land! I noticed it rained here recently, and I was curious to see if there was much grass here for the cattle. The grass is sparse over there, you know." *Maybe I could distract him with some small talk,* I thought.

"You are resisting me."

"Ah! There is nothing!" I shrugged and turned away.

I slept there that night and left for Lossom early the next morning. "Aren't you going to wait for breakfast?" my father's friend called after me, but I kept going.

Father greeted me expectantly. "Well, what do you think of her?" he asked.

"*A-a-a-a-a-a-a-a-ah!* I can't agree to this! A short thing like *that!* No! I don't want it!" I shook my head vehemently.

Father was not understanding. He shouted, "You *fool!* How dare you play around like this when you have no wealth! You are the one who will suffer!

Stay in the *aperit*! You can forget about any bride wealth from me! Do what you want! I don't have any desire for you to find a wife!"

Several months later, Loriongole came to us, concerned. "Come, look at your baby," he said. "He is emaciated, yet there is plenty of food and everything else! I don't know why he is so thin. He eats well."

"It's your doing," Father said. "I told you to bring my son here."

The next week, Chepochesondu brought Nyangaluk to our homestead. We were alarmed to see that our boy was terribly ill. Father, convinced that little Nyangaluk could be saved only by living with us and drinking our milk, decided to clarify the situation once and for all. He ordered Chepochesondu, "Leave the child here and go home to your father! I'm determined not to give any cattle for your bride price: there is no future for you here."

He finally explained to her, "The reason is this: I have seen that your mother makes a lot of noise, and I'm afraid that you, too, will nag, just like your mother. I can't have people around who shout all the time! I have even heard that you yell at people already! I will not allow loudmouthed women in my homestead! So now you know why I don't want you to stay here. Forget my son and go! If you want something—a cow or anything else— just say so, and I will give it to you if you will just leave us alone!"

He turned to me and threatened, "Now, from this day onwards, I don't want to hear that you are sleeping with this girl! If you defy me, I will cut you off for ten years without a wife. There will be no cattle for your bride price. If you obey me, you may marry quickly."

I was crest-fallen. This was the end, and I knew it.

Father, seeing this, added, more gently, "Don't you realize, Domonguria, that if you continue to sleep with Nyangaluk's mother, she'll certainly get pregnant once more? Then you'll be in the same spot. It is bad luck to go back to her! You'll end up crying, 'I'm finished! Because of sleeping with that girl, Father has cut me off for many years!' On the other hand, if you follow my advice, all will be well for you, because you are my oldest son. Even if you don't want the girl I chose for you, there are many other girls: I'll find you another, or, if you find one your heart desires, come tell me!"

My son Nyangaluk has stayed with us ever since. He soon regained his health, and my father and his third wife, Moiyoiyin, brought him up as their own child. (Indeed, until he was an adult, Nyangaluk did not know that I was his true father.)

Shortly after Chepochesondu left, she was married and went to live at her husband's homestead. Nevertheless, through the years she has continued to visit frequently at Father's homestead, just to see her son, even though Nyangaluk will never know she is his natural mother.

CHEPUSEPA

The Baringo Incident

In the spring of 1950, Lukas Pketch, a leader of the religious group Msambwa, proclaimed to the people of Churo, "I have the most wonderful ox of all! This ox will drive away the Europeans! Pay attention to my ox song!" He attracted many followers.[82]

One day, when Pketch and his disciples were eating meat together by the river at Kalowa, in the region of Baringo, some policemen came to question them.

"You have no right to examine me," Lucas protested. "Go tell your boss to come himself, if he wants to discuss something with me!"

The policemen reported this to their superiors, and four Europeans drove to Kalowa to investigate the matter. They parked their car at the base of the hill, and then, carrying guns, climbed up to confront the followers of Lucas. When they reached the crest of the hill, the four suddenly found themselves face to face with hundreds of Pokot warriors with their spears raised!

"Wait!" one European began, as the warriors started walking towards him.

"Stop!" another ordered, but the warriors advanced. "Stop, or we'll shoot!"

The Pokot kept coming, and the four Europeans opened fire. They shot three or four times into the crowd, killing many. The warriors fought back. Someone hurled a spear, killing the first European, named Simpson, and then two more Europeans fell. The fourth managed to escape to his car, where he kept a powerful gun that could kill scores of people at once. Shooting from the window, he alone killed or wounded hundreds of Pokot men, before driving away.

Following that incident, white people came from Nairobi, Nakuru and all over the country to build a settlement and outpost at Kalowa. They jailed many people and fined others. I was told they confiscated 12,000 cattle and goats! Relentlessly, they tried to hunt down all those who had taken part in Msambwa and the incident at Baringo.

Their officers asked Chief Kongolikope, of Kingyang, for a list of names, but he refused to cooperate. "I don't know any of them," he said, but the Europeans knew he was lying. They put some metal sheeting over a fire and told him, "If you are telling the truth, then prove it by walking barefoot across this fire and back again. If you can do that, we'll believe you!"

Kongolikope tried to explain, "I don't want my people to hang! Multitudes have already been slaughtered on account of these three Europeans, and many herds have been seized. Is that not enough?"

"Let's see you walk on the corrugated iron, and then we'll listen!" the Europeans retorted.

Kongolikope removed his shoes. He walked across the red-hot iron and back again. The white men were silenced, and Kongolikope became a hero amongst my people.

Some people cried over the slaughter at Baringo, but most discounted it as a matter of Tororut's Providence. Instead of moaning, we prefer to remember the incident in this popular song:

Refrain:
> *Woye Baringo, ah Baringo!*
> *Surprise the enemy!*

Verses:
> *Let's go to Tiati!*
> *Ah Tiati, surprise the enemy!*
> *Let's go to Kalowa!*
> *Ah Kalowa, surprise the enemy!*
> *The Ngidewai* fought at noon.*
> *Ah, at noon, surprise the enemy!*
> *The Ngipurut* fight at noon. Ah, at noon …*
> *People of Churo fight at noon. Ah, at noon …*
> *They killed Simpson at noon. Ah, at noon …*
> *Oh Baringo, ah Baringo! Surprise the enemy!*

> *Woye Baringo, Ah Baringo,*
> *Tingja puung*
>
> *Owun owun Tiati!*
> *Ah Tiati, tingja puung*
> *Owun owun Kalowa!*
> *Ah Kalowa, tingja puung*
> *Kiporio ngidewai saa sita*
> *Ah saa sita…*
> *Kiporio ngipurut saa sita …*
> *Kiporio ka Chura saa sita …*
> *Kikuparr Simsim saa sita …*
> *Oh Baringo, ah Baringo, tingja puung*

*(circumcision years)

A Suitable Bride

While those people were fighting at Baringo, I was falling in love with another girl very much like Chepochesondu, the mother of my son Nyangaluk. She was the daughter of Lotiom, tall and lovely, and her name was Chepusepa. She responded to my advances with affection and finally, one night I convinced her to sleep with me. Afterwards, I knew that this, without a doubt, was the girl I wanted to marry!

Chepusepa lived with her family at Lomunan, near Kadam Mountain, and it wasn't long before I had established my own homestead nearby. Our romance continued to blossom there, and the two of us dared to hope that we might spend the remainder of our lives together—if our marriage could be properly and happily sanctioned. Everything (as I had learned so painfully in the past) depended on our parents' approval.

Although we were now neighbors, I had not yet had an opportunity to meet Chepusepa's father, and I worried a lot about how to approach him. I decided to try something like: *"Sir, I'd like permission to speak with you about a girl I think is your daughter."* Then—should I tell him she had already accepted me? That we had slept together? Depending on his reaction, I would decide that later.

Nervously, I entered Chepusepa's homestead and, after questioning, found that Lotiom was inside the house of his most recent wife. I went, appropriately, to the house of Chepusepa's mother, Lotiom's first wife, and sent Chepusepa's younger sister to fetch her father. He came shortly, together with Chepusepa's mother. They sat opposite me.

I began, "Sir, I have recently moved here from Lossom. Do you know me?"

"No, I don't know you! We used to live at Lossom, but we moved away and settled here in Lomunan some time ago. That is probably why I don't remember you."

"Don't you even know my father?"

"Is he still alive?"

"Yes. Both he and Mother are very healthy."

"What's his name?"

"His name is Pturu, and my mother is Cheparkong."

"I don't remember them. What do you want?"

"I have seen your daughter—the tall one, and I want her! I need to know whether you accept or reject me as your daughter's husband." I waited, hoping.

"Well, off-hand, I reject you!" he declared. Then, seeing the abrupt disappointment in my face, Lotiom explained, "Of course, I have no reason to take vengeance on you in particular. But it would be different if my daughter was in love with you. Then I would not stand in your way."

His wife interjected, "I'll bet he has led your daughter astray!"

"No, I have done nothing wrong!" I protested, but she paid no attention. "Because," she continued, "I heard that the other day, she went with him to the homestead of Moichir. Both of them slept there in one house by themselves! Now, do you think they slept separately? Of course not! Your daughter gave in to that youth!"

This revelation made a considerable difference in Lotiom's attitude. "Well, so you and she are lovers?"

"Yes."

"In that case, I will have to consider this, but I can't answer you now."

"I only wanted to know whether you would agree to me as a person, sir," I pursued. "My intentions are honorable."

Lotiom smiled. "If my daughter loves you, then I'm not about to reject you! There is nothing else to say."

"Then, if you have no objection, sir, tomorrow I will go to my father and tell him, so that he can come and plan the exchange with you. You see, I have no wealth of my own. I merely tend to my father's cattle. If he doesn't want to pay bride wealth, there is nothing I can do about it."

"Yes, I know."

The next morning, I returned to Lossom and told my father about Chepusepa. He listened intently. "Indeed!" he remarked when I had finished. "What are the good qualities of your girl?"

"She is a person! No one yet knows her attributes," I said truthfully.

"Yes, go tell your brother-in-law I want him."

Lopedur and my sister Chelima lived nearby. I explained the situation to them, and they both came back with me. My father had beer waiting for us. We drank, and then Father asked Lopedur if he knew Chepusepa.

"I'm not sure. Who is her father, Domonguria?"

"Lotiom."

"That man has many children. Which one is this?"

"Oh, this girl is absolutely the Number One of all his daughters!" I said enthusiastically. "She is much taller than all the others."

"Oh yes! I know her!" Lopedur exclaimed. "One day your sister and I went to a dance of *laleyo* at Lomunan, and we noticed a most attractive girl there. Afterwards, on our way home, Chelima asked me, 'Which one of the girls at the *laleyo* would you want to marry?' and I told her, honestly, 'There is only one who appealed to me!' Then I asked her, 'Which one did you like?' She teased me and said, 'I'll tell you mine, but you tell me yours first!'

"So I admitted, 'There is only one wife for me there. There were two very tall girls, but forget one of them!' I described the other one and said, 'That is who I really want for a wife! Perhaps I'll take her!' Your sister laughed and exclaimed, 'That's the one I saw! There isn't any other! We both like the same one. She was my choice too!' Chelima was even more enthusiastic than I was!

"Now, Father, that is the very girl Domonguria desires!" Lopedur went on cheerfully. "It must be that all of our hearts love the same girl! I am delighted that Domonguria has chosen her, even though I know nothing about her work or her ways. If there are people who can vouch for her, then I think we should take the cattle!"

"I'll ask some of my good friends from that area what they know about her," I offered.

"Go then," said Father. "I have some work to do here. By the time the moon rises for the third time, I will be at that homestead. Take my walking stick tomorrow to her father. Tell him to hold it until I arrive to discuss the matter of his daughter."

Happily, we drank the beer until it was finished.

The next morning I awoke, feeling ecstatic over the previous day's developments. Passion and romance energized me! It was dawn, and I went to check on the cattle, still lying outside, where they usually slept during the rainy season so that they could graze at night. Suddenly, my gaze fell upon an attractive young woman passing nearby.

"Where is that girl going?" I called to Mother.

"To the gardens."

"Where are her gardens?"

"Over by the river Lossom."

"Is anyone with her?"

"She's alone—you can see that!" Mother looked at me curiously.

In those days, I was impetuous, foolhardy, and especially zealous when it came to sex. I wanted to seduce every eligible female that came near me! I charged towards that girl like a gust of wind and ambushed her.

Startled and confused, she cried, "Leave me alone!" Then, assessing the situation more realistically, she added, cleverly, "Please—the animals will eat up our gardens, if I tarry now. I really must go! Otherwise, I certainly wouldn't refuse you—you are an attractive man! Come to the gardens tonight, and you'll find me sleeping there alone." These last words saved her, even though I knew she was lying.

"Sure," I agreed, "but if I find you there, you won't escape me!" I let her go.

Laughing at the girl's ingenuity, I went back for my spear and shoes, and left for Lomunan, carrying my father's stick to present to Chepusepa's father.

Later that day, I began my investigation into Chepusepa's reputation. All those I interviewed agreed, "There is nothing wrong with that girl! She is a fine person and does good work. She is pleasant and honest. If you find her attractive, then you will treasure her." Wives can have three main faults: bickering, stealing and preparing food during menstruation. I was convinced that, as a wife, Chepusepa would have none of these bad traits.

Similarly, Father had to approve of Chepusepa's clan. As I learned, to my distress, when I tried to marry Cheparai, we must be careful to choose wives only from clans that, in the past, have successfully and repeatedly married into our own. For instance, there is one clan named Tol, or Tulin, whose daughters, named Chemutangwut, are very beautiful, but dangerous to most husbands. If a first-born Chemutangwut is a boy, the child will kill his father when he is only three or four years of age. Then, if other men try to marry the widow, the boy will kill them as well! They say one woman from this clan was responsible for the deaths of 15 husbands! Men of only three clans—the Baboon (mine), the Hyena, and the Donkey—can marry these women without fear.

Whereas everyone insists that a marriage of compatible clans has a greater chance of producing children who will thrive and escape misfortune, these considerations apply only to people who come from a pure Pokot lineage. There can be no such restrictions about marrying women of another tribe, for we only know the history of our own people. Thus, I was happy to discover that Chepusepa's family, while fully integrated into our culture, was not Pokot. They were Kadam,[83] the people of the mountain. There would be no worries about her clan!

The elders say that long ago, perhaps during the last century, when our people moved into this area, we fought three times with the people of Kadam, before we finally overcame them. When the last battle was over, we drew our peoples together and our leaders told the Kadam survivors, "Surrender to us, and we shall become one people together! Of course, if you refuse, you are at our mercy, for we have conquered you!" They agreed, naturally, and our peoples have lived harmoniously together ever since. While the Kadam elders retain many of their ancient ways, especially their magical powers, we consider the Kadam to be part of our Pokot culture. Our children have frequently intermarried.

There were other marriage taboos that I did not have to worry about with Chepusepa. For instance, we think of all aunts, uncles and father's wives as our "parents" and all of their children as our "brothers" and "sisters." Marriage to them would be considered incestuous. Yet we hear that amongst the Turkana, a man with two or four children will allow them to marry their cousin's children, even though, by our reckoning, this would be like a girl marrying her maternal uncle. Indeed, the groom himself could actually be scheduled to receive four cattle from the bride price!

Negotiating the Bride Price

So far, anyway, there seemed to be nothing to prevent a good and lasting marriage to Chepusepa. Our fate was up to our fathers and their negotiations over bride price. In preparation for this event, I collected adequate honey and began to brew beer, for it is always important to bring a gourd of beer whenever one makes a request of someone outside the family. The beer has great significance and insures that business will be conducted seriously.

Since I was about to request a wife, I needed to follow certain rules about preparing the beer, especially for my clan. First I cut some large, spongy fruits (*marotino*) of the leafy sausage tree in half and set them out to dry near the fire. They would be used as catalysts for fermenting the beer. (For weddings, we are careful to use only long, perfect fruits, discarding any with split heads. Those are considered imperfect, and will reflect on the marriage.) The beer was to be carried to Chepusepa's father in a special, large gourd: one with two necks, made into openings. Two *marotino* would be put into the large opening (it is very important to put in only two, or, if you make a mistake, four, but never three, which is extremely bad luck), and the beer would be poured from the small opening, like a teakettle.[84]

When the moon had blossomed for the third time, my father came to Lomunan.

I had gone with others to a dance of *laleyo* that day, but Chepusepa had stayed home, fearful that another suitor would try to rape her if she went. He had proposed to her before I met her, but she had rejected him. When he heard she had given in to me, he had immediately brought cattle to her father and attempted to take her by force. Even Chepusepa's mother had tried to convince her to marry him, instead of me. "That Domonguria is so big!" she had told her daughter. "If he decides to beat you, he might kill you! Why don't you consider this other suitor?" But Chepusepa had replied, "He has too many children, and none of them are mine!" and that was that.

Father arrived in the neighborhood shortly before noon and asked after me. Then he went to Lotiom's homestead and asked one mother for some tobacco. The people who were there looked him over and remarked to one another, "Who is this? Maybe this is Domonguria's father."

Chepusepa saw him and said, "I hear his father limps like that. One leg isn't good. This man is very handsome! He has bracelets all over his arms. So it must be Domonguria's father, because I hear he wears a lot of metal jewelry! Also, he is slender, and they say he has a lip plug just like that!"

Lopedur's sister was there, and she added, "I was told that Pturu's ornaments were made by a woman named Chepachikwa."

Meanwhile, one of Chepusepa's mothers ground some tobacco, put it in a container and gave it to him. She told Chepusepa to prepare food and serve it to him so that he could see what she looked like. Chepusepa ground some millet, cooked it, poured it into a bowl and whipped milk into it with a three-pronged *akiparet* stick. Then she added a little fat, and asked Father to come eat the food she had prepared for him.

Father enjoyed the meal, and went back outside to wait for me in the shade of a tree. We arrived later that afternoon. I greeted my father, but Lotiom walked past us, straight into his homestead, continuing an animated discussion with another elder. As we walked to my compound together, Father asked me, "What about that man? Did he accept my walking stick or not?"

"Yes, he took it."

"Well, I didn't see him with it."

"He has carried it every day!"

"Oh, then it must be in his house."

After our cowherd brought the cattle home, Father called me into the corral and pointed to one of the herd. He asked, "This is the calf of which cow?"

I told him. He continued to quiz me, and I named the sires and dams of all the cattle. He counted them, asked me how many calves each cow had had, and which cows had produced the largest calves. He ordered me to name them all, and I did. Then he noticed the steer whose horns I had fixed at the time I moved away from his house to establish a place of my own. (All of the steers had been calves then.)

He told me to separate the calves from the heifers, and then he counted them. Finally, he announced, "Forty heifers, 35 calves, 42 steers and 57 milking cows. If these people demand very many cattle, how many should we give them?"

"I don't know. Only you know," I replied respectfully.

"Well, if they are forceful, I won't agree to all these cattle here, but there are two other herds at Lossom. Altogether, I have three herds, numbering 285. I will need to consider."

We dropped the subject after that and went back to the *aperit*.

Father awakened me cheerfully the next morning, saying, "Come! Show me the homestead of your intended bride!"

We carried the double-necked gourd of beer I had prepared, using the two perfect *marotino*, to the house of Chepusepa's mother, who was there. At Father's request, she sent a youth to get her husband. The four of us drank the beer together, then discussed the bride price with Lotiom for a long time.

"Really, friend (Lotiom called my father 'friend' because they were near the same age), do you truthfully desire for your son to marry my daughter?"

"Yes."

"Well, since you whole-heartedly approve of the marriage, I will cut my price greatly. I don't want to haggle with you! If you say my price is high, it is high! If you say it is cheap, it is cheap! I want 37 cattle."

"There aren't that many. There are 25."

"No! 37!"

"There are 25."

"Absolutely not! I could never agree to that! Give the number I requested: 37!"

"No."

They wrangled on for awhile like this, until Father finally said, "All right, then, I agree to 30, but not one more!"

"No, but look: I'll take off two, and the cattle will be 35."

Father said, "Make it 32. Forget the other five."

"Agreed! Thanks!"

Now it was time for Chepusepa's mother to wager her part of the bargain. She demanded, "I want goats: 16 goats."

"Yes, there are 16 goats," Father replied. "Whatever you want."

Our parents had reached an agreement! Lotiom and his wife drank the rest of the beer, leaving a small amount—maybe three or four cups, and returned the gourd to me. (Custom states that you should always return a little beer to the one who brought it to you.) Before we left, Lotiom instructed me, "Go to my brother's place at Moruita, and ask him to come here tomorrow. Tell him it's about your proposed marriage to my daughter."

In the morning I walked to Moruita, remembering a recent argument Chepusepa said she had had with this uncle and his wife when she was staying with them. Chepusepa's aunt had confronted her, saying, "I hear you have had an affair with the youth from Lossom. Is this true?" When Chepusepa nodded, her aunt had snapped, "We don't want that man!"

Chepusepa had protested, "I love him very much and, yes, I have even slept with him! If you reject him, I shall have to choose which path to follow. I can either fly high, like the birds, or crawl low, under the ground, but you will never find me, even if you follow my footprints! I will be with him! So, you see, if you refuse the bride wealth he hopes to give you, that's your own undoing!"

What does that woman have against me, I wondered, as I entered the homestead of Lotiom's brother. My reception was even worse than I had imagined. When I relayed Lotiom's message, his brother flew into a rage! "No! You won't take my child!" he yelled at me.

I was insulted. "You can't stop me!" I retorted. "Just what do you want us to do? She isn't your daughter, and besides, I've already bought her! If you insist on provoking us like this, my sweetheart and I will have to run away together. Then, because of your obstinacy, you'll loose all the cattle you had hoped to get for her!"

The man's wife exclaimed, "*Ala!* Don't you remember Chepusepa's words when she came here? She said, 'If you don't want the cattle, that's your fault! I'll go away with him forever!'"

Lotiom's brother growled, "Go home! But I'll not come! I don't want you!"

I protested, "I don't understand why you want to cut me off. She loves me, and I've already agreed to pay for her, so what's the problem? Maybe you want my wife to reject me, so that you can give her to someone else. Well, you can forget about that nonsense, sir! You speak like a small child who hasn't much sense!"

Bitterly, I went back to my homestead and found Father and Lotiom there together.

"How did you find my brother?" Lotiom asked.

"He was furious!" I reported the whole incident.

To my surprise, Lotiom just shrugged and said, "Oh well, if he ranted at you like that, so what?" Then he spoke to Father, "Now, friend, please go home and let out the cattle for the wedding! Send a messenger ahead telling me when you plan to arrive in Lomunan."

"Fine! Thanks."

My Wedding

The next morning, I hiked with my father towards Lossom. We crossed the river, and walked on to another homestead, where we convinced a man to repay some cattle we were owed. Father sent me on to Losidok to claim some of our other cattle there, while he returned to his own home. I brought those cattle back from

Losidok, collected two more cows from the first homestead, and herded all of them to my homestead at Lomunan. Father had sent a message telling me to come back to Lossom the day after I returned.

When I reached his homestead, Father asked, "Did you meet two boys on the way? They requested one of our steers for their *sapana*, and they were taking it by way of your homestead."

"I didn't see them."

I noticed that my father had been busy collecting and buying a great quantity of honey, in order to make beer for the wedding feast. Some beer was already fermented. "That is for tonight," Father explained. "I have summoned the appropriate elders, and they have agreed to tell your fortune according to the customs of the Baboon Clan."

In preparation for that event, we walked up into the hills, where we cut a log and stripped all the bark until the wood was white. Then we dug a hole, put in the log, standing upright, and anchored it with earth. We returned to the homestead as the cattle were coming home.

The three elders came for me in the middle of the night. Together, we carried a gourd of beer to the place where Father and I had erected the post on the hill. We made a fire and placed the beer a short distance away. Our purpose, they explained, was to wait for those birds we call *ptieltiel*, which cry out early in the morning when it is still dark. After we had sat there about an hour, the elders began knocking on the wooden pillar. Soon, the birds awakened and said, "*Tu tu tu ta ta ta ...*," and then they cried out, "*Ptielaaaaa!*" The elders listened intently to the birds. Afterwards, they told my fortune: "Your wife Chepusepa will have nine children, and you will live happily with her. She will grow very, very old together with her husband Domonguria, until she can no longer walk around her home." When the elders were finished, they drank most, but not all, of the beer. They carried the rest home to mix with the beer that was fermenting there. The women would bring two gourds of that beer to Lotiom's homestead for the wedding.

After two days, I herded the rest of the cattle my father had selected to my homestead at Lomunan. The following day, I partied until sunset, celebrating the completion of the bride wealth for my marriage to Chepusepa. Our dreams were coming true, and my joy was unsurpassed!

When I returned to Lossom, Father reminded me, "Go find a leopard skin cape. Your wedding is near!" I was just about to leave for that purpose, when my sister's husband, Lopedur, arrived. "Why, you must use my *kalaja*!" he insisted. "My own brother killed the leopard, and I made the cape!"

"This is good!" Father exclaimed.

Lopedur loaned me his *kalaja*, some ostrich feathers, and a giraffe's tail, and Father provided another giraffe's tail and more ostrich feathers for my wedding costume. Then he instructed me, "Go to back to your homestead now, and tell

Lotiom that I will be ready on the fourth day. If he will send a message to his brother, I will do likewise, and then we will deliver the cattle."

I left straightaway for my house at Lomunan, arriving just before our cattle came home for milking. Later, as I was drinking the fresh milk, I heard singing in the distance, and left to join in the dance. It was after midnight when I finally lay with Chepusepa in her house, and in the morning, I gave Lotiom Father's message. My own family arrived at noon that very day: Father, his fourth wife—the mother of Merur, Lopedur and my sister Chelima. Together, we fetched water, made more beer and put it in the sun to ferment for three days.

It was *koiyul*, my wedding day! The beer was ready, and we poured it carefully into a large ceremonial gourd, along with two perfect *marotino*.

Now it was time to dress in the traditional wedding finery. I unrolled Lopedur's handsome leopard skin cape, the *kalaja*, and tied it around my neck. Over my chest, I wore a nicely prepared skin from the stomach of a gazelle (*akwete*)—white, with a black stripe down either side. Hanging from my nose was a glistening, white metal *aparparat*, which had been beautifully crafted out of a single cooking pot. (A man who lacks one of these will surely borrow one for his wedding day, or else the bride's mother will take offence, thinking him cheap.) I tied four tiny bells—*kurkuris*—on each of my legs, so that they cried out when I walked. Then I took a large, round feather-holder, made of twisted ligament, containing numerous holes, and attached it to the middle receptacle in the top of my clay headdress. I inserted so many white and black ostrich feathers, that one could barely see my eyes! Meanwhile, Lopedur and Father were mixing some white clay to the consistency of plaster. All of us spread this mixture on our faces, until they appeared totally white. Finally, I went in the house to get the giraffe's tails Lopedur and Father had given me (we keep them wrapped around short sticks). I tied both tails around my upper arm, and carried one of the sticks in my hand. (Some men cut a long walking stick in half and use that instead.) Now that I was dressed in the traditional manner of the groom, I had permission to let the cattle out of the corral to give to my bride's father.

I was in the process of doing just that—I had already let out 29 of the 32 promised cattle—when my father stopped me. "Let's leave the other three here and see what these people will do!" he remarked.

Triumphantly, we herded the bride wealth to Lotiom's homestead, and Chelima carried the gourd of beer. When we reached the gate, an old woman, also named Chepusepa, ran to close it on us.

"Please open the gate," I asked.

"No!" she replied, enjoying her traditional role. "If you forget that which will open this gate, it's your fault! You shall sleep there until tomorrow!"

Father bribed her, "Open the gate, and tomorrow morning, follow me, and I will find you a goat!"

Happily, she opened the gate for the cattle, which we herded in. Standing there were Chepusepa's parents, Lotiom's ornery brother, who had come after

all, the man who had married Chepusepa's older sister, and Chepusepa's mother's brother. We drove the cattle past them, and went inside the house of Chepusepa's mother. Carefully, we placed the gourd of beer on the floor at a point
midway between the mother's bed, the father's bed and the hearth. We removed
the grass stopper from the gourd and hung it from the ceiling beam, according to
custom. Soon, Lotiom and his relatives came to the door and called, "All of you
come out of the house!"

We exited, and the "owners of the bride" went in. They each took a *kalowa*,
dipped it inside the gourd and drank one cup of beer. They meditated and consulted with one another for a time, then called to us, "Come here, close to the
door!" My party drew near.

"Where are *all* the cattle?" they demanded.

Feigning surprise, Father asked, "What cattle? Don't you see they are already
here?"

"No! Three are missing!"

"Oh, *those!*" Father exclaimed, as if it was an afterthought. "Why, they were so
savage this morning that I left them home! Come fetch them tomorrow with your
child!"

"Agreed," said Lotiom.

Soon, the bride's party came out of the house and entered the corral. Lotiom
exclaimed, "Come! Your cattle tarry! Assign them to us! Where is mine—the bull
for the father of the bride?"

We brought a huge bull with mature horns that had known action, together
with a pregnant cow.

"Where are those for the mother?"

We presented Chepusepa's mother with a particularly large steer, as well as a
cow and her calf. Lotiom's irritable brother was also given a steer, a cow and a
calf. The brother of Lotiom's youngest wife received four cattle, the other in-law,
three. Chepusepa's oldest sibling received four, the one who followed Chepusepa, two, and the others, one each. The husband of Chepusepa's older sister
was awarded one.

"Now leave the others," Lotiom instructed. "I know what to do with them.
Your work is done. Come and eat! It is late, and you will want to be getting
home."

After we finished our meal, they called for Chepusepa, and all of us went into
the corral once again. Lotiom began the ceremony by arranging us in a line. We
faced in the direction of sunrise, and we stood erect. I was placed next to my
bride, to her right, and Lopedur stood on her left, as my brother. (If I already had
a wife, she would stand there too, with my brothers.) Our friends stood to one
side.

Then Chepusepa's mother and father approached us together. Her mother
held a small gourd we call *mukuh*,[85] filled with cow milk. (For this purpose, it is

important to use a very new *mukuh*, still whole and in good condition. The milk must be from a cow with a healthy, nursing calf.) She removed the cup-lid from the *mukuh* and poured some milk into it. Each parent poured a little milk first on my forehead, and then on their daughter's forehead. Afterwards, Chepusepa's mother's brother and her mother's father anointed us in the same way. When they were finished, Chepusepa's mother again took the *mukuh* and anointed us, and also Lopedur. Next, the four instructed their child, "We want you to live happily in his homestead. Don't bring them misfortune or nonsense. Be pleasant and do good work. If you fail and he beats you, it's your own fault! Certainly, if you don't follow orders, you will get quite a whipping, and we will not stand in the way. That will teach you to obey orders! Do you understand?"

Chepusepa said, "Yes."

"To tell the truth," they continued, "We don't think your husband knows *how* to beat a wife until she listens! But he doesn't want a woman who is useless, like a weed. He wants a wife who is exceptionally smart—for a woman. If you attend to your responsibilities carefully, no one will beat you. If you behave badly, you will receive the whip incessantly! You must go, now, to this man's homestead. Observe the people there. If they stand when they eat, you stand! If they sit down, you do likewise. Now, daughter, once you go out of the door of the cattle into the countryside with your husband, take care not to look behind you. You must look ahead constantly; until you reach your new home, even if the journey is long. If you look back, the marriage will be broken, and you will return home."

When this sermon was finished, Chepusepa's mother presented her daughter with a large blanket, consisting of five goatskins sewn together (a *koliko*), and a large gourd full of milk. They gave us our bride, and we took her to my homestead.

That night, Chepusepa unfastened my wedding garments. She untied the leopard and gazelle skins, and removed the bells from my legs. She loosened the giraffe tails from my arms and wrapped them around their sticks. I was filled with desire, but the wedding was not complete: Chepusepa's family had given her away, but my family had not yet married her. Therefore we slept alone, in separate beds.

In the morning, Father announced cheerfully, "Let's go now! Surely you didn't think this girl was going to stay here with *you*, son! Ha, what a fool! She can't stay here! She must see what *my* homestead is like! You can take her back later, but right now, this isn't your wife, she's mine! She's going to live with me! You can't even sleep with her freely yet—there is no compact for you!"

All of us walked together to Lossom for the second part of the wedding ceremony, in which the groom's homestead marries the new bride. Chepusepa brought her *koliko* blanket and the gourd of milk her mother had given her. When we arrived, according to custom, she presented the milk to the children in my family. Young Nyangaluk and my younger brothers and sisters drank all the milk, and the gourd was returned to Chepusepa to keep. Meanwhile, Father and I made five more gourds of beer for the wedding feast.

Chepusepa and I continued to sleep separately until the second night after our arrival. That evening, after the sun had set and it was dark, we each lay down on our own beds. Then I beckoned to her quietly, "Chepusepa, come here! Why are you staying over there?"

"What's the matter?"

"I want you to come to my bed."

"I won't come!" she declared. (I have heard that some husbands try to use force at this point, but it is proper for a bride to resist her husband's advances until he promises her a cow.)

"Sure, come! You already have one cow!" I said.

Chepusepa stood in the dark and took off all her clothes. Then she slid into the bed with me, pressing her naked body against mine. "What does it look like?" she asked sweetly.

I answered, "It is red," and then she gave herself to me.

In the morning, we waited inside the house until the sun had just begun to appear above the hills, but was not yet completely revealed. Then Chepusepa came out of the house, wrapped only in her *koliko*. It was tied with a rope at her neck, and Chepusepa was careful to hold the front of the blanket-cape together with her hands. The clothes that she had worn when she came from her father's homestead were left on her bed, never to be worn again, for today she would be dressed in the new garments of marriage.

I called my bride into the corral and presented her with her new wealth. First I showed her a white cow. She picked up some cow dung and smeared it on the cow's back, from its hump to the tail. Seven more cattle were singled out for her, and she spread all of their backs with dung. She was also given 15 goats, so that her total stock numbered 23. I told her, "Look after these cattle, for they are yours, even though you must give their calves away."

Then Chepusepa demanded, "Where is the cow you gave me last night?"

I found the red heifer I had in mind, grasped its muzzle and held it until Chepusepa came to see it with her own eyes. Then she walked to the gate of the corral and let out the *kirukuh* bull, the sire of all the cattle. The rest of the herd followed its father out of the gate.

As the cattle left, my family brought out the *minyon* skin from the house where we had slept and spread it out on the ground in the center of the corral. This special skin must come from a cow that was killed with a spear. One must not use the skin of an animal which was eaten by a hyena or which died from sickness. A husband who has no appropriate skin of his own will borrow one for this ceremony.

Chepusepa came back from the gate, stepped onto the skin, and stood very straight, with locked knees. Four children—two big and two little ones—were called to represent her future children. They stood on the skin with her, two on each side, also with locked knees. Chepusepa was handed four gourds for the four children, and she buried them in her arms. The oldest child then stepped forward to take his gourd, and the next oldest did the same, while my bride held the gourds of the little children.

After that, honey, milk and *sosion* (palm leaves) were brought. First, Father anointed the head of my bride with milk, and the children followed him, each pouring a little milk on her head. In return, Chepusepa anointed the heads of my father and of the children. Next, the women of the household tied a thin, skin rope they had made the day before around her right wrist, signifying that she was now a married woman. They presented Chepusepa with her new clothes, made from the skin of a good cow which had never been sick and which had been killed with a spear. Then, while Chepusepa held the *sosion*, one of my mothers took a long stalk of the leaves and "opened" the cape where she had been holding it together with one hand. The *koliko* was removed, and fat was spread all over Chepusepa's body, on her new clothes, and on all of her "children." Finally, my mothers dressed her in the clothes they had made for her. She would no longer wear the loose, freely swinging, beaded apron of an unmarried girl. Instead, her apron would be that of a married woman—a single skin with a border of *teroi* beads. This and her new back skirt were the clothes she would wear for the rest of her life.

When this ceremony was finished, Chepusepa picked up the *minyon* skin, carried it into the house and put it on the bed. She lingered inside for a while before coming out again to face the next part of the ritual—that of the Baboon clan.

Quickly, a large scorpion was brought out to sting our new wife with its horn. Chepusepa screamed and doubled over in pain. Sometimes the pain can be exceptional, but that is considered necessary, because the manner of the pain helps the elders tell a wife's fortune. No other clan marries wives in this way. Chepusepa recovered quickly, lying in the shade of a tree near our homestead.

Later that afternoon, a woman who was expert at making bracelets from brass wire arrived. She cut a length of the wire and began to wind it around Chepusepa's right arm, just behind the rope of marriage they tied in the corral that morning. She coiled the metal exquisitely until the wedding bracelet was complete.

All of the neighbors came, then, to eat and to drink beer in honor of our wedding. The elders started talking about different wedding customs,[86] especially those of the Karamojong. Some of the rituals are similar to ours, they said, and others are not. For instance, the Karamojong pass a *sarian* pipe, lit with tobacco, from person to person on top of the *minyon* skin. And when the Karamojong dicker over bride price, we hear the bride's family gets the groom's party so drunk that they sometimes agree to pay more cattle than they have! The next day, the groom and his people can't remember what was said, and when the bride's father tells them, they have to comply! The elders stayed, drinking and celebrating until the beer was finished.

Chepusepa and I have been happily married ever since, even though, in the beginning, she did one slightly bad thing: she stayed with me almost four years without getting pregnant. But after that we were blessed with children, although there were times when many of our babies died. It has been a great comfort to me to know that the predictions for our marriage were good. There can be no greater pleasure than knowing that I'll grow old with Chepusepa by my side.

LIVING THE POKOT LIFE

AFTER THE WEDDING

The months after our wedding were a time of harmony, as my wife and I worked side by side, warmed by the joy of our mutual commitment. The fact that our marriage had been blessed and sanctioned in every way, with the full support of our families, was a source of great security to me. Now it was up to us to strengthen our new economic base, tending our herds, our gardens and our beehives, and to honor our families and our traditions as a married couple.

Sex

We Pokot have certain rules relating to sex and marriage. I don't know how these ideas got started, but they are widespread Pokot customs. For instance, the day after a man sleeps with his wife, he must not enter anyone's house, or he could cause a small child, who happened to be inside, to vomit. Also, if you dream about having intercourse with your wife or husband, you must make love immediately, or something bad might happen to one of you. This is usually no problem, but other dreams can also cause possible harm; dreams can be the messages of ghosts.

When an elder marries a much younger woman, it sometimes happens that he becomes senile, while his wife still wants to get pregnant. In that case, the people of the household will position the husband above her until intercourse takes place. This might go on for two or three years, until the elder is completely impotent.

If a properly married woman has an affair, sickness will eventually come to her children, her husband or, possibly, her herds. When her children become ill, she will mix their urine with clay and spread the mixture on their bodies. They will recover, but the illness may reappear a few weeks later. Most women will admit to an affair readily, for fear their husband or their children will die, but if they don't, sooner or later people will begin to suspect the truth. They will confront the wife, and if she still refuses to admit her guilt, they will beat her, until she agrees to bring a goat from her father's house, slaughter it, and spread the stomach contents on the cattle, children and everyone else in the homestead. In two days, all will be well again. The husband will sue his wife's lover in a court of elders or, these days, in a government court. The man will be fined thirty cattle and will have to slaughter a sheep in the husband's homestead. This is the standard punishment.

Hopefully, I would never have to worry about such a problem.

The Beehive and the Leopard

Shortly after we were married, Chepusepa and I decided to set up a beehive in the vicinity of a well where we watered our cattle. We figured we needed to increase our sources of honey to use for making honey-beer, and we hoped to have a surplus to trade for stock, milk, tobacco and other goods. It was during the dry season, in the second month of the year, when we began the project.

First, I felled a tree and cut it into several logs. We made one log into a wedge and another into a club. We used these two to split a third log, which would be the hive. I carved a trough in each log half, made a hole in one side, and fastened the halves together with vines (sometimes we use bark rope or wire). Then we put some grass and beeswax inside and burned it carefully so that the hive itself didn't catch on fire. Finally, I climbed a tree. Chepusepa tied a rope around the hive and helped me hoist it to the top. While I was wrapping the rope and vines around the branches to anchor the hive, I heard cowbells nearby.

"Better go help water the herd now, Chepusepa," I called down. "It sounds like they are already at the well. I can finish this alone." She left, and I continued securing the hive to the tree. I covered the hive and entrance hole with thatch to keep out the rain, then surveyed my work, thinking that bees might begin to nest there in about a month.

Suddenly, I heard Lopedur's children screaming. Then Chepusepa yelled, "Come, Domonguria! The children say a leopard has killed one of the goats!"

I climbed down as quickly as I could, grabbed my shoes, spear and *panga* (machete) and ran to the children. They had startled the leopard, and it had left its kill temporarily. No one had been hurt. Chepusepa helped the children round up the animals, finish the watering and start for home, while I hauled the goat carcass on my back and dropped it under a large tree. I tied its hind legs to the trunk and climbed up. Chepusepa joined me, along with three other women who had been at the well. "Get the *panga*, Chepusepa!" I called. "If the leopard sees that, it will know a man is nearby." She took it and hid, like the other women, in the bushes nearby.

I had waited in the tree a full hour, when I began to feel terribly drowsy. I knew the leopard must be very near, for, like the lion, it has the power to put people to sleep. Just as I nodded off, the baboons in the trees around me started screeching. I looked up and noticed that one baboon was staring at the ground below my tree. Then I saw the leopard, near the goat! I poised my spear for the kill.

Chepusepa, an old lady, and the two other women took their cue and started yelling to distract the leopard. (He would not attack that many.) He looked up quickly, then lunged down to grab his meat. That was my moment. I hurled the spear with great force. It pierced the middle of his back, just behind the neck, shot through his body and stuck in the sand between his legs. The leopard started to move, but the spear trapped him, and he screeched hideously. The huge cat struggled desperately, freed itself, limped a short distance towards my wife, then fell heavily and died.

That is when I realized that Chepusepa had been there alone with the leopard, standing under the *mukatcho* tree, holding the *panga* in case she was attacked. Evidently, the other three women had run away when the leopard roared. I exclaimed, "*Ala!* What if the leopard had attacked you! You shouldn't have stayed there by yourself! Do you think leopards are docile?"

In spite of these words, I was proud of her bravery. Earlier that morning, when she had brought me two spears for our outing, I had objected, saying, "Put this one back. I'll just be working on the beehive," but she had protested, "*Ala!* Don't you know there are many dangerous animals about? One spear isn't enough!" We had argued, and she had put one spear back. Now I climbed down and said, "I was wrong. You were right about the spears."

She smiled triumphantly and demanded, "Now how are you going to approach him? You have nothing but your bare hands!"

"I think he's dead. He moaned like a dying animal."

"No, don't get near! What will you do if he's alive?"

I took the *panga,* a stick and my sheet and went to get my shoes, which were not far from the leopard—a very large male. I could see, then, that he was already somewhat stiff. I dragged the heavy carcass to a better place and began skinning it, while Chepusepa skinned the goat. The leopard's body was laden with fat, just like a hog's! While we were working, the daughter of Lokopur, my brother-in-law, came and I sent her to get her father, who was tending the cattle. Together, Lokopur and I carried the meat home.

It happened that while we were gone that day, my mother Chepusekur, the mother of Merur, had had a miscarriage. The delivery had been very difficult, and she had nearly died, saved only by the grace of Tororut. Now, as we came into the homestead, they told us that she was once again near death, for the placenta remained in the womb. My family had tried everything to no avail. As soon as my father saw the leopard meat, he took a leg, cooked it in a clay pot and fed his wife the soup in a last, desperate attempt to save her. Within minutes, the afterbirth was delivered! The leopard was her medicine! [87]

Several months later, Chepusepa and I returned to our hive with a honey vessel—a cylinder of carved wood with a cowhide base and lid. I climbed to a branch above the hive, carrying the container, and, using a rope, lowered a burning bundle of sticks to the beehive entrance. Soon the bees came out to escape the smoke and hovered behind the nest. I climbed down to the hive, removed the charred cover, filled the container with honey and lowered it by rope to Chepusepa, who was on the ground. I was pleased to see it was a productive hive, sufficient to meet our needs for some time.

White Man's Dance

One day, my wife and I attended a dance at Karemeri, where there were shops. It was the first *laleyo* celebration of girls' circumcision—the wonderful dance, in which the initiates are expected to seize their partners by force. This time, to our amazement, a white man came and joined in the dance!

He had been watching for a while on the side, when one very bold girl went over to him, seized his arms, and demanded, "Come! Let's dance!" He danced two rounds with her. Then he was taken by three girls at once! Laughing, he stripped down to his trousers and vest and seemed to dance with great pleasure and enthusiasm. All of the initiates, having spread a black ointment on their hair,[88] saluted him in the customary manner by bowing their heads so that their hair brushed against his chest. Soon the front of his vest was black!

"No worry!" he declared, when some of the adults showed concern. "It's all part of the celebration! Tomorrow, when I return to camp, I'll just wash it off with soap!"

It was a wonderful occasion! The white man asked if we could dance again when he came back with his wife. All of us agreed, and one week later we went back to Karemeri for the second dance. The man was there again, along with his wife and a camera.

"Watch me!" he exclaimed, and his wife took pictures of her husband dancing with four girls. After that, the man took pictures of his wife dancing with a man who brushed at her from time to time with a giraffe's tail tied to his arm. Then the white man tied the tail onto his own arm and hit the girls with it, all for the sake of the picture! Finally, the wife took a picture of the whole group dancing.

After that, they put the camera down and joined in the dance enthusiastically, taking time out only when their servant brought them lunch. They danced freely with all of us, but we never allowed them to dance with each other. This is because, amongst us, it is bad for a woman to dance with her husband. I don't know about other people's customs, but no Pokot man would ever dance with his own wife! A woman would no sooner dance with her husband than she would with her father!

New Songs

During those dances, we rejoiced over several new songs our bards had composed in recent years—some about people we knew.

For instance, we sang about the flippant wife Chemichen, who had a passionate affair with a visiting Kikuyu man. People teased her afterwards, asking, "Do you have any sex left to give?"

"A little," she replied.

"Well, you'd better keep it or it will *all* be gone!"

"No," she replied. "I will use it to help my people—especially the *sowa* and the *kapira!*" (circumcision years) And so we sang,

Oh you help us, oh ahay	*Okenkenei oh ahay*
You help us, ah, Chemichen!	*Okenkenei, ah Chemichen!*
Mmm	*Mmm*
What kind of thing ate you?	*Kamine kokonu?*
Sex with a Kikuyu boy, oh aya	*Kasera wero Kikuya, oh aya*
What will you give that remains inside?	*Ito ne nyo mii ori?*
I will help the sowa! I will help, yoiye	*Okenkenei sowa! Okenkenei yoiye*
I will help the kapira! aya	*Okenkenei kapira, aya*

Another melodious song was composed about a man named Rukono, from Chemwapit, who stole, maimed, killed and ate his neighbors' cattle. The animals had disappeared one by one, and people got suspicious when Rukono remarked that he had seen one of the missing oxen slip on a precarious path and fall down the mountain. Soon afterwards, Rukono was caught cooking the meat of the eighth missing ox. The carcass was right there, with cuts on the legs, just like those on the other animals before they disappeared. News of Rukono's crime spread quickly. The neighbors seized him and tied him to a tree with a nest of carnivorous insects. At first, he denied killing the cattle, but when the insects found him, entered his ears and began to cover his face and body, Rukono screamed in horror, "I ate them—all eight of them! I am a thief! Untie me before I am eaten alive!"

They freed Rukono and confiscated twelve of his cattle. Then they beat him with a stick, until he slaughtered a steer for his neighbors to eat, completing his penance. At the feast afterwards, someone asked him, "Why did you eat all those cattle, anyway?" and Rukono whined, "I was so hungry, and the sun was so hot..." His song has become very popular:

Mmm, aya, ooo, aya	*Mmm, aya, ooo, aya*
Ah aya Rukono e Rukono ah	*Ah aya Rukono e Rukono ah*
He pained so much from hunger, Rukono	*Kiwonjit kamoi, Rukono, mm*
He pained so much from hunger, Rukono	*Kiwonjit kamoi, Rukono,*
That he cut a cow's leg	*Nyo kimot teta cheptindol*
Rukono e Rukono, Rukono e Rukono ...	*Rukono e Rukono, Rukono e Rukono...*
Oh, ah, aya, ah aya	*Oh, ah, aya, ah aya*

We also sang of Cheputupalel, whose beauty was legendary. She was a gorgeous red—not pinkish red or blackish red, but in between. Cheputupalel, however, divorced two husbands, Acheya and Kayarakimat, forcing her family to return all the cattle they had paid as bride wealth. Her father was so angry that he disowned her. Cast out, Cheputupalel went to Napeyelel, where she joined some people dancing the *laleyo*. She went home with one of the men that night, declaring, "I want you to be my husband!"

"Oh no!" he retorted. "I know and fear your first husband, Acheya. I am sure he has put a hex on you to make you barren." He drove her away.

Cheputupalel then traveled on to Loro, where she allowed herself to be seduced by a Karamojong youth named Lokwi and returned with him to Morukalinga. Meanwhile, her father and brothers began searching for her. After three months, their investigations led them into the heart of Karamojong country, where they implored the local chief to send soldiers to get her. Her brothers asked her, "Did you feel that much pain amongst our own people that you had to go to a different kind?"

"No," she explained. "It was because I cut the rope of marriage from my arm, and I knew that once I did that, no Pokot man could take me again. It would be bad luck. I was afraid."

Cheputupalel's parents slaughtered a black sheep and a goat for their daughter. They made a new rope out of the goatskin and asked a man of her clan to tie it on her arm. They spread the goat's stomach contents and then sheep fat on the bracelet and all over her body, and tied some of the fat from the sheep's tail on a rope around her neck. Finally, they cooked and ate the meat, being careful not to spill the soup on the fire. Cheputupalel was cleansed in this way. From that day on, she was known as Chemutarim, meaning "she who cuts the rope," and during the rains, we made up a song about her to sing at *laleyo*:

Refrain:
Chemutarim, ohah oh aiya, Chemutarim

Verses:
    There are good men at Napeyelel, aya
    Who wear split ostrich feathers on their heads
    These are the sons of Aremule, ah
    You, Acheya, have a (bald) *head like an amniotic sac*[89]
    I go with the youth Lokwi

> *Chemutarim, ohah oh aiya, Chemutarim*
>
> *Mito muren, aya, chomi Napeyelel, aya*
> *Cho wulai palalan, oh ah*
> *Chopu werpu Aremule*
> *Miko, Acheya, ngo mut nyo lenye tupul*
> *Kopunun ngo weri Lokwi*

Singing these songs and many others, we continued dancing and celebrating the *laleyo*. Even the white couple rejoiced with us until the dance ended late that afternoon, when they bid us a cheerful good-bye and went home.

Hunting

The next day I set out to find a lion that had been harassing herds for miles around. Unlike most lions, this one seemed to kill for the joy of it. At times it would kill five cattle in a single day, leaving the carcasses only partially eaten! I began my search by walking from well to well down the large Kanyangareng riverbed looking for tracks, assuming that the lion might have come to one of the wells to drink. Six miles up the river, I not only saw a lion spoor, but, all at once, heard children yelling, "The lion got our cattle!" I ran towards them and found their dead cow under a tree of ripe fruit, which the cattle had been eating. Quickly, I sent the cowherds, with the rest of their stock, to the waterhole in the middle of the riverbed, while I climbed the tree and waited.

Within five minutes I heard the little, chicken-like *jepuikaret* birds calling, "*Kiri, kiri, kiri, kiri!*" Everyone knows that, when these birds cry out, a cat is nearby. I looked towards the sound and saw a large, male lion approaching. He crept low, looking from side to side for people. He noticed me in the tree, but saw no one else, so he came quickly to his kill. He turned the carcass on its back, took one bite, swallowed, and left. Nervously, he crouched in the bushes for some time, then trotted back quickly, intending to drag the cow by its head out to the savannah. Just as his jaws grasped the head, I speared him. The lion roared and ran a short distance, crashing into bushes and breaking the spear into three parts. Then he disappeared, leaving a bloody trail.

A man named Tudoh, who had come to the well, heard the agonized roar and called to tell me he would find some people to help me pursue the lion. (It is always dangerous to confront a dying lion alone. His last energies would be vent upon his killer.) While waiting for them, I gathered some leaves from my tree, laid them out and began to skin the cow on top of them. Soon twelve people came—six men and six women. Two old men finished the butchering, the women stayed to take the meat home, and the rest of us went after the lion. Before long we found some entrails caught on a stick, and then the lion himself, lying on his side. When I saw green flies hovering around the anus, I figured he was dead and walked up to him, despite Tudoh's warnings. We skinned him, and one man took the hide for a *kalaja* cape, while another took the tail. I ate a nice beef dinner with Tudoh that night and walked home after dark.

While we were living at Lomunan, wild herds were plentiful on the plains below Mt. Kadam, and our neighbors decided to harvest the bounty by organizing a large group hunt, along with the people from Losidok. On the appointed day, those of us from the north gathered at Kitalanengaa, while those from Losidok met simultaneously at Nangoret. Our scouts had already located the herds, and we spread ourselves into two huge semicircles around them. Slowly, the two groups began to converge, constricting the range of the animals. We could see everything—giraffe, zebra, ostrich, and lion.

First the giraffes started to run- here, then there, then another direction, only to find people everywhere. One crashed through some brush into the clearing where I was standing, then ran straight towards me. I hurled my spear at close range, and it landed in the neck. Other men came running and also threw their spears. The huge animal fell right beside me!

Just then, another charged into the clearing, and I threw my last spear. It hit the giraffe, but he kept running. I was without weapons, and more giraffes were coming! Quickly, I climbed a tree and watched in safety. I saw one of my friends kicked by a giraffe. His body was hurled high into the air, but he survived. He was lucky not to have been caught between the feet.

Those of us from Lomunan killed 27 animals that day. We feasted on meat for two weeks!

The Evil Eye

The year after we were married, Chepusepa and I traveled with four donkeys to Chemwapit. We bought maize, loaded the sacks on the backs of the donkeys and began walking them home. After two miles, we passed some people on their way to the river, and I asked, "Is the homestead of Nyangaren near the road ahead?"

"Yes," they answered. "When you come to the place where people ate a steer yesterday, follow the path to the right. It will lead you to a house, where your donkeys can spend the night safely."

We had walked on a short distance, when, suddenly, Chepusepa bent over in pain, groaning, "Oh, my throat hurts!" She lay down and vomited. I could not tend to both my wife and the donkeys, so I let the donkeys go and knelt down to help Chepusepa. Soon, four children came by with their goats, and I sent one of them ahead to ask Nyangaren to help us. Chepusepa was still suffering when he came.

"Oh, it's the Evil Eye!" he exclaimed. "Someone must have cursed her with his eyes. But don't worry. I know some medicine to counteract it. Wait here."

Nyangaren returned to the path with medicine made from a certain plant. Chepusepa ate it, vomited twice, and sat up. I brought her some water, and she bathed. Then, slowly, we led her to Nyangaren's homestead. By later that evening, Chepusepa had recovered, and Nyangaren slaughtered a goat for us to eat. The next day we led the donkeys home.

TRADING

A Ban on Ostriches

The year the Europeans seized Jomo Kenyatta *[1952]*, Chepusepa and I were sharing our homestead with Arimo, a Teso, who was a headman of the local road crew. One day, Arimo's son found an ostrich's nest between Amudat and Katabok, while he was watching the cattle. There were six eggs, and both of our cowherds took one. They brought the two eggs to our home and put them in the ashes near the fire. After two weeks, they hatched.

I remember the baby ostriches walking about, eating millet and stones. Arimo took care of them, and they grew quite large. One night a leopard got the female, but the male continued to thrive, and Arimo harvested its feathers twice. Then one day, when it was fully grown, our ostrich wandered into the town of Amudat. A European saw it and asked the people, "Where did this come from?"

"Oh, it is the 'ox' of a man named Arimo," they told him.

The European immediately summoned Arimo to Amudat. "Do you have a license to keep an ostrich?" he demanded.

"Of course not!" Arimo replied. "This ostrich doesn't belong to anyone else—it's mine. So why would I need a license?"

But the European decreed, "From this day on, you must not keep this ostrich without a license. If you do, you will go to jail for stealing from the government!"

Arimo was furious and even took his case to court at Moroto. The government claimed our ostrich anyway, but Arimo persisted, arguing, "You have no right to take my animal! I did not steal it from anyone else—it's wild! At the very least, I want to be compensated for the food I used to raise him!" They gave Arimo 50 shillings just to placate him.

That was only the beginning. The Europeans have been seizing our pet ostriches ever since. When other people heard about Arimo's trouble, they killed their ostriches so they could at least have the feathers. Lobur and Tebangar killed theirs. Another man was so angry, he killed his female ostrich and destroyed all her eggs.

Now there are no ostriches left in our part of the country—domestic or wild. We can get feathers only by trading. However, we still sing frequently about these splendid birds. During one song, which we learned from the Karamojong, we join hands, raising and lowering our arms, like an ostrich flapping its wings in the rain.

Refrain:

> *Ostrich of my ancestral father*
>
> *Ostrich, white feathers, mm*

Akalis kangidwa papa
Alakis longole uperua, mm

Verses:

> *Ostrich, small head*
>
> *Ostrich doesn't drink water*
>
> *Ostrich isn't afraid to eat rocks*
>
> *Each side is white*
>
> *Ostrich hair is black*
>
> *Ostrich,* (eats) *hardened gum of the thorn tree*
>
> *Its mother lays eggs in the sun*
>
> *Its mother stays in the muddy savannah*

Akalis jijiko
Akalia naroya
Aleke nya amur toker in
Nyakapel ya ng atoros
Akalis nyeriono otim
Akalis namude
Aoro to tokeng na kolong
A emi nitokeng nya aro

Becoming a Trader

One day, I walked to Kacheliba and bought six packets of beads. When I got home, people asked me where I had found them. "Kacheliba is too far! We want to buy them from you!" they insisted. So I sold the beads at a profit and made sixty shillings in just a short time. The next morning I hiked back to Kacheliba and bought a whole bag. As I was coming home, I could hear people calling, "Domonguria comes now, bringing many beads! Let's go buy them!" Everyone came—men, women, girls, youths and small children, and by the next morning, the beads were gone.

Lopedur told me, "Brother-in-law, you are a man of intelligence! You have become a trader! How much have you earned?"

"157 shillings from the beads alone!"

Lopedur taught me all he knew about trading, and I made my plans. By noon two days later, I was in Kacheliba again buying beads of every description: 112 packets in all. Already, the word had spread far that I was now trading in beads. The first day I earned 203 shillings! The next day I took the beads to a place near Amudat, where I had heard there was to be a *laleyo* dance. The people there beckoned me, "Come! Join us! Rest from your journey and celebrate with us until morning!" I danced into the night and slept in a nearby homestead. The next morning I sold beads there, as well as in Amudat. I earned 456 shillings in just three days!

After two months of lucrative trading in beads, I switched to cattle. One man advised me, "You had better get a license. You have done well, but you could do even better if you could attend the cattle auctions in Kenya and at Moroto and Kurikaribar." I was still ignorant and did not heed his advice. My profits were modest, and after four months of trading cattle, I decided to try my luck with ostrich feathers.

By then, Chepusepa and I were living at Alakas, where the Katabok track intersects with the road to Lodwar. To get a stock of feathers, I would have to walk a great distance to the European city of Kitale, which I had seen only once when I was a youth traveling in Mr. Pete's car. I left our home before daybreak and reached Kirengeti by nightfall. I walked all of the following day and spent the second night at the farm of a European named Mr. U, where my cousin worked as a foreman. On the third day I made it to Kitale. It had been a long walk from Alakas.

I bought ostrich feathers at the Indian shops until the feathers filled my sack, investing 1150 shillings altogether. Luckily, I was able to return to Amudat in the lorry of Kaka, one of the Indian shopkeepers. I successfully traded my entire stock at the rate of six thick bunches of black feathers or ten thick bunches of white feathers for each cow or steer. Business was successful, and after a year trading feathers, my own personal store of ostrich feathers filled two large trunks and two gourds!

While I traded in ostrich feathers, I was able, at the same time, to begin a more lucrative business in cattle by trading just outside the auctions. One European, named Mr. Smith, was an especially good customer. I could sell him six or eight steers a day for up to 500 shillings each.

For awhile I teamed up with a man named Riangole Pkurakur, who traded in Teso country, where the cattle were very fine in those days. Once, we arranged to meet in Kacheliba, where we joined two other traders and three assistants and drove in a car to a place called Ngenge, continuing on foot into Teso country. On that trip, I bought 28 cattle, Riangole bought 45, and the other men ten and seven. Then we herded them slowly back.

I left my cattle temporarily with Riangole and came home to find that my wife had also been busy in my long absence. She had bought five steers and one bull with the money we had at home and had arranged for four other steers I had previously bought in Turkana to be brought to the auction the following day! I was exhausted from my journey, and I told her, "You'd better go sell the cattle at the auction, Chepusepa. If a white man asks for me, tell him I'm sick at home"

My wife herded three of the steers she had bought to the auction, where she met the man with the four steers from Turkana. (My father and brother went along to help her during the long, all-night walk.) Inside the auction the next day, Mr. Smith began asking after me. Finally, he questioned Chief Losile, "Where is Domonguria? Please find him for me!" Losile sent a soldier to search for me, and when the man found Chepusepa, he asked, "Where is your husband?"

"He is home. He is sick," she replied.

"What are *you* doing here then?"

"I came to sell the cattle, as my husband wished."

"But the European wants to see *him*."

"Well, since he is not here, perhaps I should go."

The soldier was confused, but, seeing that my wife was surprisingly capable, he agreed to introduce Chepusepa to Mr. Smith, who asked her once again, "Where is your husband?"

"He is home, sick."

"Well, actually, I was asking in regards to his cattle. If he had brought cattle, I would have wanted to see them first." The white man shrugged and started to walk away.

"Yes, of course. I have the cattle," my wife said quietly.

The white man turned around, puzzled. "They're here?" he asked.

"Yes."

"How many?"

"Seven."

"Bring the steers for me to see!"

Chepusepa went to the place where my father and brother had been watching the cattle and brought them for Mr. Smith to examine. But Mr. Smith was still not convinced. He summoned Chief Losile and asked him, "Whose cattle are these?"

"They belong to Domonguria."

"Which Domonguria—Kaparketo?"

"Yes."

He looked them over and entered all seven into the auction for us. When it was finished, he sent a corporal to the bank with Chepusepa to pay her 2980 shillings for those seven steers. I was very proud of her!

The Death of Lorika

When we heard that the Karamojong had broken the peace and killed two children at Namosing, taking the cattle, we followed the tracks as far as Nabilatuk. We realized that further pursuit was useless, so we started taking Karamojong cattle as compensation. We had stolen three herds and had taken them as far as the water wells called Arianomunyan, in the middle of the dry Amumoit riverbed, when two policemen came, along with some Karamojong, and we took cover. Two chiefs were with them, carrying guns—Apangolekit, a Karamojong, and Lorika, a Taposa who had once spent four years as chief in Amudat. (This was the same Lorika who had once contracted with my father's friend Loram to shoot elephants so that he could take the tusks.) Knowing we were there hiding, Lorika shouted, "You must let these cattle go! We have found your Pokot cattle and the thieves that took them!"

In good faith, two of our men, Loichaon and Lorukodi, stood up to negotiate, but Chief Lorika shot them! Enraged, we sprang upon them. Kajukait speared Chief Lorika and Ngaropul speared Apangolekit. One man killed two Karamojong with poisoned arrows, and another shot the hats off the policemen as they retreated. One Pokot warrior died, and two others were wounded. We heard that one Karamojong, who was shot in the back with a poisoned arrow, died while still standing up, holding onto a tree. They say he had an erection and ejaculated after death! (Later on, people claimed that his hair and teeth fell out as well!) The Karamojong witnessed this and greatly feared the poisoned arrows.

After this confrontation, my people were constantly harassed. [90] The soldiers came to raid us, because we had blinded one of their comrades. The whole country cried over Lorika, saying, "He was such a good man." They didn't cry so much over the death of Apangolekit. In the end, we Pokot paid a fine of 2800 cattle, which was unjust, considering the loss of our own herds, our warrior, and the two children. But after they had cooled down a little, people began to laugh over this incident. Inevitably, one man made up a song about the two chiefs who caused our fine.

Lorika, Lorika, son of Karamojong wife	*Lorika, Lorika, wero chepulemin*
Refrain:	*Kilenjingo, kilenjingo nyono koronu*
Who told you, who told you to come to this country?	*Apangolekit, Apangolekit, wero chepulemin*
	Kwamun yungwun, kwamun yungwun chomi Namosing
Verses:	*Achono sonkok, achono sonkok chomi Napeyelel*
Apangolekit, Apangolekit, son of Karamojong wife	*Mi muren, mi muren chomi Napeyelel*
Eaten by the soil, eaten by the soil of Namosing	*Kwamun yunwun, kwamun yunwun chomi ariono munyan*
The safari ants came, the safari ants of Napeyelel	
They were the warriors, men of Napeyelel	
Eaten by the soil, eaten by the black clay soil	

Pregnancy and Birth

Later that year, I brewed a gourd of honey-beer and gave it to Chepusepa to take to her parents, along with a goat which had not yet given birth—the Goat of *Kirola*. *Kirola* is the ritual homecoming of a happily married woman, visiting her parents several years after her marriage. It is a happy occasion and symbol of a successful marriage. While at her parents' home, Chepusepa was careful not to drink the milk of any of the cattle her parents had received from me at the time of our marriage, for a woman must never drink her own bride wealth. Chepusepa's parents rejoiced over her and, according to the custom of *kirola*, gave her a cow, which was led to our homestead by her brother.

Chepusepa had been a good wife, and I loved her completely. Yet the fact that she had continued to be barren was a source of great frustration for both of us. You can imagine our happiness when, several months later, we realized that she was pregnant at last! As soon as I found out about the pregnancy, I asked my friend Arekai to hire a midwife to help Chepusepa at her time of birth. I sent some honey-beer with him, so that he could negotiate with the woman. She agreed, I paid her one goat for her future services.

As a pregnant woman, Chepusepa had to take certain dietary precautions to insure the health of our unborn child. She restricted her diet to about half her usual intake. Her cooking pot, utensils, plate, cup and gourd could not be shared with anyone else, and she could not eat food that anyone else had handled. A pregnant woman also must not touch the meat, milk or blood of a cow, goat or sheep which has been bitten by a snake, eaten by vultures, killed by hyenas, wild dogs or jackals, or stolen from the kills of lions or leopards. She may eat the meat of cattle that died of a fly sickness or East Coast Fever, but she must avoid all cattle suffering from rinderpest, pleuro-pneumonia, and a disease we call *loriel*.[91] In addition, she must reject the meat of animals that have died naturally and of those that have recovered from most sicknesses or sores. Because of these restrictions, Chepusepa had to be especially careful when eating food from someone else's house. I would always ask the owner of a slaughtered cow, "Is this animal fit for a pregnant woman to eat?" hoping he would answer, "Yes, I have watched this cow well. There has never been anything wrong with it. Whenever my wife wanted blood or milk, she used this cow."

When the yellow-striped *kupteluk* worm appeared—the kind that spits a green substance when touched—Chepusepa and all the other pregnant women were not allowed to eat them. After the worms disappeared about a month later, they could not drink milk until a steer was slaughtered and a cleansing ceremony performed, after which they tied grasses around their waists. If these rules were neglected, the women could starve.

During the seventh month of my wife's pregnancy, I collected honey from our beehives and made many gourds of beer for the *parapara* ceremony. (I will explain this celebration later.) All of Chepusepa's "fathers"—her mother's brothers, her mother's father and her father—came to our homestead for the feast and the important rituals that would help protect my wife and baby at the time of birth. A month later, the midwife I had hired came to attend daily to Chepusepa. She stayed in my wife's home, helping when she could, and waiting for the birth.

As those last weeks passed, I became anxious, hoping that Chepusepa's delivery would be uncomplicated, and that she would come through labor in good health. Uneasily, I remembered the song we had recently begun to sing at dances about a local woman named Cherotitch, whose mother-in-law had assisted her during the birth of her first child. While attempting to perform an episiotomy, she had cut the urinary opening by mistake! The child had survived, but poor

Cherotitch was painfully and permanently injured and, as a result, lost all urinary control. They say she cried to her mother-in-law, "If you did not want me to stay with your son, why didn't you tell me? Why hurt me? You are an evil woman! Now I must hang myself!" Luckily, people saw her in the tree with the rope around her neck, and they cut the rope just before she jumped. She nearly died from the fall. And so we sing:

Refrain:
> *Cherotitch, oh ileiya, ah!*

> *Cherotich oh ileya ah*

Verses:
> *Mother-in-law bans me from her house*
> *Mother-in-law cut me in a place of pain*
> *Cherotich*
> *Mother-in-law denies me her son*
> *Mother-in-law denies me health*
> *Mother-in-law cut my urethra*
> *Mother-in-law cut the meat of my leg*

> *Kisusion koko chi katanyi*
> *Kimultanun koko chi wolong wan*
> *Cherotich*
> *Kisusion koko chi werinyi*
> *Kisusion koko chi pulisha*
> *Kimutanun koko chi kupsuhkus*
> *Kimutanun koko chi pembuchat*

Sometimes women have problems during childbirth because of incidents that occur during their pregnancy. For instance, if a pregnant woman denies food to small children or a begging dog while she is fixing or eating a meal, her baby will not leave the womb when its time is due. People will notice this and question her, saying, "Tell us whether it was a dog or children you turned away." If she admits it was a dog, her people will call the dog at once and give it food, saying, *"You, dog! You cast a spell upon this woman for not feeding you! Let her child be born! She will not turn you away again. You are satisfied now!"* As soon as the dog finishes eating, the child will be born. Such a baby must be given one of four dog names: Kulkui or Longok for a boy; Chepkulkui or Longokwa for a girl. Likewise, if the wife refused to feed small children during her pregnancy, many little boys and girls are called to her home during her labor to be given food. When the children are satisfied, each one spits on his hands and wipes the saliva on her belly, saying, "Come, baby! We want you to come because you are our friend! We are satisfied now." The baby will be born quickly.

I heard one woman's labor was delayed because her belly longed for music. People implored her, "Tell us what your womb desires," and she answered, "I heard people singing at a dance once during this pregnancy, and I wanted to go so much that I could feel the longing in my womb." Children were brought at once to sing and dance for her until the baby came! Of course, it is not always possible to tend to a woman's desires for music during a difficult labor. If a woman said, "I long to hear the *pulkan*" (a stringed instrument), and if the musician was far away, there could be tragedy. People would have to improvise the best they could on another instrument.[92]

One evening, as I brought the cattle home, I heard someone singing faintly in our homestead. As I came nearer, I realized it was my wife, Chepusepa, singing for joy from inside her house,

> *Female genitals! Everyone hear!*
> *Oye, oyayo Oyewoye, yewoye, yewoye,*
> *Oyewoye, genitals of a girl!*
> *Female genitals! Chesokai,*
> *Oyewoye, song of the Ancient Mother Sameiwur, oyewoye*
> *Genitals of a girl!*

Happy and relieved, I herded our cattle into the corral, silently welcoming our little daughter.[93]

Only the midwife was supposed to handle the newborn baby. When our daughter was hungry, Chepusepa would lie down and the midwife would place the swaddled infant beside her. Then, when she finished nursing, Chepusepa would call to the midwife to come take the baby away. My wife was not allowed to prepare any food for at least one week after delivery. At the end of this period of rest, a hollow log was split and carved into an oblong wooden bowl so that Chepusepa could fill the bowl with water and ritually wash her hands. After that, she was allowed to prepare food, but if she had to nurse her baby before she finished cooking, she would have to wash her hands in the bowl again before returning to the food.

Chepusepa regained her strength quickly, but we soon became aware that our tiny little girl, so fragile at birth, was not thriving. In fact, she seemed to be getting weaker and more listless day by day. Desperate with worry, we decided to enlist the services of a man who knew how to conduct the ceremony of *saana*, which is intended to purify a mother who has become unable to produce a healthy child. (*Saana* is actually the name of the ritual bed, which is especially constructed for this purpose, spread with ashes and moved into the mother's house.)

In preparation for the blessing, Chepusepa and her baby began to lie together, covered with ashes, on *saana*, the bed of ashes. The next morning, I prepared beer, so that it would be ready on the fourth day, when the ritual leader would return to mix some of it with tree-root medicine and feed it to Chepusepa. My wife would use this mixture to wash the white ashes from her body and that of our infant. The bed would also be washed, dismantled and stored in a good place. Chepusepa would then drink three gourds of the beer and, hopefully, be cleansed. If Tororut saw fit to bless them, our baby girl would survive and be named either Chesaana or Cheptiren (A boy of *saana* is called either Kisaana or Ptiren), and Chepusepa would be able to have more healthy children.

But that is not how it happened. The day before the final cleansing ceremony would have taken place, I heard Chepusepa's wails of grief from inside the hut, and I knew that our baby was dead.

The Case of the Spear

Later that month I walked to Kitale, invested in more feathers, and set out to begin trading them for money or stock. I acquired several cattle on the first trip, and paid a man five shillings to take them to Kacheliba, where an auction was to be held in another two weeks. Then I went back home to rest with Chepusepa, who was still grieving over our lost child. A week later, I heard that Mr. Smith's car would be passing by Amudat soon on the way to the auction. I left immediately, spent a few nights waiting in the town for his arrival, and was rewarded by successfully hitching a ride to Kacheliba.

The auction was profitable. Mr. Smith bought two of my steers for 897 shillings and promised me a ride home later that afternoon. Happily, I carried my stool, my club, and my single spear (the government had recently forbidden us to carry two spears) to the river to drink and bathe. My bag of money was tied to my waist.

As I was walking back to the town, a police corporal called out to me, "Where are you going?

"Home," I called back.

"Where are you from?" he yelled.

"Around here," I answered, not wanting to complicate things.

"No! Come here!" he demanded. I walked over to him reluctantly.

"Hello," he began pleasantly.

"Hello," I answered, suspiciously.

"How are things?"

"Fine."

"Where is your home?"

"Oh, just over there at Koditch," I lied, hoping to end this inquisition.

"No it isn't."

"Why do you say that?" I was curious.

"Because no one here carries a spear."

"Oh? You mean it's against the law to carry even *one* spear now?" I asked cynically.

"Yes!"

Surprised and angry, I demanded, "How long has this been in effect? At which public meeting was this proclaimed? I surely haven't heard about this!"

The corporal ordered his assistant to seize my spear, but I refused to give it to him. He lunged at me, but I jumped to one side, reached down and grabbed a rock. "You will be sorry if you take my spear!" I warned. The assistant had no weapons, only the unopened can of beer he was holding.

The man's fist shot out at me, but I ducked. Then he grabbed me, while the corporal snatched my spear. I wrestled free and hit the assistant hard with my club. He started beating me with the beer can, but I knocked it away with my club and pounded it until the beer spilled out. When the assistant lunged towards me again, I banged him on the head. The blood poured out of his scalp like water in an irrigation trough.

The corporal himself then leaped upon me, wrestled me down and socked me repeatedly with his fists. I fought back, managing to throw him off. Quickly, I jumped up and hit the man twice in the gut with my club as he was trying to stand. But he socked me hard in the groin. I doubled over, then grabbed the soles of his shoes and flipped him over, hitting him four more times after he fell. That was my chance to escape. I dove for my club and ran, while the corporal blew his whistle loudly. Soon, there were three other policemen and four of their assistants following me.

I ran straight to the chief's quarters. As I entered the door, I was startled to see my friend Longol standing there with handcuffs on! He had been whipped badly; his body was covered with blood. Panting, I exclaimed, "Evidently people are being harassed on account of one spear now!"

"No!" Chief Kotit declared vehemently. "No one can accost people for carrying one spear! Even if they catch someone with two spears, they are allowed to seize only one. That's the law!"

I told Kotit what had happened, stressing that I had been careful not to hit the corporal on the head. (That would have meant trouble for sure!) Just then the three policemen burst into the room, accusing me of resisting the law. They declared, "It is not permitted for a man to carry a spear!"

"Indeed it is!" Kotit answered. The policemen seemed genuinely surprised. Chief Kotit shouted at them, "What's going on? Who gave you orders to arrest people and to seize their spears? I want to know!"

"Corporal Asea. This man was just attacking him..."

"And this man, Longol," Kotit interrupted. "Why did you whip that man? What did he steal? What did he do to justify your taking his spear?"

"He ... he was very drunk," one policeman stammered. "We took his spear because we thought he might kill someone."

"Oh really? It wasn't because of the spear alone? Did you see him quarrel with someone?"

"We did."

"Well, then it was justified."

The policemen left, and so did I, but I was not about to let this matter rest. I had already missed my ride anyway. I went to a doctor in town named Paranamba, told him about the incident and asked him to examine me. He looked at my wounds and announced pleasantly, "You're all right! I don't see anything bad."

"Look," I said. "The wounds don't matter. Injustice does. There's an important case to be made here, for the good of all of our people. Take these ten shillings and write me a good letter from the hospital." Paranamba accepted my money and gave me a letter claiming I had been given six injections at the hospital—a lie, of course. I sent the letter to the regional headquarters at Moroto. Then I asked Chief Kotit to write a letter for me to the Head Chief, Ameri, in Amudat. I put it on the mail truck myself.

Three weeks later, still in Kacheliba, I found someone who could write and dictated a second letter to Chief Ameri. This time I received a written reply from a European official named Mr. Docherty, who asked me to meet him in Amudat. I walked from Kacheliba to Amudat and met Docherty on the appointed day. He said, "Be here tomorrow morning at 8:00. I'll drive you to Kacheliba, where we will have the hearing." And so the next day we were back in Kacheliba again. A large group of men were already gathering for the court.

At my hearing, Corporal Asea claimed, "We found him fighting with another man! He was about to murder him with a spear!"

"Where is the other person? Did you detain him?" the officials asked.

"No."

"Then that's *your* problem! Now—there are 27 spears in your house. To whom do they belong?"

"We confiscated them all."

Just then a man named Lalangole stood and said, "The police took my spear without cause!" There were witnesses. "Mine too!" said another, and soon there were six men echoing the complaint.

Mr. Docherty asked Corporal Asea if he was the man in charge.

"Yes sir," answered Asea.

"Then why do you steal things from people?"

"That's a lie!" Asea shouted, but Docherty slapped him down and socked him in the jaw. "Get out of here!" he told Asea.

After the corporal left, Docherty asked me, "Do you know your spear?"

"Yes," I answered.

"Go get it."

I went to the police house, retrieved my spear and went home. A few days later I heard that Asea had been taken to Moroto and fired from his post.[94]

Purifying Our Son

It was several months after our infant daughter died that I returned from a trading expedition to find Chepusepa pregnant again. This was cause for great concern. If all went well, my Chepusepa would be given the additional name of Cheptun, meaning a mother who conceived immediately after marriage or childbirth without first having menstruated. Similarly, a mother of twins is named Chesalaa or Kamasalaa—*salaa* meaning "two things"—and a mother who has had a breech birth is called Chesowar. The first baby born in any of these ways is called Sheep, which, in Pokot, is Chemakal for a girl and Makal for a boy. Such an unusual birth calls for the large ritual cleansing ceremony we call *riwoi*.

Just before Chepusepa was due, I collected a great deal of honey for the beer that would be needed. I chose two sheep and a cow for the occasion and went to see a friend who had gone through *riwoi* with his wife. He agreed to be the ritual leader.

The evening Chepusepa went into labor, I got busy preparing the beer. After five gourds were ready, I waited in the darkness until I heard the women inside her house singing happily:

> *A very big occasion! A very big occasion! Sons of Nunu! Sons of Chepkur! ...*

> *Olileye, oyeooo, olileye! Take out the ox horns! The horns of a chepomut!*

They were songs of a boy![95] Our son Makal had been born!

I slaughtered one of the sheep and butchered it. Then, as dawn was breaking, I joined my wife and infant son inside the house. We would stay there together until the beer fermented, walking outside freely only at night. When Chepusepa or I had to go out during the day to urinate, we would cover ourselves with skins, so that the sun could not shine upon our heads. My wife and I were required to wear our sandals at all times, even while we slept. The only food we were allowed to eat was the roasted mutton from the sheep I had butchered, and Chepusepa could eat it only at night. Other meats, grains and milk were forbidden.

Early on the morning when the beer was ready, the man I had chosen as the leader arrived at the corral gate and began to sing:

Refrain:
> *Aya Makale, Chemakalo ...*

Verses:	*Aya Makale Chemakalo ...*
Oye riwoi wa oye ah	*Oye riwoi wa oye ah*
The birth is finished!	*Kupundu ainan*
Celebrate riwoi	*Kupunde riwoi*
Mother of babies, riwoi	*Kipu tongionu riwoi*
Riwoi is so dear!	*Anyen nyeso riwoi*

After he finished the song, my people brought him a gourd of beer and a tiny cup of *susinion* root medicine. He carried the vessels to our house, and we came outside. Then he sipped some of the medicine and spat it over his shoulders, under his armpits and through his legs, and he sipped and spat the beer likewise. All those present who had previously celebrated *riwoi* came forward to partake of these liquids in the same manner. Chepusepa and I were the last to be served. Unlike the others, we were not allowed to hold the cups in our hands; the ritual leader held them while we drank and spat the medicine and the beer as the others had done.

Next, Chepusepa and I went into the corral and stood near the gate, while everyone else finished drinking the gourd of beer. Then I began to sing, as I walked back to our house, followed by Chepusepa, holding Makal. I sang and danced four more songs as vigorously as I could before entering the house. Once inside, my wife and I sat down and drank a whole gourd of beer.

When it came time for us to walk out again amongst our cattle, I carried my spear and shield. All the other people quickly surrounded the cattle and started bombarding me with cow dung, while I used the shield for protection. Then the ritual leader, his wife and child gathered some of the dung together in the center of the corral and molded it into the shapes of a homestead: the corral, houses, and enclosures for calves and goats. Into the middle of this model the family placed a skin pouch containing tomato-like fruits and certain roots which have a milky pith.

The leader then led the cow I had chosen to Chepusepa. She held it, while he poured some of the root medicine and some of the beer into its mouth, making sure the cow swallowed, and he poured both liquids on the cow's back. He took four ropes made from tree roots and tied one around the cow's neck and one each around the necks of Makal, Chepusepa and myself. We could no longer drink the milk of this cow, which would be called Cheriwoi, and we could bleed it or slaughter it only at night.

Everyone began to sing, while Chepusepa, Makal and I returned to our house to consume another gourd of beer, sitting on Chepusepa's bed. Presently, the ceremonial leader came to the door of our house, leading the ram I had selected, singing.

Oye riwoi ya, Oye riwoi ya
Come to the ritual of roasted meat (x2)
Don't overlook this ritual
Come to this ritual slowly
This is a matter of intercourse
Come to the ritual of conception

Oye riwoi ya, Oye riwoi ya
Anyono tiomba chererum (x2)
Anyo tiomba makapeng
Nyono tiomba kopamot
Anyo tiomba tulungus
Nyono tiomba chepunos

I came to the door, while my friend sang again the song of the sheep, called Chemakal, which he had first sung at the corral gate. Then he led the ram away, fastened a rope around its neck and hung it from the high branch of a nearby tree.

(For a girl baby, a male goat is killed.) After it was skinned and stewed in an earthen pot, the leader's wife put the mutton on a large wooden plate and brought it to her husband to carve.

Those who had previously celebrated *riwoi* were privileged to eat their meat inside the house with Chepusepa and myself, while the others ate outside. After the meat, those of us inside the house were served soup. According to custom, as each participant took his filled soup bowl, he began to sing the song for drinking soup. (Those who waited outside did not drink soup or sing, for they had not yet been cleansed with *riwoi*.) Finally, we drank another gourd of beer, and everyone went home.

Now that our son Makal had been properly blessed, Chepusepa and I were once again allowed to drink milk, eat porridge, walk barefoot, and go out freely in the sunshine. And because I celebrated *riwoi* for my own son, I am now qualified to perform this ritual for others.

Any boy or girl healed through the ceremonies of *saana* or *riwoi* must take certain precautions during childhood. For instance, our son would not be allowed to pierce his mouth or ears with thorns freely like other children. In fact, it is ominous for such children to bleed at all. If another child hit Makal and caused him to bleed, we would have to kill a goat and wipe its stomach contents on our son to protect him from possible tragedy. Similarly, children of *riwoi* must not engage in sexual intercourse until *kitula*, a final blessing ritual, is performed, usually just before adolescence. After that, they are allowed to participate in all normal activities. [*Kitula will be explained in the chapter entitled "Sub-Chief."*][96]

Riwoi continues to remain a special ceremony for my people. Even a man who has attained the knowledge of white people would not dare to put aside this custom. Without *riwoi*, his family and herds might suffer, and he would be forced to seek a man such as me to perform the ritual in order to save his family.

WITCHCRAFT, MAGIC AND DIVINING

Witch Hunts

1955 was the year of the witch killings.[97]

Lokutamoi was the first. People discovered he had been practicing sorcery when his own brother died, asking, "Lokutamoi, why are you killing us like this?" Three days later, a band of 15 people, all relatives of his suspected victims, gathered together and marched to Lokutamoi's homestead. They seized him and pushed him outside to interrogate him.

They asked Lokutamoi, "Do you know so-and-so?"
'Yes."
"Where is he now?"
"He died."
"What killed him?"
"I don't know."

They questioned him like this about the deaths of six people, and finally someone grew impatient, grabbed a stone and threw it. Soon the whole mob joined in the slaying. Just before Lokutamoi died, he admitted, "Yes, I hexed those people—and even others you don't know!" He listed four more victims before he was silenced by a stone.

After Lokutamoi, the people purged the country of sorcery, killing 15 others in about a year. I was trading most of that time and heard many stories about the witch hunts. The men were stoned and the women were beaten to death with clubs. I was told that four were beaten, but didn't die. One of those, Chepukapai, screamed so loudly that some soldiers heard and rescued her. They say she pleaded with them, "I'll throw away all my witchcraft forever, if you will help me!" They took her into the town, and no one ever found her after that. However, we still remember her in a song that we like to sing at *laleyo*:

Refrain:
    Oh yoiye laleya Chepukapai, wife   *O yoiye, laleya, Chepukapai, korko*

Verses:
    Painful switch of the kurongora (circumcision year)   *Nguan sitot kurongora*
    Summon the soldiers! Soldier!   *Kungo kangen! Kanga!*
    Call for Sergeant (Major) *Tuwut Tongoquang!*   *Okurua sachen Tuwut Tongoquang!*
    Call for (Corporal) *Keralem!*   *Okurua a Keralem!*
    Call for (the policeman) *Lomongole!*   *Okurua Lomongole!*

One who did not get away was Apula. His fate was sealed when a powerful healer named Kalasingo Lorot, who had been called to examine a sick man, announced, "A man named Apula has bewitched this person! He keeps his magic in a cave by the river below his house. You must go and dig it up! The entrance to the cave is partially hidden by rocks."

The sick man's relatives found the cave that afternoon. They removed a lot of stones from the entrance and searched inside until they found a hole in which a pot was buried. When they opened the pot, the stench was unbearable! Inside were human fingers and skin, breasts of a woman who had suckled a child, breasts of a girl, a man's penis and the genitals of a woman. They realized that Apula was, indeed, a sorcerer who must have killed many people. Furious, they climbed up to Apula's compound, seized him and shoved him to the homestead of the sick man, where they beat him until he asked to be allowed to hang him-self. The people agreed, but since no one wanted to watch the hanging, it was decided that only those of Apula's clan would have to go. We heard later that Apula's wife and his first-born child, still doubting his guilt, held the rope and asked him, "Are you really a sorcerer?" When he answered, "Yes," they replied, "Then hang!" and he did. Naturally, at the next *laleyo*, we laughed about him in song:

Refrain:

Go away forever, you sorcerers!

Kepe kokai ponu!

Verses:

Apula, Apula, Kalasinga comes.
Apula, Apula, the son of Lopewut, comes.
Apula, Apula, Lorot comes.
Apula, Apula, the flesh of people kills.
Apula, Apula, Apula

Apula, Apula, anyono Kalasinga
Apula, Apula, anyonu wero Lopewut
Apula, Apula, anyonu Lorut
Apula, Apula, kipara soka
Apula, Apula, Apula

I was still away trading when two of my own neighbors became involved in a dispute over witchcraft. First, someone accused Woput of being a sorcerer, and several people went to beat him up. Longiro broke both of his arms. When I first heard about the incident, I did not believe the accusations against Woput. How-ever, as we later found out, my neighbor did, indeed, have a little magic, and he began to use it as revenge against Longiro.

You see, as time passed, Longiro became progressively more emaciated, and at the end of three years, he looked like a skeleton covered with loose skin, except for a huge, protruding belly. He could not even get up to go outside. Whenever people expressed concern, he would say, "I'm not sick! I feel fine!"

"You're nearly dead," we insisted. "You look horrible, and you can't even walk. Tell us where you feel sick, so we can help you."

"Maybe I don't look well," Longiro would answer. "But I don't hurt any-where."

Finally, Longiro's brother made beer and took it to Woput's homestead. Wop-ut asked him, "Where does your brother feel bad?"

"He can't tell us."

"Then he must not be sick! How do you expect me to give advice about an illness, when the person doesn't even feel bad?" He returned the man's beer.

The brother went home, made more beer, and took it, together with a cow and a sheep, back to Woput's house. Woput declared, "You surround me with your things, because you think I put a spell on your brother! But tell me, how could I have done that, if he has no pain?"

Longiro's desperate brother insisted, "Here! Take more cattle! Even if you are not a sorcerer, take them!" He left the cow, the sheep and beer at Woput's homestead and promised to bring more cattle. Woput drank the beer, then sent a message to Longiro's brother: "I want three more gourds of beer. Bring one here, put one inside your house and the third in the middle of the path—halfway between our homesteads. After I have drunk these three, I will consider helping your brother. But if he cannot even tell me where he is sick, I will be angry!"

The brother did as Woput directed. On the appointed day, Woput drank the three gourds of beer. Then he went to see Longiro in his house. "Where are you sick?" he demanded.

"I don't know."

"Then why do you thrust your things at me—your cattle and beer?"

"People think you might have hexed me."

Woput shouted angrily at Longiro, "You *broke my arms!* What had I done to you? Was there a child of yours, a brother, or a wife that I bewitched? *No!* Did I cast a spell on your cattle or goats? *No!* Yet you broke my arms for no reason at all!" He brandished his club, screaming, *"Get out! Get out of this house!"*

Longiro, for the first time in months, got up and ducked out of the door. Woput followed on his heels, beating him with the club. *"You had better run!"* he yelled, and Longiro ran, stumbling. Woput chased after Longiro, hitting at him, as if he was a small child.

After one week, Longiro started walking about and began to gain weight again. His family gave cattle, four gourds of beer, a female sheep, and six white ostrich feathers to our neighbor Woput, and the matter was finished.

Curses, Cunning and Revenge

Not all spells are equally bad: some kill and others just cause suffering. For instance, one man I know can cause people to walk very slowly, like children who are just learning to toddle. This is unfortunate, but it is not terrible. In fact, it can be a good punishment for thieves and other wrongdoers. One of our neighbors can cause an adulterous wife to pass gas constantly—when she walks about, when she sits, and even when she sleeps—making a loud noise, like a donkey braying!

A similar fate befell an acquaintance of mine, who made the huge mistake of having an affair with the wife of Ariko, a witchdoctor. Ariko cast a spell on him, giving him uncontrollable diarrhea. His feces left a trail behind him wherever he went, and whenever he sat down, he farted. No one would go near him! He was so repulsive while under that spell that even if he had died, it would have been a matter of little concern!

Many years later, a policeman named Angatun, meaning "lion", seized one of Lorikongoi's two wives, locked her up in his house and slept with her.

Lorikongoi caused Angatun to pass gas continuously for one month. He lost his appetite and became lethargic. Then one day, while on safari, Angatun fell on his loaded gun and was killed. His companions said that even as he died, he farted!

When I was a youth, living in other homesteads and taking our cattle to pasture, I would sometimes hear stories about local people who had caused mischief through the use of magic.

One was Riwongole. They say that he could not rest after his Karamojong wife, Longolan, left him and their small child to run off with Lopulungich. Even though Longolan's parents returned the sixty cattle Riwongole had paid for her a year earlier, he felt he also deserved some compensation from the man who had stolen his wife.

Well, everyone knows how cattle fear tortoises. Riwongole got his revenge by using magic to cause 200 tortoises to surround Lopulungich's homestead. Slowly, they made their way through the thorn fence and into the houses and the corral. They struck at the cattle like scorpions! Lopulungich's herd bolted, and slept that night in the bush. The next morning, 200 large birds with long legs and large bills with pouches came and perched all around the homestead. The people were horrified. They packed their belongings, rounded up the cattle and moved, but the tortoises followed, slowly and persistently. By nightfall, they were all over the new homestead, and in the morning, the birds came.

Lopulungich took two pregnant cows, six large oxen, a ewe and six ostrich feathers to Riwongole, saying, "I am giving these to you, because I wronged you. If you will remove the tortoises and birds from my homestead, so that my cattle can stay there, I will pay you for your wife." Riwongole agreed.

Lopulungich returned to find the tortoises and birds gone. Yet when he herded the cattle into the corral, the mothers began rejecting their calves. This was a grave matter indeed. Lopulungich returned immediately to the homestead of Riwongole, this time leading the *kiruk*, the bull who sired his cattle, as well as two cows.

"Now you must make an oath, for I have taken out the *kiruk*. Beware if you lie in the presence of the *kiruk*!" Lopulungich threatened. Riwongole agreed to stop tormenting Lopulungich, and they negotiated a compensation for Longolan. Lopulungich returned to find the calves nursing once again, and his people drinking milk. He paid Riwongole 45 additional cattle for his wife Longolan, and the matter was finished.

Another wizard, Lomoi, sent a hyena to sleep with an acquaintance who kept arguing with him. The hyena crawled under the man's blanket, causing him to fall into a deep sleep, and in the morning, his people were unable to awaken him. They pulled back the blanket, saw the hyena and screamed! The startled animal ran away before the people could kill it, and the man awakened.

He went immediately to Lomoi and begged him not to bring the hyena back. Lomoi countered, "Ha! You cursed me! Don't you ever insult me again!"

"We won't," the man reassured him. "Please help us. We'll remember you."

Lomoi demanded beer and tobacco. Then he mixed white clay with the milk and urine of his cattle. The hyena understood from this signal that his work for the wizard was finished, and returned to his lair.

Finally, we heard of a cunning man named Kalakas, who placed the body of his dead child at the gate of a neighbor's corral. Early the next morning, Kalakas walked by the neighbor's homestead asking, "Has anyone seen my child? He is lost!" The people there had not yet let their cattle out, and so they answered, "We have not seen him." Then Kalakas pretended to pass casually by the corral gate. He shrieked, "*Ooohhh!* He's here! Don't you see? My child has died at your gate! Your cattle trampled my child to death!" He complained loudly, and finally made a case before the elders. The neighbor was required to pay a fine, although he knew he had been deceived.[98]

Powerful Families

Magic often runs in families. When a father dies, his son inherits the power. Take my neighbor Lokudon, for instance, whose father's very presence was cause for concern. They say that when Lokudon's father would rest outside someone's homestead, people would always bring him milk and a goat to slaughter. If they didn't, the next day the cows would reject their calves and the she-goats their kids, and the animals would get lost when they went out to graze! Lokudon's father always denied that he had anything to do with these circumstances. When people came to him distressed, he would offer, "I'll ask Tororut to help return your cattle, if you wish, but when they come home, don't say it was because of me!" Yet, invariably, as soon as people took milk and a goat to Lokudon's father to ask his assistance, the cows would begin lowing and searching for their calves and the trouble would be finished.

I heard that once his cattle grazed in a pasture reserved for the dry season, and his cowherds were beaten and forced to sacrifice a steer as punishment. The following day, all but two of those who had punished the cowherds were afflicted with blindness or painful eyes. They ran to Lokudon's father and begged forgiveness, offering him tobacco. The old man spread white clay on their faces and gave them some to take to the two who had not come. Then he demanded that all of them come the next day to apologize. The young men came, bringing tobacco and beer, and they promised to slaughter a large steer for him. Their recovery was almost instant.

It was not long after his father's death that those of us who were living in the vicinity of Amudat realized that Lokudon had inherited the ancestral wizardry. It all started when Lokudon's wife ran off with a Karamojong man named Lobuin, who was living in Amudat. The lovers enjoyed a few days of pleasure, before Lokudon discovered his wife's infidelity. Then, suddenly, the Karamojong lover became impotent! He was at a loss and told Lokudon's wife, "You'd better go! There is nothing for you here!" She soon found another lover, then another, but all were equally flaccid! By the time she realized what was happening, she had earned a scandalous reputation in the town. She fled in a car to Kapenguria and then traveled on to Chepureria, where she lived with an old man who had become a sexual corpse long ago.

Meanwhile, Lokudon began searching for his wife. He questioned Lobuin in Amudat, but the Karamojong man denied stealing the woman. Lokudon warned him, "If you lie, you'll pay for it! In one week you won't even be able to leave your home!"

Sure enough, a few days after Lokudon found his wife and took her back to Uganda, a messenger from Lobuin's household reported that Lobuin's eyes were smarting with so much pain that he was unable to come himself to admit sleeping with Lokudon's wife. He was willing to pay the penalty for adultery—thirty cattle. Lokudon, however, demanded sixty—thirty because of the adultery and thirty for lying about it.

Unfortunately, Lobuin could only afford thirty cattle. When his eyes had recovered somewhat, he brought a black steer to slaughter at Lokudon's corral, spreading the stomach contents on the children and herds, according to custom. Lokudon, in return, smeared black clay on Lobuin and gave him some milk. Lobuin's eyes healed, but, because he paid only part of the fine, he remained impotent from that day onwards.

Now you must admit: that is a powerful spell! Recently, I tried to buy some of this magic from Lokudon (You never can tell what might tempt your wives while you're away), but, alas, he had died. However Lokudon's eldest son, Tomele, is my age. I think I may go to him.

Casting Spells

People sometimes contract with practitioners for certain magical services. If someone steals your cattle, goats, honey or other valuables, and if you find his footprints, you can choose to cast a lethal spell on him called *mutat*.[99] You take the dirt from the footprints and a gourd of beer to the appropriate specialist, and trust him to perform the magic for you. Then you wait. One day you will be told that the thief has died and that, just before he died, he admitted stealing from you. As soon as you hear this, you must pay 40 shillings to the practitioner you hired. This is an ancient practice, still very much in use today.

Sometimes it is even possible to buy good fortune. In return for money or cattle, certain specialists will give you whatever you want, such as riches or children. It is also, of course, within their powers to deny you these pleasures. But if such a specialist is agreeable, and if you have paid him well, you will know success.

Ordinary people can also practice certain kinds of magic. I have told you how my family has been successful in asking our stolen cattle to cast spells on the families of Makal and Munyan. And we, like others, have used oaths to threaten and punish those who were lying against us.

There are several forms of oaths. An accused person may drink a mixture of milk, blood, clay pigments, or other prescribed liquids. A cow may be split in half and the blood scattered on the parties concerned. I have already mentioned some of the others—jumping over a hyena head or accepting earth together with a shaving knife. A defendant is suspected if he refuses to participate in an oath, but the consequences are severe for those participants without a clear conscience. Death will surely come to those who lie.

Animal Magic

It is possible for domestic animals to have powers of sorcery, and there are ways to tell whether certain animals in a herd are affected. Goats, for instance, will vomit, bleed through the nose, and nearly die, then completely recover. There are five manifestations of sorcery in cattle: vomiting, nosebleeding, looking up and sticking out its tongue, wrapping its tail around a stick, and getting its head caught tightly in branches. Of course, a cow may do all these things without being seen, and will acquire the power to kill—especially sick people. Typically, the victim will become deathly ill in the afternoon, recover by evening, take a turn for the worse during the night, recover in the morning and relapse that afternoon. In such cases, the elders will plead with their herds to show them the sorcerer, for if the evil cow is not found, the person will die, regardless of medicine or doctors' efforts.

Three birds in particular have magical powers. The *ptieltiel*, a friendly woodpecker with a red head and rump, which drills holes for its nests into very hard trees, comes to people in the daytime, speaking to them and bringing them good luck on their journeys. Their cries can also help the elders prophesy about the success of an impending marriage.[100] However, if a *ptieltiel* flies around a walking person and then dies, bad luck will certainly follow. The long-tailed *siririt* and the *biukook*, with its human-like ears, cast their spells in darkness. If either of these birds perches on top of a house and sings during the night, people will die.

Divining

Divining is not magic, but a skill which is passed down from generation to generation, often within a family. We know of three ways to tell the future and see distant events: reading milk, throwing sandals, and studying the intestines of cattle or goats. All three are used to answer the same sorts of questions. I have also seen the Karamojong and the Turkana make predictions with intestines and shoes. These divining practices are good. Not only do they occasionally save a

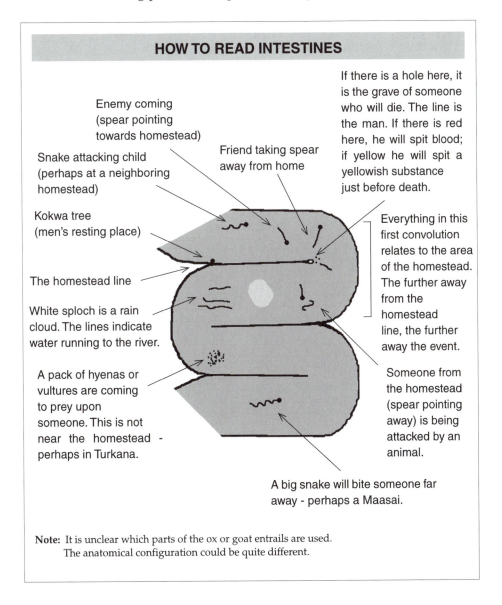

HOW TO READ INTESTINES

Enemy coming (spear pointing towards homestead)

If there is a hole here, it is the grave of someone who will die. The line is the man. If there is red here, he will spit blood; if yellow he will spit a yellowish substance just before death.

Snake attacking child (perhaps at a neighboring homestead)

Friend taking spear away from home

Kokwa tree (men's resting place)

Everything in this first convolution relates to the area of the homestead. The further away from the homestead line, the further away the event.

The homestead line

White sploch is a rain cloud. The lines indicate water running to the river.

A pack of hyenas or vultures are coming to prey upon someone. This is not near the homestead - perhaps in Turkana.

Someone from the homestead (spear pointing away) is being attacked by an animal.

A big snake will bite someone far away - perhaps a Maasai.

Note: It is unclear which parts of the ox or goat entrails are used. The anatomical configuration could be quite different.

life, but they let us know what to expect, so that we can be prepared and avoid disaster, if possible.

A diviner of milk is known as Chepukapul, literally, "person who reads water." When someone is ill, Chepukapul goes out very early in the morning and milks a cow which has calved once and whose calf is healthy and present in the herd. He or she takes this milk and some tobacco to the sick person's house. After studying the milk, Chepukapul might say, "Someone has cast a spell upon this man. Go find a white goat and kill it." (The milk will reveal which kind and color of goat will cure the person.)

The diviner who throws sandals will place one shilling on each sandal. Then he puts tobacco on the fire and waits ten minutes. When he begins tossing the shoes, he studies the way each lands. The positions of the sandals tell him whether a sorcerer has made trouble, if the cattle are threatened, or if someone will be sick, among other things.[101]

When I was still a child, I remember people coming to my father, who knew the art of reading intestines. He could tell them if an enemy was coming or if Pokot from other areas were raiding and how many were to be killed in those incidents. The intestines would tell him about the rains, the cattle, and whether the year would bring a good harvest. If a man was sick, Father would kill a cow to see whether he would die. He might have to kill several cattle before finding one that said the man would live, thus influencing Fate in favor of his cure. Through the years, Father has taught me this art, and now I have also become a knowledgeable reader of intestines.[102]

Once my father read a goat's intestines and exclaimed, "Look! There are people fighting near here! There is a spear from our homestead—the spear of an adult, and he is fighting a dangerous animal. I don't know who it is, but I don't think it's bad." Then, on second thought, Father decided he'd better kill another goat just in case. He studied the intestines and found them clear. And that was how he saved me from being killed by a lion that was mauling me!

I heard that long ago in Kupkomo, a diviner read the intestines of an ox and told the people, "Enemies have come! There will be much bloodshed! At Kamatira, the victory will be ours, and the cattle saved, but later there will be a massacre, unless you do as I say: you must sacrifice four red steers, two red goats and two red sheep at the place I will show you. The blood of these animals will take the place of the human blood that will otherwise spill there."

At that time, two groups of *tios* were living in their circumcision house at Kupkomo. Unimpressed with the predictions and thinking the elder a fool, they decided to prove themselves as warriors. They declared, "If there is danger, we want to be there! Nothing can kill us!" They collected their spears and hiked to the locality the elder had mentioned, where they encountered two groups of Maasai youths sitting together. Others had gone to Kupkomo early that morning, raided Pokot cattle and killed many people. When they saw the Pokot warriors, the Maasai yelled, "Come meet us here! Then you will know that we also are youths who have come out of the fire, just as we see you look like boys have come from your circumcision house!"

"Yes! We are!" the Pokot warriors challenged.

The fighting was grisly, and when it was over there remained 16 wounded, exhausted Pokot youths and one very fit Maasai giant named Lounun. At first they just stared at each other. One of the old survivors of that battle told me, "If some other Pokot reinforcements had not come just then, Lounun would have killed us all! He was the largest man I have ever seen. Only Sakwar could equal him in breadth, but not in height! Lounun was finally killed by a poisoned arrow, but even as he died, he lunged towards us with his knife and his spear. Then his hair came out and he fell. One poisoned arrow was sufficient."

After the battle, people followed tracks to Kamatira and found that the cattle had already been returned. The Pokot there had killed many Maasai, and the others had run off.

The archer who shot Lounun was called Sesiamoi, after a Karamojong woman he had once killed. Sesiamoi told everyone about the fight and about the size of his victim, Lounun. Many came to see the body, lying there among the dead and wounded who were too weak to go home, and they were amazed. Some speculated that Lounun might have been a son of Tororut. They dug holes and erected huge stones to mark the height and breadth of the body, so that they could show their children the size of the enemy they had fought at that spot. The stones are still there today, and the place is called Lounun. The soil is red and barren, devoid of trees or grass, as if pools of human blood, like petrol, burned the area into a wasteland. We have not seen the Maasai since. Evidently, the Europeans took over the country at that time and chased them far away.[103]

CELEBRATIONS

After Makal's birth, I continued to profit handsomely from my cattle trading business. Our little son grew quickly, and Chepusepa began to wean him to a mixture of cow's milk and root juice. (Babies under about a year and a half should not drink cow's milk or eat certain meats without first mixing it with the root medicine.) Soon Chepusepa was pregnant again!

Songs of the Bards

One day the three of us attended a *sapana* celebration for our friend's son. After
we had feasted, sung and danced for a while, one of our elders, a talented com-
poser of songs, told everyone to be quiet. Soon the crowd was hushed, and we
waited eagerly to hear our bard's latest creation. His abilities were well known.
People sometimes came to him for help when they were making up songs, and
he never failed to find the appropriate words. Now he declared, "I'll put in a song
of mine you've never heard before! Tell me what you think of it!" And he sang:

> *O yoiye Chepuseipei oye*

O yoiye Chepuseipei oye

Refrain:
> *Reveal the baby goat*
> *Reveal the baby goat*
> *Chepuseipei, the baby goat*

Ho porua wawa,
Ho porua wawa
Chepuseipei wawe

Verses:
> *Daughters of the white monkey clan*
> *Daughters that tie* (cords around their newborns') *ankles*
> (Ending with a high-pitched trill)

Oye tipiko kundoro oye
Tipiko kuna kel

Everyone cheered and began to sing and dance to the new song, including my
friend, Chepuseipei's brother, who was there. We have rejoiced in song ever since
over his sister.

Chepuseipei ran away only a week after she was married. Her husband found
her and brought her back, but, alas, after two more weeks, she was lost again!
Her husband searched for her throughout Moruita, but to no avail. Then a friend
confided, "I think your wife is quite safe. In fact, there is reason to believe she is
having an affair with a certain man. You must be very clever if you hope to find
her." Chepuseipei's husband thought this over. He knew he would never find his
wife if he went around broadcasting that he was searching for her. She would
only hide or run away. He would need to think of another pretence.

He arrived at the homestead of his wife's supposed lover the following morning with three of his companions. The cattle were standing just outside the corral.
"Friends!" he called to the men there. "I've lost a goat! Have any of you seen
it?"

"No."

"It's a kid of one of your goats," one of his friends explained. "We've searched
everywhere for it. Maybe it wandered back here." He continued talking, while
Chepuseipei's husband slipped into the homestead and began searching all the

houses. It was a large settlement: five men and their families lived there. When the people asked what he was doing there, Chepuseipei's husband claimed he was searching for his baby goat. Finally, two houses remained. "Well, if it's not in either of these, it must be lost in the bush," he declared casually. "Perhaps it will come back tonight. I'll have to come back later, but first I'll look in these two homes."

He entered the largest house. It was three or four times the size of a typical dwelling, with a place for the goats to sleep, a compartment for their kids, a place for the calves, and one for the people. It took his eyes a long time to adjust to the darkness, especially on one side of the house. A woman was there, holding a small baby.

"Woman!" he called into the darkness. "Where is my baby goat? I hear it wandered into your herd."

"You are mistaken," she answered.

"Perhaps you just aren't aware of it yet," he remarked, as he continued looking around. In one particularly dark place near the wall, he saw a large skin draped over something.

"What is this *koliko* hiding?" he asked, lifting it. There was Chepuseipei! He seized her, pushed her outside, and called to his companions to help him take her home. Chepuseipei eventually settled down and had a large family, but we have danced to her song ever since.[104]

Later that afternoon, we sang about another young runaway bride that many of us knew, but whose story had quite a different ending:

Even though her father had been paid 29 cattle and 30 goats for her, poor Cheptai was so repulsed by her husband, she would run away at night after he fell asleep to hide in other homesteads for days or weeks at a time. Yet, no matter how hard she tried to hide, her husband inevitably found her and forced her home. This went on for six months, and Cheptai became increasingly desperate.

There was only one person to whom she could confide—a youth named Malowor, who lived in a neighboring homestead. Whenever they had a chance, the two would meet in an isolated place, and Malowor would try to comfort his frustrated friend. In fact, it was Malowor who finally talked Cheptai out of hanging herself or running away to the Karamojong or the Turkana.

"No! Please don't go! Don't destroy yourself!" he had pleaded with her. "If you can only love me, I promise that one day you will rejoice over my words. Death has no reward, but life can bring you happiness—trust me! Believe me! Stay even here in the wilderness, and I will tend to you. One day your father will feel enough pain to return the cattle of the man you despise, and you will be my wife!"

Thus Cheptai went to live in the bush. She slept in a small cave at the top of a mountain, where her family stored surplus food in a large woven *adulaa*. She knew her family often visited their other, much bigger, cave, where they kept four *adulaa* filled with millet and sorghum, but they hardly ever used the food in the small cave. With plentiful food, a cooking pot, and a vessel for carrying water, Cheptai was able to survive undetected for six more months. Malowor, now her lover, came frequently to comfort her at night, leaving secretly before each dawn.

As the months went by, Cheptai's family became increasingly concerned over the extended disappearance of their daughter. "Why has no one seen her?" her mother worried.

"Where would she sleep?" agonized her father.

"It must be the child has hung herself!" Cheptai's mother concluded, and no one could console her. She cried incessantly, and everyone feared that she, too, would hang herself.

One day after a storm, a youth from that homestead was walking on a path below the small cave, when he recognized Cheptai's footprints in the drying mud. He followed the tracks for perhaps 100 yards and lost them on the rocks which led up to the small storage cave. Quickly, he ran back to tell Cheptai's mother. She climbed the mountain the next day. When she saw that the *adulaa* in the small cave was nearly empty, Cheptai's mother knelt beside the basket and wept tears of joy, for she knew that her daughter was alive. Then she hurried back to tell her husband, who was just as relieved and thankful.

Cheptai's brother was sent to keep watch on the cave every day after that. On the second afternoon, he saw his sister come into the shelter. From his hiding place in the bushes, he called, "Where did you come from?" Cheptai froze. "Where is your house?" he asked, still partially hidden.

"On ... on top of that hill," Cheptai stammered.

Her brother now revealed himself, saying, "Leave the food. Come, let's go home."

Cheptai withdrew, distressed, but he continued, "You've lived out here all these months! Aren't you coming home?"

"No! I'm not coming!" Cheptai protested. "If I did, you'd take me to that man. I can't stand him! I tried to hang myself, but I couldn't take the pain. Oh, please let me live in the wilderness! If the wild beasts eat me, that's all right! If a snake bites me, fine!"

"Let's go. I won't strike you," he said gently.

"I'm not going."

The brother exploded. "How dare you disobey me!" he shouted, leaping at her. He grabbed her arms and snarled, "You either come with me right now, or I'll beat you up and drag you home!"

Defeated at last, Cheptai whispered, "I'll come." She descended the mountain silently beside her brother, thinking, *Surely, death would have been better than this. If only I had had the courage to hang myself. If only I had not listened to Malowor. They* reached the homestead after sunset. Cheptai knew the cattle would be home and her father would be there. She felt ill as she entered the corral gate.

What happened then was totally unexpected. The women shrieked with delight when they saw her. Her mother ran to her, crying, and embraced her over and over. Then her father came. Cheptai bravely raised her eyes to meet his and was shocked to see him smiling at her! She gaped at him, and the women stepped aside to leave the two of them alone. There was a long, tense pause, and then he said in a loud voice, "We will return the herds of that man!" Everyone cheered, and the loudest voice was that of Cheptai.

It was not long before Malowor appeared to offer her father cattle for her hand in marriage. The wedding was a joyous occasion! And when the long rains came and the celebrations began, people said to one another, "That girl was a fugitive in the wilderness for nearly a year! Someone should make up a song about her for the dances! A well-known bard did, and we began to dance to the song of Cheptai:

Maiden, sleeping in the bush, Cheptai	*Cheptonyo cherruw wui, Cheptai*
Maiden, I was going into the wilderness	*Cheptonyo, kolintan opelnai*
Maiden, the son of home will return me	*Cheptonyo konyokuo wero kao*
Maiden, I have my helper, Malowor	*Cheptonyo otingeto remburan Malowor*

Parapara for Pregnancy

While I was dancing, one of the other guests called me aside and confronted me with some unexpected news. "Say Domonguria!" he greeted me. "You know that girl from Arol who stayed here for three months recently? Well, she's pregnant! She claims she slept with no one but you, and her family wants you to come for *parapara*!"

Parapara, as I have mentioned, is the ritual we perform for pregnant women to insure success in childbirth. It is very important, and only a fool would disregard it. However, my participation would mean I had accepted responsibility for fathering the child. I went back home and told my father, but he just shrugged, saying, "Well, that's your problem, and you'd better go see about it. You should have known this could happen, Domonguria. You should have waited until her "days" arrived to be sure she wasn't pregnant. Ah, but now it's up to you—you are a grown man! You don't need me to help you anymore. You are old enough to handle your own problems!"

I thanked him for his implied sanction, took 100 shillings and left. The next morning I made it to Ortum in time for the cattle auction, where I had four steers waiting, along with those of my partners. I was lucky. By the following morning, all four were sold. The largest drew 488 shillings, the smallest 240, and the others 350 and 295. I took my cash and hired a car with others to Sigor, planning to walk the rest of the way to Arol. When people in that region cautioned me about wild animals, I thought it prudent to buy a couple of spears from a man for ten shillings to carry on my journey.

As I neared Arol late that afternoon, I passed two women carrying water from the river. They must have spread the news of my arrival quickly, for soon a man came to question me. I explained that I had come from Uganda and was searching for the homestead of Maile (the girl's father). "Why, that is Maile's homestead," he remarked, indicating the nearest homestead.

I entered the corral and looked around for the *aperit*. Finally, a child took me to an area behind one of the houses. I waited there, and soon I saw Chesinen, my pregnant girlfriend, coming. She seemed very happy to see me. "Hey! Look how my stomach swells!" she exclaimed. "Uh huh! Thank you very much, Domonguria! It is wonderful!" She went to announce my arrival to her mother, who came quickly to welcome me. I found out later that she had been surprised to discover I was a fully-grown man and delighted to find out I was married.

While Chesinen lit the fire in the *aperit* and spread skins on the ground where I was sitting, I took my spears and belongings into the house, as they suggested. Chesinen's brother looked in at me briefly, and, as soon as I returned to the *aperit*, he came over to greet me. He asked my name, nodded, and questioned me, "Did you come here innocently, or because you heard the news?"

"I heard a report."

"Thank you! So it's true!"

"Yes."

"Oh, good!" He seemed very relieved.

I sat there in the *aperit* awhile longer. When the goats came home, I could hardly believe my eyes: there must have been over a thousand! Three houses on one side of the corral could hardly contain all the pregnant females! The goats kept coming and coming and I could see no end to them—they were like grains of sand! The people in the homestead hurried out to milk the goats and to round up all the kids. Then the cows came—over 50! and the calves—about 100!

"Ha! They're RICH!" I almost exclaimed aloud.

At last the steers came—all 200 of them! I was amazed. The homestead was now bustling with activity, especially milking. Chesinen came to ask me, "Which kind of milk do you prefer? Camel milk?"

"I'd like to try some camel milk! I've never tasted it!"

She explained, "Well, we have milk from two types—those that have finished nursing and those that are nursing now."

I was dumbfounded by the good fortune that surrounded me! "I am ignorant," I admitted. "Which is better?"

"Personally, I like the milk of the nursing mothers," Chesinen said as she walked off happily. Soon she returned with a gourd full of steaming camel milk. I drank until I was satisfied, and finished the whole gourd later.

That night, my girlfriend's brother told her to take my things into one of his houses, which was empty. There, she brought me more milk from the nursing camel, along with stiff porridge, which I ate ravenously. We slept together, quite satisfied.

The next day, the brother questioned me again, "What is your reaction to the situation? Do you accept responsibility for the pregnancy?"

"Yes, but only if she slept with me alone. If there were others, I don't know."

"She claims it was you alone. What do you wish to do?"

"There is only one way."

"Yes. Thank you. Are you ready now?"

"I don't know, but I'll try. I would like to see my brother Kokwa (my uncle's son), who also lives in this region, and have the ceremony in his homestead."

He said, "We will have to ask my father when he comes back. If he agrees to have the ceremony there, fine. If he orders it here, it must be so."

"Of course, but I'd prefer to do it there."

I spent three days at that homestead, having sent a message ahead to Kokwa to expect me on the fourth evening, as his homestead was far away. When I arrived, Kokwa had a huge gourd of beer waiting for me. I greeted his wives, Chepindaing and Chemalin, and Kokwa went to slaughter a goat for us. We drank and ate throughout the night, catching only a few hours' sleep just before dawn. After I had been there two days, I told Kokwa about the girl and how she wanted *parapara*. My cousin readily agreed to sponsor the ceremony.

"Here are 100 shillings for honey," I offered.

"Oh, that won't be necessary," he declared. "I have plenty of honey—seven huge gourds by the hive, three in Chepindaing's house, four in Chemalin's house and five others in a cave. But we could use the money to buy a heifer the Turkana wanted to sell us yesterday. They wanted 90 shillings, but the most any of us could offer was 86."

The next morning Kokwa and I bought the Turkana calf and then walked to Maile's homestead together. Maile considered our proposal and agreed to have the ceremony at Kokwa's homestead, provided that he was given two gourds of beer to drink first in his own homestead.

"Of course," replied Kokwa. "Even if you want three, we'll bring them!"

Having reached this agreement, we walked back to my cousin's house to prepare the beer. When it was ready, we sent the gourds to Maile's homestead with four women, two to carry each gourd. One of the women stayed overnight to wait for Chesinen, who had gone to buy maize and cassava, and brought her to Kokwa's homestead the next day.

Meanwhile, Kokwa and I collected ten gourds of honey and managed to find 22 empty gourds for making the beer. We prepared the mixture, and when it had fermented for three days, we summoned Maile and the man who had agreed to be the ritual leader for the ceremony.

On the day of *parapara*, Kokwa's family and I waited until we heard in the distance the sounds of Maile's people approaching (they had tied strings of bells on their legs), so that we could carry beer to them on the path just outside the homestead, as is the custom. Ten of Chesinen's people came: her father, his three wives, his brother, his son and their wives. They had spread white clay on their faces, like we do at weddings, and both the men and the women had decorated their heads with ostrich feathers (The women put theirs in the decorated head-bands we call *tenda*). Maile and his party drank the first gourd of beer sitting there on the path, and then we brought them another—the beer for taking off shoes. When that one was emptied, we fetched yet another gourd—that of greeting. We held it at the gate, as our households repeated greetings to each other. First were the men's greetings. We sang and answered each other many times, like this:

Greetings, girl's father, mm ...	*Takwes, kapikoi mm ...*
Greetings, father-to-be ...	*Takwes, soye ...*
Greetings, child's family, greetings ...	*Takwes monechi takwesa ...*
Greetings in-laws, greetings	*Takwes orotin takwes*
Health! to your health!	*Chemgech chemgecha*
Health, father-to-be, health ...	*Chemgech soya Chemgecha*

Next, the women began sang their greeting to each other:

Come here! Greetings, greetings	*Nona! Kongoi, kongoi a*
Greetings, family of mother-to-be, greetings	*Kongoi soye una kongoi*
Greetings girl's mother, greetings	*Kongoi pokura kongoi*
Greetings, Greetings ...	*Kongoi takwesa, kongoi ...*

After this greeting song, we presented the third gourd of beer to Maile's family. They drank, then washed their hands together with me and Kokwa, keeping the palms straight, according to custom. Afterwards, we spat, taking our time, and began to sing two more songs. The first one, *Alangana Alangitokona*, I don't know well. The second one goes like this:

Refrain:

Eko, eko, ah eko!	*Eko eko a eko*

Verse:

Say the parapara words for the mother-of-child	*Aparpar kama monung e*

Refrain:
>   *Ah eko e karawoiya*

Verses:
>   *Go to Emba Sotot* (where the ancestors) *came from*
>   *To find words that are there* (at the river)
>   *Go to Cheptulel*
>   *Ah, the people* (of long ago) *are there*
>   *They came from the hill Ipet*
>   *They are at Tokiss*
>   *They are the people of parapara*
>   *Say the parapara words that are taken away*
>   *Say the parapara words. Go.*
>   *We say these words* (so that) *the mother-of-child*
>   *will give birth* (easily) *like a donkey*
>   *Say parapara words* (so that) *the mother-of-child*
>   *will give birth* (easily) *like a rabbit*

>   *Ah eko e karawoiya*
>
>   *Kepe Emba Sotot kangunan*
>   *Kenyoru ngale cho kimi atoni*
>   *Kepe Cheptulel*
>   *Ah, kimi pichoni atoni*
>   *Kangunan kaipu Ipet*
>   *Kimito Tokiss*
>   *Kimi pichoni kaparparat*
>   *Aparpar choni kachengan*
>   *Aparpar chona. Awesta.*
>   *Keparpar kama monung koyo*
>   *koyei ta sukiria*
>   *Aparpar kama monung*
>   *koyei ta tutuiya*

We continued drinking and singing or saying the words of *parapara* until the following morning.[105] (There are many other songs for *parapara*.) Only Chesinen did not drink, for it is said that if a woman drinks the beer of her own *parapara*, all of her children will become thieves!

After dawn, the elders beckoned to Chesinen and me, and directed us to remove our clothing. The two of us sat naked on the ground, side by side, with our legs spread apart, her one leg overlapping mine, while they bathed us and washed all of our garments. Then we got up and walked into the corral. One old woman exclaimed loudly, "This mother is about to give birth! Oh look! She has delivered now, and we can hear the newborn baby cry!"

The other women all joined in, shouting, "Good! It's a girl! You've given birth to a girl!"

The elders countered, "No! A boy!"

"Wrong! A girl!"

They teased like this while Chesinen walked to the center of the corral and stood on the skin that had been laid there. She was given some *sosion* grass to hold, while we serenaded her with the four circumcision songs—two for girls and two for boys. When we finished, two small children—a girl and a boy— came with their mothers into the corral, each child holding a tiny gourd of milk and singing. The little children were led to their places, one on each side of Chesinen. (Sometimes there are four children instead of two, with a girl and a boy standing on each side of the pregnant woman.) She took their hands, turned them around four times, and the three of them sat down. Then an old woman brought a cup of honey and one of milk. She dipped the *sosion* into the milk, fed it to Ches inen, then dipped it into the honey and fed her again. She fed each of the children in the same way. When this was over, I joined them, and the people tied Chesinen and me together briefly, using a rope made out of roots. The ritual ended when Chesinen carried the small gourds back into the house.

The only happy challenge that remained after this was consuming the rest of the huge quantity of beer my cousin and I had prepared. Afterwards, Maile and his family went home, leaving his daughter at Kokwa's homestead for another two weeks. Before I left, I gave Chesinen 70 shillings: 60 for her own food and ten for her mother.

I traveled, then, to the Kerio valley to resume my trading. I bought six cattle, twelve goats and two donkeys with the remainder of the money I had earned at the auction. When, at last, I returned home, I found my wife, Chepusepa, with a new baby girl!

A few months later, I received word from Kokwa that Chesinen had given birth to a healthy daughter she had named Maile, like her father. After another year or two, I was sent greetings from the elder Maile, along with the news that his daughter had been married, and that our little girl was healthy and was living in her grandmother's house at the homestead I had visited.

I remained in Uganda throughout this daughter's childhood, while my cousin tended to all of the fatherly duties. One year, he sent me a report that Maile had been circumcised in his homestead, and I sent him my thanks. Shortly afterwards, a man requested my daughter in marriage, and Kokwa accepted the proposal. He received 20 cattle and 30 goats at the wedding, then sent me the news that our daughter's bride wealth was complete. Only then did I return to Kokwa's homestead. Maile's mother, Chesinen, came to greet me there and stayed four days with us. Before she left, she suggested, "Perhaps there is something you would like to give me?"

"Of course, I shall give you a present!" I responded quickly. "You are as a wife to me, the mother of my daughter. To refuse you anything would be abhorrent, for Tororut has blessed us with a child. We shall feast on good fortune until our demise!"

"Good!"

"First I need to go to Baringo, where I have relatives. When you hear I have returned, come to bid me good-bye and receive your gift."

"I will come."

I traveled along the banks of the Kerio until I had rounded up twelve of my cattle and ten goats from various households. I herded them to my cousin's home, then traveled to another area near Turkana, where I acquired six more goats. When I returned to Kokwa's household, Chesinen came once more, and I presented her with two goats and 15 shillings. She thanked me profusely. I left, then, for Uganda with my stock, including 15 cattle and 20 goats from the bride wealth.

I had given five cattle and ten goats to Kokwa for his help in raising my daughter.

Several years later, I returned to that region again and found my daughter pregnant. She already had another small child! We visited, and Maile remarked that she had a wish to see my home. "I want to see the homesteads of my father and my grandfather and to meet my grandmother," she said. I have waited for her ever since, but she has yet to come.

FAMILY CHANGES

Times were good. My cattle trading had been profitable, greatly increasing the family herd. My marriage was happy, and my children were thriving. Nyangaluk, now considered my father's child, was old enough to tend the goats, while our son Makal played happily around the homestead. I had received the welcome news of my daughter Maile's successful birth at Arol, and Chepusepa's infant daughter was nursing well. We were content.

Misfortune

Then, suddenly, our good fortune plummeted.

First, I became terribly sick. The illness was so severe and unrelenting that I finally consulted a diviner of sandals, who told me, "I see that you took six cattle that already belonged to another trader. He found out and threw a stick in your direction, casting a spell to make you ill."

I had, indeed, bought six cattle recently from a man named Loinyan but, alas, I had not known that they really belonged to another man! Many months later, after questioning Loinyan's neighbors, I would discover that a Somali named Adam Niworial had already bought those particular cattle before my arrival and had left them in Loinyan's corral with the intention of collecting them on his return trip. Then, when I arrived in the area, people had told Loinyan, "The son of Pturu is a good man. He buys lots of cattle for a better price than the Somali. We should have him sold our cattle!"

Loinyan had answered, "Show him the cattle anyway, but don't tell him they are already sold, or he won't consider them. As a trader, he would consider it dishonest." And so I had bought the cattle, and when the Somali returned, the people gave him back his money and he cast his spell on me.

The diviner cut open a white goat for me, but his treatment did not work. The illness progressed rapidly, and soon my cattle saw that I was dying. Desperate, my father went to town to consult Chief Losile, and Losile discussed the matter with his sub-chief, Amiri, who had some knowledge of Somali witchcraft. Amiri said he would try to arrange something for me through a local Somali man, if Father would bring 36 shillings for the treatment.

Father took me to Amudat that very day and paid the Somali who had agreed to try to counteract the spell. The Somali, assuming the trader had used a book for his magic, reasoned that if we read from a certain other book, I would no longer be under the spell's power. That evening he read some words and prayed to Tororut over me, but I didn't know exactly what was going on, because of my condition. By the next morning the fever had broken! The illness had so depleted my energy that I had to rest at home for half a year, before I felt strong enough to go trading again.

It was during my time of recovery that our baby daughter, who had been toddling about so happily, suddenly got sick and died. *Why,* I wondered painfully, as Chepusepa and the other women grieved over her little body. *Why are we being denied our children?* It was hard on Chepusepa, but, thankfully, her spirit remained strong. Some women threaten to hang themselves when a child dies.

Several weeks later, our son Makal tried to kill a lizard with a bow and arrow. The arrow hit its mark, but the lizard was not killed. It crawled, half-dead, into our house and stayed there. This was an *extremely* bad omen, and there was absolutely no alternative but to set fire to the structure with everything in it. All of my money—I figured 6800 shillings—burned with the house. My mother's hut was also destroyed in the flames. After the fire, I gathered perhaps 300 shillings in change from the rubble. I took the charred coins to town, but the shopkeepers rejected them because the numbers on the coins were illegible.

There was nothing else to do but start over. I sold some of the family cattle and began trading donkeys with a Luo man named Apollo. Luckily, it was the time of year when the government was demanding 12 shillings in tax from each adult. People were happy to sell me a donkey for the 12 shillings, instead of selling a cow or a steer, as they would have to do otherwise, in order to raise the money. We herded our sizeable herd of donkeys all the way to Kisumu and sold them for 68 shillings each. I made the journey twice, and left a Luo girl pregnant.

My travels home from those ventures led through areas of great turmoil. Several years earlier *[1952-3]* the Kenya Government had apprehended the powerful Kikuyu leader, Jomo Kenyatta, and locked him up at Lokitaung. The news of this action had caused protests and violence throughout the land.[106] In fact, Kenya became so dangerous during that time, that I was reluctant to return to Kisumu again. I joined, instead, with two other men, Mangusio and Ngoroko, and began trading goats in our own country of Uganda. My two associates had licenses to sell at Mbale, so we herded the goats there on three occasions. (I mingled with the crowds and sold mine without a license.) Unfortunately, during the last trip, Mangusio's money was stolen, and he became so upset he threatened to hang himself. He calmed down only when we agreed to share some of our profits with him.

After that incident, I stopped trading in goats and turned, once again, to cattle, a business I continued for several more years, until the time Jomo Kenyatta found his Chair, becoming the first President of Kenya.

My Bride Chepto

I am a man from around Amudat, but my second wife, Chepto, comes from the hill Tingirich, near Chepropul. Chepto was married once before, but ran away from her first husband. He pursued her for a full year, before he realized she would never come back to him and allowed Chepto's father to return the cattle he had paid as bride wealth. Chepto was sent to live with her brother-in-law, the former Chief Todile Losile, in Amudat. I met her there, and we quickly fell in love. Two months later, I asked Losile's permission to marry Chepto, but he told me, "I can't take this responsibility while her father is alive, Domonguria. You must go find him."

I set out immediately for Tingirich and found the homestead of Akumaris, Chepto's father, without difficulty. When I announced my intentions, Akumaris asked me, "Whose son are you?" and I answered, "I am the son of the Elder Pturu."

"Very good," he replied. "If you are Pturu's son, I want some cattle from you! You may have your wife after you give me 30 cattle!"

"There are not that many," I protested. "I have 20 cattle."

"He countered, "Yes—*at least* 20! We'll make it 25."

"Yes, done! It will be as you say."

"And 19 goats."

"Yes, I have them."

"Good! Take your future wife home and then summon me. I will come, and you will give me my cattle there."

My happiness over the prospect of marrying Chepto soon turned to anger, however, for when I reached Amudat several days later, I was shocked to find that another man, Nyoale Langarikamar, had taken Chepto by force four days earlier! He had tried to romance her, but she had fought him off. Then he had tried giving her cattle, but she had refused them. He was trying to marry her without even going to see her father!

Incensed, I went home, got my spear and started off for his homestead. Chepusepa was worried, and my brother and my brother-in-law ran after me, arguing, "They will outnumber you! You have no chance!" Just then, a boy caught up to the three of us with a message from my father: "Tell Domonguria to come. His wife is at my homestead."

Chepusepa and I went at once to Father's place. We were told that Chepto had run away from her tormentor and had arrived the night before. She had gone to the farms early in the morning and would be spending the night and the next day there.

By then it was getting dark, so Chepusepa and I decided to spend that night in my father's homestead. The following evening, Chepto came back from the gardens, and I welcomed her as my bride. Since it was her second night at her new family's homestead, I slept with her then, consummating the marriage and promising her a cow.

In the morning we tended to all the rituals of marriage. I gave her cattle and goats, she stood on the skin, and we stung her with the scorpion. (Unfortunately, Chepto suffered horribly from the sting.) Because of the haste of the wedding, due to our problems with Langarikamar, we did not have the opportunity to have her fortune told, as I had with Chepusepa. However, that's not so bad, since it is more important for a man to have a good fortune with his first wife anyway.

Two days later, Langarikamar came. The two of us fought, and I beat him until he was nearly dead. Finally, he gave up and stumbled home, but our contest was not over. Several months later, when Chepto was pregnant, she became critically ill. It was obvious to me that this was because of a spell Langarikamar had cast on her. I intended to kill him, but my family talked me out of it. Finally, I walked to his homestead and told him, "If my wife dies, you will die with her." It was a very serious threat, and Langarikamar knew it. Soon afterwards, Chepto recovered and gave birth to a healthy baby girl. We named our daughter Cherel.

Chepusepa and the Spirits of Kadam

Meanwhile, I was increasingly concerned about the children of my wife Chepusepa. Her first child, born after four years of marriage, had died in infancy. Our son Makal had survived, but we had to perform the *riwoi* ritual at the time of his birth to protect him. Then we lost our third baby when she was less than two years old. Now, shortly after Cherel was born to Chepto, a baby died while still in Chepusepa's womb. Within weeks, a young man appeared in our homestead with a strange message for Chepusepa: *Your children have perished because of the ghosts of Kadam.* I was instructed to bring honey, a steer and tobacco to a place called Kamaret, on the mountain.

Chepusepa, as you know, is a child of Kadam. Her people and those on Moroto share the same heritage, and their ways can be very mysterious, yet frequently helpful to us. For instance, by examining certain plants high on the mountain, certain Kadam elders can predict the rains, and by listening to them, we Pokot know how much to sow each season. The Kadam also call forth spirits to bless their gardens in times of need, and their rituals are known to be extremely potent.

But the spirits of Kadam are also to be feared. When a Kadam man dies—even if he dies far away, his soul will return to the mountain to join his ancestors in the cave where they live. Of course, many of the caves on Mt. Kadam are inhabited by living people, and others are used as food storage, but some are known to belong only to the ghosts, and if a person goes near one of those, he will die. The spirits prefer to remain unseen. If you hear one on the mountain, you must be careful not to get too close to it. There are only a few Kadam elders who can actually talk to the ghosts and call upon their powerful services without fear of death.[107]

Knowing these things, I responded immediately when the message came to me from the elders of Kadam. I collected honey from our hives, bought some tobacco, gathered all the necessary supplies for beer making, and packed them on the backs of two donkeys. My two wives and I led the donkeys and the steer to Kamaret, where I made the beer and, after it was fermented, killed the steer. An elder came just then and warned me to leave that spot at once, for many ghosts would come, and I—but not my wives—would be in danger. And so, apprehensively, I left Chepusepa and Chepto at that mysterious place and went to spend the night at a friend's house.

Early the next morning, both of my wives ran into my friend's corral to tell me the news. The ghosts had spoken to Chepusepa! She would be blessed with more children, and she was to call her next son Moru.

Chepusepa became pregnant immediately after we returned! Since she had lost her last baby during childbirth, she tied ostrich eggshell beads around her stomach and wore them throughout the pregnancy to increase her chances for a healthy delivery this time. It worked, and when our daughter Akimat was born, Chepusepa untied the eggshell beads and fastened strands of them around the baby's neck, waist, wrists and ankles. Our little daughter thrived, and so did all the rest of Chepusepa's children. A few years later, our son Moru was born. He was followed by our daughters Naowal and Naokut, our son Lokero, and, finally, our little daughter Chepetoi.

A Practical Decision

By then I was a veteran cattle trader and had known success in many lands. But times were changing. In those days, when I traveled with my associates—four Nandi and two Sebei—to Korosii, where cattle were being sold, all of us wore western-style clothes, and I even shaved the clay from my hair in order to fit in with the crowd and increase trust in our business.

One day at the market in Korosii, when we had made our selections and were in the process of buying several fine cattle, one of the sellers looked at me, recoiled, and questioned my associate, "That one—what tribe is he?"

"He's just one of us," my Nandi partner replied, trying to get on with the business. But the merchant would not desist. "No," he protested irritably. "What kind of people would do *that* to their mouths?"

It was my lip plug. I had not thought anything about it when I had shaved my head for the trip and bought clothes to try to look like the others. It was the same beautiful ornament the ironsmith had given me as a child when I first pierced my lip, and I had worn it with pride ever since. Now it had become my enemy.

"You are mistaken ..." my associates were protesting.

"How many cattle did that man buy, and for how much?" His assistants told him. "Then return those six cattle and give him back his money!" the merchant demanded.

"But sir," I interjected. "What do you have against me? I am an honest trader!"

He reclaimed his cattle, handed me back my money, and glared at me. "I don't want to do business with your kind! Go get cattle in your own country!" He spat and walked away.

"Truly, your lip plug gave you away," my partner Ndiwa said.

"I know. It's true." I thought about it, sadly, for the rest of that long, unproductive safari.

Right after I returned home, empty-handed, I walked resolutely to Amudat to see the white doctor who had come to work there. I told him, "My lip plug has begun to torment me. Please sew up the hole in my mouth." He agreed wholeheartedly, and within a few minutes it was done. I walked back home and gave the old ironsmith's exquisite piece to my wife Chepto, saying, "Put this decoration in your mouth."

She looked at me incredulously. "What happened?" she asked.

"Ah—it brought trouble to me" was all I could say.

I have not worn a lip plug since. My friends and relatives were amazed at my action, for I had such a beautiful ornament.

Leopard and Lion

At that time we were living at Lossom, and we spent a lot of time working in our gardens. During the first months of the year, my wives worked there every day, hoeing and preparing the soil. I joined them whenever I was home. When the rainy season came, I prepared beer to celebrate the cultivation and planting of our fields.

Usually, we made three very large gourds and one small one, so that when the beer in the small one began to ferment, we knew all of it was ready to drink.

The rains of that year caused some curious things to happen. First, a hard rainstorm split the rock above the cave Cheptorogoin, where we would often go with others to dance at night, and the entire cave collapsed! Luckily, no one was in it at the time, but we wondered if, perhaps, Tororut did not like people playing there. Then, during another storm, Tororut caused a giant boulder to be moved, leaving a gaping hole where it had stood! No man could have done this. Finally, as during any rainy season, predators, such as leopards, hyenas and lions, began to prowl in increasing numbers about the homesteads in search of goats or cattle to eat.

A few weeks after my safari to Karosii, it was raining hard during the night, and all of us were having trouble sleeping, so Chepusepa got up and lit the fire. That was a mistake: our baby daughter saw the goat kids resting nearby and crawled out of bed to play with them! We decided to let her stay there a little while, until we got drowsy again. Then Chepusepa held out her arms to little Akimat, saying, "Come, let's sleep now."

"No!" Akimat retorted, and she toddled in further among the baby goats.

Try as she might, Chepusepa could not get her baby into the bed. There is no persistence quite like that of a small child who wants to play! My wife cajoled, and, finally, demanded that her daughter come, but tiny Akimat only started crying and whining, "I want to see the baby goats! I want to see the baby goats!" At last, in exasperation, Chepusepa picked her up forcefully and wrapped her completely inside the blankets. She was still crying when I dozed off.

I awoke to the sound of the kids bleating. The fire glimmered, and I became aware of something big moving in the room. It was a leopard! He was trying to get in the small door to the alcove where we kept the baby goats. I sat up and yelled, while the leopard knocked the gate down, swiping at some of the kids with his paw. They scampered in terror under the beds. He glanced at us (Chepusepa was also yelling now), then ducked quickly out of the house. My wife and I waited, and when we were sure the leopard had gone, we rounded up the goats, fixed their gate, and put them back in their alcove.

We had no sooner lain down again, when Chepusepa screamed, "The leopard is back!" She threw a skin over our baby Akimat, just as the leopard leaped towards them. I lunged across the room, grabbing the leopard's tail, as it stood over my wife and child on the bed. For a moment it strained against me, digging its claws into Chepusepa's face and arm. Then it turned, urinating all over me while I still clung to its tail, and bounded out the door, knocking me off balance. I got up, drenched, and ran to Chepusepa. "Did it hurt you?" I asked, panicked.

"No, it was just the claws." She was bleeding profusely from the gashes in her temple and arm.

'What about the baby? Did it crush the baby?"

"No." Chepusepa rocked our heavily swaddled infant and laughed in spite of the blood. "I guess it's a good thing I wrapped her in all those blankets to make her behave! They saved her!"

A week later, while I was sleeping in Chepto's house, I was awakened by the bells and lowing of the cattle. "What's going on?" I mumbled, but I saw that Chepto's bed was empty. Then I heard her calling from the corral, "The cattle have gotten out! I think a hyena or a leopard is here in the corral!"

I bolted outside and found only two steers—my father's most recent ox of ropes and Lemaluk's ox—standing in the corral, looking towards the gate. The rest of the cattle were wandering restlessly among the houses. Then I thought I saw a large shape passing just outside the corral gate. I opened it and stepped outside, watching for any movement in the shadows. Something did move, very slightly, and I realized it was the tail of a lion. Quickly I went back in, secured the gate and called to the other men.

Six of us got our spears and went out. We split into two groups and circled the homestead. I could hear the lion running ahead of us. Finally, it loped off, and we pursued it into the bush a good ways before going back to guard the homestead. None of us slept until, just before dawn, we heard a roar far in the distance.

How I Lost My Finger

One morning, towards the end of the fourth month, my wives and I left just after dawn to work in the gardens as usual. We called at the gate of each homestead on our way, as is our custom, so that by the time we reached the fields there were 15 of us—eight men and seven women, along with some children. One of the women announced the news that a cow had just been killed by a lion on the high land above the river Lossom. A few men were already tracking it, she said. That was the first I heard of the beast that was to challenge my life before the day ended.

When we reached the fields, which were very long, we spread out to perform our various tasks. Some of us were hoeing, some were harvesting the grains, and others were planting corn. The heat from the sun became oppressive as the morning progressed. Then, suddenly, I heard the growl of a lion! It was quite close—within the boundaries of our farm—at the opposite end of the field from where I was working. Quickly, I grabbed my spear and ran with the other men towards the noise, keeping my eyes on the people and watching the grains carefully for any movement. The women and children began to flee.

Finally we saw the lion, but a woman was trapped on the other side of him. In fact, the lion was gnawing on the hoe she must have dropped in her fright. We stalked him carefully, hiding in the grain. The lion raised his head, looked from side to side and saw that all the people had vanished except for the woman standing motionless only a few yards away. Her luck held. The lion, probably sensing the need to escape, ran past her into the bush.

We pursued the lion that day for about 16 miles. His trail did not go straight, but in circles. We followed it backwards, then ahead again, then around corners. The lion went snakelike, and we pursued him relentlessly in the heat. Then we heard a terrifying roar, which shook our souls, for we were very, very close. We ran towards the noise, but almost stumbled over the bloody, mauled bodies of two of our friends!

Wokolay's left arm was destroyed, and the meat had been ripped off his forehead and above his eye, so that only a piece of skin hung down to cover his eye. We were relieved to discover he was still alive. The other man was my best friend, Arekai. He was exhausted and bloody, but had fared much better than his companion. When he saw me, he still had enough wit to demand, "Why have you left us alone to the mercy of this animal, Domonguria?"

"Where is he now?" I asked

"Beneath that tree," Arekai pointed, and I noticed a bloody trail.

"Whose blood is this—man's or lion's?"

"It's from the lion. We've been stalking him all morning." Arekai explained. "After the first two hours, we finally got close enough to throw our spears. One wounded him, but the lion outdistanced us again, running in the direction of the fields, then circling back, perhaps another ten miles. By then, he was exhausted and suffering from the wound, so he decided to fight it out with us here. He sprang first on Wokolay, then threw Longoritudo down with a slap of his paw and bit at his back. That's when I ran to help, throwing my spear. The lion wrenched it in two, but Longoritudo had a chance to run away. I think his arm is broken. Then Samson, the schoolboy, got a spear and threw it, tearing the edge of the lion's mouth. He charged, but Samson leaped into a tree just in time and climbed to the highest branches. The lion jumped up at him, but Samson was too high up. That was the lion's last effort. He managed to go about 100 yards to where you can see him now. He's dying."

I studied the lion in the distance and remarked, "He's lying as if he is dead."

"I don't know."

"Well, if he's lost that much blood, he's not about to go anywhere. We should leave him alone. He has already mauled two people and has done enough damage to others! We'll let him stay there and come back later to see if he's dead." I figured I knew what I was talking about, having killed several lions myself already.

"No! He is is dead now," one man protested.

"We don't know that, and no one is about to go close enough to see," I countered.

All of us fell to bickering about this. Most of the men insisted that the lion was dead and wanted to finish the hunt then. Finally, I became exasperated and said, "All right, all of you stay low and I'll go find out."

I crept closer and closer to the lion, until I was standing just behind him. He was breathing. I turned to go back and almost bumped into a man who had been following me.

"Well?" he asked.

"He is alive," I whispered. "We'll come back later. The spear of Arekai will finish him off."

"You're crazy! This animal's dead!" He said angrily, and with a short run, he threw his spear at the resting lion. It missed, but grazed the hairs on the lion's back.

Instantly, the startled cat awoke, jumped up, and reeled around to find me standing there! (The other man was further back.) He lunged at me, and I threw my spear, hitting him in the muscle between his legs, below the neck. But that didn't stop the lion. He made a great leap and landed on top of me.

He bit at my right leg, but I managed to grab his huge head with my left arm, and so he left my leg alone and began chewing my arm. Desperately, I grasped his ear with my right hand, and he started after my right arm, which I rammed between his teeth, deep into his throat, trying at the same time to seize his neck with my left arm. The lion was now biting at my head, but my right arm saved me, for he couldn't close his jaws while my hand was in his throat.

My friends ran to save me. One man began bombarding the lion's head with orange-like fruits and his spear. The lion rolled over, ripping my hand from his throat and squashing me beneath his back. I could see a spear hit him in the head, and he roared in pain, the vibration of his agony rumbling through my mauled body. He died on top of me.

I struggled to move, feeling like a ragged piece of paper under a great rock. I could feel the stabbing pain of the lion's claws stiffening into me. "Push him away!" I gasped. Then one man grabbed his head, a second got the tail and a third tugged at the feet, and together they dragged the carcass off my crushed body.

With a great effort, I managed to stand and take a few steps, but I saw that inside the gash in my right leg one blood vessel—the one that connects the leg and the waist—was nearly severed. I begged my friends to help me make it to the clinic at Amudat.[108] (Even though we were closer to home, I knew I needed more help than my people could give me there.) We started from that area of Lossom at midday and struggled to make it to Amudat by evening.

As soon as I arrived, the white doctor began to work on my mauled body. First he tended to my finger, which had been bitten off when I was pushing my hand into the lion's mouth. He cut away the hanging tissue, vessels and scabs, cleansed the wound and stitched it up. Since that time my finger has carried the mark of that lion—it is a mere stub.

The doctor then turned his attention to my leg, remarking on my good fortune that the blood vessel had remained intact. If it had been severed completely, he explained, my leg would have had to have been amputated. Then he told me, "Domonguria, this animal has wounded you so badly that it is impossible for me to treat you here. I lack the facilities I need to diagnose your condition. For instance, I need an X-ray. The hospital at Mbale has X-rays, and I would like to take you there. Do you consent?"

I nodded and he continued, "Tomorrow I will drive you to Mbale. Try to convince your friend to come along with us. His arm is badly broken."

When I was taken to the ward, I saw that Longoritudo was also there. The doctor had already spoken to him about Mbale, but he was apprehensive. Not only would the city be foreign to him, but he did not know Swahili. He would be unable to communicate or even know what was happening to him. "Don't worry," I assured him. "I learned Swahili when I began trading in distant places. We will go to Mbale together, and I will translate for you." Longoritudo trusted me.

My family—the children, both my wives, my mothers, brothers and sisters—came to the clinic that night and saw me languid and wasted. They could not have known, then, that I would return from Mbale in good health, for that day I was in terrible shape! I couldn't walk, sit, or even feed myself. I lay on the bed like a man with a broken back. I even had to eat my food lying down. I could see the anxiety on their faces.

I tried to ease the children's distress somewhat by telling them, "There is no reason to worry about me. I won't die! You'll see! And when I've recovered my good health, I'll go back to fight again! I'll battle lions, leopards, other animals, and enemies! I'll not shirk my duty! I'll fight strenuously, as is our custom, for such has been the role of men since the time our elders gave us life long ago. Now, I know you are worried, because of the man who was killed yesterday while fighting the lion near the shops at Kwangao, but you are forgetting that men fight beasts every day! Why? Because it is our duty!"

I could see they were not entirely convinced by my bravado, so I added, "Besides, even if I never regain enough strength to hold a spear and shield in my hands, I'll survive. The doctor will take me somewhere else for a while, but don't you think I'm going to die there. It is impossible, because my spirit resists it! Now you must go home and look after our place for me until I come back." But the children could see my suffering, and some of them left crying.

Early the next morning, the European drove Longoritudo and me to Mbale. Two days after we entered the hospital, they took the X-rays, and I saw in the pictures that my hand resembled stew meat in a pot! The lion had crushed my hand like a thing smashed by the blow of a stone, and the bones were unrecognizable.

The doctor at Mbale was very attentive. Longoritudo's arm was fixed, and he returned home in a few weeks. But four months passed before the doctor finally told me, "You are now healed!" The next day, a hospital vehicle took me as far as Moroto, where I was met by a car from the Amudat clinic and was driven home.

ENCOUNTERS WITH
GOD AND ENEMIES

ILAT, THE THUNDER GOD

After my fight with the lion and subsequent recovery, I turned once again to cattle trading, traveling through all of the areas inhabited by my people: the West Pokot district of Kenya, parts of Turkana, and my own Southern Karamoja region of Uganda. During those safaris, many sights, tales, and events were revealed to me. For instance, in Pirirol I was amazed to see that all the cattle turned red after each rain. The color would wear off by mid-morning. This phenomenon only occurred in the small area called Pirirol, meaning "something red." People no longer live there.

In 1962 I traded for a while with my brother-in-law Lokolikwa, who lived at Sigor. The two of us acquired a supply of the red medicine used for treating a cattle sickness named *kubliss* and sold it throughout the province, using our profits to buy cattle to sell elsewhere.

Ilat's Chosen Neighbor

Once I arranged to meet Lokolikwa in Chepropul at the house of Chepto's brother, Lokwado. That night, Lokwado told us an amazing story about his neighbor Lolingangyan's recent encounters with the thunder-god, Ilat.

Evidently, Ilat appeared to Lolingangyan three times in the dark, saying, "I have chosen to live with you. We will be neighbors, and you and your family will be my people. Do you agree?"

Lolingangyan was so startled, he could not answer the first two times. Finally, Ilat awakened him in the house of his second wife, demanding, "Why are you procrastinating? What don't you like about me?"

Lolingangyan had protested, "I only met you a few days ago and I have yet to see you clearly. How can I make an agreement with someone I can't even see?"

But Ilat had answered, "Be assured, I am good. If you need to see me, come outside the door and we will talk there."

So Lolingangyan went outside and sat on his stool, while Ilat sat on his. He tried to look at the thunder-god, but his mind was aware only of the shape of a man's body. He realized later that he had not even noticed whether the man was clothed. He could not focus on Ilat's head or his face. (This always happens to people in the presence of Ilat.)

Ilat explained, "I want your homestead. You must remove nothing, for I wish to live in my friend's home as it is. You will live nearby and we will be neighbors."

When Lolingangyan asked, "Where shall I build my new homestead?" Ilat replied, "You will build just beneath the small hill over there, on the lower side."

Lolingangyan agreed then, but Ilat continued, "There is one more matter which concerns me. Yesterday, a girl came to the place where I cultivate at Choda[109] and picked one of my ripe gourds from the *selangwa* vine. Instruct the girl to leave that gourd, as well as a gourd of milk there tomorrow. She can claim the two gourds later in the morning, when she sees that the one is empty. That is all for now."

The next day, Lolingangyan told his people about the arrangement with Ilat. He found that the girl who had picked the gourd at Choda had become quite ill. He explained Ilat's instructions to her family, and they left immediately with the sick girl for Choda. She placed the ripe gourd she had picked by the *selangwa* vine, along with a hollowed gourd full of milk, then waited a short distance away with her brother. After about two hours, they went back to the vine and found that the milk had disappeared, so they took the two gourds and began walking home. They had gone only a few steps, when a sensation of health surged through the girl's body! Indeed, she was feeling so spry by the time she reached home, that she joined in a neighborhood dance! The cure was so spectacular that, ever since, people have continued the custom of leaving milk whenever they harvest the ripe gourds of Choda.

That night, Ilat showed Lolingangyan the site for his new homestead, telling him, "Tomorrow you will find two signs in this location. The one which is standing will mark the center of your corral. A baby goat will be resting at the place where you will build your goat house. The gate for the goats shall face over there, and that of the cattle shall face this way."

Accordingly, the next day, Lolingangyan found an unsheathed spear standing on end at the spot where he had stood with Ilat the night before. A rabbit was lying down a short distance away. He walked over to the rabbit, reached out his hands and grabbed it. Incredibly, the creature did not bite or even try to get away! He put it down gently, saying, "*Ala!* This must be the 'baby goat!'" and the rabbit hopped away. Lolingangyan and his wives began cutting branches for their new homestead that day.

After Lokwado finished telling us this tale about his neighbor and Ilat, he remarked, "Just before you came, I heard they had finished the houses and were about to put thatch on the roofs."

"Ha! That is a good story!" Lokolikwa and I told Chepto's brother. He saw that we had not believed it, and he challenged us, "OK, go see for yourselves!"

We did. The next day, we spoke with Lolingangyan's wife, then went to see the new homestead, which was exactly as Lokwado had described. We were shown the spear of Ilat, and we met the girl who had been cured. Later, we spent the afternoon with Lolingangyan himself at a prayer ceremony. After considering the evidence and the obvious sincerity of the people concerned, we were convinced that Lokwado's story was true!

Several years later, I had the opportunity to ask Chepto's brother what had become of his neighbor Lolingangyan, and he told me the rest of that strange story:

Lolingangyan did, indeed, move to his new homestead. Soon Ilat appeared to him again and said, "Tomorrow I will move into your old homestead. You must stay here as my neighbor. Do not move away without asking me first!" Curious neighbors went to see Lolingangyan's old homestead, now supposedly the household of Ilat, but found only an abandoned settlement. But when Lolingangyan himself went there, he claimed he could see people in the homestead!

One day, Lolingangyan was searching for lost cattle near his old home, when he heard someone calling, "Children! Take these cattle to my friend Lolingangyan's homestead! They belong to him!" Lolingangyan went up to the gate and asked, "Are my cattle here?"

Ilat appeared and exclaimed, "Friend! Where have you been? I have been waiting for you to come to get your cattle!" He opened the gate to let the missing steers out, and Lolingangyan saw that Ilat's corral was filled with cattle! When he told his friends about the incident, they were incredulous. Some of them had been near the abandoned homestead that day. They had seen no cattle and had heard no people. The neighbors considered this and figured that Lolingangyan's cattle must have been hidden amongst the invisible ones of Ilat!

Eventually, however, Lolingangyan moved away. He had no sooner built his new house, than Ilat appeared and demanded, "Friend, why did you move without first asking me? Since you have erred, you must leave this home and build another one as I advise you. Do not move again!"

Once again, Lolingangyan followed the instructions of Ilat. Then, during the tenth month of that year, the well near his homestead ran dry, and Lolingangyan and his neighbors dug a new one at Choda. Two days later, Ilat came, declaring, "Because you have disobeyed me, this well will no longer yield good water!"

In spite of this warning, all of the local families continued to water their cattle at the well. Soon the animals began falling over, their stomachs heaved, and their throats split open! Nearly three herds—65 cattle and many goats—succumbed. Lolingangyan prayed, "Please, my friend! Spare some of my herd!" The rest of his animals recovered.

Nevertheless, one month later Lolingangyan moved again, and once more Ilat chided him. "My friend, you have rejected me! Come back! Don't cross me again!" But Lolingangyan refused to return. Ten days after that, Turkana raiders murdered Lolingangyan and stole all his cattle, harming no one else.

That is the story I was told by Lokwado, who heard it from others. I really don't know which parts are true, or whether a person will indeed die if he refuses to obey Ilat, but perhaps it is worth considering.

Punishment for Profanity

Many people have had encounters with Ilat, for he is, after all, the intermediary between people and Tororut in matters related to rain, and, therefore, all of the natural things of the earth. When I was a boy, I think I saw him on the hill Kapchok. Then, several years later, as I have told you, my childhood friend Kokwa disappeared. Many assumed he had been taken by Ilat.

Kokwa's brother, Petorr, later married a friend of mine named Harikudi, meaning "road." Petorr called her by her clan name, Chemun.[110] They were a fine couple, in excellent health, and lived only three miles from my homestead at Lossam. Often my wives and I went to dance near their homestead, and we always enjoyed their company. But one night, while we were dancing, we heard that Petorr's wife was missing.

They say that the day before she disappeared, Chemun had been impatient with the cattle and had cursed at them. Instantly, a dust devil had appeared, whirling towards her! The biting sand had slammed into Chemun, and she was thrown down by the force of the wind. After the whirlwind passed, she managed to get up and herd the cattle home, but, by the time she reached the corral, she was feeling chilled and too sick to milk the cows. Petorr took the cattle to pasture the next day, leaving his ailing wife alone in the house to rest. When he returned that evening, she was gone.

As soon as it was light enough to see, Petorr began to follow Chemun's footprints. They led to the hill named Kapchok Lomuk Chao, which is about two miles from Kanyao and known to be one of the dwelling places of Ilat. People are careful not to say bad words while walking there, for it is well known that Ilat often punishes those who profane against the creatures of nature, which are ignorant and innocent. When Chemun's footprints disappeared at the rocks there, Petorr remembered his wife's admission that she had been angry at the cattle, and he was worried.

That afternoon, Petorr returned to find Chemun at home, but critically ill. She had lost her hearing and speech and could acknowledge him only with her eyes. Petorr immediately sent for a diviner, who came to throw his sandals. "It was Ilat who took your wife," the diviner concluded. "Find a white goat and perform the *kilokot* ritual." Petorr followed his instructions, and his wife recovered, although she has remained deaf to this day. My friend Harikudi, an intelligent woman, has been forced to go about like a fool ever since. Even her speech is garbled.

Nevertheless, Chemun stayed with Petorr until his death, giving birth to two sons. (Petorr married a second wife, who could help her.) Then she was taken as a wife by Loikok, Petorr's paternal brother and my friend Kokwa's next youngest brother by the same womb. Loikok, Chemun and my family shared the same homestead for many years, while Loikok was working as a foreman in Amudat. We are very close friends.

SUB-CHIEF

I n 1963, the year Jomo Kenyatta became the first President of Kenya, the local elders selected me to be the assistant to the sub-chief of our area. After six months of performing those duties, the sub-chief left and I took over his job until 1965.[111] As sub-chief, I had to travel around the countryside collecting taxes and registering young men who would pay taxes in the future. It was a terrible job, and it made me poor.

A Stranger's Calf

One day, my father met a traveler named Nangaromit and invited him to our homestead to rest. As soon as this stranger entered our corral, a nursing calf walked over to him and started licking him! The man shooed it away, but the calf persisted. We hit it with sticks until it ran back to the other calves, but as soon as our backs were turned, it came back to Nangaromit. Then we shut it in the calf house, but it cried loudly and continuously, and when we let it out again it raced to the traveler, licking him joyously. My father was worried and said to his brother, "This calf brings us bad tidings. It knows this man."

Father questioned Nangaromit about his father, his clan, and possible mutual stock acquaintances. They found they had one friend in common. "Do you have any business with his family?" Father asked him.

"Well, not any more", Nangaromit explained. "Years ago, we married one of their daughters, but she rejected us, so her father returned all of the bride wealth except two—a cow and its nursing calf, which he promised to send as soon as the calf was weaned. They did bring the cow later, but said the calf had died. Why do you ask?" The calf nuzzled him as if to answer. "By the way, where did you get this calf?"

"That is why I asked," Father said grimly. "This calf is descended from a heifer given to us by that same man nine years ago. We paid him a steer and goats, and we have given him goats twice since."

"*Ala!* Then this must be my calf!" Nangaromit exclaimed. "I do not know you or your cattle, sir, and you do not know me, but this calf has recognized me—that cannot be denied! You had better send for your associate and tell him to expect some powerful words from Nangaromit, if he insists on concealing my cattle. They will not allow it!"

Father was disturbed. He promised to pursue the matter and asked Nangaromit to return in one month. Before he left, Nangaromit was followed once again by that calf and also by its mother. He told them, "Yes, we know each other! I must go now and you will stay here with these people, but I will return for you. Go now!" As soon as he said this, the cattle left him and mingled with the herd.

Father sent for his associate immediately. When the man came, Father made beer, according to custom. Later, as they were drinking, Father asked him, "Where did you get the heifer you gave me?"

"Why, that cow and its line were ours since my father's time!"

Father told him about Nangaromit's visit. The man insisted that the cow was his.

"In that case," Father declared, "I want a steer and 29 goats, such as I gave you when we first became cattle associates, and I, likewise, will return the cow you gave us at that time, as well as all of its offspring. Our arrangement will be finished, and you will be free to tend to your own business with Nangaromit. I want no part of it!"

"Agreed. There is no reason for you to be implicated in any disagreement I might have with Nangaromit. I'll bring your goats and steer in three weeks." They parted cordially.

A month later, we told Nangaromit we were still waiting for our goats and steer. He was perturbed and demanded, "Send a child to tell that man I am waiting for him at my own homestead. I shall not return here." We complied.

We heard later that there was a large case made before the elders over the ownership of the cow. In the end, we were told that Nangaromit asked his rival to swear upon a magical object in the presence of his herd that the cattle in question were his. A lie would give the cattle power to kill him and all his people. He refused, and finally conceded, "The cattle are now yours, Nangaromit. Truly, I was told by a child that your calf had died, but I was traveling at the time. I did not honestly believe these cattle could really be yours. I'll go return the steer and goats to Pturu immediately, as I had promised, and you can go claim your cattle."

Nangaromit persisted, "I demand an accounting of all of the offspring of my cow since the day you took her, 36 years ago. The cattle in Pturu's corral are not all."

"That is true. But I must ask my brothers and the children, for I do not know myself."

When Nangaromit came to our homestead to collect his cattle, which had sustained our family for nine years, Father protested, "I have no vengeance on you! We are good people! Let us keep your cattle!" He agreed. Father then gave him beer to drink, according to custom, and the next morning Nangaromit left with the two cattle that had cried out to him, together with 27 of our goats, leaving his other 15 cattle with us. He has been our cattle associate ever since.

"It's Nothing—the Gun"

The Turkana have always made trouble, even for white people. Once, long ago, a white man named Crampton[112] came to our land. He organized a huge army, consisting of all types, including Pokot, Karamojong and Marakwet, to march upon the Turkana. For once, the renowned Turkana warriors suffered great defeats. In fact, they were almost annihilated. But they recovered, and these days the Turkana are once again a fearsome enemy, since so many of them have acquired firearms from Ethiopia, the Marille, or the *ngoroko*, a group of Turkana bandits.

During my term as sub-chief, the Turkana raided the Tepeth (So) near Moroto, but the Tepeth, with the help of the Pokot, were able to recapture their herds, killing several Turkana in the process. One brave Tepeth man, named Lothiepari, speared two Turkana men who had guns, before a third saw and shot him. The bullet pierced right through Lothiepari's shield. That gunman, Lopuronito, was killed with a Pokot arrow.

Following this incident, one of my friends made up a song, saying, "Be brave in the presence of guns. They are nothing, although they bring trouble." Ever since, when we are pursuing enemies who have stolen our cattle, we join together and sing:

Refrain:
> *It's nothing*
> *It's nothing, my men.*
> *It's nothing—the gun.*

Verse:
> *It's nothing—its cry.*

Verses:
> *The gun of Achila* (a Turkana chief)
> *Guns of the Turkana*

Hwa akiding a
Hh akiding ngikilioko
Akiding i nyatoma

Akiding i nyeruo

Atome Achila a
Nyatom ngi Turkana

My men
Men, don't let Lopuronito get away
Men, don't let Tengan get away
Men, don't let Lotonya get away
It says, "Da da da da"

Ngkiliok o lu
Ngkiliok, nyelakak i Lopuronito
Ngkiliok, nyelakak a Tengan ya
Ngkiliok, nyelakak a Lotonya
Nyeba da-da-da

Spell on a Car

I was doing some work in Loro one day, when a car drove in from Amudat and stopped at the shops there. While the driver was shopping, a local elder named Ariongole begged him to take his sick wife to the hospital in Amudat, but the stranger refused. When the man came back to his car, Ariongole tried again, offering to pay him, but the man shook his head and drove away.

It was not long before that driver was back in town again—this time on foot, saying that his car had stalled without reason half a mile outside of town. One local man considered this and asked him, "Are you quarreling with anyone?"

"No," he answered.

"Has anyone asked you for a ride in your car?"

"Yes, but I don't know his name."

Others volunteered, "It was Ariongole. He has a sick wife."

The driver sent for Ariongole and told him, "My car won't go. I'll give you 50 shillings and will take your wife if you will help."

Ariongole agreed. He ordered the driver to bring the car to the shops. The car worked perfectly, and the wife and elder got in for the ride to Amudat.

A Blessing Completed

During my last year as sub-chief, we decided it was time to perform the second half of the *riwoi* ceremony, *kitula*, for my growing son. Makal, you will recall, was one of those babies born under unusual circumstances (a mother conceiving before menstruating, a breech birth, or twins) who must be blessed in the *riwoi* ritual immediately after birth. We had taken the necessary precautions during Makal's childhood (protecting him from injury, not allowing him to pierce his ears or nose), and he had grown tall. Indeed, Makal was eager to have the final ceremony performed, so that the blessing would be complete and he could lead a normal life.

In preparation for this event, during the third and fourth months of that year, I requested a steer, collected gourds of honey, and bought a great quantity of sugar. I brewed almost twenty containers of beer and poured most of it into a large cow-skin sack, sewn for the occasion. Then, on the first day of *kitula*, I sent for the same ritual leader who had conducted *riwoi* for Makal when he was born.

When they were within a half a mile of our homestead, the leader and his family began to sing, and I brought them a gourd of beer to drink there on the path. Afterwards, they continued to the door of our corral, where they served Chepusepa and me a cup of beer, together with the medicine we had boiled in a small pot for the occasion. Turning their attention to Makal, they draped four strands of *teroi* beads over his chest—two on each shoulder, crossing in the middle. Then the family walked together to one of our houses, where we had removed everything, except for one of the beds—the "bed of children". They sang and drank more beer inside, sitting on the bed, and when they came out, a goat was slaughtered for them to eat.

As the cattle filed into the corral that evening, those who had come for the ceremony seized the steer I had chosen and punched it on both sides of the head with their fists until the creature fell. Before they killed it by striking its head with a club, they cut off the long, narrow piece of hide extending from the steer's neck to between his legs. This skin, called the *yopa*, was presented to Makal and his mother, Chepusepa. One side of the beef and the front leg were given to our guests to cook and eat, along with all of the beer in the large skin sack. The ritual leader and his family were content with the goat meat and the gourds of beer I had given them. The eating and drinking and singing continued all night long.

In the morning, the rest of the carcass was butchered, and the other side of beef, along with the breastbone, was cooked in the corral where the cattle lay. While the meat roasted, Makal's ears were pierced with the *terema*, the arrow we use for letting blood from our cattle, and small pieces of metal were inserted into the holes. Then, just as during the *riwoi* ceremony, the women went with Makal to hold a large cow, while it was fed root medicine and beer. I joined them there, and we lifted Makal over the cow's back four times. Afterwards, the rest of us— Chepusepa and I, and those who came to officiate—jumped over the cow four times as well. During this time, our friends and other family members were singing, and they continued to sing until the *teroi* beads were removed from Makal's chest, thus finishing the ritual. The family who had led the ceremony gathered their possessions, while I walked ahead with a gourd of beer to await them on the path about a mile from our house. They drank the beer there, then went on their way.

Following the *kitula* purification, a child may take part in all normal activities. There are no more worries about bleeding or sex, and girls of *kitula* may now pierce their ears again with thorns. Kitula is really not a very big occasion for us, but we consider it necessary to continue to protect a mother and child from sickness, if they have been though *riwoi* or *saana* after childbirth. I was glad to have completed this obligation to Makal and to my wife Chepusepa.

COMETS AND DISASTERS

The Comet of 1965

When my job as sub-chief was over, we moved our cattle to Losidok to graze, because the rains had not come for four months and the pasture around Lossom was depleted. At that time, a comet appeared in the sky, with a long tail pointing downwards towards the earth. This was the first comet I had seen, but I knew from stories told by my father and other elders that it was, most likely, a bad omen. Even our ancestors noticed that comets rarely bring peace or good fortune, especially if they appear frequently.

As you know, when my father was very young, he saw a huge comet named Taruh, with two very long arms sweeping upwards. Soon afterwards, the new disease called smallpox struck our land, causing widespread, random deaths. Most of my father's family perished during the two epidemics.

The elders say another comet, Tpsaro, with its single long tail pointing upwards and to the right, foreshadowed continuous, unrelenting rains. All peoples—Karamojong, Turkana, Pokot, Maasai, and Nandi—suffered a lot, and the Maasai came to raid us.

These and other stories were remembered and retold by the elders when the comet appeared to us in 1965. All agreed it was an omen, but no one knew how the fate of the comet would be manifest. So, like our ancestors, we joined together to sing and pray to Tororut to save us from the misery that was about to descend upon us. First, we sang certain songs—including the male and female circumcision songs—for four consecutive nights.

On the fifth morning, we took our cattle to a predetermined place, midway between all the homesteads in the area, and mixed them with the other herds that were gathered there. All of the men, women and children of the surrounding settlements brought their cattle and came for the ceremony. Together, we sang two songs, and the members of a designated clan killed the two steers that would be used for the blessing. At Losidok, there were four people in this clan, and they each had a part in the ensuing rituals. One skinned the carcass, one gathered firewood, another made the fire and gathered the leaves on which to serve the meat, and a youth spread the stomach contents on the bellies of all of the people. The chyme left over was used to anoint all the cattle. When the first meat cooked by this clan, the *alamachar*, was taken from the fire, the rest of us began to cook our beef. Then the elders of Losidok joined together to pray for Tororut's intercession during the troubles that awaited us, while everyone else sang and danced for the rest of the afternoon.

In spite of these efforts, as soon as the comet disappeared, Pokot cattle succumbed to disease by the hundreds, and people began to die of jaundice, a horrible sickness that yellowed their eyes, nails, tongues, urine and sputum. Nineteen of our own cattle died, and my soul felt great pain. I declared, "Let me cover my eyes and open them in another country! I cannot stay here, watching my cattle die!"

In Turkana

I left my siblings and moved, with my two wives and my mother, to a place called Kotoru in Turkana, where we stayed with a respected Turkana man named Lokorokaa. There were several other Pokot families in the area, and we settled in peacefully at first. But three months later, four Turkana bandits—ngoroko—murdered two of our Pokot cowherds, the sons of my friends Lochelipus and Longoringyan, taking their cattle.

Crazy with rage, we Pokot banded together and tracked our cattle to Kakadungole. There we came across a Turkana elder with two small children, seven or eight cattle, and 25 goats walking upon the very tracks of our stolen cattle on the road the enemy had used. They symbolized everything we had lost, and we attacked them like vipers. I wrenched the old man's spear away, as Karole, a Pokot youth and friend of the slain cowherds, cursed at him, screaming, "Where are *our* children now?" He whirled around and plunged his spear into the Turkana boy's heart. Then Lotanyale seized the arms of the shocked elder, I grabbed one of his legs and Lokworo got the other. We forced him to the ground, and Lotanyale slit his throat. The terrified little girl ran away, and we let her go. Then we took the Turkana cattle and goats back to our homestead.

A great assembly of Pokot men and youths were waiting at the corral, ready for revenge. But when Lokorokaa, my Turkana associate, heard what we had done, he shook his head sadly and exclaimed, "Ah! You have killed the good elder Atikitik!" He told us that Atikitik had recently taken some of his cattle to Chepropul to trade for goats, but he had been able to sell only one steer for 25 goats. He had been returning home with his children and small herd, when we attacked him. Our victim, we now learned, had been a peaceful man, who could not have known that people had been murdered or cattle stolen. "We must not go on killing people!" Lokorokaa proclaimed emotionally. "Two of yours and two of ours will be enough!"

That day, we raided a Turkana settlement, taking many cattle, and perhaps 100 goats and 25 camels, but we killed no one. After that, we learned that a powerful Turkana leader ordered his people to follow the tracks of the *ngoroko* and return our cattle to us, so that they would not have to continue paying for the crimes of the bandits. Eventually, the cattle were recovered.

Three months later, in August, the Turkana descended upon a Pokot homestead in Chepropul early in the morning, killing three women, two youths, and four small children. Two other women and a child were wounded. They took 200 cattle.

As soon as we heard the news, a group of us began to pursue the raiders. We tracked the cattle first to Lomopus, the riverbank opposite Kaputir. Then it became obvious from the tracks that the Turkana had split the cattle into three sections. We knew that, eventually, they would have to go through the same pass, so we ran ahead to lie in wait for them.

When the first contingent came, one Turkana man saw us and shouted to his gunman. We charged. The father of one of the slain children drove his spear through the gunman, an *ngoroko*. Another Turkana grabbed the dropped gun, but Kamuta shot him in the nose with an arrow. We shot another man in the stomach and another in the back, but they all escaped, except for the first gunman. Some of our warriors left to return the cattle, while we awaited the rest of the Turkana.

Soon, the second group of raiders came, and we ambushed them. Their gunman tried to shoot, but the gun jammed. We chased those *ngoroko* to the riverbed, killing one man, then gave up the pursuit, so we could send those cattle on and be ready for the final assault.

Finally, the last of the raiders entered the pass with our cattle, and, once again, we cut them off. They also had one gunman. He shot six times, wounding Longnyolamela in the leg, and our men killed two Turkana with spears and wounded two others with arrows as they ran. We chased them, and Kamuta was about to kill the gunman, when he was speared in the ear by a Turkana, who had been hiding behind some rocks. That man escaped with the others. We returned the last of our cattle, then, and carried our wounded home. Kamuta, who had miraculously survived, was taken by his people to the hospital in Amudat.

After that incident, I decided it was too dangerous to go trading, even though my stock had been seriously depleted by disease and, before that, during my unproductive years as sub-chief. I stayed in my Turkana home and watched over my children and my herd.

During the next *laleyo* dances, we sang about a Pokot hero named Kupkatam, son of Mole Tumara, who had been much more successful in dealing with Turkana raiders. They say it was still dark one night, when Kupkatam climbed a tall lookout tree beside his hilltop home and spotted a Turkana camp. He ran to awaken and warn his people, calling, "Alert! Awake! The enemy have come! I saw their fire in the valley! They must have spotted our fires from down there!"

Woyo e ...

Refrain:

The son of Mole calls out, the son of Mole calls

Verses:

He cries to the newcomers
Kupkatam, left-handed man
The son of Tumara calls out
He calls to the newcomers
Woye ... (trills)

Woyo e ...

Kirir wero Mole

Kirir chi punotoi
Woe Kupkatam wachelan
Woe kirir wero Tumara
Woe kirir chi punot
Woye ...

There were only ten men to protect the village, many of whom had just moved there. The path leading up the mountain had an upper and a lower section, separated by a long, narrow stretch along the edge of a great cliff. "They say that a person who falls from that cliff can die before he hits the bottom," Kupkatam said, as he assigned half the men to each part of the path.

Soon the Turkana came, and the two Pokot groups signaled to one another. The first group let the enemy pass, and pursued them quietly from the rear. As soon as they reached the cliff, the Pokot warriors shot at them from behind with arrows. The Turkana ran ahead for cover, only to encounter the second Pokot war party. The confused raiders stumbled backwards and fell to their deaths—all except six, who managed to escape to their homeland.

Raiding and Revenge

While I was living in Turkana, our family experienced a tragedy from which we have never fully recovered. It started when my brothers Lopeyok and Merur, along with seven other neighbors, raided some cattle from the Karamojong. The two cowherds fled, hopelessly outnumbered, but Lopeyok pursued them for a mile or so and almost ran into a Karamojong man returning to his homestead. Reacting instantly, Lopeyok threw his spear, wounding the man in the shoulder. The brave, but weaponless Karamojong warrior actually wrenched the spear from his own body and hurled it back at Lopeyok. The blade ripped through the muscles in my brother's back, then fell to the ground. As Lopeyok lunged to recover his weapon, he was tackled hard by his opponent. They wrestled, and Lopeyok somehow managed to throw the Karamojong down next to the spear. Quickly he grabbed it from the ground and drove it into the man's stomach. But that courageous warrior, incredibly, extracted the spear from his gut and cast it again at Lopeyok, who dodged it. They fought furiously hand-to-hand for a moment, and then Lopeyok's opponent died.

One of the other Pokot raiders had followed my brother's tracks, knowing that once Lopeyok starts pursuing an enemy, he will never lose him or give up, and might, in his zeal, track the cowherd into the midst of Karamojong warriors. Everyone knows that there is something wrong with Lopeyok's mind, and his persistence is legendary. I once hunted eland with him and tired after stalking them for two miles. After another two, I quit, but Lopeyok continued the hunt for six hours and finally killed one. At the feast, people told him, "You shouldn't hunt so relentlessly that your body suffers! You must be very tired," but Lopeyok replied, "I am not tired," and I believed him.

The Pokot warrior finally caught up to Lopeyok, as he was stripping the body of its beads, shoes, and other ornaments. He called out a greeting, but Lopeyok instantly grabbed his shield and spear, ready to kill what he thought must be a new enemy. The man had to identify himself repeatedly, before my brother recognized him, put down the spear, and turned again to his dead enemy. Noticing the terrible, flooding wound in Lopeyok's back, his friend suggested, "Come, we must find some bark-rope to tie off the blood."

"No," said Lopeyok. "Use the sheet of my enemy to bind the wound."

When the bandaging was completed, already stained with blood, Lopeyok, as is customary, placed the sheath of his spear on the body. Then he and his friend stood by the corpse and sang first to the hyena and then to the vulture, telling those scavengers to come get the food a warrior killed for them:

Give to the hyena to eat (x2)	*Eba nyebu tarakinai* (x2)
To kill, to eat, and then go. Ooo	*Tarakinai, tarakinai kithiyoto. Ooo*
Give to the vulture to eat (x2)	*Eba taruku tarakinai* (x2)
To kill, to eat, and then go	*Tarakinai, tarakinai kithiyoto*
Mm, Ooo	*Mm, Ooo*

The two finished singing, and turned to leave, giving the traditional Pokot call, a high-pitched "*ku-ku-ku-ku.*"

When you kill an enemy, you are forbidden to drink any water, until someone who has previously killed an enemy of the same sex as your victim mixes clay with water and spreads the mixture on your right arm and chest, if the enemy was a man, or on the left arm and chest, if you killed a woman. He then spits into the air, under the armpits and on you. If you find no one to spread the clay on your arm, you must go without water, even if you die of thirst. Thus, it was a lifesaving blessing that Lopeyok's companion had previously killed a man and had been cleansed through ritual, for Lopeyok was badly weakened from loss of blood. The two walked slowly to the river Lokilim, where my brother was washed and anointed by his friend. Then he drank deeply.

They decided to follow the path by the riverbank, instead of that used by the cattle, since Lopeyok would have no strength for a second fight. Near Atongai, they heard the noise of a battle between the other Pokot raiders and their Karamojong pursuers. Later they would learn that the Pokot archers killed three Karamojong in that battle, and the rest fled.

Lopeyok was nearly unconscious from thirst and weakness by the time they met the others at Achorichor that afternoon. The men had already divided up the cattle and had slaughtered one to eat. They gave Lopeyok some blood from the carcass, along with the liver, to help bolster his strength. Earlier, it had been decided that Lopeyok should get 14 cattle, but now some protested that his share should be increased to 17 because of his prowess. As it ended up, Lopeyok was awarded 19, while all the others, including Merur, took 15. When the meal was finished, the Pokot raiders went their separate ways. Merur took our family's two shares home, while Lopeyok, who was suffering, followed slowly behind.

As soon as Lopeyok reached his homestead, he began to follow all of the procedures required of a warrior who has just killed. This was necessary for his own purification, as well as for the protection of our family and friends. First, a door was cut into the fence at the back of the homestead, on the lower side, exclusively for him to use; he could not enter through the corral gate. Then the front part of his clay headdress, the *atero*, was shaved off, and red pigment was applied there and on other parts of his head. After that, Lopeyok killed a very old female goat outside the homestead, spread its stomach contents all over his body, and ate its meat.

The next morning, a ritual leader came to slaughter a white male goat and to cut and twist its skin into long white ropes (about ten), which he wrapped around Lopeyok's waist, neck, arms and legs. He placed the beard of the white goat on top of Lopeyok's head at the place of the atero, where it had been shaved. (This is very handsome.) Later, Lopeyok collected strands of ostrich eggshell beads and asked a very old woman to tie them around his waist and neck, next to the skin ropes. (The Turkana and the Karamojong also use ostrich eggshell beads for this purpose.)

My family was worried about Lopeyok's extensive wounds, but they knew that if they took him to the clinic at Amudat, the police might seize him, suspecting the truth. Instead, they tried a traditional treatment—placing boiled butter inside the sores. It worked, and the wounds healed rather quickly, leaving a large scar across my brother's back.

For the remainder of the month, Lopeyok could not enter the corral, sleep or converse with his wife, or let his shadow fall upon women, girls or small children. He was not allowed to drink cow milk or to hold bones. He could eat only boneless meat and maize meal, if there was any, and could drink only goat milk.

He was required to live alone, on one side of the homestead, sleeping on grass, not skins, using only the cloth he wore for bedding. Whenever a young child came near while he was in the homestead, Lopeyok had to duck inside a hut until the boy or girl passed by. If children approached while he was outside the homestead, Lopeyok would have to sit down so as not to cast a shadow, warding off the children with his stick, and calling for someone to take them away. This is because his shadow could cause illness.

If, by accident, an unpurified killer's shadow falls upon a woman, he must treat her by mixing red and white clays separately with milk and dung from the *kirruk* bull, the sire of the herd, and painting red and white markings on her body. (This is very pretty.) It sometimes happens that people are unaware that a dangerous shadow has been cast. A practitioner may advise a sick woman, "The shadow of a man who has killed someone and is not yet purified is in your body. You must search for him and bring him a mixture of milk and *kirruk* dung so that he can cure you."

Meanwhile, the police had followed the cattle tracks and were conducting their own secret investigation, learning quickly that Lopeyok, son of Pturu, had killed a Karamojong man and stolen cattle. When he heard the police were looking for him, Lopeyok decided to cross the border into Kenya as soon as his purification was complete. Since the raid had taken place towards the end of the month, the entire ritual period would last only a few more days. He had just enough time to prepare beer for the final cleansing.

On the first day of the new moon, the ritual leader returned. All of the necessary items were assembled: several gourds plus one small pot of beer, a container of root medicine, a mixture of ox and goat bloods poured into both a clay pot and a wooden basin, and milk from both animals. A model of a homestead was constructed out of cow dung in the corral, including miniature houses and shelters for calves and goats. Seeds were put inside the enclosures, and *sosion* and certain other grasses were stuck into the dung. A similar model was made just outside the corral gate.

The men walked around each of the models six times, then divided into two groups and ran around the perimeter of the outside dung homestead four times. These "raiders" then met at one of the two doors of the model, and each man threw his spear at the entrance, saying, "Now I kill a husband, leaving a wife!" or "Now I kill a wife, and her husband survives." Finally, Lopeyok stabbed into the pot of blood with his spear, piercing it and spilling the blood.

After this reenactment, the ritual leader poured some of the root medicine into a small gourd cup and gave it to Lopeyok. He spit the juice upwards, downwards and to each side, and did the same with the beer in the small pot. The leader sipped some as well. Then Lopeyok poured both cow milk and goat milk into the wooden basin containing the blood of those two animals and drank it all.

He completed the ceremony by running around the fence of the homestead four times.

Now that he was cleansed for the moment (after one year, there would be another, final ceremony), Lopeyok was allowed to enter the corral and resume normal activities—speaking with his wife and children, eating in his own house, sleeping with his wife and walking about the compound. All of the eating utensils used during his time in isolation were thrown out and beaten until they broke.

Losing Our Cattle

But Lopeyok's life was in danger, and so he fled from the Ugandan police and came to live with me in Turkana for a few months, until the search was over. By that time, I had moved to Nabuor, about 15 miles from Kaputir, where there are shops and Kenya police. Lopeyok was safe there, but the family herds, unfortunately, were still in Uganda. Although they never found Lopeyok, perhaps presuming him dead, the Uganda police, along with some Karamojong, descended upon my father's homestead, confiscating all the Karamojong cattle, as well as 130 of ours and 89 goats, leaving only 30 sheep and six donkeys to support the entire extended family. In an instant, we became poor.

Thus, when Lopeyok returned home, he found all the cattle gone and heard the terrible news that some of his little children were dying of starvation. His wife and children had fled to her father's house, and Merur's wife had also left. Only our father Pturu, his wives and his older children remained. Father was in a state of depression, having seen his life's herds vanish and watching the children suffer from hunger. He had considered suicide, but my blind brother Apur had pleaded with him and assured him that he and his brothers would go find cattle. By the time Lopeyok arrived, they had already left to claim two milk cows from one associate and one more from another homestead.

Nevertheless, Father saw that those three cows would not suffice for everyone, and so he decided to move in with me for a while. He told his wives, "Even if my eldest son has cattle, I will still try to go hungry to preserve the herd, but if I stay here, I'll wind up killing myself, due to worry over the starvation of our children. When I was a youth long ago, I experienced great hunger like this, but Tororut helped by keeping the lions, leopards and hyenas away at night. Perhaps he will help us all again now."

Father arrived at my homestead in Nabuor, together with my brothers Apur and Lorot and my first son Nyangaluk, now considered my father's son, who had recently been attending a mission school. They stayed with me two months, before returning to find the other children starving at Lossom. In desperation, they sent Lopeyok back to Turkana to ask me for help, and I managed to find 25 shillings to give him so that the children could buy a little food until I could move, with my small herd of cattle and my family, back to Lossom to try to save Father's homestead.

Attack on Lopedur

Before he left, Lopeyok told me the alarming news that the Karamojong had recently come to raid our brother-in-law Lopedur's homestead, as well as three others in the region around Alakas. The raiders had fired a gun into the homestead one morning and everyone had scattered, including our sister's four young boys, who had run out in front of the Karamojong. The enemies had taken all the cattle, but everyone was most immediately concerned about the children. Chelima had been frantic, fearing her sons had been shot. Luckily, Tororut had shielded them, and the boys were found unharmed after a short search.

The men then ran after the cattle, and soon caught up with the enemy. Lopedur fought apart from the others. His shield was pierced by five different spears, before the sixth entered his left arm! "Friends, where are you?" he had shouted. Serowatch, his brother, heard and ran to him just in time to throw his spear at Lopedur's opponent. The Karamojong man ran off, gashed in the back. The rest also got away, along with Lopedur's cattle.

They took Lopedur straight to the Amudat clinic and reported the incident. Quickly, two policemen and the Pokot chief of the Moruita area drove in a Landrover to the hill Cholol to await the cattle thieves. Serowatch and several men from the other raided homesteads hurried on foot to join them there. As they approached Cholol, Serowatch later told us, they sang the two songs often sung before fights over cattle:

Mm, the cattle low - They cry on the large hill	*Mm erua aite -*
Ah, the cattle low - On the hill covered with clouds, ah	*Erua mura polonia*
Ah the cattle low - On the hill with ekuno trees, ah	*Ah erua aite -*
	Ah ekothi moru nyedo, ah
	Ah erua aite -
	Ekothi moru ekuno, ah

My men are strong, mm ooo	*Ewo winyo nyekile, mm ooo*
Very strong are you, Lokilelo	*Nyewo winyo, wo Lokilelo*
The song is very strong, eyo	*Atama ewo winyo, eyo*
Don't go, you good Pokot men, ee	*Nyikilotoyo, upe nyekile ejok, ee*
Don't go to Turkana, you good men	*Nyikiluthiong Turkana, nyekile ejok*

They waited quietly with the police at Cholol, and within an hour they heard the cattle lowing. As soon as the Karamojong came within range, one policeman, a Jie, shot two men. Then the Pokot joined in the battle. One Karamojong man, who was about to shoot a policeman, was speared twice, and three more were killed, including their gunman, Lotomanimoi. As soon as he fell, Serowatch seized the gun and hid it. He was taking the ammunition from the corpse, when a policeman came to ask, "Where's the gun?"

"What gun? He threw it to someone else, who ran away with it."

"Well, maybe so," replied the policeman skeptically. And so we have the gun to this day. It's a shame we got only half the ammunition, but at least we have that and its mother, the gun.

News of the raid spread quickly, and about forty people, mostly from the homesteads of Lopeyok and Merur, came to Lopedur's homestead in answer to the alarm. They were certainly surprised to find all the cattle contentedly mooing in the corral and preparations being made for a feast! (Serowatch had decided to kill a steer to celebrate the return of the cattle.) The honored right hind leg, according to custom, was given to Lopeyok and Merur, since they were the brothers of Lopedur's wife, Chelima. Everyone partook of the feast and enjoyed the telling and retelling of the story of the raid and the recapture of the herd.

On their way home afterwards, Lopeyok, Merur and the others came across some strange, fresh footprints, indicating rubber-soled shoes, which they knew to be a sign of Karamojong, since none of their neighbors wore shoes of rubber. They followed the tracks for almost two miles and came across a Pokot corpse, which had been set out in the bush recently. They stopped to put the body up in a tree, then continued following the footprints to the river, where they found two sets of tracks. Lopeyok followed one trail, while Merur and his men followed the other.

Suddenly, Lopeyok was startled by a gunshot. At first, he thought he had been hit and ran for cover. Then, recovering his senses, he ran towards Merur and the others, who were also fleeing. A bullet grazed Merur's headdress, and another whizzed by Lopeyok, who instinctively dropped to the ground and began inching towards the gunman. He had gotten quite close before the gunman saw him and whirled around. Instantly, Lopeyok jumped up and threw his spear. The blade cut deep into the man's thigh muscle. A moment later, the gunman disappeared into the thicket, spear and all. Now other Karamojong were closing in and shooting. Weaponless, Lopeyok called to his neighbors, but no one heard because of the deafening gunfire. Somehow all of them managed to avoid the enemy and make it back to Lopedur's homestead, where they reported the incident. By then it was dark.

The following morning Lopeyok went with ten men to follow the Karamojong tracks once again. Some distance from the site of the skirmish they noticed that bark had been freshly stripped from a tree in two places, presumably to tie off wounds. After that, the tracks led to the road and then to a hill named Kameris, near Nangalitabaa, where it was evident that they had wrapped a wound again— probably that of the gunman Lopeyok had speared. Next, they came across a giraffe-skin shield discarded by the path, and figured its owner must have been too weak to carry it further.

Indeed, as they later discovered, the enemies had walked all the way to Amudat that night and had slept at the door of the clinic. According to witnesses, the white doctor found them and asked what had happened. The Karamojong explained, "We came from Karamoja to see our brothers, who are police in Amudat, but the Pokot attacked us!"

"Maybe you really came to kill Pokot in their homesteads," the doctor suggested.

"Oh no! Not us! Three Pokot men attacked us, we tell you!"

"Then why did they let you get away to come to the hospital?"

"I outdistanced them," the wounded man offered.

Evidently one of the police vouched for him and he was allowed to stay at the hospital. When he recovered, his people came to take him back to Moroto. He has limped ever since.

Helping My Family

A week after Lopeyok's visit, Chepusepa, Chepto and I packed our donkeys and moved with our 15 head of cattle to Father's homestead at Lossom. The milk from my cattle sustained our desperately hungry family there, while three of my brothers and I journeyed around the entire countryside trying to accumulate stock for them. One associate gave us goats, another cattle, another goats, and so on. After two extensive trips we had gathered together 21 cattle and 39 goats. They were enough to save the family.

Nevertheless, ever since the government seized our cattle, we have been poor. Because of lack of stock, I have been unable to marry again. At least Lopeyok and Merur have wives, but our younger brothers have had to suffer greatly. Where could they find the extra cattle with which to marry wives? Ultimately, we have had to rely upon Tororut to help our cows calve abundantly, and we have worked hard in the gardens, hoping that Tororut would find us a little food there. And, most importantly, we always help one another. When I have a job and earn some money, I help my brothers. They help me in other matters.

A few days after I brought the last of our cattle home, I was in Amudat visiting with friends, when a boy from our neighbor Lorien's homestead approached us. He was trying to recruit men to help him move a dead lion from one of their houses!

He told us that Lorien had recently moved his cattle and some of his family to another homestead, leaving only the goats, a few boys and their mothers in the old settlement. The night before, the youth Arekai was sleeping in a goat house, when a lion entered the skin door, pounced on him, and bit him. When he screamed, the lion leapt over the small wall separating his sleeping area from the goats and started mauling the animals. Luckily, a stranger heard the screaming and ran into the homestead with his spear and shield.

A woman stopped him at the door of the hut, warning, "Don't corner the lion like that! Here—use a poisoned arrow." She opened the quiver she was holding and gave him two arrows and a bow. Quickly, he ducked into the house and shot the lion, while the woman grabbed the boy. They waited outside until they heard the lion vomit. Then there was silence. After awhile, the woman and the stranger made a small hole in the side of the house, looked in and found the lion was dead.

It took five of us to lift the dead lion. He had killed many goats and his body was lying on several of the carcasses. Presently, the police and local chief came, wrote down the facts and took the boy and the lion skin to Amudat. Arekai recovered after two weeks in the hospital.

Purification

Later that year, Lopeyok completed his purification for killing an enemy. First, he begged an ox from a friend and slaughtered it, catching the blood in a wooden trough. While the meat was cooking, he removed the ceremonial goatskin ropes that had been tied around his body during the first ritual, along with the goat-beard headpiece. He cut them up and burned them in the corral. Then he untied all of the ostrich eggshell beads he had worn during the period of cleansing and gave them back to the women.

Many people came to eat the meat of the ox and to drink milk at the purification ceremony. An elder served Lopeyok a rib of the beef with the skin attached. He chewed a little, then spit downwards, upwards and to each side, and the elder did likewise. When Lopeyok broke the rib bone with his teeth, the elder gave him the name of the enemy he had killed—Atukole. He would use this name, along with his old one, from then on. (The Karamojong also have this custom. It reminds me of how missionary teachers assign our children new names when they enter school.) Finally, Lopeyok was given two cuts of meat to eat, and the ritual was finished.

Lopeyok now was allowed to dye an ostrich feather red to wear in his headdress for the next five or six years —especially at dances. People who have killed often go to dances with red pigment spread on their skin, wearing the red ostrich feather and a white goatskin rope, using no colors other than red and white. They are called *kololot*.

Lopeyok also chose to have decorative scars cut into his body, symbolizing the killing of his enemy. To be scarred, a warrior takes ten shillings to the local man or woman who knows how to cut skin in this manner, together with a white ostrich feather, which is said to prevent the practitioner, who has seen so much blood, from going blind. Before the incisions are cut, the patient drinks milk, mixed with blood. The practitioner draws the pattern in red clay, then incises each mark with the needle we call *seduk*. The small rows of wounds extend from the stomach to the biceps of the arm. When he gets home, the warrior's children rub butter into the sores each day, until they heal and stand out nicely. His wife will think his scarring very handsome when she sleeps with him and will enjoy caressing his marks of bravery. One who has killed two people will let the first set of sores heal, before returning to have the other arm and chest cut. If he has killed more, a small set of scars will be cut on each of his sisters' arms until enough blood has been spilled to suffice.

FIGHTING FOR THE HERDS

Our Karamojong Cattle

We had no sooner finished building our homestead near my father's home at Lossom, than we heard that the Karamojong had raided cattle near Loro, killing about 40 Pokot. This time, we avenged them well. About 300 of us descended upon a Karamojong homestead near Kakamongole one evening during a driving rainstorm. I would guess we killed over a hundred men, women and youths and captured 1200 cattle. I still remember coming across one Karamojong wife who had been killed in the raid. She was the most beautiful woman I have ever seen. We drove the cattle back across the river that night. By the time the Karamojong came in pursuit, the river had flooded and several were swept to their deaths trying to cross it. The rains covered our tracks from there.

By the next morning, helicopters were circling above us. My brothers and I took our shares of the cattle and ran. I was allotted 15 cattle, Lopeyok seven, and my other two brothers five and two. We hid the cattle at Kapchok, in Kenya, for a week until the aircraft left. They never found us, but our fellow raiders were not so lucky. We heard the government seized many of their cattle, swooping down in their helicopters like fierce birds.

During the week we were in Kenya, the Karamojong raided at Aparipar, killing 260 people, including a storekeeper named Munuia, his wife, his cook and a servant. The Pokot there fought all night and, with the help of the soldiers, brought back some of the cattle. Kenya Army troops eventually seized numerous Karamojong cattle in retaliation and gave them to the Pokot.

The day after I got home from Kapchok, I went to Kanyao to tend to some matters. Chief Ameri stopped me there and demanded, "Where did you come from?"

"I've just returned from Kenya," I answered truthfully.

"Do you mean that when they raided near Kakamongole, you weren't in the country?"

"I had already gone by then," I lied.

"What were you doing in Kenya?" he persisted.

"I was trading—buying goats and donkeys."

"Oh yeah? Then where are these animals now?"

I had to think fast to answer that one. I said, "The river was flooded and I had to leave them on the other side. I tied them up by the small wooden foot bridge and left a boy to watch them. I hope the waters recede before long!"

"Ah, there is so much trouble here now," Chief Ameri informed me. "The soldiers are everywhere, harassing people, confiscating their weapons. You're lucky you were on safari then!"

"Yes!" I agreed heartedly, glad to have a believable alibi.

Nevertheless, soldiers continued arresting people who had gone on the raid and, finally, they also seized me and took me to Amudat to be questioned. One corporal was assigned to examine two of us. He glared at me and demanded, "Did you go to kill Karamojong?"

"I was in Kenya on a trip. In fact, I was on my way to Ortum, when I heard people had gone to fight. When I came back to Kanyao, I met Chief Ameri, and he questioned me. You can ask him."

The corporal sent another soldier to summon Chief Ameri, while he interrogated the other man. After some time, the Chief arrived, and they told him what I had said.

"It's true," Ameri said earnestly. "I met him coming from Kenya. He looked like he must have been gone a long time."

Someone in the crowd objected, yelling, "No! He was on the raid!"

"I didn't go," I insisted.

There was a great deal of commotion, and finally the corporal sent me to stand with a large group of other suspects who were bound for jail in Moroto. It took me very few minutes to work my way to the edge of the group, where I slipped one of the soldiers 30 shillings. He pretended to take no notice when I ran off and left my companions to their fate.

Two weeks later, I was summoned to Moroto to stand trial three times. Throughout the hearings, I stuck to my story about trading in Kenya. Chief Ameri and even the corporal backed me up. I was released, but most of the other men in my family were sent to jail for the next four years.

Four nights after my return from Moroto, I was awakened by the sounds of a goat bleating frantically. I ran outside and found that the sounds were coming from the sheep house. I realized that a goat must have gotten mixed in with the sheep, and it was a good thing, because sheep are remarkably stupid and won't cry out easily when threatened by a predator. My father's homestead was next to ours, and I yelled to them, "Trouble in the sheep house!" Just then I heard something crashing through the corral fence.

My family came to examine the damage with me. There was a hole in one side of the sheep house, and a lot of carcasses inside, including the goat. We figured it must have been a hyena.

The next morning we skinned one of the dead sheep and the goat outside. I disassembled my spear and set the blade upright on a small stick I had buried in the ground. I covered the spear tip with grasses and hung the viscera of the animals from a tree limb just above it. Then I constructed a small fence around the trap to warn people. We ate some of the mutton there by the trap that afternoon, leaving the bones.

In the morning we found the dead hyena caught on the spear. He had tried to run, tearing out his own viscera. Father was especially pleased. As he watched, I cut off one of the hyena's legs and stood it upright on a stick. (I had seen my father do this whenever he killed a hyena—I have no idea why. We don't cut the legs of lions, leopards or any other predators.) I left the rest of the hyena carcass suspended on the spear blade. Then we went home and feasted on mutton until sunset.

It just happened that, two days later, soldiers came to search our homes for spears, which had been declared illegal on account of the raids. We had hidden ours well, and they were not found. However, just as they were about to leave, one of the soldiers noticed birds feasting on the carcass of the hyena. There, in the middle of the kill, exposed by those gluttonous birds, was the bloody tip of my spear! They confiscated it and left.

Following those Pokot-Karamojong raids and counter-raids, soldiers policed our country constantly for a year. The Karamojong in the Army tore up any Pokot complaints, ridiculed us, and shot people without cause. We felt justice often favored the Karamojong in raiding incidents. The soldiers seized all the spears, arrows and even the machetes they saw, sometimes beating up people in the process.

One day the soldiers went to the homestead of Parenge and Purkitch, where they raped two women. Then they grabbed a third—a woman who had recently given birth. She struggled, until one soldier hit her with the butt of his rifle, knocking her to the ground. In spite of her pain, the woman jumped up and grabbed his gun. Her assailant slapped her and cuffed her with his fists, but she would not let go. As they wrestled for the gun, a bullet was fired, hitting another soldier, who had been watching. The wounded man, enraged, began kicking her and stamping on her like a maniac, until blood poured from her birth canal, from her smashed nose and from gashes all over her body. At last the man stopped to tend to his own wound, and the soldiers left. My people carried the woman to Amudat hospital, and, with the help of four injections, she survived.

The wounded soldier brought the case to court, accusing the woman of shooting him! However, even in such strange surroundings, that woman was not one to be easily intimidated. She told her side of the story with conviction, while the soldier, now on the defensive, indignantly denied beating anyone. The judge sensed something was wrong and dismissed the case.

Turkana Raids

Not long after those incidents, I decided, like many others, to move my family and herd away from this constant fighting with the Karamojong. The only problem was that we were living together with a man named Laposikanar, whose mother, Chemaring, was so old that she could no longer walk about. She stayed inside her house day and night, and had no bowel or bladder control. It was, of course, impossible for my friend Laposikanar to move with Chemaring. He pleaded with us, "Please don't leave me. If you move, the Karamojong will surely come and kill me. Wait—tonight I will anoint my mother's head with milk."

Since long ago people have done this. When a person is so old that he is unable to make a necessary move with the family to escape drought or enemies, the eldest or, if that is not possible, the youngest of his children will anoint his head with milk. The parent will fall asleep peacefully, never to awaken.

That evening Laposikanar poured milk from a perfect, unbroken gourd onto his old mother's head, saying gently, "You have become very old, my mother. But now you will rest well with the milk of your cow." He waited until Chemaring nodded off to sleep, then came to the *aperit* and told us solemnly, "I have tended to my mother. We will see tomorrow if it works."

The next morning Laposikanar went into his mother's house and said, "Wake up, Mother, and eat your food!" She did not respond, and he found that she was dead. We helped him dig the grave and bury her. Then we slaughtered a goat and spread ourselves with the stomach contents. The next day we moved to Kaseipa, in Kenya, where we completed the ritual for the dead. Luckily, Laposikanar had a black ox to slaughter, along with the necessary goat. We paid an old woman 55 shillings to tend to the procedures for distributing Chemaring's worldly goods.

In September of 1968, Chepto gave birth to our son Chepunos, named after the hill on which we were staying at the time, just above the locality called Lopet. At that time, Chepto had three living children. Having lost her second baby to illness after only nine months, she had given us a healthy son, Kakuko, and now this baby, Chepunos. Meanwhile, Chepusepa, now free of the curse of Kadam, had produced five healthy children. We rejoiced that our homestead had been blessed with new life!

However, our short stay at Chepunos was marked by disturbing events. One day lightning struck the wife of our neighbor Lokokwang while she was herding the calves and goats. Lokokwang found her lying face down on the side of the hill, breathing heavily. He rolled her over, and was horrified to see her freakishly disfigured, almost like a bird! Lokokwang tried to round up the calves, but they began stumbling and falling down. Only two survived the trip home. With the help of a practitioner named Muriako, Lokokwang's wife eventually recovered, but the scars remained.

Very early in the morning several weeks later, while Chepusepa and my mother were staying at the garden and I was at home, sleeping with Chepto and the children, our daughter Cherel came into the house to get some fire to carry back to her own house. She paused at the door and asked, "Father, do you hear something?"

"No, what ..." but I was interrupted by the sound of gunfire. My daughter was terrified. She ran out, screaming, "The Turkana are killing people!"

I took my shield and spear, let out the cattle and goats and called to my children: "Run up the hill! I'll take the herds!" They ran together up the path, while I herded first the goats, then the cattle to the top of Chepunos. There was only one way up, and I guarded it carefully. When I felt they were secure, I told the children, "Stay here and keep watch in that direction. If you see any Turkana, run and hide! I don't think they'll find you here."

I sprinted down the hill and climbed to the top of another one just above the gardens. I yelled down to warn my mother and Chepusepa to take cover, then ran back towards our homestead. On the path I came across fresh footprints of cattle and goats, so I followed them. At Kaisakat, I was joined by others. We continued following the tracks until we caught up with the Turkana and the stolen Pokot herd at Dapar. My companions killed three Turkana with their arrows, before the surprised Turkana raiders began shooting back. When we saw how many guns they had, we ran, leaving the cattle. One of our men was killed.

Later we continued tracking the cattle to Nachacha, on the wild, open Turkana plains. Although we could see the raiders, there was insufficient cover to allow us to get close enough to attack them with our spears and arrows. As we considered this predicament, one of the raiders spotted us. His companions gunned down six of us while we were still far away, and we were forced to leave the cattle once more.

The third time we tried to retrieve the cattle, we found our enemies camping on a dry island in the river Suam. Again, we had no place from which to mount an attack, so we left the herd for good and returned home.

Those Turkana warriors had killed a woman and her child in a homestead very close to ours, four uncircumcised sisters in another homestead, and seven men on our forays. Altogether, 13 people died as a result of the raid.

After that event, my family and I packed our belongings again and moved to a high hill at Parakaswa, where grass was more plentiful. I was sick for several months after the move. Then, in February, a messenger came to tell us that my sister Chelima was gravely ill after giving birth. The baby had survived, but Chelima had been taken to the Amudat hospital.

Chepusepa, my mother and I left immediately for Father's homestead at Lossom. The morning after our arrival, we walked to Amudat to see Chelima. We were distressed about her condition and decided to take her home from the hospital and have her treated by a practitioner. Thankfully, this worked and she recovered.

While in Amudat I took a bag of the free maize meal the government was providing at that time.[113] I borrowed one of my father's donkeys, loaded it with the sack, and was about to set out for Parakaswa, when the rains came and we changed our plans. Instead of traveling, my wife and I decided to spend the afternoon preparing our termite hills, because we knew the delicious insects were about to fly. Chepusepa and I alone managed to catch more than a maize-sack full of termites! We brought them back to Father's homestead and dried them in the sun. A few days later, we loaded the termites, maize meal and our other belongings on four of Father's donkeys and set off for home, spending the night at Kasei.

As we approached our homestead, our daughter Akimat came running out to us, exclaiming, "The Turkana have just killed people near Korsitch!"

I left the donkeys burdened, grabbed my spear and shield, and ran to Chebunbun, along with others. We searched in vain for evidence, then went back to Lopet, where we were told our efforts would be of no use. The Turkana had killed 17 children and two women had disappeared, along with twelve cattle and some goats.

Later that week, I returned three of my father's donkeys, loaded the fourth with another sack of maize meal at Amudat, and took it back home.

The following month we heard the terrible news that there had been a Karamojong raid on my brother Lopeyok's homestead in Uganda. The cattle had not been recovered, and, once again, Lopeyok was faced with the imminent starvation of his family. After moving his household to a safer location, my brother went alone to try to steal some goats from the Karamojong in order to feed his wife and children—at least temporarily. We were told that when he finally returned with a single goat, his people were so hungry that they met him in the bush country, killed the goat, and ate the stomach raw!

Two days later, Lopeyok joined with some others on a larger raid. Failing to find an entrance to a Karamojong corral, the warriors broke through the fence. Lopeyok and two others prodded the cattle out, while three men guarded the gate to the houses. When the cattle began lowing, awakening the homestead, Lopeyok heard a Karamojong man calling for help. Another ran out and was speared in the mouth. Meanwhile, Lopeyok and his partners managed to chase the cattle up and over the hill into our country.

At dawn a police vehicle came searching for the raiders. They drove right by Lopeyok and his companions, who were lying in the bush beside the track, before they spotted the cattle and stopped the vehicle. A policeman and a Karamojong man got out and started towards the herd. Lopeyok and another warrior grabbed their bows. Their arrows grazed one policeman in the legs, and when he turned to run, Lopeyok shot him in the back. Another man shot the Karamojong man in the head, and he fell. The wounded policeman staggered back to the car and drove away. He eventually recovered in the hospital.

Instead of going home, Lopeyok herded his share of the cattle all the way to Chepropul, well into Kenya, where they stayed for three months, while the government was actively searching for them. When he heard the investigation was called off, he herded his cattle home. They have been in his homestead ever since.

In July, the Turkana came again to Parakaswa, where we were living. My son Moru heard yelling and ran to find that Turkana had already taken cattle and were raiding the fields at Chemukuh for millet, sorghum and maize. I left with another man for the gardens, but my companion vomited when we were half-way there, and I had to bring him home. By the time I finally made it to the fields, everyone had left. I followed them to Chebunbun, where I noticed vultures circling and diving ahead of me. This was unfortunate, as it is considered bad luck whenever a vulture passes overhead and rests in front of you, although if it comes to rest behind you, it is considered good.

Nevertheless, as I continued on the path, I came across a stray cow, then about twelve stray donkeys. Next, the birds flapped up at my approach and I saw in their wake a dead Turkana, shot in the head. I knew this had to be the work of Loterok, who had just returned from service in the Kenya Army, and who, apparently, had a gun. Just then, six gunshots announced the place of fighting.

I ran to join the battle, meeting two others on the path. The three of us passed another corpse, and also a Turkana man who had a broken leg. We finally caught up with Loterok and the others at the edge of a vast area devoid of trees. I remembered our other experience with armed Turkana in such a place and told my companions, "We will never get them now! They can kill us at will, like police, here on the plains. If we can't fight on the hills, we will have to let them go."

Even Loterok agreed. He and his men had managed to salvage about a hundred animals, but the Turkana had taken several hundred more and had murdered about ten children. Frustrated and bitter, we turned back. As we passed the Turkana with the broken leg, one of the men killed him. Then we rounded up the stray stock and brought them home.

Peace

Our battles with the Karamojong and the Turkana had been continuous and devastating, ever since the appearance of the comet several years before. In Uganda, especially, the Pokot-Karamojong bitterness had reached a peak that had exhausted both our peoples. Finally, after Lotomanimoi, the crippled gunman, was killed in the ambush at Cholol, the Karamojong leaders earnestly offered to make peace. In addition to their troubles with us, the Karamojong claimed to have been harassed by the Kenya Army, which, they said, had seized their herds, shot and detained their people, and even run over children with their trucks.

A huge Pokot-Karamojong peace council was called by the Karamojong elders at Moruita. The Karamojong proclaimed, "We must make an oath, as our fathers did long ago, so that we may live peacefully together. We must produce more children, in order to compensate for those who have died." They brought out a white steer, then held out two ostrich feathers—one red and one white—to the Pokot elders. "Which of these do you want?" they asked.

The Pokot leaders chose the white feather symbolizing peace. The Karamojong elders presented the Pokot elders with a *lukutia* belt (the woman's skin belt, decorated with cowrie shells, worn by a mother several years after giving birth to insure the health of her baby). Each side killed a white steer, and the blood of the two animals was mixed. Finally, certain revered and very old elders from each tribe assembled the items of peace: the mixed blood and combined bones of the two steers, a razor-like knife resembling an arrowhead (used for shaving our heads), the red ostrich feather, a Pokot spear and a Karamojong spear. They took the solemn oaths of peace, while the symbols were buried about six feet deep. The Pokot, who had accepted the peace offer, kept the white ostrich feather and the *lukutia* belt.

After the peace, our peoples finally quit fighting for a while. At last, everyone could walk about freely, without threat. Pokot and Karamojong began to live side by side, intermarrying, and even sharing gardens in some areas, as they had after previous peace ceremonies.

In the olden days, such a ceremony would insure peace for as long as five to ten years (that is ten to twenty years by Pokot reckoning, for we count two years for every one of yours), but these days there have been times and places when a proclaimed peace lasted only a few months.[114] It is dangerous for men to begin fighting without first removing the peace tokens, for many of them will die, and that is why younger men and youths are not allowed to witness the ceremonies. They might decide to remove the articles of peace and resume the fighting without justification.

When I heard, with great relief, that a Pokot-Karamojong peace had been proclaimed, I moved my family far away from the Turkana, back to the region of Lossom. We arrived in August of 1969.

One of our new neighbors there was a man named Pkiror Lomuna, about whom people told a scandalous story, enjoyed by all. Pkiror, who is of my mother's buffalo clan, grew up in an isolated homestead, shared by his father, Tenaita, and his father's brother, Mikale. There were no other people around and, hence, his only companions were his own brothers and sisters (We consider cousins to be siblings as well.).

This was very hard on Chemuren, daughter of Mikale, who wanted a boyfriend. She convinced Pkiror to sleep with her one night, just to satisfy her desire, but, alas, she got pregnant! Her parents were perplexed. "How could this happen?" they asked.

"It is a matter of Tororut," she replied. "There has been no man. Tororut has blessed me with a child."

One small girl heard this and tattled, "I saw Pkiror lying with Chemuren!"

Chemuren denied the accusation, but her parents were not convinced. They questioned Pkiror, who admitted the truth, saying, "We have sinned greatly."

When Chemuren heard this, she ran away, never to be seen again. Even Pkiror never knew whether she gave birth to a boy or a girl. Some say she went to the Europeans to become a prostitute. Nevertheless, people made up a song about her, which we like to sing at the time of *laleyo*. (Many of the lyrics refer to the clan totem, the buffalo, with its horns, tossing head and lashing tongue.)

Aya, her brother is appealing	*Aya kemulanan werang nyu*
Refrain: 　*Chemuren, mmm aya, Oh Chemuren, ah*	*Chemuren na aya, uh aya* *Oh Chemuren*
Verses: 　*He is appealing to that daughter* 　*Chemuren, daughter of horns* 　*Appealing Pkiror* 　*Appealing son of Tenaita* 　*Chemuren, mmm, buffalo daughter* 　*Appealing buffalo man* 　*Appealing man of horns* 　*Chemuren, he is a man of the tongue* 　*Appealing boy Lomuna* 　*Her appealing black brother*	*Kimulanan mondengnyo* *Chemuren mondo kui* *Kimulanan Pkiror* *Kimulanan wero Tenaita* *Chemuren mm mondo lalin* *Kimulanan chi to lalin* *Kimulanan chi to kui* *Chemuren, nyi chi to mulia* *Kimulanan weri Lomuna* *Kimulanan weri kuptoi*

Elephant Hunt

After the peace, for a time, we were able to enjoy hunting and other outings, without worrying about the safety of our herds and families. Many of the young men at Lossom were eager to go hunting for dangerous wild animals, such as lion, elephant, rhino or buffalo, so that they could take back souvenirs of their kill and cut notches in their oxen's ears as symbols of their prowess. A successful hunter can cut one of the ears of his ox-of-ropes for each dangerous animal he helped to kill. If he kills two elephants, he will cut decorations in both of his ox's ears. When women see these handsome signs on his name-ox, they know he has the courage of a bull.

And so, not long after we moved back to Uganda, 28 of us took our spears to Kokwokoliong to search for elephants. But when we asked a Kokwokoliong man if he had seen any elephants about, he warned us, "There's only one elephant in these parts—a dangerous bull that has already killed several people. No one dares to use that path these days!"

"Which path?" we asked. "Can you take us there?"

He exclaimed, "Oh no! I wouldn't show that to anyone! But you can see it in the distance from the top of Kokwokoliong hill." He hurried off.

I climbed the hill with another man, while the rest waited. We could see the footpath half a mile away. Our hunting party started down to the path quietly, and after a mile or two we saw the great bull standing beneath a tree.

"We're in luck! He doesn't see us," one man whispered.

"I'll scout ahead and find the best place," said Nakapor.

While we waited for Nakapor, we bolstered our courage with comments like these: "We must go carefully, in fours. We can't run. We want him to come to us. We'll try to hit him before he reaches us. We'd rather die than show our backs, right?"

"Right!"

"If he kills us or if we kill him, it's all the same!"

"We should watch one another. If anyone runs, we'll bring his wife here and tell her, 'See? This is where your husband ran off! Why did he run away, while the rest of us were here? Why did he not stay here to die with us? Why did *he* want to be spared? Ha! Any decent man would rather die with his comrades, yet *your* husband said, "Let me run and I'll be saved!" Did he think he should recover alone, while everyone else died? He's a coward!'"

"Yes, yes! That's the way it should be! That's what we'll say!"

We lashed out at cowardice!

After Nakapor came back, we fanned out slowly, in groups of four, until we had formed a semicircle around the bull. He still had not seen us. It was important for him to face us, so our spears would hit true.

"I'll get his attention," said a man near me. He threw his spear. He missed, but the elephant opened his eyes, alert. A second spear hit him in the flank.

Instantly, the beast was upon us, screaming, trumpeting. We hurled our spears like one great, multi-armed hunter. The bull's face was soon covered with spears, with one in the forehead. The circle closed around him, but he still came at us. The spears of our neighbors brushed past our faces. Finally the great beast whirled around, trying to retreat. Then he crashed down, almost at our feet, dying in agony.

The people of Kokwokoliong rejoiced when they heard the news and rushed to thank us. The elephant had recently killed two Turkana and one Pokot man. Before that, it had trampled to death two Somali women and injured their husband. Nevertheless, it had been a typical hunt. We stalk rhino and buffalo in the same way, creeping up very closely and killing the animal quickly. If we see a dangerous animal first, we have a chance. But if that bull elephant had seen us first, some of us might have been killed.

Since it was impossible to know who had thrown the first or the killing spear, we divided the bounty equally. The tusks were sold, and several men requested some of the skin for shields. Others brought strips of the elephant's hide home to their wives for making shoes, a source of great power for a woman.

To make shoes, each wife dries a skin in the sun, then covers it with donkey dung for two days to soften the leather. After that, she carves a paddle and beats the skin until it is pliable. Finally, she cuts the soles, using a spear point, and ties leather strips over the tops to complete the sandals. Then she watches her husband. Whenever he wears the shoes she made for him on a journey and brings back stock, this bounty is hers! Even if he chooses to give his other wives smaller presents, the cattle belong to her, because she claims, "I was the source of my husband's strength on these raids. I made the shoes he wore! If anyone wants a share of this fortune, they will have to ask me first." The other wives are happy for their co-wife, for each knows that her time, too, will come. One day her husband will present her with skin of a giraffe, buffalo or elephant for making new shoes, and henceforth, the bounty will be hers!

Sometimes after a hunt, a man who has been insulted by his lover will dip his garment in the blood of the kill, take it to the house of the girl's mother, and shake it at the woman, spattering her with blood. But there are other, more pleasant, traditions. One of our companions at Kokwokoliong had borrowed his girlfriend's skin apron (*atela*) to take along on the hunt. On our way back, he stopped at her homestead to announce proudly to her father, "We have killed an elephant for this skin! Be ready! We will come to celebrate in two months!"

On the appointed day, several weeks later, all of us put on our best garments and decorations. We covered our heads with ostrich feathers, wore beads and giraffe tails, and walked in unison to the girl's home for the ceremonial returning of the *atela*. As we expected, a party was waiting for us, and we feasted, danced and celebrated until the next morning. Five *atekerai* (wooden bowls) had been filled with a mixture of milk, blood and fat for us. In return, before we left, we killed a steer for the women of the homestead to eat. We went to our own homes to satisfy our hunger.

Simba

In January, 1970, I met Simba in Amudat ...

[See the Preface for descriptions of Domonguria's work for "Simba" (Larry Robbins) on the archaeological dig and the subsequent taping of these stories with Pat Robbins.]

DESTRUCTION AND HOPE
IN A CHANGING WORLD

RETURNING HOME

Tororut's Will

Early in 1970, while working for Simba, we saw another comet. This one, like Tpsaro, had a tail pointing upwards, but to the left. And there were two of them: one visible at Moroto and one on the Kenyan side of the border. The one above us gradually drifted until it joined its brother in Moroto, which would appear in the evening. The strange nature of this comet caused the elders to wonder if sickness would not come again to our people and, perhaps, a drought or other disaster as well. Most of them believed the cattle, at least, would be spared this time. But why, they asked each other, did this comet appear only five years after the last one? As before, all the people and herds from each neighborhood gathered to sing, pray, and be anointed with the stomach con-tents of ritually-sacrificed steers. We hoped that Tororut might choose to spare us this time.

In March, I heard of another strange happening. It was raining hard at Aparipar, when two men were sitting beneath a tree watching their cattle. One of them, the son of Loweita, yelled curses at a few of the cattle for some reason, and instantly, Ilat struck him, throwing him a great distance. Simultaneously, Ilat struck his companion, the son of Muria Loker, on the head, leaving a scar like a rainbow of red, yellow and green. As he regained his senses, Loker's son, dazed, became aware of a man asking, "Why did you curse the cattle? They can't understand you. They are beasts of little intelligence. Their work is to eat, to go home, and to sleep. If you want milk, a cow won't deny you. Why, then, do you curse at them? I see you have not heeded my constant teachings. Hence-forth, watch your tongues!" When the apparition left, Loker's son got up and saw his friend lying on the hillside, looking quite dead. He ran away.

Eventually, the son of Loweita regained consciousness, feeling excruciating pain throughout his body. He had been badly burned, like one who has been scalded with boiling water. With a great deal of trouble, he managed to walk home, where he collapsed. His people carried him to the hospital at Karita, where he eventually recovered from burns and dehydration. However, the skin on one side of his body peeled off completely, leaving him white, like a Euro-pean!

My Sister's Death

After my work for Simba was finished, and while I was far away in Nairobi recording this book for you, alas, my dearest sister, Chelima, was dying. My family told me later that they had been alarmed by Chelima's sudden and mysterious illness. When she failed to recover, they had decided that her agony must be due to the sorcery of her old suitor, who, even after she was married to Lopedur, had never given up the hope of having Chelima for his wife. Obsessed with his thwarted love for my sister, he was always saying, "She'll return to me one day!" Perhaps he finally realized she never would, so he decided to kill her.

My brothers forcibly brought that man to Lakalaa's homestead, where my sister was suffering, and warned him, "If our child dies, you will die with her! We will beat you to death!" Just then, my sister's condition worsened dramatically, and while my family's attention was diverted, the man ran off. Then Chelima died.

In my absence, my brothers had to bury Chelima without me. When someone we love very much, like Chelima, dies, we call our people together to help dig a grave in the corral. (If there is no one to help, a man will grieve and dig it alone.) My brothers sadly placed our sister's body in the grave, covered it with dirt, and put a small mound of stones on top. They cried to the spirit of our cherished sister, "Sleep now, Chelima, and watch over the end of life." Then, because she died of sorcery, they prayed to Tororut earnestly on her behalf, asking for the punishment and death of the sorcerer. After the burial, those of my brothers who had helped with the grave killed a goat and covered their bodies with its stomach contents, then spread the partially digested grasses of a second goat on the bodies of their children. (It is important for this to be done the day a person dies. It is a family matter, and no outsiders are permitted.)

I was on my way home for a visit a few days later, when I heard this sad and shocking news. My brothers, I learned, were in seclusion, awaiting my return, so that the final ceremony of the black ox and the distribution of beads could be completed. After some agonized thought, I decided not to go home yet. If I did, I would have to slaughter a goat, spread myself with its stomach contents, and stay in seclusion for nearly a week. Then I would have to search for a black ox, for there was none in our herd. We had a black cow, which had just calved, but that would not do. If I earned more money, I could afford to buy a black ox for the ceremony. Then I would have to find an old woman and hire her to perform the ritual of dividing the beads. There were so many matters awaiting me, I knew that if I went home, I would not return. Therefore I stayed with friends instead, and returned to Nairobi to finish this recording.

Meanwhile, my brother Lopeyok marched to the sorcerer's house, filled with anger over Chelima's senseless death. She had taken nothing from this man, whom she had once loved—no cattle or even goats, and yet he had killed her! When Lopeyok arrived, the man's wife claimed she had no idea where her husband had gone. Frustrated, Lopeyok beat her.

When my brothers inquired further, they discovered that other people had already taken the sorcerer away the day before, claiming he was responsible for other deaths as well. They had dragged him into their homestead and begun to beat him, but he had pleaded for mercy, saying, "Let me go hang myself! Don't beat me like this!" They had agreed. And so Chelima's former lover and murderer had climbed a tree and tied one end of a rope to a branch and the other end around his neck. Then he had jumped.

When I finally returned home in July, after you left for America, I found that some of my cattle had died unexpectedly. My wives had been distraught over my long absence and had even begun to talk of moving elsewhere until I came back. To make matters worse, Chepusepa had become terribly ill. I took her to the hospital immediately for treatment, and she stayed there, recovering, for the next two weeks.

Meanwhile, I busied myself tending to the remaining matters concerning my sister's untimely death. Having spent the first week in seclusion, I found and purchased a black ox with the money I had just earned, and hired a very old woman for 50 shillings to oversee the ritual of distributing Chelima's beads. The night before that ceremony, we slaughtered the black ox and ate it. The next morning about thirty people came, and I provided them with beer and tobacco.[115] Then all of my sister's beads and ornaments were placed on the skin of the black ox, together with grass, water, milk, honeycomb, and *moikut* (small, round sedge-root tubers). The old woman washed them with water, rubbed them with the beeswax, and washed them again in milk, before dividing them among the relatives. Each heir chewed the *moikut* and spat the juice of this medicine, in order to ward off any spells of the sorcerer that might still be attached to his share of the beads.

Sometime later, Chelima's widower, Lopedur, asked our sister Chepchalup, daughter of my father's third wife Moiyoiyin, to cleanse him. She went to his homestead, together with her husband and her children, to perform this ritual. She washed Lopedur first with water, then rubbed his body with honey-fat, and washed him twice more, first with beer and then with milk. For this, she was given five goats and a cow we call *korukuk*, which would be hers alone and could never be given to anyone else.

Once a widower is washed in this way, he is free to marry again. To marry before he is cleansed would bring death upon a new wife. In addition, each time he marries after that, he must slaughter a black or red sheep the morning after he brings his bride home, then anoint her with its stomach contents. When he cooks the mutton in a pot, he must be careful not to let any of the soup spill on the fire.

A Curse

I brought Chepusepa home from the hospital, and she recovered quickly. At last, I saw my household was in order, and I decided it was a good time for a walk to Amudat with some friends to spend the afternoon drinking beer at the "club." Chepto's father and brother, who were visiting in the area, met us on the way and gladly joined our party.

Just as we were passing the main shops in Amudat, I heard a man call out, "Domonguria!" I looked around, expecting to see another friend, but came face to face with a man who seemed ready to fight!

"Where's my wife?" the man yelled accusingly at me.

"What wife?" I asked, confused.

"My wife you are living with!" he shouted.

"I don't know your wife," I said quietly. I thought the man was a lunatic at first, but as he continued his insults, I stared at him with increasing recognition. This was Nyoale Langarikamar, the man who had tried to marry my wife Chepto long ago! He had forced her to his homestead at the very time I was at her father's house in Kenya, asking for her hand in marriage! The memory rankled me. He was trying to claim my Chepto!

"I want my wife," he taunted, and I slugged him in the jaw as hard as I could. That was just what he wanted, and he punched me back. We lunged at each other, but some men from the gathering crowd around us pulled us apart. I struggled against them to get at Nyoale, but my friends held me back. I could taste blood in my mouth. I seethed, "If you ever insult my wife again, I'll ..," but I was drowned out by people in the crowd yelling, "He's a sorcerer! He wants to cast a spell on that man's wife!"

Chepto's father and brother were alarmed by what they were hearing, especially remembering the recent fate of my sister Chelima at the hands of her former suitor, turned sorcerer. They seized Nyoale by the throat, and Chepto's father threatened him so that all could hear, saying, "If our child dies, all of your children will die! If ours thrives, yours will too." Then they let Nyoale go, and we proceeded, somewhat shaken, to the club to drink our beer.

After that incident, a cow died unexpectedly, and I began to worry. However, Chepto and our children remained healthy, and Chepusepa, fully recovered, became pregnant.

Then around the ninth month, at the time of the rains, my mother—the middle one, Chepusuchon—became ill. I took her to the hospital in Amudat and watched over her there for the next two weeks. Five days after I brought her home, I was called to Katabok to tend to one of my sick in-laws. When I returned a week later, I was alarmed to find my mother Chepusuchon convulsed in pain. She kept screaming, "My head! My head!" clutching at her head and her throat.

She vomited and continued writhing, screaming in agony. It was already getting dark. I knew I would have to get help for her as soon as possible in the morning—at dawn. But that night Chepusuchon spat out something dark blue, and then she died. I sat down and cried over this dear mother I loved so much. Our household was once again engulfed in grief and the matters relating to death.

As the months went by, we continued loosing more and more cattle, and there seemed to be no reasonable explanation. By the time Chepusepa's baby was born, most of the milking cows had died. This was a desperate situation for the children, and Chepusepa, in particular, needed strength and nourishment.

I walked several days to the home of a cattle associate and brought home an ox I intended to sell for money for food. While I was in Amudat searching for a buyer, a neighbor came to tell me that the same ox had just died! Astonished, I asked, "What killed it?" He answered, "We don't know. Yesterday afternoon the cowherd ran to tell us that it just lay down and began to die. By the time we got there, only its eyes were still alive." As I walked back to my homestead that day, I puzzled over the unexplained deaths of my cattle. The idea grew in my mind that perhaps Nyoale Langarikamar had had something to do with it. True, he had not harmed Chepto or the children, but perhaps he was seeking to punish us indirectly. There were too many unexplained deaths.

There was nothing left to do at that point, but to beg for money from friends in order to save Chepusepa, who was increasingly weak from hunger and soon would be unable to care for our infant daughter, Chepetoi. My father helped by sending a youth to sell one of his remaining steers in Kacheliba. As soon as the boy returned, my father gave me 200 shillings, and I bought a large sack of maize meal in Amudat. Chepusepa began to recover visibly after the first few meals, so I went back to Amudat for more maize and, one by one, carried the heavy sacks home. However, this food arrived too late for my daughter Cherel. Feeling pain from hunger, she decided to leave our home and go to live far away in Tingirich with her mother's father, who had food. It saddened me greatly not to be able to provide for my own child.

Ironically, the Karamojong were responsible for a new infusion of cattle for our herds in 1971. Already, the peace was being broken, as we started hearing reports of raids in the surrounding areas. Then, one evening, our own cattle did not come home. We waited, and our hopes sank with the sun. At daybreak, we found the two murdered boys, who had been our cowherds. Another man's herd had been taken along with ours, and it was easy to follow the tracks, which headed straight for Karamojong territory. However, the raiders had a day's head start, and by the time we reached their homeland, the tracks had dispersed and were lost to us forever.

There was no choice but to find two herds of Karamojong cattle to replace the ones we had lost. This was not difficult. We spotted two groups of grazing stock almost instantly. I was greatly relieved when both sets of cowherds saw us at a distance and ran away unharmed, leaving the cattle to us. We herded all the cattle together and began to move them, keeping a nervous watch for the owners. They would be alerted by the cowherds soon.

We had gone nearly three miles before they came and the battle began. I was in the front, near the side of the herd, and the Karamojong attacked from the rear on the other side. I did my best to keep the cattle moving and under control, while my companions fought the enemy. It was over quickly. My friends killed two Karamojong men with spears, and the others ran off. We continued to push the cattle as fast as they could go, knowing we had not seen the last of our pursuers. For awhile, I thought we just might make it to our lands without further incident.

Suddenly, two Karamojong men appeared on my side, brandishing their spears. The man on the left leaped off a rock and started to rush me, spear poised, then he tripped and fell! I threw my spear at him, but it fell short. I glanced up to see that a group of cattle now separated me from the other attacker, so I hurled my second spear at the first man. He rolled to one side and the spear narrowly missed. Defenseless, I lunged for my spears, but the Karamojong man grabbed them, stood, and was about to thrust them into me at close range, when an amazing thing happened. Instead of feeling the certain pain of death, I saw my enemy fall, with a Pokot spear imbedded in his chest! I nodded thanks to the neighbor who had just saved my life, and he called, "Let's get our weapons and take our cattle home!"

Soon we were in familiar land and were relatively safe, but I was obsessed with other thoughts which kept pounding in my brain: *the killing ... the killing. We only kill because of trouble. They come to harm you—to kill your children, to steal your cattle which are your very life. Enemies continually plague our home, but when we follow them and try to kill them, I always fail! Even in battle I am unable to draw blood. Why am I forbidden to kill my enemy? It has always been like this. I have fought many, many enemies, yet I have never killed a man.* When I was a child, I remember the elders saying that Tororut sometimes prevents certain men from letting the blood of others, no matter how hard they try. I have thought this over many times, and have now come to the conclusion that I must be one of those men, and I give thanks because of it, for it is not good to kill someone. Because of this, unless the lives of my family are endangered, I have decided I will not go again to fight.

My share of the cattle from the Karamojong raid was enough to save our family from starvation. Most of the new animals remained healthy, but as the calves from my original herd matured, they continued dying, one by one. At the end of two years, only one of them was left, and I knew that my extensive losses had, indeed, been due to the curse of Nyoale Langarikamar.

"I might as well go hang myself," I ranted. "Even if I find other cattle, he will kill them! Why don't I just take a spear and kill Nyoale instead!" But my family refused to let me kill a man and suggested I go instead to a witchdoctor for medicine with which to break the curse.

As it turned out, Nyoale's own neighbors settled the problem for me early in 1976. We heard that two brothers had consulted a witchdoctor after their father and many of their extended family and acquaintances had perished in a short period of time. "The reason your father died," the practitioner had told the sons, "is because Nyoale Langarikamar killed him! When you return, you will find yet another—a woman—ill because of his spell. After she dies, he will begin preying on each of you. So it is your decision: if you don't kill him, he'll kill you." The brothers brought this news to their mother and to the other wives and children of their deceased father. Together they went to Nyoale's home and beat him to death.

Now that the curse was removed, I set out with determination to assemble a new herd—to beg from my associates, my in-laws, my uncles and my brothers. One gave a goat, another a cow, until I became a man of security once again. The cattle are still few, but I will husband them until they are as numerous as in the days before the curse of Nyoale Langarikamar.

IDI AMIN

Evil

The Karamojong and the Turkana, we understood. We fought one another, raided herds, and occasionally lived together, because we agreed on what was important—our cattle and our customs. Yet, in 1971, there came to our lands a more insidious enemy than either of our tribes had ever experienced, for this enemy was evil, without reason.

It began when the new leader of Uganda, Idi Amin,[116] sent orders to our community, forbidding us to wear clay in our hair or skins on our bodies. "You must shave your heads and buy your clothes in shops," the directive said. "Furthermore, the days of courts and jails are over. The law of these days is the knife!"

People were outraged. The new code of dress disregarded the most cherished customs of the Pokot and of the Karamojong. Our leaders objected, and Amin listened. "I want to know what bothers you," he said. He called a huge meeting of both of our peoples.

A Karamojong man was the first to speak. He said, "Since long ago, if a man removes his headdress, it is only because a relative has died. If a woman shaves her head, it is because her husband has died. The orders to shave our heads are repugnant to us." Then he sat down.

"I have heard from the Karamojong," Amin said. "Is there a Pokot man who will speak?" A tall man, respected by our community, stood and fervently explained our dilemma, ending thus: "We beg you to hear our cause, sir. We do not wish to be disrespectful, but a breach in these customs would be too painful for my people."

"So I have heard!" the fat man exclaimed. "You have both said the same thing, even though you come from different tribes. Now I want to hear from the women." He sat down on the platform and folded his hands over his large belly.

One Karamojong wife began to speak. "The only time we shave our heads is when our husbands die, or our fathers, or our children. It is a very bad thing for us ..."

"Thank you, mother," interrupted Amin. "You have said enough and you may sit down. I want a Pokot woman now."

A Pokot woman stood and repeated what the Karamojong woman had said.

Amin stood up, now agitated, and began pacing. "I have heard your side. How many spoke? Four! Soldiers, bring those four people up here and question them some more!" He sat down, while his soldiers went into the crowd, seized the four and brought them to the front. There, in front of all of us, they stabbed the two men and the two women to death, then threw their bloody bodies in a heap on the ground.

Revulsion and terror swept through the crowd. We looked around to see ourselves surrounded by soldiers. The fat man stood up with a slight smile and asked, "Well, have you seen what happened to your spokesmen?" There was complete silence in the stunned crowd. This angered Amin, and he shouted, "I said, have you seen these people?" All of the soldiers raised their guns and pointed them at us. "Yes, we have seen," we replied.

"All right, now who would like to add to what they said?"

One brave, very old elder stood up. He said in a clear voice, "We will say no more. We will obey your orders. We will shave our heads now."

"Good! Now everyone applaud!" He clapped his fat hands. The guns were aimed again at the crowd, and the people began to clap. "Again!" Amin called, and we clapped again. We were made to clap four times. "Thank you," said Amin. "From now on, whoever does not obey my orders will follow these four." He left the platform and walked away.[117]

A few days later, the soldiers of Amin drove out to the small settlement of Katabok, where you and I and Simba lived together, while doing the archaeological excavations on Kadam Mountain, early in 1970. The people—our friends there—fled with their cattle, and the soldiers followed them up the slopes of Mt. Kadam. There they captured ten people, tied them with ropes and slaughtered them. They confiscated all the cattle they found.

Our family was one of the first to move across the border into Kenya, which was only a mile away from our previous homesteads. After news of Amin's terror spread, multitudes of others followed. Most never returned to Uganda. Those who stayed in Uganda continued to be persecuted. Amin's soldiers seemed to delight in killing people, as if they were baboons.

My Children

In 1972, there was a solar eclipse, and this time it was advertised widely. Even the soldiers told us, "on Saturday afternoon from 3:00 until about 4:30 the sun will die. Turkana will be the darkest. In Pokot areas, there will be some light." But the most frightening part of the message was this: "You must patch your houses so that no light can enter, and you must stay inside. Beware, any of you who look at the dying sun! The globe of your eyes will be removed and you will be blinded!" Luckily, Tororut prevented this horrible thing from happening.

My boy, Nyangaluk, who has been known as Simon ever since he entered school, was granted permission by his school in Thompson's Falls to come home the day before the eclipse so that he could instruct our people. He called a meeting, and about thirty men came. He told them, "You must bring the cattle home after midday tomorrow and be sure they are in the corral by mid-afternoon. The sun will be gone for about an hour, but it will return and will not go out again." The next day, Simon himself took our cattle to graze, for he wore a watch. I went along with the children to herd the goats. Simon brought the cattle back at about 1:00, and at 3:00 he instructed the cowherds to bring the animals inside. Before we entered our houses, we noticed the country becoming dim, but we trusted Simon, and when we came out again, there was light.

By the end of 1973, Chepto was very large with child, and I said to Chepusepa, "Come, let's go find food to sustain Chepto and the baby after birth." Together we herded two donkeys and some goats across the river Suam and on to the hill Chepinyan, where people grow a lot of maize. We made our purchases, bartering with the goats, then loaded the donkeys with the grain and started home. When we reached Kanyao, friends greeted us with the news that on the morning after we left, Chepto had given birth to twins! I worried the rest of the way home.

Chepto was so sick after the birth that other women had to nurse our babies— our son, Turu, and our daughter, Chepkerket. I knew it was urgent to have the *riwoi* ceremony for twins, so that the babies and their mother could regain their health quickly. Chepusepa and the other women helped Chepto, while I gathered honey from my hives and sent my younger brother to find a sheep for the ritual. We brewed six gourds of beer from the honey. Then I went into seclusion with my ailing wife Chepto.

When all was ready, my family summoned a man who had previously fathered twins to perform the ritual. Just as we had previously celebrated *riwoi* for our son Makal, because Chepusepa had become pregnant with him without having menstruated since her last childbirth, now we performed the same ceremony because of the birth of our twins. The sheep was slaughtered, the beer was drunk, and the same songs were sung. A root was boiled in a small pot to produce the medicine which would liberate my wife and me, for we had stayed inside together, always with our shoes on, until that moment. We sipped and spat the medicine and the beer, together with the ritual leader and others who had performed *riwoi*. Then we went outside with our babies, and the sun saw us. We completed all the rituals to bless my wife and babies.

My wife's recovery began at *riwoi*, and she gained back her strength quickly. She was now called Chesalaa, Mother of Twins, in addition to her other name. The twins also have prospered. Like Makal, we will watch over them, taking precautions whenever they bleed, and teaching them not to pierce their mouths and ears with thorns like other children until their *kitula* purification, which I shall arrange when they are about seven or eight years old. For that ritual, I will call back the man who conducted the first half of their ceremony, the *riwoi*, and he will bring his wife and his own twins to help with *kitula*. The procedures will be the same as in the *kitula* we held for Makal. Hopefully, these rites will continue to protect Chepto and our twins from sickness during their lives.

One happy afternoon, my wife's father brought our beloved daughter Cherel back to us again. It had been three years since she had left to find food at her grandfather's home, when our cattle were dying as a result of Nyoale's curse. We rejoiced over her homecoming, but were alarmed to see that Cherel was covered with sores. One of my relatives, who had already removed all his ornaments and his clay headdress so that he could safely cross into Uganda, volunteered to take her to the hospital in Amudat. He left her there for treatment.

A week later, a messenger told me that a "Sister Ruth," who lived in Amudat, wanted to see me about teaching my daughter to read.[118] I found a small piece of paper and took it to a literate man to write my reply: "I cannot come there, because you know I am now a man of Kenya. If we go there the soldiers will question us." I gave the note to Sister Ruth's messenger, who left again for Uganda. Two days later, the man returned with another message from Sister Ruth: "Tell him I want his daughter for school." I replied immediately: "Impossible! How could I pay the school fees for this daughter you want, Sister?" The nun wrote back, "I will ask nothing from you, only your permission for your daughter to attend school."

After considering this for a few days, I went again to the man who could write and dictated a long reply: "Providing that you never ask me for school fees or other support, you may have *temporary* custody of my child, Cherel, and she may attend school. Ask her if I am wealthy, and she will tell you that our herds were so decimated recently that I wished to hang myself, and she was forced to flee to her maternal grandfather in order to find food. I cannot sell soil or stones in order to pay for her school fees! But I believe that anyone who is still living can eventually find wealth, and I am determined that one day she will be my child again!"

I was told that as soon as Sister Ruth received my letter, she took my daughter out of the hospital and enrolled her in school in Amudat, where she was renamed Mary.

Uganda

These days, Amudat has become a ghost town. The shops there are unable to stock supplies, and grass has begun to grow over the road, once the major link between northwestern Kenya and the rest of East Africa. In spite of this, those of us on the Kenya side of the border still find it necessary to cross into Uganda, for there is no other clinic or school nearby, and our cattle still must graze there during the hot, dry season. But Amin has declared that if we enter his country, we must abide by Ugandan rules. We must remove our beads and headdresses, and our wives must take off almost all of their jewelry. Women have to exchange their skin clothing for dresses at the border, and men must find a shirt and pants to wear. We must also disguise the brand symbols on our cattle to minimize the danger of their being seized by the authorities.

Even white people are being prosecuted in Uganda now. Dr. Webster, the only physician at the hospital in Amudat, was forced to move his wife and children into Kenya for their own safety. During his absence, two Pokot men died of spear wounds inflicted by the Karamojong, because they claimed no one but Webster knew how to treat them. Dr. Webster returned for a time, but now even he and his staff are gone. There is no other doctor at the hospital, and the town leaders have also disappeared.[119]

Recently, I walked to Amudat to visit my daughter, Cherel. She begged me, "Please Father, go to Kenya. Sell a goat or ox for money to buy us books and paper for writing." I was outraged to find that not only are there no instructional materials at the school, but the children are also without basic necessities, such as soap or needles and thread for sewing the tears in their cotton clothes. They have neither butter nor salt for their vegetables, and occasionally the maize meal runs out altogether.[120]

When I walked to Karita to visit some of our relatives who had stayed behind in Uganda, I witnessed an atrocity. There is a huge hole, like a well, dug into a rocky outcrop there, and during the rains it becomes a small lake. Many people pass by the area in the morning, and that is where I saw Amin's soldiers stopping and questioning some of them. I heard one soldier demanding, "Where are you going and with whom?" The people tried to cooperate, but many were pushed to one side for further questioning. I walked by as unobtrusively as possible, glad that I had shaved my head, removed all my beads and put on an ill-fitting cotton shirt and shorts for my journey into Uganda. When we were a safe distance away from the commotion, my companions and I found a place in the rocks where we could sit and watch unnoticed. To our alarm, we could see, from our high vantage point, that the people who had been pulled aside were being taken, one at a time, to a group of soldiers at the side of the water, where they were quietly stabbed to death, and their bodies cast into the standing water. We watched perhaps twenty murders, before we could stand no more and went home.

Chiefs

The extent of Amin's persecution has depended, to some extent, on the personality of the particular chief for a region. For instance, in one area of Karamoja, the people had a very good working relationship with a chief named Angela. When they wanted to go on a raid, the Karamojong in the neighborhood would kill an ox and call Angela to the feast, presenting him with gifts of money. In turn, Angela always pretended not to notice when they raided the Pokot, Teso or Sebei. However, when Amin's man Masiniko was appointed to take over Angela's job as chief, everything changed. Having been told about the situation with Angela, Masiniko was not surprised when the local people asked to meet him at a nearby homestead. He agreed, but also telephoned his headquarters to ask for a contingent of Amin's soldiers to accompany him to the meeting. On the appointed afternoon, Masiniko walked up to the homestead, ostensibly alone. Sure enough, an ox had been slaughtered and the meat was roasting. There were scores of people. Masiniko greeted them and asked, "Why have you called me?"

"We wanted to meet you—to get to know you," they answered.

"But it is *I* who should call *you*!" he yelled at them. "I thought it was *my* position as a government official to call the meetings—not you! But I already know the real reason you wanted to talk to me. You wanted to bribe me, just as you bribed my predecessor, Angela, so that you could go on raids without interference! Well, it's time you learned that this sort of proposition won't work with me!" He called out to his soldiers, who had quietly surrounded the village, "Seize the men and get rid of the women!"

The soldiers grabbed the unprepared men quickly and corralled them into a group at gunpoint. Then, in full view of the men, the soldiers pushed all the women together and shot them all. Some of the men went berserk watching the massacre of their wives, daughters and sisters, and they, too, were killed. When it was over, Masiniko addressed the shocked men. He said, "Observe your wives! There will be no more meetings." And he left.

In the Pokot area of Southern Karamoja, it was the procedure, before Amin, that when a new administrative chief was needed, the people would choose a Pokot man from among those who had finished school and nominate him to the government officials, who would usually cooperate. But Amin preferred his own henchmen. Therefore, in 1974, the Pokot elders decided to take a big chance and nominate Kapuriel, one of Amin's big men, who was also Pokot. The soldiers agreed, and Kapuriel was sent home.

Although he intended to be the uncompromising arm of the government, Kapuriel was, in fact, truly alarmed by what he saw amongst his own people. What disturbed him the most was the fact that the women, who were forbidden to wear skins of any kind, had been forced to remove even the leather bracelets by which they had been married. People could see that this bothered him.

In addition, whereas the previous authorities in the area had softened the iron law enough to allow a youth to celebrate *sapana*, he could put clay on his hair only for the duration of the ritual. The boy's father was required to ask permission from the authorities ahead of time and to register the celebration. Then Amin's soldiers, the chief, and the District Officer would come to police the festivity, and the decorated youth would be allowed to walk about without fear of death for those few days. But, at the end of the celebration, all the colors would have to be washed off, along with the clay, and the youth would be left with no visible proof that he had become a man.

Likewise, the celebration of women's circumcision had to be reported. People were allowed to wear jewelry and feathers without fear only during the first day of the post-circumcision ritual, *lupol*, always under the watchful eyes of Amin's soldiers. Yet, even during those times of temporary freedom, coiled wire jewelry and the marriage bracelets were not worn, for they required careful wrapping and twining—too much to remove or replace in a day's time.

Four months after his return, Kapuriel was officially appointed to attend a youth's *sapana*. There, amidst the very traditions which had formed him and made him a man, Kapuriel summoned what courage he still had and made an emotional speech:

"Everyone hear! Women are women, and girls are girls, and there *is* a difference! Yet even grandmothers have been required to go about dressed like girls here, and I find this offensive! Now that I have become a leader in our country, I am proclaiming that you have six days to put the wedding rope back on the arm of each married woman! On Monday of this week, when a woman comes to town, I want to know whether she is married or single! I will be the first. I will tie my wife's marriage band back on today! If this is considered wrong, I say, 'So what! It is our custom!' This decision is mine alone. I may die because of it, but I will not go back on my word!"

Kapuriel did keep his word, and our wives once again wore the ropes of marriage, like their ancestral mothers. They were also allowed to wear up to six brass or aluminum bracelets. Copper jewelry of any kind was not allowed.

The following year, Kapuriel was transferred to Karamoja country, and the government brought a Karamojong man to be our administrative chief in Amudat. However, that man made so many mistakes, they replaced him after only three months and installed a Pokot man again. We have watched nervously for any change in policy, but the marriage bracelet has been allowed to stay.

A Famous Turkana Bandit

While trying to cope with government harassment, the Karamojong, especially, have also continued to suffer at the hands of Turkana gunmen. Even Amin's soldiers have tried to help the Karamojong on occasion, but with little success. This is because parts of Karamoja are flat, with no relief, such as hills or rocks, and there is nowhere to hide from the bullets. To make matters worse, the cunning Turkana often station some armed warriors only a few miles from the site of a raid, while the rest go ahead with the stolen herds. Then the unsuspecting soldiers and cattle owners, assuming they will have to cover many miles before they catch up to their cattle, are ambushed and pumped with bullets while still in their own neighborhoods. This has happened time and time again.

The Ugandans have recently made overtures for peace, and, in fact, there are Turkana and Karamojong living side by side around the other side of Mt. Moroto. Some Karamojong have gone to live peacefully in Turkana country with the real purpose of acquiring guns to bring back. Others have even sold their daughters or second wives to the Turkana in exchange for guns.

One Turkana bandit, Losike, became famous and is feared in every country—Pokot, Karamoja, Dodoth, Jie, Rendille and Samburu. We heard that he once walked into a corral in Nawiapom, and demanded goats for his companions to eat. The owners complied, but alerted the local army. The soldiers followed Losike past Lokwakipi, where he had also taken meat, but the Turkana saw them coming and shot one of Amin's soldiers dead. Vowing a personal revenge, those soldiers tied their dead companion on a camel's back and took him back to town, where they forced the local chief to disclose the location of Losike's homestead.

Forewarned, Losike promptly moved, but he was told that when Amin's soldiers arrived at his old homestead, they were aided by a man named Lolukangyan, whose donkeys he had once stolen. A few days later, Losike, along with two Kenyan soldiers, who were also Turkana, spotted Lolukangyan and others watering their cattle at a well. One of the soldiers walked over to ask, "Where is the man who told Amin's soldiers where to find the cattle of that thief Losike, who stole his donkeys?" They pointed to Lolukangyan, and the soldier promptly aimed his gun and riddled Lolukangyan with bullets. The others fled, and the soldiers shot after them, then divided their cattle three ways. I heard that the soldier who shot Lolukangyan was later disciplined, but, of course, nothing happened to Losike.[121]

Losike came to terrorize the Pokot in 1972. First he killed my acquaintance Lokeris and his three children, taking 15 cattle. Then he murdered two very old women and a youth, and wounded a young girl in Kasei, trying to steal more cattle. Our people killed many of those Turkana raiders with poisoned arrows, and the arrow of the youth Lunyori even grazed Losike's head, but the poison was not sufficient to harm him. He broke his leg, we heard, trying to escape, but, with typical resilience, he hobbled into a cave, where his gang found him a few days later.

Finally, in 1974, the Kenyan soldiers from Kapenguria came to him personally to beg for peace. Losike said, "I'm not the one who is crying, but if you are so desperate, I suppose I'll agree, as long as you don't bother me or my herds." The soldiers and Losike's people met at Lodwar, where they buried the ancient items of peace—a spear, a razor for shaving one's head, etc., as well as bullets this time, and covered the hole with fresh cement. They even assigned a corporal to guard the spot. All of this was to restrain one man! Losike is still alive, but he has participated in no raids since the peace, content to watch others do the work for him. After all, a bargain is a bargain.

Witchdoctor

In 1975, perhaps 35 sorcerers were killed, mostly due to the advice of a man named Lochero, who lived in Kenya. A Karamojong by birth, Lochero had become one of us long ago, and he was widely respected for his extrasensory powers.

For instance, Pkile consulted Lochero after three of his children died and a fourth became sick. Lochero told him, "One man has killed all your children, and he will continue to kill your entire family if you let him! Even now, there is no hope for your fourth child. He will die."

"If I knew who it was, I would murder him!" Pkile had cried.

Lochero had answered, "I cannot tell you his name, but, among your neighbors, is there not one who lives alone? His house is apart from the other homesteads, near a small hill, and his garden is on the slope above his house. Now I suggest that you go home and wait for your child to die, for you can do nothing to prevent it. But don't dig a grave. Throw the body into the bush, then watch carefully. That man will come to cut the scalp and sexual organs from the corpse. Perhaps you already know which man this is."

The child died the next morning. Pkile sadly placed his son's body in the bushes and went home briefly. When he returned to watch the body, he was too late. The corpse had already been mutilated, as Lochero had foretold.

Pkile gathered his people and they followed tracks from the corpse to the home of Murangole, who lived alone. They found him in his garden and seized him, yelling, "We followed your footprints, Murangole! Where have you just been?"

"I only came from my house to my garden."

"Did you go anywhere else?"

"No."

Murangole was tied up and taken to the place of the body, while his neighbors searched until they found human parts buried by the edge of his garden. When this news was reported, they beat Murangole until he was nearly dead. That afternoon, Pkile's three wives came to finish the deed.

Word of Lochero's expertise spread after that. The sons and brother of the ailing chief Sewat Longolemuk came to consult him, and Lochero told them, "A man has cast a spell on your father. His home is at the bottom of the road, across the river from your homestead." An investigation revealed that two men there had indeed conspired against the chief. One was beaten to death on the spot.

Not all of Lochero's advice resulted in death. My mother's uncle, who lives near us, consulted Lochero after the first two babies of his new wife wasted away inexplicably and died in infancy. Lochero speculated, "It must be that long ago your wife's father asked your father for a steer and, in exchange, loaned him a heifer. Then your father deceived his associate by claiming that the cow and all its descendants had died when, in fact, its own heifer remained in your homestead. Of course, you know that neither a woman nor her children can drink the milk of her father's cow in her husband's homestead without harm. So when your wife milked that cow and gave the milk to her baby, it was inevitable that the child would die. Therefore, because it was your family that stole the cattle, you alone must take responsibility for the evil which has befallen your household. There still remain three unlawful cattle in your corral—one cow and her very small calf, about two weeks old, and the red cow that was the one responsible for the deaths of your babies. Go now and return the cattle to their rightful owner, and your wife will henceforth live in health." He followed Lochero's advice, and it appears to have worked: his wife's third child seems to be thriving.

As Lochero's reputation soared, his business also boomed. They say he was responsible for the deaths of more sorcerers in any year since the purges of the 1950s. The government officials at Makutano heard of his powers, but remained skeptical. Finally they sent for Lochero, pretending to ask for his advice in solving a theft. They said, "A hat was stolen. You figure it out and find the thief."

Lochero just laughed at them. He scoffed, "Are you trying to scandalize me or make fun of me by telling me half-truths? You left the hat out on purpose and told someone to go steal it. In other words, you stole your own hat! Then you have the nerve to summon me? Ah! Go! I am not a child." The officials were left dumbfounded.

The District Commissioner at Kapenguria tried the same trick—arranging for something to be stolen, and calling Lochero to solve the mystery. Lochero shook his head with disdain for the D. C., saying, "You figure that you, an important man, have the power to discredit me? Really! You can't fool me, and I would appreciate it if you don't waste my time with trash like this. Maybe there is something worthwhile I can do for you instead."

"Yes indeed!" the D. C. exclaimed coolly. "If you are as intelligent, clean, and straightforward as you claim, you should be able to grasp the lesson of your own profession. Obviously, you must believe that those who are responsible, however subtly, for the deaths of others should be sentenced to death themselves!"

Now Lochero, as the official had recognized, was no fool, and the meaning of the D. C.'s words was not lost on him. He left as quickly as he could. It wasn't long before government officials appeared at his home to close down his business. They told him, "If you continue to give advice, many more people will be killed, for the country is certainly full of sorcerers. If this happens, it is *you* who will be charged with their murders."

There were very few witch hunts after that.

1976

This year, 1976, has been a year of stress, changes, and new responsibility. My people have been harassed by Turkana and Karamojong raiders and persecuted by the thugs of Amin, while my own family has had to endure great sorrow and to assume new roles.

Raids and Murders

First, Turkana raiders hit Musol, stealing about 50 cattle and goats. My brother Lopeyok and his friends pursued them and managed to shoot four raiders with poisoned arrows, killing three. They confiscated two guns and two spears, before the government troops from Sigor arrived, killed ten more Turkana, and returned the cattle.

No sooner had this battle finished, than Lopeyok and his companions heard that cattle had just been stolen from Lokut and Arekai. In spite of their exhaustion, and knowing the Turkana had nearly a day's head start, the men followed the tracks of those cattle until sunset, and continued the next two days. By the fourth morning, well into Turkana country, they found the herds. Four unsuspecting Turkana men were busy eating meat, while two more were lying down, guns at their sides. Lopeyok and the others crept up very close. They shot one man with an arrow and speared another as he was grabbing for his gun. The other Turkana warriors ran, but one tripped, dropping his gun, and they killed him. My brother's band was successful in reclaiming the Pokot cattle, but, unfortunately, as they were herding their cattle back home, they met some soldiers, who confiscated the guns they had taken.

One very dark night that same month, two youths set out to visit their lovers, who had just moved to a new homestead. After some effort, they were able to locate the gate, and they entered the corral. One boy stayed there with the cattle, while the other sneaked around the houses, trying to discover where the girls were sleeping. Suddenly, the first youth heard someone pulling out the thorn bush, which served as the corral gate. Quickly and quietly, he ran to the opening and raised his spear. Sure enough, in walked three Karamojong warriors, obviously trying to raid the cattle. The youth stabbed the first raider, who cried out, waking the entire household. His startled Karamojong companions fled without their shields or spears, which they must have put down when they opened the gate. The homestead rejoiced, and the girls and their parents heaped praise upon the youths who had saved their herd and killed the enemy. I'm sure those youths returned many nights after that to bask in the adulation of their lovers!

In Kenya, most Pokot continue, with good reason, to be worried about Turkana or Karamojong raids, but in Uganda and near the border, where we live, the worst raiders and murderers, by far, are the troops of Amin. Whereas the intentions of the Turkana and the Karamojong enemies are straightforward—indeed, the same as ours—Amin's men can be sadistic and devious.

Early this year, Amin's soldiers raided Karamojong cattle from an area called Lokalis, killing seven women and ten children, as well as a man named Longolingyan, and burning their stores of maize. Longolingyan's neighbors managed to escape into Kenya during the attack. After this, the government spread the word among the Karamojong that the Pokot were really the ones who had stolen the cattle and that the army had recovered them! All of the owners were asked to claim their cattle at Chepsokunyan on the appointed day.

Desperate for their herds, the Karamojong returned from Kenya and reported to Chepsokunyan, where they saw a huge corral of cattle guarded by Amin's soldiers. "Look over the cattle and tell us how many belong to you," each man was told. Some claimed as many as five head of cattle, others none. Altogether, 35 Karamojong made claims and were asked to stand in a group, awaiting their herds, while the other people were dispersed. Then, instead of receiving their shares, these 35 were surrounded by soldiers with guns and tied to a tree in the hot sun, while the soldiers decided what to do with them. The next morning, they were pushed into the back of a truck, driven to a small lake and shot. Their weighted bodies were thrown into the water. Afterwards, the soldiers returned to feast on their cattle, unchallenged.

Another day, some soldiers stopped the son of my friend Lokongoria at Lokuss and asked him, "Where are the people who herd their cattle here every day?"

The youth told them that the owners were at a meeting in Karita.

The soldiers ordered, "Go tell your fathers that we have killed a giraffe over there by those trees. They should come tomorrow to get the meat."

The boy did as he was told, and the next day, my friend and five other men went to check on the kill. They followed a vulture to the carcass, and sent for their families to help with the meat. As they were skinning the giraffe, three soldiers appeared, and some of the men ran away.

"Why do you run?" Lokongoria called after them. "They said the meat was for us!"

But his neighbors kept going, and my friend and the others who stayed never returned with the meat. One witness said a long rope was tied around their waists and they were herded in the direction of Karita, presumably to be killed.

Until this year, those of us on the Kenya side of the border had considered our herds relatively safe from the raiding soldiers of Amin, who were destroying our Ugandan neighbors. However, in April, Amin's men tried a new tactic—raiding Kenyan cattle by helicopter! Indeed, no one would have believed it, if they had not seen it happen with their own eyes. The helicopters landed in the Kanyao region at Nangalitabaa. Soldiers killed six people, and stole many head of cattle. They slaughtered Lopeta and his two children in their own home, along with an elder and two youths, and wounded another. The heads of the decapitated victims were brought to Kanyao, so that people could see for themselves the evil that had infested Uganda.

In July, we heard that the Karamojong had raided Sebei cattle, killing two men. The Sebei reported the incident to the authorities, and Amin's men, together with the Sebei, followed the tracks to Karamojong country, where the trail was soon lost, because of heavy rains. Instead of giving up the search, the soldiers found some local Karamojong eating beef in their *kurket*, and ordered them at gunpoint to leave their spears and come outside for questioning.

"Where are the cattle?" the soldiers demanded.

"Ours are grazing. We've seen no other herds."

"Then what is this meat you're eating?"

"It is ours! If you think this is stolen meat, ask the owners of the stolen cattle to look over our herd. They will know if the animals are theirs!" The Sebei warriors agreed. They examined the Karamojong cattle carefully, then told the soldiers, "They are not ours."

The head officer flew into a rage. He screamed at the Sebei, "You are nothing but trouble! We try to help you, but it's not good enough for you!" He ordered his men, "Tie all these people up! They aren't worth the trouble!"

The soldiers made both the Sebei and the Karamojong ranchers lie down in the road and lashed them together with rope. Then the captain, quite berserk with anger, jumped in his truck, gunned the motor and ran over the heap of bodies. A few of the men who were cut free by the car got up and ran. But the captain, having turned his truck around, sped after them, running one man down. The rest escaped, along with the women and children of the household, and it was they who told us the story.

One night we saw three very large airplanes pass overhead, and we wondered about them. Two days later, we heard that men of unknown origin had landed those planes at the Entebbe airport to fight with the Ugandan authorities briefly, and that the incident had left Amin in a state of furor.[122] He would no longer allow people the small freedoms they had begun to gain, but followed his original motto: "If a man ignores or disobeys, don't ask questions; converse with bullets!"

A Pokot man, who was studying in Kampala, claimed that Amin's men confiscated half the herds of all successful ranchers in that area. There was very little food in the city, and almost no supplies or petrol for transporting any goods that remained. Most of the white people had fled the country. The student told us many stories of barbarism in other areas that echoed the nightmares we had been experiencing at the hands of this murderer. Amin has truly become an enemy of the Ugandan people and is responsible for the destruction of the country.[123]

Mourning my Parents

Late last year, I traveled all the way to Kapenguria to buy a quantity of maize for my family, and, upon my return, I found my natural mother sick. We assumed she would recover quickly, but during the next two months, she continued suffering from stomach pains. Soon she was too weak to travel. There was no one left at the Amudat hospital who could treat her, and we would only find danger and humiliation in Uganda. And so she died. I dug her grave in sadness at the side of the corral, washed her fragile body, and laid her carefully in the grave in the customary way for women—on her left side, as if in sleep. We mourned, as we had for my sister Chelima and for my mother Chepusuchon, and attended to all the rituals of death.

My father was unable to recover from her death. He would say, "Now that this woman has died, I will die with her. If she had lived, I could have gone on for many more years. But now my first wife has died before me, and I see that my time has come, for I cannot go on without Cheparkong." Then he declared, "Before I die, I must tend to the circumcision rituals for my two girls who are now ready and find homes for them. Then I will be finished."

As he promised, Father arranged the ceremonies for the two girls, Naowal and Adunga, and negotiated a marriage for Adunga, his daughter by his fourth wife. Then a man came to him to request my daughter Naowal in marriage, and my father gave his blessing. He told the girls, "Now I have found homesteads where you can give birth to your children and live happily until you die. May you live to become very old with your husbands and children. Yes, live well, for you have shown me respect. Adunga, you accepted your husband without protest, and now, Naowal, you have accepted yours. Thank you, my beloved children."

The day my daughter Naowal left us to go and live with her husband's family, Father called all of us together and said, "I have fulfilled my promise and found homes for these two children, and now my responsibilities are over. You, Domonguria, will be in charge of the family and will sit on my stool. You will lead the little children of our homestead on the right path, and when they have grown, you must find homes for each of them. And soon, you must find a bride for your brother, my son Aluka. I cannot do it. I am too old. You, Aluka, must follow your older brother now. He is in my chair and you must obey him. If you are disobedient, you will suffer, but if you show respect, Domonguria will do well by you. I shall remain for your *sapana*, but Domonguria will find the steer and make all the other arrangements for you."

Thus, I became the head of my family.

I busied myself in the next months with all the arrangements for my brother's *sapana*, while my father watched approvingly. Shortly after the ceremony, however, Aluka began an affair with a girl my father scorned, and Father could no longer refrain from judgment. He called to me and said, "Tell your brother to forget that child. I don't want her!"

I spoke with Aluka, and he stopped seeing the girl. But when Father heard that Aluka had taken another lover, he summoned my brother directly. He ranted at him, "You, Aluka, have erred! If you want to marry, go to your brother and he will tell you which clans to choose from. You must not select a girl freely!"

This was too much for Aluka. He took his girlfriend "by force" (without proper settlement) and brought her home.

Father was irate. He summoned me from my homestead at Murua Len and ordered, "Tell your brother to forget that girl at once! You must think of another girl he can marry."

I spoke with Aluka. "How can you disregard Father's command?" I asked.

But Aluka was adamant. He said, "I went along with his wishes the first time, but this is too much! I don't want to leave this girl too."

So I went to the girl. "Leave us and go home to your father," I commanded. "I don't want you here. You should never have come in the first place, without our having consulted with your parents. Now the Elder has refused you, and you must go!"

She protested, "Why do you deny me my husband? Am I not like the other women of this household? What don't you like about me?" Then she added, "I'll be frank, sir. If your brother says to me, 'Come, let's go,' I'll go! If we see we are rejected here, we will be forced to leave this homestead and have our children elsewhere!"

These were familiar words. I went home and let the matter ride for a week. When I returned, she was still there, and I asked her, "What are you trying to do to your husband?" To Aluka I said, "You know Father warned you against taking a bride by force. Passion has made you disrespectful!"

Father, who was nearby, intoned, "You have chosen to ignore me in my old age, and I can do nothing about it. Because of this, you shall not prosper like my other children, or like me. From the time I married your mother until now, I have rejoiced in life. But you will not grow old like me, unless you leave this girl! I hope my other children will not follow Aluka's example."

I went back home in frustration.

Three days later, Father sent for my younger brother, who had been renamed Peter in school. Peter approached him respectfully, saying, "Father, I have come. What do you wish to say?"

"Is Aluka still with that child?"

"Yes, he is."

"I have said what I feel about such a girl being in my family, and I shall not change my mind. Tell your brother Domonguria that it is now up to him and his wife. I fear that Aluka will seal his own fate, because of disrespect for me. Maybe he thinks that, because I'm about to die, she can stay, but I don't want her here when I'm gone!"

Father became silent, and Peter left to report his words to me.

Early the next morning, a small child came to our homestead to say, "Father has died." I stood there in silence. *So, it has happened,* I thought. *Just like he said.*

"But why?" I asked the child. "Was he sick?"

"No, there wasn't any illness. He just died." Then the boy added, as an afterthought, "Last night, as I was passing by, I heard him say, 'Please send for my eldest son.' I heard his wife ask, 'What do you want to tell him?' and he repeated, 'I want him to come here to see me.'" But no one went to get you, and he was quiet after that."

These words pained me greatly. Father had known he was about to die. I should have been there.

I helped my brothers, Aluka and Merur, dig his grave in the center of the corral, where elders and other very important men and women are buried, and we performed all the burial rituals befitting an elder. We washed Father's body, removed his ornaments, and laid him carefully in the grave on his right side, taking great care that his head was propped as if he were asleep, for it is bad if one is facing straight up or downwards into the grave. We anchored the body in position with rocks, until it was enclosed, like a box. Then we spread leaves and grasses, and then dirt on top, and covered the entire grave with stones, forming a small hill. Finally, on top of the mound, we put a little dung from the family herd.[124]

When the burial was complete, we slaughtered a very old mother goat. Its stomach contents were spread on the bellies and on the arm and leg joints of Pturu's children, including me. Then the leg bones of the goat were cracked, and we were anointed in the same way with the marrow. After this, according to custom, we mourned in silence. Even small children were taught not to cry. We did not converse with anyone, and no one visited my father's homestead. When our children were greeted by neighbors, they kept silent. Plates, gourds and utensils were not washed for three days. These are our traditions. It was the same for my mothers and for Chelima.

After five days, we selected a cow with a surviving calf and milked it. We mixed tobacco with a little soil and took it, together with the milk, to give to the spirit of my deceased father. All of my brothers and sisters, even those who had married and established homes of their own, came to milk the cow and to bring him tobacco and soil, saying, "Father, drink your milk and accept this tobacco we bring you. We ask your blessing on us, our children and our herds. Help us to marry, to raise our children well and to live peacefully in our homes. We ask your guidance now, for in life we never wronged you."

When an important man dies, his brother comes to his homestead to select one of his large steers—his ox-of-ropes, if there is one—for the memorial feast called *kinduh*, which is held at the month's end. Since Father had no living brothers, it became my duty, as the eldest son, to select and slaughter the steer for his friends and relatives to eat. There are many rules about cooking and serving the meat of *kinduh*. The cooking fire is lit on the western side of the homestead, the direction of the setting sun, and the leaves upon which the meat will be served are put some distance away. While cooking the meat, one must remain solemn and gaze in the direction of Mtelo. Then the men are called, and they come to eat silently in two's and three's, sitting on the ground instead of on stones or stools. The beef is laid directly on the leaves, which are spread on the ground in front of each person, and it must be eaten there and not held in the hands. During the memorial feast, everyone remains perfectly silent. People greet a newcomer only by taking his hand quietly. Any leftover meat is carried home boneless, for the bones must be left at the site. The only exception to this rule is the left leg, which is cooked whole and taken home for the children of the deceased to eat alone.

After the feast of *kinduh*, we divided Father's herds amongst his heirs, according to tradition. First, the Cow of the Grave, Chepurim, was given to my brother

Merur, who helped with the burial. Next, the Cow of the Memorial Feast, Chep-kinduh, was awarded to me, for I had killed the steer for kinduh. These two cows must never be given away. Finally, Father's other relatives came, and each was given a cow or a goat. The inheritance was distributed in a single day. No one is allowed to come afterwards to request stock.

Thus I buried both of my natural parents in a single year. Like the others who died before them, they will not be forgotten as long as any of us are alive. Even after moving away, whenever any of us—children, grandchildren or remaining wives—pass by one of their graves or a place of death, we will pick up a little dirt, stones or leaves to throw on the site, saying, "Give us your blessing," or "Help me with my children," or "Guide me on this journey," or, simply, "Stay in your grave and look after us."

Two months after my father died, I began to cast out the girl who had caused us such grief. My brother and I argued for two weeks, making a racket, and I was adamant. The girl cried throughout the ordeal and finally left for her own home. After that, Aluka moped about a great deal.

"I don't even want to talk to you, until you bring me a girl who can be my wife!" he snapped. "You banished the one I chose."

"Am I not your father now?" I reminded him.

"I don't know," he countered. "If you find me a wife, you will be my father, for you are the eldest. But if I am left without a wife, you will not be doing your duty as head of the family."

I gave him my assurances, and he quieted down somewhat, but he still harbors ill will towards me. Just the other day, as I was leaving, he told me he had approached yet another girl, but she had put him off, saying, "I'm flattered by your overtures, but I have heard about you. If I have a love affair with you, I will be banished just like those others. Don't lead me on!"

"You are not to search for a wife on your own," I chastened him.

"Yes," he acquiesced, "but come back soon. I want your opinion."

At last, I see, there is hope for Aluka.

Karamojong Attack

We had just settled down again after Father's death, when another incident threatened our household. It was a normal mid-afternoon at Murua Len, when Chepusepa and two other women decided to fetch water from the river. I was in the corral when they left, and I could hear Chepusepa call out to a neighbor, "Come with us!"

"We'll follow," her friend answered, and a few minutes later I saw her go by with a little girl.

Two old women were sitting and talking under a shade tree just outside our fence. Suddenly, I heard one of them ask in surprise, "Who are those men—the one in green and the other in black?"

"I don't know," the other replied. "Maybe they came from Kanyao. They're following the path to the water. They're probably thirsty."

About a half-hour later, the same little girl I had seen earlier ran into our corral shrieking, *"The Karamojong have killed us! They've killed us!"*

Panic flooded through me. *"Chepusepa! No ... No!"*

"No, not Chepusepa. The woman I was with!" the child sobbed. "Chepusepa and the others were ahead of us. My shoe came undone, and I stopped to tie it. My aunt went on, but I heard her scream. When I looked up, I saw a man pulling a spear out of her back. Chepusepa and the others saw it too, and they ran ahead to the river to tell the men. I ran back here."

"You're lucky your shoe came undone," I told her. "Rest here with my family."

I took my spear and sprinted towards the river. To my relief, Chepusepa was unharmed, kneeling by the dead woman on the path. She said the other men had already left in pursuit, so the two of us walked home together. That evening the search party returned unsuccessfully, having tracked the Karamojong as far as Kiwawa.

At noon the next day, we heard that fresh Karamojong footprints had been spotted by the dry riverbed at Lossom, so we left immediately. After about two miles, I spotted one of the warriors creeping through the bush by the riverbank just ahead of us. I could see that his intended victims were two little boys, who were playing together while they watered their small herd at a well in the riverbed. I yelled loudly to warn the children. The startled Karamojong man started to flee, but my friend Lorimo hurled his spear, killing him. Kidarile chased another warrior and killed him. A third Karamojong escaped.

A few days later we heard that ten Karamojong had attacked six cowherds at Kiwawa. The brave youths had managed to wound three of them during a fight—two with arrows (one through the eye) and one with a spear. The cattle had been taken, but were recovered again at Charicha, where three of the Karamojong were killed.

The following week, a Pokot cowherd was killed at Nangalitabaaa. The boy cried out before he died, warning the others, who managed to kill two of the raiders. Some people on their way home from Amudat saw the other Karamojong warriors running by and gave chase, killing them before they reached the town.

The situation with the Karamojong clearly has been worsening. Just recently a contingent of 15 Karamojong came to Moruita to offer peace again to the Pokot, but the Pokot elders refused to honor them, claiming, "You say this every day. It means nothing!" However, the Karamojong returned the following month, after both sides had consulted their chief elders. The Karamojong contingent admitted to lying in the past, but asked for one more chance to make their word good. Our elders assented, but the people are skeptical and place no faith in it.

PLANS FOR THE FUTURE

Because of the Karamojong incidents and my father's death, we have moved our homestead once again, and Lopeyok and my other brother have built their homesteads nearby. I have decided to remain in the general region of Lossom for the present, but one day I would like to join some of my clan in the countryside west of Ortum.

Meanwhile, these are the plans for my children:

Long ago, Father ordered, "Let the eldest son, Simon Nyangaluk, go to school. Makal's work shall be to look after my cattle. Lopedur takes care of the goats. Kakuko watches the calves. Now these children, along with Lopeyok's son Kiror, will suffice for taking care of the herds. I will not give permission for these four boys to go to school. If other children, like my small boys Chepunos, Lokero or Psinun, want to go to school, I won't object, for my herds will be tended. Consider the girls—Naowal, Cherel, Akimat, Naokut, Chepkeriket and Tutoko. Alas, there are not enough cattle in our homestead! I want Chepkeriket to help me with the cattle. When a man marries her, he will pay cattle to me! When a man marries Tutoko, he will bring cattle to me! When another takes Akimat, I will have cattle! Cherel will bring more and Naowal and Naokut as well. My strength is here!"

Over the years since my father's proclamation, my family has experienced both good fortune and extreme hunger. Not long ago, two of my children had to flee to other homesteads in order to find food. But recently, I have managed to find new sustenance for my family, and I have brought back my son Kakuko and enrolled him in school with Simon Nyangaluk at Kanyao. I have also allowed my daughter Cherel to remain at school in Amudat. For I have seen the value of education.

However, it worries me that many of the school children and others who have been in association with Westerners have begun to reject the words of our elders. They neglect customs that have been handed down to us since ancient times. The school children are told, "It is best for you to disregard your traditions." But is this possible? Will Tororut approve? For it is he who has shown us the way since the beginning of time. Only Tororut has clear knowledge of all things and of all people. Humankind has never been able to discover his Word. Which man or woman can say, "It is I who have created the cattle, food of all types, the rain, trees, stones and earth"? It is essential that we know that Tororut is the one who has done all this work.

You see, in the beginning all people were ignorant, knowing only that which Tororut had taught them. Their thoughts were like dreams. Nevertheless, they did not go about their work blank-minded. They considered everything in their environment, until they came up with ideas that appealed to them. Gradually, with Tororut's help, the traditions of our ancestors were born. As time went on, these customs began to differ slightly from place to place, and smart people learned to seek out those who knew the old traditions well, so that they could be sure that what they were doing was correct.

Now, however, I see some of our children are growing up literate and well educated, aware of the history and customs of foreigners, but ignorant of the traditions and legends of their own people, disregarding the words of their elders! Yet most of these readers can't honestly say, "I know this is so, because I have seen it with my own eyes." They have only learned through the written words of foreign elders. It is time for our Pokot traditions and history to be written down as well, so that our school children can read about their own heritage, and others can understand and appreciate our culture. That is why I recorded this story.

I am thankful, Pat, for the work we have done together. We completed the initial taping in 1970, and met again six years later to find three new children at my house and two at yours! We have been blessed with good fortune! I trust that your work on this material will be productive and that you will examine carefully its good and bad points, keeping me informed, so that in the end we will rejoice over our work together. I hope that this record of our customs will become valuable to the children we send to school and will eventually benefit both of our peoples.

Now we pray for guidance as we depart once again for our separate lands. May Tororut bless us, our work, our children, and our herds, so that we may live long and happy lives until our final year. May he show us the good paths to follow and watch over us, even when we sleep at night, so that we may wake to find the country good.

EPILOGUE

Pat Robbins

Shortly after we parted in August, 1976, Domonguria's eldest son, Simon, wrote, "Father had an accident after falling into the hands of a gang of robbers at Kapenguria just two days after leaving you. He was badly beaten and all the money he had was taken. He went to Kapenguria hospital, where he was treated before he came home, but he is now all right." Four months later Simon reported that his younger brother had been badly burned after falling on the fire, but was treated successfully at the hospital in Kapenguria. A sister's eye infection was also treated there. Disease took its toll. Domonguria spent most of 1992 suffering from tuberculosis.

Simon reported severe drought and famine in his area during 1979-1982. This disaster was widely publicized by international news organizations, resulting in a huge relief effort and establishment of NGOs (nongovernmental organizations) to monitor the situation. In April, 1981, Simon wrote, "The people are now fed through the famine relief program which supplies the yellow maize imported from the U.S.A. However, the supply is not so adequate and irregular; sometimes it reaches people when they are badly off from hunger." Simon closed one letter with familiar words: "The weather here is very hot and the place is dry, there's a lot of famine and people are suffering from starvation. There was not enough harvest last season and it seems there's no hope also for this year. Please convey our sincere love and best of our greetings to your family, relatives and friends. Yours affectionately, Mr. and Mrs. S. Pturu"

The first in his family ever to read or write, Simon graduated from a teacher's training college in 1978. After teaching one year in Kanyao, he was appointed headmaster of a new church-sponsored boarding school not far from his father's home at Lossom, Kenya. Under his guidance, the school quickly expanded to include six grades (standards) with 134 children and five teachers. By 1982, he and his father had struggled to find enough school and uniform fees to send nine of the family's children to school. Sadly, one of them, Domonguria's son Kakuko, was speared to death by some Karamojong raiders while herding goats during his school holidays. Another son died of malaria three months before he was to graduate from Technical School. Simon and his wife, a pastor's daughter, have at least six children and hoped to educate them all. In 1987, he was appointed to lead and develop another new school in the nearby hills.

Indeed, schools have become much more prevalent and locally acceptable in the years since this recording. Many more Pokot have been educated and have entered alternative careers. Tarmac roads connect previously remote areas. Government decrees, relief programs, and the efforts of churches and NGOs encourage or demand a more sedentary lifestyle, no raiding, less stock, western clothes, and village centers with schools, shops and a cash economy. Capitalism, materialism and individual successes challenge the egalitarian, communal ideals and power structure of Pokot society. Clearly, the options for Domonguria's children and grandchildren are dramatically different from those of their elders.

We continue to be distressed over the terror we know our friends along the Kenya-Uganda border have been facing daily. At least 300,000 Ugandans were reported murdered during Amin's rule, which ended, finally, in 1978, after a Tanzanian-supported invasion. As Amin's forces fled, Karamojong warriors pillaged the Moroto armory of guns and ammunition, some of which were sold to the Pokot. Amin's cruel decrees, violent government intrusions, and the new prevalence of powerful guns left permanent scars on Pokot society. In 1980, Obote returned as president, but army violence and atrocities, along with droughts, livestock diseases, and cholera caused widespread death. Obote was overthrown in 1985 by the army, and Museveni became president in 1986. The economic and political situation in Uganda improved under Museveni's rule, but new waves of violence flooded the north. For many years, the Sudan-based Lord's Resistance Army terrorized millions and forced many populations to flee. The profusion of weapons from these conflicts allowed Karamojong warriors to trade cattle for more guns. Government policing efforts resulted in more violence.

Across the border in Kenya, the well-armed Turkana *ngoroko* bandits continued harassing the Pokot, who found they could now easily obtain guns for protection and conduct their own murderous counter raids. Harsh government disarmament campaigns resulted in temporary moments of peace, followed by increased violence, as people rearmed.

Jomo Kenyatta, the first President of Kenya, died in 1978. He was succeeded by Daniel arap Moi, a Tugen, who in the later 1950s had represented West Suk District and surrounding areas on the colonial Legislative Council. Unfortunately, Moi's rule was punctuated by graft, corruption, a collapsing infrastructure, ethnic violence and natural disasters (flooding, malaria and cholera in 1979-80, and drought in 2000). After his retirement due to term limits, Mwai Kibaki won the presidency, promising to end corruption. A long-anticipated, but flawed new constitution was defeated by the people, and corruption reforms faded. A drought in 2006 was followed by ethnic violence after the 2007 hotly-disputed election results.

The widespread use of AK-47s along the Kenya-Uganda border has had disastrous effects on East African pastoral societies in this region. While many aspects of traditional hierarchy reportedly remain intact, bands of armed thieves now act independently and powerfully. Arms' dealing is lucrative, and guns are necessary for self-defense. Guns are even valued as bride wealth payments. The cattle exchange relationships, supporting the traditional egalitarian culture, are undermined by the power of the AK-47, sometimes eliminating the need for widespread camaraderie and making possible immediate enrichment and self indulgence. Government disarmament raids have resulted in violence, displacement, confiscation of livestock, school closures, and vulnerability to attack, while communities scramble to rearm. Enemies must raid and protect their cattle with guns, or their herds vanish. Policing efforts have mostly failed, and armed vigilantes, while effective, often become raiders themselves.[125] With decimated herds, struggling pastoralists are increasingly forced to rely on external sources of aid and development programs.

Sadly, we lost touch with Simon and his family after 1992, and I have been worried about their safety and health. The border area has been oppressed by constant violence and suffering, and I had feared the worst. However, after reading this manuscript in 2008, my son Michael surfed the internet and found Simon's real name mentioned in an obscure report of the Constitution of Kenya Review Commission, documenting a hearing in Kacheliba in June, 2002. This was one of the many meetings held across the country to hear comments from the Kenya constituency regarding the proposed constitution. Simon spoke in English and also submitted a written report, outlining his proposals for government administration, security, education and health programs. He advocated a "government as from the grassroots," beginning with a Village Administration for each ten household villages, overseen by a Locational Administration, then Divisional, District and Provincial Administrations. He said, "The new Constitution should provide the types of security that makes every citizen of Kenya free, feel free, and comfortable in any part of the country." This would require complete disarmament, the closing of black markets for arms, and an enhanced border security police force, well-equipped with phones, vehicles and arms. Simon proclaimed, "Education should be free for every Kenyan, for both girls and boys, and also adult education should be changed from the Ministry of Social Services to the Ministry of Education, Science and Technology. Adult classes should also sit for national examination..." He submitted his suggestions for health reform in writing.

I am encouraged that Simon is a dedicated leader and educator in his local community, championing reforms for his tormented people. I hope to be able to see his family again one day. It is also my hope that in spite of ongoing and unprecedented cultural changes, their rich and lively Pokot heritage will not be forgotten.   O

NOTES

PREFACE by Pat Robbins

1 The 1969 *Kenya Population Census* listed 93,437 Pokot. The 1969 *Uganda Population Census* listed 34,654 people living in the mostly-Pokot Upe area of Karamoja. Thus the total 1969 figures equal about 130,000. Later estimates range from 220,000 (Elisabeth L. Meyerhoff, "The Threatened Ways of Kenya's Pokot People", 1982; Elisabeth Hasthorpe, *A Study of Pokot Songs*, 1983) and 250,000 (Jannick Maisonhaute, "The East Pastoral Pokot Sapana Ceremony", 2000) to over 300,000 (total figures for Kenya and Uganda in Kjartan Jonsson, "Pokot Masculinity: The Role of Rituals in Forming Men", 2006).

2 Rev. Thomas Wakefield, a missionary at Mombasa, was told by a man from the Zanzibar area that the northern Baringo Lake area was avoided by caravans, because, "the Wa-Suku are feared on account of their ferocious and barbarous character. They are brave and daring, but guilty of many horrible and brutal deeds. They do not hesitate to give battle to the Maasai …" He describes torture and maiming of enemies and their animals. "They do not eat fish, though they abound in the water near them. They are agriculturists, and also pastoral … Their weapons are light spears, which they throw with much dexterity and precision." See T. Wakefield and Keith Johnson, "Routes of Native Caravans from the Coast to the Interior of Eastern Africa, Chiefly from Information Given by Sadi Bin Ahedi, a Native of a District near Gazi, in Udigo, a Little North of Zanzibar" (1870), p. 326.

3 Joseph Thomson, *Through Maasailand: A Journey of Exploration Among the Snowclad Volcanic Mountains and Strange Tribes of Eastern Equatorial Africa. Being the Narrative of the Royal Geographical Society's Expedition to Mount Kenia and Lake Victoria Nyanza, 1883-1884* (1885), pp. 312-3.

4 Count Samuel Teleki, Unpublished *East African Diaries of Count Samuel Teleki* [1886-95], translated by Count Charles Teleki Sr. and Vera Teleki (1965), pp. 6-69. See also Ludwig von Höhnel, *Discovery of Lakes Rudolf and Stefanie: A Narrative of Count Samuel Teleki's Exploring and Hunting Expedition in Eastern Equatorial Africa in 1887 and 1888* (1892), Vol. 2. Teleki and von Höhnel named the Lake Rudolf, after the crown prince of Austria.

PROLOGUE by Domonguria

5 Rinderpest arrived in Eritrea on an Italian steamer coming from India in 1889 and caused widespread losses throughout eastern and southern Africa during the 1890s (Michael Bollig, *Risk Management in a Hazardous Environment: A Comparative Study of Two Pastoral Societies*, 2006, p. 122). According to C.A.Turpin ("The Occupation of the Turkwel River Area by the Karamojong Tribe", 1948), a devastating rinderpest epidemic in 1894 killed 90 percent of the cattle belonging to Karamojong herdsmen in northeastern Uganda. The Karamojong told Turpin, "The Suk lost cattle also but not to the extent we did, because they kept their stock on the hill tops. [Rinderpest] also took its toll of Turkana cattle. Donkeys and small stock were not affected much … and camels also escaped … [In 1896] the rains failed in Karimojo and a disease called *emitina* [scab] accounted for large numbers of our small stock" (p. 163). Turpin as well as Barber (*Imperial Frontier: A Study of Relations between the British and the Pastoral Tribes of North East Uganda*, 1968) report that travelers in the region at that time encountered people who had lost all their stock and existed only by hunting and gathering. Barber writes that a smallpox epidemic began in the area in 1899. By 1902 it had killed many of the Pokot living north of Lake Baringo. These events are described in more detail in the section "Youth", this book.

CHILDHOOD

When the Sun Died

6   Maps of solar eclipses in Richard Gray "Eclipse Maps" (1965) indicate total eclipses would have been seen in the area on January 14, 1926, and before that on September 29, 1894.

7   According to Domonguria, *Tororut* is the Pokot name for God, the creator and supreme immortal being, judge, caretaker and guide. Tororut is manifest in natural phenomena such as the hills and mountains, the sun, stars, rain, and thunder. Prayers are sometimes addressed to these phenomena individually, as aspects of Tororut, especially the sacred mountains. Thunder *(Ilat)*, which also influences the rain, can take human form and mediates with other natural manifestations on behalf of humans. Ilat will also discipline humans who transgress on the rights of other animals, like cattle. In addition, it is believed that the spirits of certain elders continue to exist after death, and one must be careful not to offend them. John G. Peristiany ("The Ideal and the Actual: The role of Prophets in the Pokot Political System", 1975) has described a much more elaborate Pokot cosmology than that inferred by Domonguria's account, and John Russell (*Kenya, Beyond the Marich Pass: A District Officer's Story*, 1994) and Meyerhoff ("The Threatened Ways", 1982) were also told about celestial families. Jonsson ("Pokot Masculinity", 2006) describes the religious beliefs and rituals of Cheptulel residents, which include many similarities to Domonguria's descriptions, but there appear to be differences in use, importance and interpretation. Bollig (*Risk Management*, 2006, p. 19) states, "The basis of the Pokot religious system is a well formulated morality and a detailed code of honour."

8   Jonsson (op. cit., p. 319) describes this *Moy* ritual as a means to curse the evil spirits that might be infecting the sick person, but Domonguria's description is more prayerful. Jean Brown (Unpublished list and description of a collection of Kurut Agricultural Pokot artifacts at the Michigan State University Museum, 1975) notes that these prayer drums can also be used at times of difficult or delayed birth, massive stock deaths, or sickness of secluded circumcision initiates, as well as for divining causes of illness.

9   Domonguria said the sun has two names: *Chepukopukwa* and *Asis*.

10 Harold K. Schneider ("Pokot Folktales, Humor and Values", 1967, p. 310) reports that he heard this "hole in the wall" story (with a few variations and no names mentioned) in 1952. Domonguria told me this happened in his childhood homestead, and he seemed well acquainted with the families concerned.

11 There appear to be some exceptions to this rule. For instance, meat and milk are consumed together during initiation rites. Schneider (see op. cit., 1967; and "The Pakot (Suk) of Kenya with Special Reference to the Role of Livestock in their Subsistence Economy", 1953) notes that he was told that mixing milk and meat in the stomach "will cause the milk cows to dry up," but the two may be eaten together if the meat is from an animal which was skinned before being butchered. Otherwise, the milk is drunk by those without meat or saved for the next day. There are other eating taboos, especially relating to pregnancy. Men generally eat separately from the women and children.

12 As in many African communities, the Pokot use the word "mother" to designate not only their biological mother but also the other wives of their father.

13 All men and boys who are circumcised at the same time belong to the same age set. Age sets have names like sowa, kurongora, kipkoimet, etc. Members of the same age set are bonded to each other in certain ways. This is described in more detail in the section "Cattle and Romance", chapter "A Son" (*Circumcision*).

Thunder God

14 Schneider, in his PhD dissertation "The Pakot (Suk) of Kenya" (1953), remarks that the donkey packs (panniers) resemble "tennis rackets without handles, two of which are hinged together with thongs on one side. A set of these is hung on either side of the donkey and the goods are carried lashed into them."

15   Brown (Unpublished list and description, 1975) says the clay (her informants use yellow) helps to
     keep wild animals away during a journey. White clay, mixed with water, is also spread on the face
     and chest of a sick person and on the face of a bridegroom for good luck. The mixture can be
     drunk to counteract certain evil spells. Other pigments are used as charms to protect against
     lightning (red), illness following childbirth (orange-red), or sorcery (black, red, light grey).
     They can also be buried by sorcerers in order to inflict harm (red, yellow). Peristiany ("The
     Ideal and the Actual", 1975) and others have speculated about the use of Pokot color symbol-
     ism, associating white with purity and the sun; red with blood, war, lightning; etc. He notes the
     ritual of smearing red and white clays on the bodies of warriors preparing for battle (red on the
     left side). This is mentioned by Domonguria in the section "Coming of Age", chapter "New
     Developments" (*Thunderstorms*). A similar ritual is used to counteract a curse in the section
     "Youth", chapter "Sorcery and the Family Herds" (*Scandal*). Bollig (*Risk Management*, 2006)
     writes, "the blessing with grey and then with white colored earth symbolically removed the
     danger of disease: white, symbolizing peace, health and harmony, displaces grey, symbolizing
     disease, sin and bad luck."

16   *Tapogh* is also used by Domonguria later in this narrative to refer to the bright heavenly phe-
     nomenons "comet" and "meteorite", as opposed to the term *kokelion* (sing.), *kokel* (pl.), which
     means "star". J. P. Crazzolara (*A Study of the Pokot (Suk) Language*, 1978) defines this term as "the
     'largest star in the sky', Sirius", noting the word can also be used for the morning star or the
     evening star. Meyerhoff, for her PhD dissertation on the roles of Pokot women (1981), collected
     stories about a celestial family including Venus (*Tapogh*), who brings the rain, Mars, and the
     small stars around them. Pokot sometimes use the position of the stars to forecast rain.

17   Beer is traditionally consumed before any important negotiations take place.

18   David Webster writes in *The Shimmering Heat: Memories of a Bush Doctor in East Africa* (2007), p.
     108, "In rainy weather, flying forms of termites emerge from their anthills to mate and start new
     colonies. The flying forms have swollen sausage-like abdomens, full of a protein-rich goo,
     much loved as a delicacy by the Pokot. They are eaten either raw, after first removing the legs
     and wings, or roasted, having a pleasant nut-like taste. During rainy weather, when the flying
     ants were emerging in their thousands, the Pokot would cover the exit holes of the anthills with
     skins, and direct the flying ants into pits from which they could scoop them and feast."

19   P. Randall Baker ("Development and the Pastoral People of Karamoja, North-Eastern Uganda:
     an Example of the Treatment of Symptoms", 1981) and Neville Dyson-Hudson (*Karamojong
     Politics*, 1966) write that during the 1920s the government restricted the seasonal movements of
     herders in Karamoja District in order to collect taxes and to provide compulsory labor for road-
     building. An Intelligence Officer for the King's African Rifles wrote in 1927 that "some 250 Suk
     were working on the Lodwar-Kacheliba Road" (King's African Rifles Intelligence Report,
     1927).

The Year the Earth Shook

20   The January 6, 1928 Subukia Valley Earthquake, in the Kenya (Gregory) Rift Valley, recorded a
     magnitude of 6.9. "The earthquake triggered rockfalls and minor landslides and exhibited
     long-period effects at large distances" (Nicholas N. Ambraseys, "Earthquake Hazard in the
     Kenya Rift: the Subukia Earthquake of 1928", 2007, p. 253).

21   There were a series of Pokot-Karamojong raids in 1928, beginning when the renowned Pokot
     warrior Lokitare (or Logitare) took some Karamojong cattle after six (6) of his were missing.
     During the retaliatory raids, it is estimated that 3000 cattle were stolen and four people killed.
     This period followed a drought in 1927, along with boundary changes and grazing concessions
     to the Pokot in former Karamojong areas (see David Eaton, *Violence, Revenge and the History of
     Cattle Raiding Along the Kenya Uganda Border*, 2008b). Lokitare's death nine years later is de-
     scribed in the section "Youth", chapter "Bad Luck and Work", this volume.

22   According to Brown (Unpublished List and Description, 1975) and Meyerhoff ("The Socio-Eco-
     nomic and Ritual Roles of Pokot Women", 1981), *rataw* was used mainly for contraceptive purposes
     in the agricultural communities they studied. A woman's hair, nail clippings, menstrual blood,

urine, etc., would be sealed in an animal horn to prevent pregnancy in a run-away wife or an un-married daughter. Conception could occur once the horn was opened. Brown was told that charms using horns or hollow stones, filled with items and sealed with wax, were also used to protect against other physical problems and diseases.

Making a Homestead

23 According to J. Brasnett ("The Karasuk Problem", 1958), the building of the Kitale-Lodwar road (unpaved) in 1928 coincided with a westward expansion of the Pokot in search of more grazing for their expanding stock.

24 Adolescent girls sometimes have their own hut or sleep in the house of an older widow or grandmother. They must not sleep in the same hut as their fathers, nor may adolescent boys stay with their mothers. (Meyerhoff, "The Socio-Economic and Ritual Roles of Pokot Women", 1981)

25 The diagram relates to the homestead Domonguria had in 1970 in Uganda, in the Lossom area, and it was drawn under his direction. It had to be made narrower, however, in order to fit it on the paper, and the corral should be much wider and larger, especially at the bottom end (by the door). Homesteads change all the time, and so do the people living in them. This is meant to be an example of a Pokot homestead—one that Domonguria's family actually built, not the format of every Pokot homestead. Most Pokot homesteads I have seen seem to have the houses more congregated on one side, with the corral extending out from them.

26 In 1916, the Karamojong told Turpin (see "The Occupation of the Turkwel River Area", 1948, p. 162) "that the country between Depasien [Kadam], Elgon, and the Suk hills was formerly in-habited by a tribe called the Oropom, which was similar to us in habits, customs and language. The Oropom had nothing in common with the Suk group; they did not circumcise and the lan-guage of the latter was not understood by them ... Finally our grandparents decided it would be to our advantage to capture the Oropom and dispossess them of their country and property ... that raid broke up the Oropom and many of them were captured and absorbed by our tribe ... some took to the Suk hills." Charles D. Laughlin and Elizabeth R. Allgeier (*An Ethnography of the So of Northeastern Uganda*, 1979) list *eropom* as a So clan name. Its equivalent Karamojong clan is called *ngioropom*. For further discussion on the So (also called Tepeth, Tepes and Ka-dama), see chapter "Chepusepa" in the section "Cattle and Romance":

27 Schneider ("The Pakot (Suk) of Kenya", 1953) was told that the *merkutua* (circumcision initiates) invented this irrigation system on Cheptulel; afterwards the idea spread to surrounding hills. He observed that "irrigation in the District does in fact occur in a continuous line from Chep-tulel all along the east side of the south mass, turns through the Marich Pass and continues around the west side of the south mass. Elsewhere it is found only in Seker as far as is known." A 1935 agricultural survey by Colin Maher (cited by Schneider) noted that hollowed logs were used to carry water across stream beds and ditches. G.W.B. Huntingford (*The Southern Nilo-Hamites*, 1969) speaks of irrigation furrows three to four miles long. Russell (*Kenya, Beyond the Marich Pass*, 1994, p. 41) mentions the "ingenious network of furrows ... skillfully using the contours of the land to maximum advantage" seen in Sigor.

28 Russell (op. cit.) says the children on platforms would hurl stones or mud balls at birds in the gardens. They "would be stuck, one at a time, onto the end of a long pliable stick. A flick of the stick would launch the ball a long way and, with practice, surprisingly accurately" (p. 41).

29 Specifically, the traditional crops grown are *eleusine coracana* (called finger millet or eleusine) and *sorghum caudatum* or *sorghum vulgare* (called sorghum or millet). G. H. Chaundy, principal of the Government African School at Kapenguria from 1931-43, tried to introduce many new crops and to teach modern agricultural practices by means of demonstration plots. In spite of his efforts, the only new crop adopted by Pokot farmers was maize, which is somewhat similar to the traditional crops (G.H. Chaundy, "The West Suk of Kenya: Teaching a Primitive Tribe to be Better Farmers", 1948). See also Harold K. Schneider, "Pakot Resistance to Change", (1959).

Life in Lossom

30   Brown (Unpublished list and description, 1975) was told that blacksmiths, who belong to the *Chepochesundu* clan, teach their sons the art of smithing and give them the necessary tools (tongs, chisel, hammers, bellows and possibly mandrels) during a graduation ceremony. Her informant used a wooden bowl bellows with a goatskin diaphragm and a cow tail nozzle, and made four clay *tuyeres* (blowpipes) at a time. These *tuyeres* can also have magical powers.

31   Brown (op. cit.) says these necklaces are made from wild asparagus twigs. A pendant of tortoise shell pieces and goat hooves is sometimes attached. For earrings, women wear three or four rings in the upper ear and large metal coils in the lobe. Lip plugs are frequently made from *muchukwa* wood or aluminum from old pots.

32   Bollig (*Risk Management,* 2006, p. 347) writes that the colors and color sequences of beaded jewelry are often fixed, and some color combinations are restricted. Red, yellow and dark blue are popular. He also found (in Baringo) that the type of metal used for coiled jewelry, like bracelets, earrings and rings, alternates from one generation to the next (see his paper on "Pokot Social Organization Structures, Networks and Ideology", 1994, p. 69).

33   Mervyn W.H. Beech (*The Suk: Their Language and Folklore,* 1911) collected a similar Pokot story about why the Endo, or "Chep-bleng" (later called the Cheblen in this book), moved to the south of Cheptulel. He writes that, "when the whole tribe were celebrating a ceremony under the shade of a lofty pillar of overhanging rock, a bird came and perched above them and warned them all to flee. Those who heard the bird and listened to its advice migrated to Endo, but all the rest were crushed by the pillar, which broke in half and fell upon them" (p. 3). Nearly a century later, Kim de Vries ("Identity Strategies of the Agro-Pastoral Pokot: Analysing Ethnicity and Clanship within a Spatial Framework", 2007) was told a version of the story, in which a white-necked crow, *kukai,* warned people at a rain ceremony "that a rock would fall from the sky." This rock was identified in this tale as Tapar Mountain, in the Cherangani Hills. Most of the dancers were crushed, but "the few who survived became the Talai" (p. 63). Barbara Bianco ("Gender and Material Culture in West Pokot, Kenya", 2000) writes that "one of the *Talai* clans puts two horizontal rows of cowries on its (*lökötyö*) belts to show respect for the white-necked crow that warned it to flee an encampment about to be crushed by a massive boulder." (p. 31). According to a drawing I made with Domonguria's guidance, this bird appears to be the white-naped raven *(Corvus albicollis).* The species is 22-inches and black, with a crescent-shaped white marking behind the neck. (John G. Williams, *A Field Guide to the Birds of East and Central Africa,* 1963). It is found on rocky hills throughout East Africa and is reputed to be very intelligent by some who have tamed it.

34   It is likely that this white couple was Mr. and Mrs. Rogers. In 1928, Rogers, the District Commissioner, "spent 192 days on 'safari' during which he walked the staggering distance of 1,614 miles" (Barber, *Imperial Frontier,*1968, p. 213). According to David K. Patterson (*The Pokot of Western Kenya 1910-1963: The Response of A Conservative People to Colonial Rule,* 1969), the first European woman in the Pokot region arrived in 1926 at Kacheliba. Before that time, the only Europeans seem to have been the early explorers: Thompson in 1884, Teleki and von Höhnel in 1888 and Johnston in 1902; then a succession of lone District Commissioners who seldom stayed in the post longer than a year. They were expected to spend half their time touring the district on foot (horses were used in later years). The first non-official Europeans, five mica miners, came in 1928, while the first missionaries (the Housdens, then the Tottys) and the first school teacher (Chaundy) arrived in 1931. Even by 1936, the entire European population of West Suk consisted of only six men and four women (Patterson, op. cit.). Karamoja was administered by only two colonial officials until World War II, and there were no resident white police officers. They tried to address local security issues without alienating the people, "with almost complete autonomy" (Eaton, "Violence, Revenge and the History of Cattle Raiding", 2008b). Several government officials expressed frustration over the resistance or indifference of the Pokot to any reform efforts.

35   Peristiany ("The Ideal and the Actual", 1975, p. 200) says that the Kopembich, ancient enemies of the Pokot, "have become, in Pokot fantasy, one-eyed ogres who prowl around huts at night kidnapping their children ... they identify the 'Kopembich'...with the Marille". (The Marille—or Marle— are a people living northwest of Lake Turkana. They are also known under the names Dassanetch

and Galeba.) De Vries ("Identity Strategies", 2007, p. 56) reports that some residents of Kapenguria and Cheperaria described the Oropom as "huge enemies, giants, some even termed them as man-eating monsters (*kapompich*) that harassed the Pokot." She heard another "frequently told story in which the *Orkom* had once cut a ladder to a cave wherein Pokot were living. In the north of Pokot, this story was identified as something that had happened to the *Chemkea* sub-clan, which comes from Tepeth, although the harasser was believed to be a cannibal, they could not tell if he was someone of the Oropom descent" (p.56 n71). Domonguria discusses the Oropom in the chapter "Making a Homestead" (*Building Our Homes*) as previous inhabitants of the area who were defeated and assimilated by the Karamojong and Pokot, and who may be responsible for excavating rock wells. He makes no connection between the Oropom and the Kopembich.

Turkana and the Year of the Locusts

36 "Mr. Major" was probably a Major in the King's African Rifles (KAR), which maintained a presence in the region from as early as 1908 to 1937 for the purpose of guarding the passes against Turkana raids and generally containing Turkana expansion (see Barber, *Imperial Frontier*, 1968). The KAR also confiscated livestock to compensate the Turkana or Pokot for animals raided. It was widely believed that the army kept many of the confiscated animals (Bollig, *Risk Management*, 2006).

37 Miscellaneous correspondence and annual reports filed in the Kenya National Archives for 1929-1931 mention generous rainfall at the end of 1929 and locust problems. Large swarms were reported at Riwa in 1929 and west of Kacheliba in 1931. A Locust Control Officer, Mr. Wisdom, coordinated a team of locust officers in the field (when their trucks were working). Schneider, in "The Pakot (Suk) of Kenya" (1953), mentions drought and locusts occurring in 1928.

38 The elders sit in a semi-circle in the *kurket* (the shade of a tree just outside the homestead) for rituals according to a prescribed pattern: the oldest in the middle, flanked by seniors and then juniors in descending age-set order (Bollig, *Risk Management*, 2006). The opening always faces Mt. Mtelo.

39 When I asked Domonguria to recite a typical prayer which might be said during a Pokot male prayer ceremony, he said the invocation which is reproduced in the text. However, near the end of the prayer, he added the words: "*Some people have heard that a Child of God was killed, yet he recovered and went to heaven. So we know you are strong enough to help a man recover, since you yourself died and surpassed death!*" This is an obvious, and fascinating, reference to Jesus. However, since I chose to insert this prayer in the story of Kokwa, which would have taken place before the first missionaries arrived (1931), I decided to eliminate those sentences in the text.

YOUTH

Sorcery and Family Herds

40 Peristiany ("The Age-Set System of the Pastoral Pokot: The Sapana Initiation Ceremony", 1951a) and Schneider ("The Pakot (Suk) of Kenya", 1953) write that the *tilia* (cattle associate) economic bond continues until all female descendants of the original cow are dead. Stock friendships are spread over a wide geographic area, an additional precaution against localized disaster.

41 Bollig (*Risk Management*, 2006) writes, "The moral obligation to redistribute property is a cornerstone of Pokot ethics and underscores the egalitarian system" (p. 386). Food is shared, not horded, even during famines, according to his informants. Bollig argues that large-group social control efforts failed partly because they interfered with social and economic networks. "A free-rider was not punished because everybody had a more immediate interest in the relation to the accused than in the common good" (ibid., p. 392). Before the colonial government appointed chiefs, there were, traditionally, no elite groups or chiefs within the Pokot pastoralist economy.

42 The Time the Country Became Dark refers to the period 1880s and 1890s, when the Pokot area suffered through a number of disasters, including a rinderpest epidemic, other stock diseases, drought, mass starvation, and smallpox.

43 The low side of the corral (the burial place) is a metaphor for death. This means that only through a curse of death will the cow (and her descendents) eventually be allowed to leave with her rightful owner.

Wandering Years

44 Possibly *longorichinuh* is sleeping sickness. Huntingford (*The Southern Nilo-Hamites*, 1969) writes that 2/3 of the eastern plain was infested with tsetse fly in 1932. The 1933 West Suk District Annual Report (Kenya National Archives, Kenya Government, 1924-1960) mentions outbreaks of East Coast Fever (*lokit*, caused by ticks) and rinderpest (*molmoltai*, caused by a virus) among Pokot stock.

45 A December, 1931, meeting at Lobubure about the boundary issue is mentioned in the 1932 West Suk District Annual Report (Kenya National Archives, Kenya Government, 1924-1960). The new boundary was set along the river Suam, and the Pokot were formally granted access to grazing areas they had used across that border in Karamoja. This area west of the Suam, known as Karasuk, had been administered since 1926 by Kenya Colony's West Suk District Headquarters, located first in Kacheliba and, after 1930, in Kapenguria, while the rest of Karamoja had been administered by the Uganda Protectorate from the Karamoja District headquarters in Moroto. Thus, conflicts between the Pokot and the Karamojong over this territory had often developed into conflicts between the two British administrations. In 1928, after an increase in inter-tribal raiding, the King's African Rifles joined the police in patrolling the border. This led to the tense situation Domonguria describes. The 1931 agreement put all the disputed land under one administration (Moroto) and abolished the political border between the two tribes. The changes took effect in July, 1932, and resulted in improved Pokot-Karamojong relations and a large migration of Pokot to Uganda, where the taxes were lower: 7 shillings in Uganda vs. 9 shillings, or 4 goats, in Kenya. Pokot tax collectors in Uganda recruited Pokot from Kenya, since they received a portion of the taxes they collected. See Ton Dietz, *Pastoralists in Dire Straits: Survival Strategies and External Intervention in a Semi-Arid Region at the Kenya/Uganda Border: Western Pokot, 1900-1986* (1987), p. 193. Karapokot was eventually integrated into Kenya again after independence.

Dance, Songs and Stories

46 Several researchers have commented on the *amumur*, which seems to have been held more frequently in the past. The *amumur* dances and songs often center around animal imitation. Beech (*The Suk*, 1911, p. 24), who called it a war dance, says the warriors sing, then "all join hands and run round sideways in a circle, stamping their sandaled feet as loudly as possible, then pairing off ... all imitating the habits of some animal ... accompanied by the cries thereof ... Individuals emerge from the crowd and rush madly about, stopping to kneel on one knee and brandishing a spear at the others, the while uttering a weird war cry. Blasts from a wooden trumpet ... giving forth a noise similar to that produced by a bassoon ... women walk around the outside of the ring indulging in obscene contortions and uttering weird shrill bird-like warblings." Peristiany ("The Age-Set System", 1951a) and Richard Owen Hennings (*African Morning*, 1951) describe an elephant dance, in which the stomping dancers hold their spears like trunks. Peristiany reports that animal dances occur during *sapana* celebrations. Four alternating rows of men and women form a half circle, which revolves slowly around the corral, while other women come to anoint the chests of the warriors with butter. As the dance continues, "... the warriors suddenly swerve to the right while the women swing to their left, dealing a glancing blow at the men with their pubic aprons. Each file then weaves in and out of the other" (ibid., p. 196-7). Hasthorpe ("A Study of Pokot Songs", 1983, pp. 60-61) witnessed variations of *amumur* dances during *sapana* ceremonies in Cheperaria. During one, girls are "captured" one by one and brought into the middle of a rotating men's circle, where they form their own ring and dance with joined hands. During another, men and women face one another, lock arms, and the line advances (with some walking backwards) to one end and then to the other end of the corral. The warriors then dance to perform their salutations at the *kurket*. In addition to this descrip-

tion, Hasthorpe presents an analysis of Pokot songs and dance patterns performed in the Chepareria and Ortum areas. Maisonhaute ("The East Pastoral Pokot Sapana Ceremony", 2000) also describes in detail the dances she witnessed during *sapana* ceremonies in 1994.

Pokot dances I have observed include circular jumping dances, initiated first by the women, then by the men, followed by the ox dances, as described in the section "Youth", in chapter "Call Me Red-Spotted Ox" (*Ox of Ropes*). A variety of linear dances are frequently held in the evening. During one of them, after the singing begins, girls point their long dancing sticks to choose a partner, then couples line up in a row facing one another, bobbing in time to the singing; the male holds his partner above the waist, while she holds her dancing stick. I have also witnessed the a children's line-dance and the *Semna Kengeiwa*, already described, and another, in which each dancer in turn ducks under the joined, raised hands of the next two people in line. Dancers are accompanied by their own singing, clapping, stamping and leg bells. Occasionally, sticks are beaten or a hollow tube blown while jumping. I have not observed drums or other musical instruments used in the dance.

47   District Commissioner, R.K. Dundas wrote in his "Notes on the Tribes Inhabiting the Baringo District, East Africa Protectorate" (1910), p. 61, "Lowalan, a great Suk warrior, has on more than one occasion invited his enemies to a conference and then treacherously massacred them." Beech, the District Officer for Baringo from 1909-1910, described Lowalan as the "Chief *ki-ruwok-in* [leader] of the Southern Suk and their most renowned warrior." See page 329 and the Photo Essay (Pokot 100 years ago) for photographs of Lowalan. In 1923, Lowalan was suspected of falsely accusing two of his Turkana enemies of planning a raid, in order to provoke British action against them. (David Eaton, "Violence, Revenge and the History of Cattle", 2008b).

48   Hasthorpe, who studied West Pokot songs for her ethnomusicology dissertation (1983), notes that older people and older songs use many more Karamojong or Turkana words, and ox praise songs, in particular, describe oxen using those languages. She found Pokot songs are distinguished by their antiphony (with a repetitive, often droning chorus accompanying an expressive, melodic, and often extemporaneous solo part), an absence of drums and sparse use of other instruments, simple rhythms, and the frequent choice of a pentatonic scale (e. g. C, D, E, G, A).

Clans

49   Surrogate calves are made and used to encourage a cow to give milk after her calf has died. One collected by Brown was a calf skin with sticks in its legs and the body stuffed with straw (Unpublished list and description, 1975). Bianco ("Gender and Material Culture", 2000) collected a different version of the origins of the *Siwetoi* clan, who sew cowrie shells on their *lokotyö* belts to indicate buffalo horns: "long ago a buffalo came and impregnated the clan's cows because there was no bull in its herd" (ibid., p. 31).

Call me Red-Spotted Ox

50   This shooting star may have been a bolide, an especially large meteor. The October 9, 1933 Giacobinid (also known as Draconid) meteor showers were among the most spectacular of the last century, with "rates in excess of 1000 meteors/hr" (Neil Bone, "Sky Notes: 2005 October and November", 2005). Intense meteor activity could have been seen as the Earth plowed through the debris of the comet (Giacobini-Zinner) in the morning. Another possibility is the famous chondrite meteor that fell in Ramurute, in Kenya's Rift Valley "on January 28, 1934, at 10:45 p.m. According to handwritten records at the Museum Für Naturkunde in Berlin, Germany, the shower of a few pounds was accompanied by dazzling light followed by several loud explosions. Fragments were collected over an area of approximately 1.2 km. One almost completely preserved stone of 67 g has been analyzed (see H. Schulze et al., "Mineralogy and Chemistry of Rumuruti: The First Meteorite Fall of the New R Chondrite Group", 1994). This is a tempting reference, except for the time.

51   Steers with horns fixed this way (one horn up and the other trained down and forward) are called *kamartin* (sing. *kamar*), and are highly prized by Pokot. In his 1984 article, "A Unique Surgical Operation on the Horns of African Bulls in Ancient and Modern Times", Calvin W. Schwabe traces the

history of bovine horn fixing, particularly relating to the *kamar*-type configuration, back to ancient Egypt. Schwabe says this practice has continued in the Nile River basin for at least 4500 years, probably starting in Nubia or the surrounding desert region. (The appearance of such bulls in ancient Egyptian art coincided with periods of intense association with Nubian peoples.) Evidently, the operation is unknown outside of the Nile River basin. Schwabe feels that the long history of this specific cultural practice demonstrates the continuous, deeply-ingrained cultural and aesthetic appreciation for cattle in the region.

Unlike the long-horned steers depicted by the ancient Egyptians, Pokot cattle are the short-horned, hump-back Zebu type. Brown (1975) writes that horns are shaped using two stones. The blunted end of a ground stone axe is used to smash the skull in the sinus region, and the pointed end is used to hold it in place, while a small, heavy rock is used to pound the horn into position. The end of each horn is then placed in a hole, which is bored partly through the rock, and pulled into shape. The horns are tied in place until the bone heals.

52 Domonguria's bull song is a mixture of Pokot and Karamojong words. *Domo* refers to spots on the head of his ox, and *nguria* refers to the red spots around the eyes. During the boast songs I witnessed, people in a circle began to sing a slow, chanting chorus, punctuated with claps. As the chorus continued, the man performing his ox song in the center sang a different melodic solo at a faster, higher and louder pitch, holding his arms in the position of his ox's horns from time to time. After singing, he jumped very high with straight legs three times, and three women jumped (almost a shuffle) forward and nodded their heads to one side to honor him. Then the next ox dancer began, and the chorus changed to honor him.

53 The 1934 West Suk District Annual Report (Kenya National Archives, Kenya Government 1924-1960) lists Kalebon (probably the same Kadabon) as an assistant to the headman Loduk in Batei location. According to Dietz (*Pastoralists in Dire Straits*, 1987), "from 1934 to 1936 all men between 18 and 45 years of age had to work for a period of one month in a year on government projects" (p. 70). Domonguria was younger and worked longer.

54 Bianco ("Gender and Material Culture", 2000) writes that *ptangtang* is "an ailment that can lead to excessive bleeding, miscarriage, or the delivery of a 'greenish or skinny' child" and "pregnant women might be given vomiting medicine a few months prior to delivery" (p. 33). I have been unable to identify this illness.

55 In 1936, the District Commissioner of West Suk District wrote in his Monthly Intelligence Report, "Circumcision ceremonies are taking place all over the Suk Reserve at present. There appears to be no regular period for holding such ceremonies, and it is six years since they were last held. The reason given for holding the ceremonies at present is the good rains and consequent surplus of crops ...Youths from 10 years of age upwards are undergoing circumcision" (Kenya National Archive, Kenya Government 1936-1951).

56 Lokitare was involved in the 1928 raids. See in section "Childhood", chapter "The Year the Earth Shook" (*Herding with Kilowan*), when Domonguria's childhood friend was murdered. Eaton ("Violence, Revenge and the History of Cattle", 2008b) observes that the period between 1928 and 1953 was relatively peaceful, because of arranged councils between group leaders and "through the efforts of local communities and administrative forces to investigate thefts and apportion blame individually rather than collectively."

COMING OF AGE

Independence

57 According to Harold K. Schneider ("Pakot Resistance to Change", 1959), young men frequently worked as herdsmen for more wealthy stock owners. They were paid in livestock, which they could use for *sapana*, bride price, etc.

58 Before the *sapana* initiation into adulthood, symbolized by the painted clay headdress, a youth might wear an intricately-sewn string cap incorporated into his hair with the assistance of a friend. This coiffure is well-tended and often decorated with ostrich-feather pompoms, chains and other ornaments. According to Brown (Unpublished list, 1975), red clay may be plastered over it, but no

other colors can be used. A nice picture of a youth's clay and pompom headdress can be seen in Mirella Ricciardi, *Vanishing Africa* (1971), p. 62-63.

59 This game is played all over Africa and is variously known as *bau, omweso, mancala, ingiless* (Turkana), etc. Schneider, in "The Pakot (Suk) of Kenya" (1953), p. 129, spells it *kachich*. Some peoples use carved game boards, but the Pokot and Turkana dig four rows of holes in the ground (two rows belong to each team), moving numbers of pebbles from one hole to the next in an effort to capture pebbles from the opposing side according to the rules.

60 Thirty years later, as Domonguria recorded this story, his eyes brimmed with tears.

61 Grazing areas were traditionally set aside and policed by young men, according to Schneider ("The Pakot (Suk) of Kenya", 1953). Anyone who violated the restrictions had to sacrifice an ox for a communal feast. The colonial government later superimposed its own rotational grazing schemes, which were not very effective until around 1948. By 1959, 237 000 acres were officially protected. (Patterson, *The Pokot of Western Kenya*, 1969).

62 Neville Dyson-Hudson ("The Karamojong and the Suk", 1958, p. 197) describes a blood-letting procedure: the ox is "held in a standing position by one or two men: a leather noose is pulled tight round the neck, temporarily distending the jugular vein; a blocked arrow is shot into the vein, and several pints of blood (depending on the animal's condition) are allowed to pour into a receptacle. The thong is then released, whereupon the bleeding stops; and possibly after the application of a little mud to cover the incision, the ox wanders quietly off to resume grazing." Webster (*The Shimmering Heat*, 2007, pp. 55-56) adds, "The blood was stirred with a stick to encourage clotting and the separation of the fibrin (which was eaten). The cow would then be milked, and the milk added to the blood, providing a smooth, nutritious, pink yoghurt-like drink. The initial taste was the sweet taste of milk fresh from the cow; the lingering taste was the salty taste of blood." Unfortunately, this practice "often gave them brucellosis or tuberculosis, both prevalent in their cattle."

Becoming a Man

63 Pokot horns are side-blown, made out of wood or of cow horn. They are used to warn of attacks, and to call people to meetings, ceremonies and feasts.

64 For more detailed descriptions of *sapana* celebrations, see Peristiany ("The Age-Set System", 1951a and 1951b), who attended four *sapana* rites at Ortum in 1947; Maisonhaute ("The East Pastoral Pokot", 2000), who participated in 12 celebrations in Baringo District in 1994; and Jonsson ("Pokot Masculinity", 2006), who wrote about West Pokot *sapanas*, also in the 1990s. They describe dances, games, and competitions, blessings and songs, the apportionment of the meat, the reading of the intestines, mixing and ritual spitting of the blood-and-milk mixture and meats, the spreading of chyme, creating the headdresses, and *sapana* age sets. Maisonhaute (op. cit., p. 45) observed, "the east pastoral Pokot sapana-classes organisation is nearer the Turkana's, the west pastoral Pokot sapana is made on the Karimojong pattern, and the mountains Pokot are still the holder of the traditional circumcision-classes organisation." *Sapana* is one of the few occasions when milk and unskinned meat can be eaten on the same day.

65 Muruasikar is also the name of the place in Kasauria, a mountain near Sigor, from which the pigment is obtained, according to Peristiany (op. cit., 1951a). Brown (Unpublished list, 1975, pp. 18-19) writes that men often prepare the clay for their own headdresses, crushing it in a bowl and adding water to make a smooth paste. This is used by the hair dresser to coat the carefully divided strands of hair, which are then criss-crossed into a neat mud pack. The *waria*, an implement which has a flat surface in the middle and shallow combs at both ends, is used to smooth the clay, and all the hair around the headdress is shaved, except for the *atoro* area on top of the head. "Holes are made for the feather container by pushing the end of a stick through the mud and hair, the wire coils are then pushed into the hole with a piece of string through them which is used to sew them into the mud-pack ... using the wire flea-scratcher (worn by all men with a siolop to itch under it) bent up to pull the wire through ... The whole mud-pack is wetted to finish it off smoothly and then patterned all over with the waria" (ibid.).The comb patterns are vertical in the center and horizontal around the edge. The colors (ground pigments) are painted on while the clay is still wet using the frayed end of a small stick. According to Brown (ibid.), "The whole operation takes about 4 hours. The blue used

nowadays is Reckitts washing blue. The old colour was obtained by burning a tree and using the ash." Sometimes strands of hair from dead relatives are incorporated into the front diamond (*atoro*) before colored clay is applied. Bollig ("Pokot Social Organization", 1994, p. 69) writes that the colors and ornaments reflect the relative seniority of *sapana* age sets, and "juniors have to ask seniors for permission to wear certain feathers and paint special lines on their mud-cap."

66 Nakere is listed as a locality of the Ngalacata River Unit of the Ngipian section of the Karamojong in Dyson-Hudson (*Karamojong Politics*, 1966). Peristiany ("The Age-Set System", 1951a) was told a story about a Pokot warrior named Merkol, who introduced the custom of *sapana* to his neighbors in Tiati (in the far eastern region of Pokot settlement) after learning it from the Karamojong. Merkol was said to be of the *kerongoro* circumcision set which, Peristiany assumed, immediately preceded that first *sapana*. Thus it seemed possible to date the circumcision, by calculating approximate age-set cycles, and the first Pokot *sapana* to the 1870s. This date corresponds well with the stories told here. Domonguria saw Cherotwa, then an old woman, when he was a child (1920s and '30s). Cherotwa was a baby at the time of the first Pokot-Karamojong *sapana* ceremony at Nakere. A number of elders told Peristiany in 1947 that they had once attended an *amuro* (*hamura*) ceremony with Karamojong, and that such times were marked by inter-tribal peace ceremonies and ritual instruction of new elders.

67 This comment on *sapana* applies mainly to the pastoralist Pokot. Brown (Unpublished list, 1975), who interviewed the Kurut agricultural Pokot, reports that "The Sapana ceremony is not so important to the agricultural Pokot and nowadays very few men wear the Siolop (mud-pack hair-do) except a few conventional elderly men" (p. 18). The pastoralist headdress has apparently become much less elaborate over the years. Travelers from Thompson (1884) to Joy Adamson (*The Peoples of Kenya*, 1967), who collected her material around 1950, describe a large bag-like "chignon of shoulder length hair, molded with a special bluish clay into a thick pad which hangs down the neck. At the bottom a flexible spiral ... carved from the horn of an Oryx antelope, wrapped tightly around with hair from a giraffe's tail. It is very resilient and where its end touches the chignon again, the fur of a hare is attached like a pompom ... Until recently, it was the custom of the eldest son when his father died to cut off the chignon and add it to his own ... one sometimes saw chignons hanging down to the waist" (Adamson, op. cit., pp. 21-22). By the early 1950s, according to Schneider, ("The Pakot (Suk) of Kenya", 1953) this longer hairstyle had almost disappeared in the Ortum area. Brown (Unpublished list, 1975, p. 20) writes that the spiral decoration, now made of wood instead of horn, and with a pompom "made traditionally of the soft hair from under a donkey's tummy" is still used sometimes on ceremonial occasions.

68 J.P. Crazzolara (*A Study of the Pokot (Suk) Language*, 1978) defines *sosion* as a palmyra palm, which can also be called African fan palm, or Borassus aethiopum.

New Developments

69 Major E.F. Whitehead ("A Short History of Uganda Military Units Formed during World War II", 1950) reported that some 77,000 Ugandan Africans were enlisted during World War II, most during 1939. The 4th (Uganda) Battalion King's African Rifles of the 2nd East African Infantry Brigade was formed in 1940. It was garrisoned in Lokitaung, in Turkana, and fought the Italians in Abyssinia (today's Ethiopia). Schneider ("The Pakot (Suk) of Kenya", 1953) reports that conditions improved during the war for the Kenya Pokot, who sold about 300 head of cattle to the army in 1941. The District Commissioner in Kapenguria, on the other hand, reports in 1942 that Uganda Pokot were crossing into Kenya, partly because of "unwillingness to provide oxen for the War effort and antipathy towards being recruited for Military Units". See West Suk District Monthly Intelligence Report, 1942, by District Commissioners N. F. Kennaway and R. D. F. Ryland (Kenya National Archives, Kenya Government 1936-1951).

Chelima: Becoming a Woman

70 This description of female circumcision differs in many ways from the account given by Meyerhoff in "The Socio-Economic and Ritual Roles" (1981) of female circumcision among the agricultural

Pokot from the Kataw region of the Cherengeni Hills. The Karapokot girls stay in a single hut during seclusion, whereas the Kataw initiates return to their homesteads. Karapokot sexual restrictions are more limited and the initiates more aggressive in their pursuit of beads. They emerge in new clothes, not new cloaks, like their Kataw cousins. Meyerhoff does not mention the *karemba* ritual and never uses the term *laleyo* (perhaps another name for *kipuno*), while Domonguria does not speak of the washing ceremony inside the hut or of the secret bead ceremonies at the river and later at *sewo* (all of which are private women's rituals and may have occurred). Hasthorpe in "A Study of Pokot Songs" (1983) also describes similarities and differences in the styles of the female circumcision ceremonies she witnessed between the Cheperaria and the more northern Ortum regions of Kenya. The variance in detail in this, and other rituals described by Meyerhoff, Hasthorpe, and other ethnographers, may reflect differences in geography, distance, economy (agricultural vs. pastoral orientation), and outside influence between the communities, as well as in the sex of the informants.

71 Hasthorpe recorded several girls' circumcision songs. She writes (op. cit., pp. 102-104), "The night before circumcision, songs are sung to test the girl's stamina and ... remind her of all her responsibilities to her family and imply that the welfare of almost every man, woman and child depends on her bravery ... Praise-songs for the newly-circumcised girls... are slow and pensive, reflecting the physical discomfort ... as well as the transition they are undergoing from child to adult." Songs for the dances are "energetic ... boastful and confident. In the songs the initiates praise themselves and look forward to the future."

72 Once a newly-circumcised girl in Karamoja proudly showed me her incisions, which were clean and precise, resulting from the removal of the labia minora. I swabbed the incision with alcohol. Meyerhoff (1981), who witnessed 15 initiation ceremonies in Kataw, writes in "The Socio-Economic and Ritual Roles" (1981), pp. 136-138, that the circumciser "cuts off the prepuce and part of the labia minora in one or two quick slashes." Later, in a private place, older women inspect the cuts, "making sure that both sides of the labia are cut straight and evenly so that the two sides are able to heal together and form a smooth and even scar ... the shaft of the clitoris is not cut." The World Health Organization classifies such practices as Female Genital Mutilation (FMG) Type II—Partial or total removal of the clitoris and the labia minora, with or without the excision of the labia majora. Brown (Unpublished list, 1975) says the circumciser, who inherits her job, uses a curved, tanged blade and applies sisal juice to stop the bleeding and pain. She receives a goat in payment. Webster (*The Shimmering Heat*, 2007, p. 86) says this practice resulted in scarring that "caused the narrowing of the introitus, making subsequent childbirth more difficult". Other complications he witnessed included blood loss and infection.

73 A circumcision stick collected by Brown (Unpublished list, 1975) is about 10 feet long, with the top half wrapped in bark. It is painted white. Brown says initiates also carry shorter, thin, white sticks, which they use to scratch at the door of the hut before entering. Male circumcision initiates have similar sticks, which they rub with red ochre.

74 There are many subtle differences in the descriptions of the *lapan* rituals—Domonguria's is just one of them. Crazzolara (*A Study of the Pokot (Suk) Language*, 1978) defines *lapan* as the concluding ceremony of taboo. Meyerhoff ("The Socio-Economic and Ritual Roles", 1981) says it is the feast for the women who participate (they sing obscene songs to each other, give advice, feast and dance). Jonsson ("Pokot Masculinity", 2006) says *lapan* is a feast held during the seclusion period of circumcision when the initiates have reached the stage of being allowed to eat unassisted with their own hands.

CATTLE AND ROMANCE

Deception and Love

75 According to Ruto Pkalya et al. (*Indigenous Democracy: Traditional Conflict Resolution Mechanisms: Pokot, Turkana, Samburu and Marakwet*, 2004) the *kokwa*, "is made up of respected, wise old men who are knowledgeable in community affairs and history. The elders are also good orators and eloquent public speakers who are able to use proverbs and wisdom phrases to convince the meeting or the conflicting parties to a truce. Every village is represented in the council of elders ... Both the accused

and the accuser are allowed to narrate their story before the panel". Community members share their insights about the conflict, and "traditional lawyers (eloquent members representing the plaintiff and defense) can speak on behalf of the conflicting parties. The *Kokwa* deals with major disputes and issues and is mandated to negotiate with other communities especially for peace, cease-fire, grazing land/pastures and water resources. The *Kokwa* is the highest traditional court and its verdict is final."

76 *Somongi* are large gourds with the tips cut and lashed with bark thonging, used for beer, milk or tobacco.

A Son

77 Peristiany ("The Age-Set System of the Pastoral Pokot", 1951a, p. 205) writes that in 1946 the pressure on pastoralists to circumcise by their extended families in the hill country of Kenya "was so great that over one hundred uncircumcised pastoralists were housed in one circumcision hut not far from Kacheliba" on the Suam river. He noticed that "a number of uncircumcised pastoralists who had already made sapana, married and had children joined the initiates in the circumcision hut."

78 Juxton Barton ("Notes on the Suk Tribe of Kenia Colony", 1921, p. 91) writes of the circumcision house: "... this hut is not a circular erection, as might be expected, but a large rectangular hut with a two-sided sloping roof of grass ... It is situated in the depths of the bush, it has two doors, the right for those already circumcised ..., the left for the candidates ... at the opposite end of the building." At Cheptulel in the 1990s, boys built two houses "of very poor quality with flat roofs made of branches … the house of the elders has two doors." The boys slept in the other house (see Jonsson, "Pokot Masculinity", pp. 148-149).

79 Brown (Unpublished list, 1975) says three belts are worn: two as bandoliers across the chest and one around the waist. These belts were called *pompos* by her informants. The iron bells sewn onto the *pemoi* necklet do not have clappers. In addition to these, mothers of circumcision initiates wear fringed leather headbands *(tenda)* sewn with ostrich eggshell beads and blue beads. Jonsson (op. cit.) says a white ostrich feather is sometimes put in the front of the headband, and bells are worn on their legs (pp. 160-161). Bianco ("Gender and Material Culture", 2000) examines the cultural implications of the woman's *lökötyö (lukutia)* belt, which is decorated by sewing cowrie shells in meaningful designs to signify the clan, birth of twins, etc. It is tied around the mother's waist after a successful birth as a blessing and protection for her infant and is thereby thought to have spiritual powers. It is untied after infancy, stored in a pannier *(asacha)*, and worn again for special blessing for other births and for circumcision.

80 For more detailed and somewhat varied accounts of male circumcision, see Barton ("Notes on the Suk Tribes", 1921), Meyerhoff ("The Socio-Economic and Ritual Roles", 1981) and Jonsson ("Pokot Masculinity", 2006). Like the *chemerin*, the *tios* sit on stones during the surgery, threatened by their fathers, and do not use their hands for eating until after a cleansing ceremony, followed by beer drinking. Brown (Unpublished list, 1975) says initiates collect beads from girls by placing decorated sticks in their path (It is forbidden to cross the sticks). Bollig (*Risk Management*, 2006, p. 289) says secluded initiates wear women's clothing, borrowed from an elderly female, in exchange for a sheep, forming a stock friendship. Barton (op. cit.) mentions a mock battle inside the circumcision house, during which mothers are told their sons have been "killed." He describes encounters with a symbolic beast, modeling figures out of grass, and a cleansing ceremony at a stream, during which initiates are lectured about personal conduct. During the final ceremony, amidst singing and dancing, the veiled initiates crouch together under their blankets, protected by a ring of elders with locked arms. Their mothers struggle to get to their sons and dress them in women's beads. The initiates are symbolically promised stock by young women or relatives and blessed by their mothers and aunts. Jonsson (op. cit.) gives a thorough and detailed account of these and other circumcision rituals performed in Cheptulel during 1992-1995. Meyerhoff (op. cit.) found that the timing and rituals of circumcision vary from one area to the next. In the agricultural areas where Meyerhoff and Jonsson worked, male circumcision was considered far more important than *sapana*. By contrast, Beech (*The Suk*), as early as 1911, and Barton ("Notes on the Suk Tribe") in 1921 note that circumci-

sion had been abandoned by many Pokot living near the Turkana and Karamojong, who do not circumcise.

81 There seem to be differences in the frequency and importance of circumcision between pastoral and agricultural Pokot communities. Pokot circumcision age sets have been discussed by Beech (op. cit.), Schneider ("The Pakot (Suk) of Kenya", 1953 and "The Subsistence Role of Cattle Among the Pakot and in East Africa", 1957), Peristiany "The Age-Set System of the Pastoral Pokot", 1951b and "The ideal and the Actual", 1975), Meyerhoff (op. cit.), Bollig ("Pokot Social Organization", 1994), Maisonhaute ("The East Pastoral Pokot", 2000), Jonsson (op. cit.), and others. Several report that age set names change every 9 to 16 years and each consists of three or four circumcision sub-sets (called sections by some authors). Thus, there can be living members of, perhaps, five age sets at any one time. They seem to occur in this order: *merkutwa (merkutwo), nyongu (nyongi), maina, juma (chumo, chumwo), sowa (sowo), kurongora (korongoro, kerongoro, kurongoro, koronkoro), kipkoimet (pkoymot), kabelach (kaplelach)*. Peristiany and Maisonhaute give a shorter list; Jonsson (op. cit., pp. 193-194) gives a longer one. He observes, "The system was copied from the Marakwet people and the Pokot elders have to acquire information from them about when to start and close age-sets." They "do not always have the same names everywhere in the district so that there may be two or three names for each of them depending on the district." Beech, writing in 1911, says the most recent initiates were *maina*. Barton ("Notes on the Suk", 1921) writes that youths were circumcised into the *juma* age grade in 1918-19. Following *sowa, kurongora* began in 1936 in some areas. In 1947, Peristiany (op. cit., 1975) heard that some elders wanted to eliminate the name because previous *kurongora* periods were marked "by droughts, rinderpest, the infection of circumcision wounds, the disobedience of the young Kerongoro warriors, the folly of their leaders, and defeat at the hands of their enemies," but this did not happen. Maisonhaute (op. cit.) says there were no circumcisions between 1957 and 1988 because of raiding, and the *kaplelach* age set began in 1988. Jonsson (op. cit.) says *merkutwo* was closed in 1990, and *nyongu* was still open in 2003, so there is some disagreement between these reports. Bollig (op. cit., 1994) claims that the pastoral Pokot around Baringo circumcise only every 25 to 30 years and the "generation sets" he lists span fewer years.

Chepusepa

82 Lukas Pketch, once expelled from a Catholic school, became the local Pokot leader of a larger, southern Rift Valley province movement known as *Dini ya Masambwa* (DYM), founded by a Kitosh man named Elijah Masindi. Pketch encouraged members to defect from Christian churches, avoid schools and other European institutions, ideas and objects, and, eventually, drive all non-Africans out of Africa. Arrested in 1948, he escaped a year later and began organizing anti-European rallies and song-fests. Local chiefs refused to aid British efforts to capture him. Patterson (*The Pokot of Western Kenya*, 1969, p. 37) writes, "Finally, on April 20, 1950, Rev. T. Collins of the African Inland Mission heard of a DYM meeting in Baringo District. He found the gathering, which he estimated at two hundred men and women and talked with Pketch. Rev. Collins reported to the Baringo District Commissioner, A. B. Simpson ... Two intrepid tribal policemen tried to arrest Pketch who told the policemen to tell the D. C. to come and make the arrest in person. Simpson, joined by A. J. Stevens, who had just arrived to take over the district, gathered a force of two European and forty tribal and Kenya police and set out ... in two lorries. Singing was heard at a point near Kolloa; the police dismounted and moved into the grove, to confront 200-300 Pokot, armed with spears. Lukas Pketch and nineteen of his followers were killed and the remainder scattered. Stevens, two European policemen and one tribal constable died ...". Reinforcements and armored cars were rushed to the scene. Finally, under pressure, chiefs turned in more than 200 suspects. Bollig (*Risk Management*, 2006, p. 151) lists the following harsh punishments: 176 imprisoned, 8 hanged, military and police presence, fines, 5000 head of cattle confiscated, forced labor constructing roads and landstrips, and confiscation of spears. A detailed description of this event is also found in Russell's memoir, *Kenya, Beyond the Marich Pass* (1994), pp. 46-54.

83 The Kadam (or Kadama) are a branch of the So, or Sorat (also known as the Tepeth, or Tepes), an indigenous people who inhabit three mountains in the region: Kadam (also known as Debasien), Moroto and Napak. Informants told John Lamphear (*The Traditional Life of the Jie of Uganda*, 1976,

p. 203) that the Tepes lived by hunting and trapping on Mts. Toror and Nyanga as well, before the Karamojong drove them south in retribution for raiding. According to Laughlin and Allgeier (*An Ethnography of the So*, 1979), there is no evidence that the So migrated into the area, like the Karamojong, Pokot or Turkana. Their language is related to the Ik and the Nganga, both of Northern Karamoja. Mt. Kadam remains the religious and linguistic center of So life. In 1933, the government initiated efforts to remove the So from their mountains in order to protect the forests. This policy caused the Kadam people to move to the valley floors and lowest slopes, thus bringing them into more direct contact with the Pokot. Both the Pokot and the Karamojong have been awed by the mystical powers of the So.

84 *Marotino* refers to the cucumber-like fruit from the *rotin* tree (sausage tree, *kighelia africana*). A beer making gourd *(logh)* collected by Brown (Unpublished list, 1975) has a basketry-edged hole near the tip of the neck for pouring and another, larger one just below the neck on the opposite side for putting in the ingredients: honey, water and *marotino.*

85 The *mukuh* is a special calabash for milk. The cap rim is woven and sometimes ornamented with cowrie shells (see Schneider, "The Pakot (Suk) of Kenya", 1953).

86 Marriage customs of the Karapokot, as described by Domonguria, apparently differ somewhat from those of the agricultural Pokot studied by Schneider ("The Pakot (Suk) of Kenya", 1953), Meyerhoff ("The Socio-Economic and Ritual Roles", 1981) Francis P. Conant ("Frustration, Marrage Alternatives and Subsistence Risks Among the Pokot of East Africa: Impressions of Co-Variance", 1974 and "The External Coherence of Pokot ritual Behavior", 1966), Jonsson ("Pokot Masculinity", 2006) and others. Bride wealth among the agriculturalists is much lower, sometimes involving only beer, honey, grain, blankets, money, or goats (symbolically representing cattle). Gifts of stock are periodically promised to the bride on the way to the groom's corral, although few are actually delivered. Schneider (op. cit.) was told the groom's family can later claim back some calves of bride wealth cows and expect other stock gifts when visiting the bride's family. He says bride wealth cattle are rarely shared with others unless debts are owed, yet Domonguria includes distribution of the bride wealth to key family members as an integral part of the ritual. Bollig ("Moral Economy and Self-Interest: Kinship, Friendship, and Exchange Among the Pokot (N.W. Kenya)", 1998, p. 140) says about half the promised bride wealth of the Baringo area Pokot is paid at the wedding, and the rest is paid over a period of years and distributed throughout the father's "personal network". Conant (op.cit., 1974) writes about elopement and kidnappings sometimes being allowed during the summer solstice in some Kenyan farming communities.

LIVING THE POKOT LIFE

After the Wedding

87 Barton ("Notes on the Suk", 1921) was told that passage of the afterbirth is often stimulated by causing the mother to vomit. He also noted that leopard fat is "conserved by all Suk" and observed that it was given to male circumcision initiates (ibid., p. 92).

88 Specifically, this was probably seed oil mixed with ground black stone. The ointment can also be spread on clothes for beauty (Brown, Unpublished list, 1975). In the late 1940s, according to Adamson (*The Peoples of Kenya*, 1967), the only Europeans in Kapenguria, the government headquarters, were the District Commissioner's family and an agricultural officer.

89 The word *tupul* (spelled variously) is defined as bladder by both Beech (*The Suk*, 1911) and Crazzolara (*A Study of the Pokot (Suk) Language*, 1978). However, Domonguria explained, "this is the sack the baby is in, and when it comes, it is bald, and we know the baby will come soon."

Trading

88 Dyson-Hudson (*Karamojong Politics*, 1966, p. 243-248) writes that Kanyangareng River grazing rights had been a source of contention between the Pokot and the Karamojong since the region was officially opened to the Pokot during the drought of 1949. The two small Pokot cowherds were

speared in that area in March of 1953. In May, when Pokot raiders were intercepted by Karamojong, "the Government chief and native Government agent with them were both speared to death by the Pokot, and the remaining Karamojong fled" (ibid.). Immediately afterwards there were massive raiding and counter-raiding on both sides, involving thousands of cattle, with the Government in hot pursuit. Fines were levied on both peoples, and, according to Brasnett ("The Karasuk Problem", 1958), the Kanyangareng area was subsequently closed to the Pokot. The 1953 fine for the Upe Pokot was 3 cattle per taxpayer and the Ngipian Karamojong paid one, "giving the government a welcome booty worth 700,000 shs." (Dietz, *Pastoralists in Dire Straits*, p. 189).

Docherty, the British official Domonguria would soon meet in court, eulogized Lorika, who died after this incident: "A Toposian (Sudanese) by tribe, he was an outstanding leader with astonishing breadth of vision and depth of intelligence, considering his very humble background. His murder by the Suk in the 1953 disturbances created a gap that will be felt for many a long year—even the Suk regretted what they had done in the heat of battle; for he held the unique reputation of having been the only chief in the history of Karamoja who was loved and respected with equal sincerity by both tribes ... Lorika was convinced that the only solution to the bitter enmity between the Karamojong and the Suk was assimilation ... Lorika was an idealist ..." (Docherty, "The Karamojong and the Suk", 1957, p. 38-40). Nevertheless, violent cattle rustling and revenge attacks continued during the 1970s and 1980s between the Pokot and Lorika's son, Athiyo, who was assisted by the heavily-armed Uganda army.

91 Specifically, Domonguria mentions *lokit, loukoit, molmoltai, and loriel. Lokit* and *loukoit* are Karamojong terms defined as East Coast Fever and pleuro-pneumonia by J. M. Watson, Agricultural Officer, Karamoja, quoted in Turpin ("The Occupation of the Turkwel River Area",1948, p. 165). *Molmoltai* is identified as rinderpest by Schneider ("The Pakot (Suk) of Kenya, 1953). *Loriel* remains unidentified. East Coast Fever has been endemic in mountainous regions inhabited by the Pokot. It first appeared in the Kadam Mountain area around 1934, thereafter depleting the southern Karamojong herds at a time when Pokot were given temporary grazing rights in Karamoja because of drought. The resulting tension contributed to numerous Pokot-Karamojong conflicts (see V. Rada Dyson-Hudson, "East Coast Fever in Karamoja", 1960).

92 The *pulkan* is a 6-stringed lyre, traditionally made from a large tortoise shell with cow skin stretched over it, using sinews from the back of a cow for strings. Some are made with a wooden base, and even tin boxes and wire strings have been used. Brown (Unpublished list, 1975, p. 30) says the "pakan" is usually played in the evening "to make people happy ... the musician sings as he plays, and his tunes are some of the most delightful and varied in Kenya (to a European ear!)." Another instrument played alone for pleasure is a 2-holed flute, which can be side- or end-blown. Schneider ("The Pakot (Suk) of Kenya", 1953) says it is usually "a temporary variety, made on the spot." Leg bells (kurkuris) and, occasionally, whistles (store-bought) are used at dances. According to Hasthorpe ("A Study of Pokot Songs", 1983), a wooden, side-blown horn, about 30-35 inches, is played by men at *sapana*.

93 The Pokot version of this song is included in this book's section "Coming of Age", in the chapter about female circumcision, "Chelima: Becoming a Woman" (*The Karemba Ritual*). David Webster (*The Shimmering Heat*, 2007), for many years a doctor in Amudat, writes, "Pokot women deliver their babies in the squatting position, and they are encouraged by the village 'midwives' to push from the onset of labour. To add to all this downward pressure the 'midwives' squat behind the mother and, wrapping their arms around the woman's abdomen, press on the uterus ... Very generous and mutilating incisions are made in the perineum, to compensate for tight circumcision scars and to aid the baby's exit. And Pokot women generally have wide pelvises, which offer little resistance to the progress of labour. All this leads to the frequent occurrence of total prolapse (procidentia) of the uterus..." Another problem Webster noticed was the occurrence of tetanus in newborns as a result of cutting the umbilical cord with a dirty instrument. "The simple act of distributing new razor blades and a piece of clean string meant a considerable reduction in neonatal tetanus" (ibid., pp. 52, 90).

94 There was a tightening of colonial government control in Kenya during the 1950s. Because of increased raiding, spears were impounded and Special Force units were set up "to follow up raids and ensure payment of blood money" (Baker, "Development and the Pastoral People of Karamoja", 1981, p. 75). Hennings (*African Morning*, 1951) argued that stock owners who moved out of their

administrative tax districts for grazing should be brought back. Dietz (*Pastoralists in Dire Straits*, 1987, p. 70) mentions that there were "modernization attempts," including dams, boreholes, ox ploughs, irrigation, missions providing education and health services and many more white people (increasing from a few in 1950 to over a hundred in 1959). Docherty, whom Domonguria met, proposed measures to save the land from overgrazing: dispersing cattle from water holes, providing additional boreholes and pumps, enforcing rotational grazing, and buying and exporting cattle. A quarantine on sales of cattle to the European-settled Trans Nzoia was lifted in 1952, and by 1954 Kenya instituted compulsory cattle sales, giving each location a quota and providing auctions. This was continued throughout the 1950s, meeting increasing resistance, which was countered by military force and prosecutions. By contrast, the Karasuk area governed by Uganda, where Domonguria lived, was "almost unadministered" (Patterson, *The Pokot of Western Kenya*, 1969, p. 34). It was against this backdrop that Domonguria gained success as a cattle trader.

95 The Pokot versions of these songs are included in the section about male circumcision.

96 Hasthorpe ("A Study of Pokot Songs", 1983, pp. 67-69) describes another version of these ceremonies as practiced in Cheparia, West Pokot, where they are called *yatat* and *kitunga*, instead of *riwoi* and *kitula*.

Witchcraft, Magic and Divining

97 In the West Suk District Annual Report, 1955, District Commissioner A. D. Shirreff noted that in 1955 six men were condemned for witchcraft at a single meeting, tied to a tree and beaten to death. In addition, the government jailed another sorcerer. "This decision was widely welcomed and the killings ceased" (Kenya National Archives, Kenya Government 1924-1960).

98 Schneider ("Pokot Folktales, Humor, and Values", 1967, p. 292) collected a similar tale about a mother who placed her dead child at the gateway of a neighbor's corral. "When the cattle were let out in the morning they would walk over the child and the mother would raise a great cry and say the man had killed her child. Then her husband would come and take all the man's cattle ... All this used to happen during the time of the *Sowa* age-set long ago."

99 The *mutat* and *muma* rituals, using witchcraft to find thieves, are described in varying forms by Pkalya et al. (*Indigenous Democracy*, 2004), Jonsson ("Pokot Masculinity", 2006) and others. Pkalya et al. write that a permit to perform those rituals could be obtained from the government in West Pokot District, "thus validating and legitimizing the ritual(s)" (pp. 27-28).

100 Beech (*The Suk*, 1911, p. 25) says it is a bad sign if the "tieltel bird" whistles on a man's left on a journey, unless he is searching for a wife, when it is propitious. These woodpeckers are also mentioned in the section "Cattle and Romance", chapter "Chepusepa", *My Wedding* when they tell the fortune of Domonguria's bride-to-be.

101 Brown (Unpublished list, 1975, p. 17) explains, "The sandals are held soles together in one hand and flipped. If both land upright it is a good portent. If both land face downwards it is very bad. One landing on top of another indicates good marital relationships ... Blessings are called for ... by placing the green leaves of *seret* on top of the sandals whilst intoning the blessing."

102 See the diagram showing "How to Read Intestines" according to Domonguria. The veins, blotches and spots are interpreted by the diviner as events, features of the landscape (rivers, mountains), diseases, etc. Locations are judged by the distance of markings from the designated homestead line of the intestines. Peristiany ("The Age-Set System of the Pastoral Pokot", 1951a, p. 193 fn) was told that "Names are given to the intestines, for example, names of rivers ... Black spots indicate rinderpest. They are the crows and birds of prey which hover over the dying cattle. A white line ending in a red spot is a long file of enemy warriors coming to raid the Pokot. A large round spot is a grave and is a sign of sickness among human beings. According to the 'river' where these signs have been found the locality of the event is ascertained." When the intestines show potential threats, the diviner may distribute thin strips of the ox hide to be worn for protection against calamity. Sometimes another ox or a goat is slaughtered, and its intestines read, in order for the diviner to clarify a worrisome prediction or, perhaps, to influence Fate, as Domonguria mentions. A picture and diagram of the Himba method of reading intestines is found in Bollig (*Risk Management*, 2006, p. 260).

103 In another version of this story collected by Schneider ("Pokot Folktales", 1967, pp. 308-9), an old archer killed many Maasai raiders from the roof of his hut. Pokot warriors pursued the rest to Cheperaria, where a stream flows down the Kamatira escarpment from the Mnakei plateau. There they "killed a Maasai raid-leader who was twelve feet tall and whose name was Lowunon. That is how the stream got its name ... Thereafter the Maasai never came back to Pokotland ..." Kim de Vries ("Identity Strategies of the Agro-Pastoral Pokot", 2007) reports that a Lounun story, told by elders at a 1996 workshop sponsored by the Pokot Language Committee at Nsakuta was "about Uas Nkishu Maasai who were heavily defeated by the Pokot around 1850. The military leader of the Maasai at that time, Ole Lounon, was killed at Kamatira in the present day Chepareria Division. His grave can still be found there today, and the place is known as Lounon village" (p. 52). The 1850 date appears too early to agree with both Domonguria and Schneider's versions that state that the Maasai never returned to fight the Pokot after this incident.

Celebrations

104 Chepuseipei and her family lived near the Robbins' campsite at Katabok. She is in the group picture in the Photo Essay.

105 The *parapara* ritual cleanses young parents and their baby from misfortunes that could be caused by unatoned sins of their ancestors and themselves. During the night of a *parapara* ceremony Meyerhoff ("The Socio-Economic and Ritual Roles", 1981) attended, the elders sat in a hut by the fire chanting about the histories of the families involved, each man using his fingers to stir the "words" into a wooden bowl containing red earth and water. This "mixture of words and blessings" was then placed between the legs of the pregnant girl and tipped over, thereby absolving the parents of all past sins which might prevent a healthy birth. Jonsson in "Pokot Masculinity" (2006) also writes about stirring water with clay from an anthill in a trough, into which people spit blessings, as songs and confessions take place, before the mixture, placed between the girl's legs, is spilled, symbolizing the birth. Bollig (*Risk Management*, 2006, p. 343) writes, "Pokot believe that if a murder—no matter how long ago—between two clans has not been properly atoned this results in a very specific sin called *moriyon*, which is not attached to an individual but to all members of the respective clan ...Whenever people of these two clans engage in marriages or other relations that involve close physical contact (like circumcision or sexual intercourse) they run the risk that their children will die or be crippled, or they themselves may become sick and die because of *moriyon*." Hasthorpe ("A Study of Pokot Songs", 1983, pp. 62-65) also describes a *"barabara"* ceremony. Each *parapara* description varies somewhat in ceremonial details and songs, but the cleansing purpose is clear.

Family Changes

106 Those turbulent years of unrest in Kenya, especially in Kikuyu areas where Mau Mau activities were prevalent, became associated with the drive towards independence in 1963. Even in Pokot regions, in 1956-7 at least 293 people were arrested for anti-government activities, supposedly sponsored by the Pokot version of *Dini ya Masambwa*, including a group on Mt. Kadam. Shirreff, the District Commissioner, suggested in the 1956 West Suk District Annual Report (Kenya National Archives, Kenya Government 1924-1960), "... in dealing with a menace of this kind ... replace the fear of witchcraft by a greater fear of government". There were stock fines, long prison terms, exiled leaders, a military tour through the district, a purge of non-cooperative chiefs and "whole locations were forced to labor on roads and other public works" (Patterson, *The Pokot of Western Kenya*, 1969, p. 39-40). Increased raiding in Karamoja District in the late 1950s and 1960s resulted in large collective fines, inflated to enrich government officials (see Dietz, *Pastoralists in Dire Straits*, 1987, pp. 72, 190).

107 The oldest men on Kadam and Moroto mountains are initiated into the powerful So (also known as Tepeth) "ghost cult," or *kenisan*. The *kenisan* serve as a link between the ancestors and living people and form the ruling body, both politically and judicially, among the So. They can call forth

ancestors by name, ask their assistance to help or punish, control the rain, bless the crops and cast out disease. The most important rainmaking ceremony for all So is held periodically on Mt. Kad- am, whenever the leaves of the *poiyo* plant wither from severe drought. So dreamers can also foretell events and prescribe actions (Laughlin and Allgeier, *An Ethnography of the So*, 1979). John M. Weatherby ("A Preliminary Note on the Sorat (Tepeth)", 1969, p. 78) notes that when women are called to be present, "they are kept out of sight in a special hut near the place of ritual."

108 In the late 1950s, the British government agreed to build and fund a hospital in Amudat if the Bible Churchmen's Missionary Society (BCMS) would provide the staffing. Its first physician, Peter Cox, arrived in 1957 and treated patients under a thorn tree while the building began. His replacement, Dr. David Webster, wrote in his memoir, *The Shimmering Heat* (2007) "By the time we arrived in 1967, Amudat Hospital ... served an area of about 5,000 square miles of remote bush country ...". Although crowded at night, during the day "the two open-sided twelve-bedded wards, male and female, were virtually empty. Apart from very ill patients everybody—patients and the relatives caring for them—was outside. Scattered under the acacia trees around the hospital were groups of people, patients and carers, cooking on open fires. The hospital provided a basic diet of maize meal, but everybody cooked for themselves ... water was very short ... The hospital was staffed by two BCMS nurses" and "six 'dressers'—local young men who had been recruited after a few years of Primary schooling, and had then been trained on the job. This small band of staff was caring for about 1,500 in-patients a year, and 36,000 out-patients. The wards were always over-full, with pa- tients and their relatives sleeping at night in, under and between the beds." There was a small op- erating room with a single light bulb, and Dr. Webster added an examination room to replace the former process of squatting to see patients lined up on benches. By 1970, they were treating over 52,000 patients a year. (ibid., pp. 37, 38, 90). Both Doctors Cox and Webster were valued and re- spected by local Pokot.

ENCOUNTERS WITH GOD AND ENEMIES

Ilat, the Thunder God

109 Similarly, Barton ("Notes on the Suk Tribe", 1921, p. 89) noticed that "a certain small plot of to- bacco, apparently growing wild and untouched, is always unviolated, as it is the garden of Ilat. Again, a certain aerated spring of water bubbling from the rocks is called 'the water of Ilat.'"

110 It is not proper for husbands and wives to address one another by their given names. Instead, clan names are often used.

Sub-chief

111 Both Kenya and Uganda were, at the time, divided into Districts, each headed by a District Com- missioner. Districts were divided into Divisions, led by District Officers, and they were, in turn, subdivided into Locations, run by government-appointed Chiefs. Each Chief supervised Sub- Chiefs, who governed small regions within his location. This system of chiefs is not indigenous to the Pokot, who have no traditional governing hierarchy, other than councils of elders (*kokwa*) and the ritual leaders who announce the timing of circumcision rituals. The first Pokot "headmen" (chiefs) were appointed by the British District Officer Juxton Barton after 1918. He also established locations, a representative council and a government court system. Threats were used to force re- luctant elders to accept the positions, and later, young, educated Pokot were appointed. These in- novations were largely ignored by most Pokot, with the exception of the courts, which were useful for disputing issues under government control. Most disputes were still handled, as always, by elders in their *kokwas*. Chiefs and Sub-Chiefs were responsible for government matters like tax col- lection and labor for government projects. They did not seem to enjoy any increased social prestige. Government officials and observers have noted that, although the Pokot willingly paid taxes, they had little interest in waged labor, government appointments, or hierarchical political power, pre- ferring to live the egalitarian pastoral life of their ancestors.

112 Crampton, affectionately remembered by the Pokot (including Domonguria) as "Karamdi", was the District Commissioner from 1913 and during the World War I years (fighting actually occurred in East Africa between the British and Germans in Tanzania.) During that time, the colonial government headquarters was at first Ngabotok, then Kacheliba. From a camp at Wakor, near the Marich Pass, Crampton organized and led the Pokot on a series of highly successful, government-sanctioned raids to subdue the powerful Turkana. Easily the most renowned local British official, Crampton reportedly lived amongst the Pokot and married a Pokot girl with the cattle he raided from the Turkana. The fact that he rewarded and respected the Pokot, defeated their enemy, and did not attempt to interfere with their customs probably accounts for the initial Pokot acceptance of a British government presence (see Schneider, "Pokot Folktales", 1967, p. 291, and Patterson, *The Pokot of Western Kenya,* 1969, p. 14). Ann C. Muir in "Response to Maendeleo—Changing Perceptions Amongst the Pokot of Nginyang in a Period of Transition" (1985), p. 21, speculates that the Pokot, unlike their neighbors, peacefully accepted the British presence in Kenya and paid the imposed taxes "in return for protection from raiders who surrounded them. Since their boundaries were now fixed by a government this was perhaps a very reasoned decision."

Figthing for the Herds

113 Although food was distributed occasionally in Pokot areas since the 1940s, distributions became more regular and expected after the late 1980s, regardless of hunger or prosperity. Politicians have gained influence by bringing in food. This reliance on maize as a substitute for meat, milk, blood and other foods has led to increasing malnutrition (see Bollig, *Risk Management,* 2006, pp. 379-382) and, some feel, has undermined indigenous survival strategies, causing, instead, dependence on government or religious programs.

114 In 1920, a peace meeting between Pokot and Karamojong leaders, including Turkana and Sebei representatives as well, was held at Lokales, near Kacheliba, and was attended by the two District Commissioners, Captain Chidlaw-Roberts of Uganda and Juxton Barton of Kenya. The "right thigh bone of an ox was broken in two. Then, while the tribes' representatives placed their hands on the bones and held up 'native razors', a peace oath was taken, after which the razors were buried." (Barber, *Imperial Frontier,* 1968, p. 199). Barber claims raiding was "greatly reduced" during the next three decades, but Brasnett ("The Karasuk Problem", 1958, p. 118) says the raiding started again in May, 1921 "and continued at a greater pitch than before ..."

DESTRUCTION AND HOPE IN A CHANGING WORLD

Returning Home

115 I have omitted a sentence here, because I was uncertain of the translation. On the tape, Domonguria seems to say, "We took out the fat that we call *siromu* and fastened it around each person's neck." Earlier, however, in the section describing his *sapana,* Domonguria told me that *siromu* was "the bag that holds the stomach." As for Beech (*The Suk,* 1911) and Crazzolara (*A Study of the Pokot (Suk) Language,* 1978), they both define it as "kidney". It is thus unclear what is put around the neck.

Idi Amin

116 Idi Amin was once a Sergeant in charge of an army detachment in Amudat. He was remembered as "a soldier who had been only too happy to shoot up the locals" (Webster, *The Shimmering Heat,* 2007, p. 106).

117 Webster (*The Shimmering Heat,* 2007, p. 110) reports that the Uganda Army "despised the Pokot. Amin had already made his edict about clothing, and any Pokot seen naked or in traditional goat skins was shot on sight. Most of the victims we saw at the hospital were women and children." A similar event was described by Karamojong elders to Dr. Mirzeler "... Amin himself went to Kara-

moja with his soldiers, and gathered people near Moroto: he told them to divide into two groups, those who wanted to wear clothes and those who did not. His soldiers were then instructed to gun down those who refused to wear clothes" (Mustapha Mirzeler and Crawford Young, "Pastoral Politics in the Northeast Periphery in Uganda: AK-47 as Change Agent", 2000, p. 416).

118 Ruth Stranex, originally from South Africa, was one of the two dedicated nurses at Amudat hospital who worked with both doctors Cox and Webster. In about 1970, she "established a hostel for girls, where girls from remote mayattas could live and be cared for while attending the local primary school. Until then, education, such as there was, was almost entirely the preserve of boys." Dr. Webster's wife, Rosemary, also taught "Ruth's girls" sewing on the veranda of their home, each week (Webster, *The Shimmering Heat*, 2007, pp. 34, 84, 127).

119 After Dr. David Webster and his family left Amudat in 1973, Dr. Wattis and his wife, a nurse, ran the hospital until the end of 1975. The dedicated, long-serving nurse Ruth Stranex was deported, the wife of one of the dressers was shot, and a new doctor died in a road accident. Because of the dangerous situation, further doctors were not appointed, but the Ugandan staff tried to maintain the clinic during turbulent times. More recently, Médecins Sans Frontières has worked there. (Webster, *The Shimmering Heat*, 2007, pp. 196-199)

120 Dietz comments, "Amin's take-over in 1971 meant the end of all 'developmentalist' plans. Lack of funds, lack of foreign exchange and lack of expertise, resulted in a virtual breakdown of most facilities … Trade in general collapsed with the expulsion of Indians from Uganda and the breakdown of transportation … Karamoja suffered under a military occupation, with soldiers and co-opting civil servants who used the proceeds of plunder and cattle raiding as their major source of income." (Dietz, *Pastoralists in Dire Straits*, 1987, p. 73)

121 A 1973 anonymous report in *Africa Today*, "Uganda under Military Rule" (Vol. 20, 1973, p. 15), claims, "For over the past year the cattle-keeping Turkana in north-west Kenya have raided almost daily into Uganda for livestock, going as far as one hundred miles inside Uganda ... and the Uganda Army has be unable to deal with them," but also states, "A number of times the (Uganda) Army in pursuit of raiders has crossed over into Kenya, shooting, bombing, and taking revenge against Kenyans on their own territory…"

1976

122 The "men of unknown origin" were Israelis. On July 3 and 4, 1976, Israeli commandos descended on Entebbe airport to free the passengers and crew of an aircraft hijacked by pro-Palestinian radicals and held hostage with Amin's support.

123 At the time I taped this section, the heinous rule of Idi Amin was at its peak. The local District Commissioner showed us photographs of a captured helicopter, which had been used to raid Kenyan cattle. The former school teacher at Katabok, where we had camped, told Domonguria how the residents, our friends, had been hunted down and slaughtered. He had managed to escape.

124 Barton in "Notes on the Suk Tribe" (1921), p. 98, describes a burial: "The sons dig a deep grave in the cattle kraal, make a thatched stick bed, place the body thereon together with his sleeping mat of hide; the head of the corpse is rested on his pillow stool, honey-beer, tobacco and other food beloved by the deceased is placed in the grave by the body. Above the body are laid rafters of sticks; on this upper platform grass is placed, above the grass earth, then stones, then a mound of cow dung, and finally a zariba of thorns to keep away the hyenas and jackals. Suk are buried on their side so that the stomach lies towards the mountain called Mutelo in the Sekerr Mass." According to most researchers, the oldest son usually inherits most of his father's holdings, while the youngest inherits most of the mother's stock. Jonsson in his dissertation "Pokot Masculinity" (2006), pp. 259-263, describes more recent burial practices near Cheptulel, in Kenya.

EPILOGUE by Pat Robbins

125 See Mirzeler and Young ("Pastoral Politics, 2000), Eaton ("Violence, Revenge", 2008b), Dietz (Pastoralists in Dire Straits, 1987) and news reports.

BIBLIOGRAPHY

Commentary by Pat Robbins

The first European explorers to pass through Pokot country were Thomson, Teleki and von Höhnel, whose comments were included in the Preface. After Kenya—together with Uganda—became part of the British East African Protectorate in 1895, travelers and some early government officials made attempts to record their observations about the Pokot. Major Austin ("From Njemps to Marich, Save and Mumia's", 1899) and Colonel Macdonald ("Journeys to the North of Uganda", 1899) appreciated the friendly and helpful individuals at Marich, who decided not to attack their caravans in 1897. Austin mentioned their skillful irrigation system, and Macdonald speculated about their origins. In 1907, Hobley credited the government for stopping Maasai raids on the Pokot. In his 1910 article on the inhabitants of the vast Baringo District, K. R. Dundas described the early migrations of the various peoples who came to be known as "the Suk" and listed some of their customs. Mervyn W. H. Beech, District Officer of the Baringo region from 1909-10, published a general book on Pokot culture and language.

Kenya became a Crown Colony in 1920, while Uganda remained a protectorate until independence in 1962. While supervising the new Kapenguria government post in 1921, Juxton Barton studied and outlined the divisions of Suk culture and politics in order to create and superimpose a British government organization. Twenty-six years later, John G. Peristiany, working as a Government sociologist, conducted fieldwork among the Pokot for six months, sometimes taking excursions from a base camp at Kongolai, near Kacheliba. He published a series of articles on *sapana*, age sets, spiritual beliefs, and other aspects of social structure. John Russell published a charming memoir about his experiences as a District Officer in Sigor from 1957-9.

Harold K. Schneider completed a more extensive anthropological field analysis of the Pokot after living in the Ortum area for ten months in 1951-2. A decade later, Francis P. Conant studied the agriculturalists and pastoralists in the Masol region for a year, observing some customs not mentioned by Domonguria. Robert B. Edgerton examined the values and attitudes of Pokot communities in that area, using interviews and psychological assessments. Our friend David Webster has published a fascinating memoir about his tenure as the lone doctor in Amudat and the surrounding area of Uganda from 1968-73, and his later experiences in Marsabit, Kenya. Anthropologist Elizabeth L. Meyerhoff lived in Kenya's Cherengeni Hills near Sigor from 1972-9 and wrote about the role of Pokot women and the male/female concepts of sexual identity among the agriculturalists. Elizabeth Hasthorpe collected and studied 1000 Pokot songs between 1974 and 1982 in the Chepareria and Ortum areas for her thesis in ethnomusicology. Ann Muir (1985) analyzed a change in power dynamics, resulting from the acceptance of a more sedentary, cash-based, "progressive" lifestyle by many Nginyang Pokot and the marginalization of the egalitarian, pastoral traditionalists. Ton Dietz (1987) listed survival strategies and external interventions in Pokot areas along the Kenya/Uganda border. Michael Bollig, who studied the Pokot in the Baringo District of Kenya from 1987 to 1993, wrote about their egalitarian social and economic ideals, their adaptations to disasters, the more recent destruction wrought by raiding with AK-47s, and impoverishment due to population growth and diminished herds. Historian David Eaton interviewed hundreds of Pokot during 2005 and 2006, and wrote about the history of raiding and peace-making efforts along the Kenya-Uganda border, finding that government interventions were much less effective when the focus turned from individual to communal punishments. Kjartan Jonsson's dissertation recorded in detail many rituals practiced by agrarian Pokot living in Cheptulel, based on three years of research and 11 years as a pastor in that area until 1995.

When I began this project, there were very limited sources about the Pokot, and I never encountered a person who had been interviewed by a researcher. The area is now more accessible, and times have changed. In "Violence, Revenge and the History of Cattle Raiding Along the Kenya Uganda Border, c. 1830-2008", Dr. Eaton comments, "During a market day in Namalu I found myself at the back of a queue of researchers seeking interviews with local elders … In Karamoja, it was rare to meet people who had not been somehow involved in an earlier project regarding raiding or its consequences, and they were often quite aware of contemporary scholarly theories on the subject."

Many other references I have listed relate to specific cultural topics and are self-explanatory. Superb photographs and illustrations of the Pokot and their neighbors appear in the works of Jones, Riccardi, Meyerhoff, Adamson, and Russell. Chesaina Swinimer wrote a beautifully-illustrated children's book about the Pokot. I have also included in this bibliography a selection of references on neighboring peoples mentioned in the text.

When judging the relationship of these works to the present text, it is important to understand that Pokot rituals, songs and folklore will differ somewhat between the residents of the southeast region of the Pokot homeland and the Karapokot of Uganda, like Domonguria, who live in the northwestern corner of

Pokot settlement. Historian Eaton comments, "By the early 1900s, the Kapchorop-ko Pokot may have had more in common with the Pian Karamojong than the Baringo Pokot living further east." Similarly, most authors have recognized variations between the customs of the pastoral Pokot (many of whom, like Domonguria, also farm) and the agricultural Pokot (who also keep stock). Finally, certain rituals described in the literature were more prevalent in the past. The ceremony of the colors so painstakingly described by Peristiany, for example, ceased to be practiced, he says, around 1916, being displaced, somewhat by circumcision-set cycles. At the time of my writing, circumcision, in turn, was no longer a wide-spread prerequisite for either sex or *sapana* among the Karapokot, and a general-ized correlation between age sets, cycles, etc., of the two ceremonies could be misleading. At the time I collected it, Domonguria's autobiography was, I be-lieve, the first detailed account of the "Karapokot" of Uganda. Since then, more people have written about their way of life, while the Karapokot have been bom-barded by outside influences that have threatened and destroyed aspects of their traditions.

List of References

Adamson, Joy
    1967 *The Peoples of Kenya*. London: Collins & Harvill Press.
Africa Today
    1973 "Uganda under Military Rule" *Vol. 20*, No. 2 (1973).
Andersen, Kaj Blegvad
    1977 *African Traditional Architecture: A Study of the Housing and Settlement Patterns of Rural Kenya*. Nairobi, New York: Oxford University Press.
Ambraseys, Nicholas N.
    2007 "Earthquake hazard in the Kenya Rift: the Subukia earthquake of 1928". *Geophysical Journal International* 105(1): 253-269.
Austin, H. H.
    1899 "From Njemps to Marich, Save and Mumia's (British East Africa)". *Geographical Journal* 14: 307-310.
Baker, P. Randall
    1967 *Environmental Influences on Cattle Marketing in Karamoja*. Occasional Paper #5. Kampala: De-partment of Geography, Makerere University College.
    1981 "Development and the Pastoral People of Karamoja, North-Eastern Uganda: an Example of the Treatment of Symptoms". In *Contemporary Anthropology: An Anthology*, edited by Daniel G. Bates and Susan H. Lees, 66-78. New York: Alfred A. Knopf.
Barber, James P.
    1964 "Karamoja in 1910". *Uganda Journal* 28:15-23.
    1968 *Imperial Frontier: A Study of Relations between the British and the Pastoral Tribes of North East Uganda*. Nairobi: East African Publishing House.
Barton, Juxton.
    1921 "Notes on the Suk Tribe of Kenia Colony". *Journal of the Royal Anthropological Institute* 51: 82-99.
Beech, Mervyn W. H.
    1911 *The Suk: Their Language and Folklore*. Oxford: At the Clarendon Press.

Bianco, Barbara
   1991 "Women and Things: Pokot Motherhood as Political Destiny". *American Ethnologist* 18: 770-785.
   1996 "Songs of Mobility in West Pokot". *American Ethnologist* 23(1): 25-42.
   2000 "Gender and Material Culture in West Pokot, Kenya". In *Rethinking Pastoralism in Africa*, edited by Dorothy Hodgson, 29-42. Oxford: James Currey.

Bollig, Michael
   1994 "Pokot Social Organization Structures, Networks and Ideology". In *Sprachen Und Sprachzergnisse in Afrika*, edited by T. Geider and R. Kastenholz, 63-86. Cologne, Germany: Rudiger Koppe.
   1998 "Moral Economy and Self-Interest: Kinship, Friendship, and Exchange Among the Pokot (N. W. Kenya)". In *Kinship, Networks, and Exchange*, edited by T. Schweizer and D. White, 137-57. Cambridge: Cambridge University Press.
   2000 "Staging Social Structures: Ritual and Social Organisation in an Egalitarian Society. The Pastoral Pokot of Kenya". *Ethnos* 65(3): 341-365.
   2006 *Risk Management in a Hazardous Environment: A Comparative Study of Two Pastoral Societies.* New York: Springer Science and Business Media, Inc.

Bollig, Michael and Matthias Osterle
   2007 "We Turned our Enemies into Baboons: Warfare, Ritual and Pastoral Identity among the Pokot of Northern Kenya". In *The Practice of War: Production, Reproduction and Communication of Armed Violence*, edited by A. Rao, M. Bollig and M. Bock, 23-51. New York: Berghahn Books.

Bone, Neil
   2005 "Sky Notes: 2005 October and November". *Journal of the British Astronomical Association* 115(5): 298-299.

Brasnett, J.
   1958 "The Karasuk Problem". *Uganda Journal* 22(2): 112-122.

Brown, Jean
   1975 Unpublished list and description of a collection of Kurut Agricultural Pokot artifacts at the Michigan State University Museum, Accession No. 4434. East Lansing.

Chaundy, G. H.
   1948 "The West Suk of Kenya: Teaching a Primitive Tribe to be Better Farmers". *Canadian Geographical Journal* 36(2): 94-101.

Chesaina Swinimer, Ciarunji
   1994 *The Heritage Library of African Peoples: Pokot.* New York: The Rosen Publishing Group, Inc.

Conant, Francis P.
   1965 "Karok: A Variable Unit of Physical and Social Space among the Pokot of East Africa". *American Anthropologist* 67(2): 429-434.
   1966 "The External Coherence of Pokot Ritual Behavior". *Philosophical Transactions of the Royal Society of London,* Series B, 251(772): 505-519.
   1974 "Frustration, Marriage Alternatives and Subsistence Risks Among the Pokot of East Africa: Impressions of Co-Variance". *Anthropological Quarterly* 47(3): 314-327.

Crazzolara, J. P.
   1978 *A Study of the Pokot (Suk) Language.* Bologna: Editrice Missionaria Italiana.

Dietz, Ton
   1987 *Pastoralists in Dire Straits: Survival Strategies and External Interventions in a Semi-Arid Region at the Kenya/Uganda Border: Western Pokot, 1900-1986.* Netherlands Geographical Studies; 49. Amsterdam: Koninklijk Nederlands Aardrijkskundig Genootschap; Instituut voor Sociale Geografie, University of Amsterdam.

Docherty, A. J.
   1957 "The Karamojong and the Suk". *Uganda Journal* 220: 76-89.

Dundas, K. R.
   1910 "Notes on the Tribes Inhabiting the Baringo District, East Africa Protectorate". *The Journal of the Royal Anthropological Institute* 40: 49-72.

Dyson-Hudson, Neville
    1958 "The Karamojong and the Suk". *Uganda Journal* 22(2): 173-180.
    1966 *Karamojong Politics*. Oxford: Clarendon Press.
Dyson-Hudson, V. Rada and Neville Dyson-Hudson
    1969 "Subsistence Herding in Uganda". *Scientific American* 220: 2-11.
Dyson-Hudson, V. Rada
    1960 "East Coast Fever in Karamoja". *Uganda Journal* 24(2): 253-259.
Eaton, David
    2008a "The Business of Peace: Raiding and Peace Work along the Kenya-Uganda Border, Parts I and II". *African Affairs* 107: 89-110, 243-259.
    2008b "Violence, Revenge and the History of Cattle Raiding Along the Kenya Uganda Border, c.1830-2008". PhD Dissertation. Halifax: Dalhousie University.
Edgerton, Robert B.
    1971 *The Individual in Cultural Adaptation: A Study of Four East African Peoples*. Berkeley: University of California Press.
    1994 "Pokot Intersexuality: An East African Example of the Resolution of Sexual Incongruity". *American Anthropologist* 66 (6): 1288-1299.
Edgerton, Robert B. and Francis P. Conant
    1964 "Kilapat: the 'Shaming Party' Among the Pokot of East Africa". *Southwestern Journal of Anthropology* 20(4): 404-418.
Gray, Richard
    1965 "Eclipse Maps". *Journal of African History* 6(3): 259-260.
Gregory, Robert G., Robert M. Maxon and Leon P. Spencer
    1968 *A Guide to the Kenya National Archives: to the microfilms of the provincial and district annual reports, record books, and handing-over reports, miscellaneous correspondence, and intelligence reports*. Syracuse, N.Y.: Program of Eastern African Studies, Syracuse University.
Gulliver, P. H.
    1955 *The Family Herds, A Study of Two Pastoral Tribes in East Africa, the Jie and Turkana*. London: Routledge & Kegan Paul.
Gulliver, Pamela and P. H. Gulliver
    1957 *The Central Nilo-Hamites*. London: International African Institute.
Hasthorpe, Elizabeth
    1983 "A Study of Pokot Songs". PhD Dissertation. London: School of Oriental and African Studies.
Hennings, Richard Owen
    1951 *African Morning*. London: Chatto and Windus.
    1961 "Grazing Management in the Pastoral Areas of Kenya". *Journal of African Administration* 13(4): 191-203.
Hobley, C. W.
    1906 "Notes on the Geography and People of the Baringo District of East Africa Protectorate". *The Geographical Journal* 28(5): 471-481.
Höhnel, Ludwig von
    1892 *Discovery of Lakes Rudolf and Stefanie: A Narrative of Count Samuel Teleki's Exploring and Hunting Expedition in Eastern Equatorial Africa in 1887 and 1888*, (Vol. 2). Translated by Nancy Bell, 1968. London: Frank Cass & Co.
Huntingford, G. W. B.
    1969 *The Southern Nilo-Hamites*. London: International African Institute.
Jonsson, Kjartan
    2006 "Pokot Masculinity: The Role of Rituals in Forming Men". PhD Dissertation. Reykjavik: Faculty of Social Sciences, University of Iceland.
Jones, David Keith
    1984 *Shepherds of the Desert*. London: Elm Tree Books.
Kenya Government
    1970 Kenya Population Census 1969, Vol. 1. Nairobi: Statistics Division, Ministry of Finance and Economic Planning.

Kenya National Archives
1965   Kenya Government Papers. Nairobi: Kenya Government Printing Office. (Accessible in microform in the Michigan State University and Syracuse University libraries).
   1913-1920 Turkana and Suk Annual Reports 1054-1059.
   1920-1941 West Suk District Handing Over Reports 1087-1100, 1111-1112.
   1922-1927 Rift Valley Province Intelligence Reports. Suk-Kamasia Reserve (Kerio Province): West Suk District 84, 91, 97, 104.
   1924-1960 West Suk District Annual Reports 1062-1099, 2557-2561
   1930-1954 West Pokot District Miscellaneous Correspondence 288-311.
   1936-1938 Turkana District Monthly Intelligence Reports 469-472.
   1936-1951 West Suk Monthly Intelligence Reports 115-126.
   1939   Rift Valley Province Intelligence Report (Baringo District) 106.
   1947-1952 Rift Valley Province Handing Over Reports of West Suk 1048, 1051, 1053, 1061, 1064, 1072.
   1957-1962 West Pokot District Handing Over Reports 950-958.
   1961   West Pokot District Annual Report 2565.

Kipkorir, B. E.
   1973 *The Marakwet of Kenya: A Preliminary Study*. Nairobi: East African Literature Bureau.

Lamphear, John
   1976 *The Traditional History of the Jie of Uganda*. Oxford: Clarendon Press.
   1992 *The Scattering Time: Turkana Responses to Colonial Rule*. Oxford: Clarendon Press.

Laughlin, Charles D. and Elizabeth R. Allgeier
   1979 *An Ethnography of the So of Northeastern Uganda*, Vol.1 & 2. New Haven: Human Relations Area Files, Inc.

Maisonhaute, Jannick
   2000 "The East Pastoral Pokot Sapana Ceremony". *Rites et Religion: Les cahiers de l"IFRA* 18: 1-47. Nairobi: French Institute for Research in Africa.

Macdonald, J. R. L.
   1899 "Journeys to the North of Uganda". *The Geographical Journal* 14(2): 129-148.

MacDougall, David and Judith MacDougall
   1978-1981 *Turkana Conversations Film Project: The Wedding Camels, Lorang's Way* and *A Wife Among Wives*. Berkeley: University of California Extension Media Center.

McCabe, J. Terrence
   2004 *Cattle Bring Us to Our Enemies: Turkana Ecology, Politics, and Raiding in a Disequilibrium System*. Ann Arbor: The University of Michigan Press.

Meyerhoff, Elizabeth L.
   1981 "The Socio-Economic and Ritual Roles of Pokot Women". PhD Dissertation. Cambridge: Lucy Cavendish College.
   1982 "The Threatened Ways of Kenya's Pokot People". *National Geographic* 161(1): 120-140.

Mirzeler, Mustafa, and Crawford Young
   2000 "Pastoral Politics in the Northeast Periphery in Uganda: AK-47 as Change Agent". *The Journal of Modern African Studies* 38(3): 407-429.

Muir, C. Ann
   1985 "Response to Maendeleo – Changing Perceptions Amongst the Pokot of Nginyang in a Period of Transition". M. A. Thesis. Edinburgh: Centre of African Studies, Edinburgh University.

Patterson, K. David
   1969 *The Pokot of Western Kenya 1910-1963: The Response of A Conservative People to Colonial Rule*. Syracuse University Program of Eastern African Studies, Occasional paper no. 53. Syracuse: Syracuse University.

Peristiany, John G.
   1951a "The Age-Set System of the Pastoral Pokot: The Sapana Initiation Ceremony". *Africa: Journal of the International African Institute* 21(3): 188-206.
   1951b "The Age-Set System of the Pastoral Pokot: Mechanism, Function and Post-Sapana Ceremonies". *Africa: Journal of the International African Institute* 21(4): 279-301.

1954 "Pokot Sanctions and Structure". *Africa: Journal of the International African Institute* 24: 17-25.

1975 "The Ideal and the Actual: The Role of Prophets in the Pokot Political System". In *Studies in Social Anthropology*, edited by J. H. M. Beattie and R. G. Lienhardt. Oxford: At the Clarendon Press.

Porter, Philip W.

1963 "Suk Views on Suk Environment". *Annals of the Association of American Geographers* 53: abstract.

2004 *Indigenous Democracy: Traditional Conflict Resolution Mechanisms: Pokot, Turkana, Samburu and Marakwet.* Nairobi: Intermediate Technology Development Group—Eastern Africa.

Ricciardi, Mirella

1971 *Vanishing Africa.* New York: Reynal & Co./William Morrow & Co., Inc.

Robbins, Martha E.

2005 "Pokot Dance". *The International Encyclopedia of Dance.* Selma Jean Cohen and Dance Perspectives Foundation. Oxford: Oxford University Press.

Robbins, Lawrence H. and Martha E. Robbins

1971 "A Note on Turkana Dancing". *Ethnomusicology* 15(2): 231-235.

Russell, John

1994 *Kenya, Beyond the Marich Pass: A District Officer's Story.* London, New York: The Radcliffe Press.

Schneider, Harold K.

1953 "The Pakot (Suk) of Kenya with Special Reference to the Role of Livestock in their Subsistence Economy". PhD Dissertation. Evanston, Illinois: Northwestern University.

1955 "The Moral System of the Pakot". In *Encyclopedia of Morals*, edited by V. Ferm, 403-409. New York: Philosophical Library.

1956 "The Interpretation of Pakot Visual Art". *Man* 56: 103-106.

1957 "The Subsistence Role of Cattle Among the Pakot and in East Africa". *American Anthropologist* 59(2): 278-300.

1959 "Pakot Resistance to Change". In *Continuity and Change in African Cultures*, edited by W. R. Bascom and M. J. Herskovits, 144-167. Chicago: The University of Chicago Press.

1964 "Economics in East African Aboriginal Societies". In *Economic Transition in Africa*, edited by M. J. Herskovits and M. Harwitz, 53-75. Evanston, Illinois: Northwestern University Press.

1967 "Pokot Folktales, Humor, and Values". *Journal of the Folklore Institute* 4(2/3): 265-318.

1974 "Economic Development and Economic Change: The Case of East African Cattle". *Current Anthropology* 15: 259-265.

1979 *Livestock and Equality in East Africa: The Economic Basis for Social Structure.* Bloomington: Indiana University Press.

Schulze, H., A. Bischoff, H. Palme, B. Spettel, G. Dreibus, and J. Otto

1994 "Mineralogy and Chemistry of Rumuruti: The First Meteorite Fall of the New R Chondrite Group". *Meteorites* 29(2): 275-286.

Schwabe, Calvin W.

1984 "A Unique Surgical Operation on the Horns of African Bulls in Ancient and Modern Times". *Agricultural History* 58(2): 138-156.

Teleki, Count Samuel

1965 "East African Diaries of Count Samuel Teleki" (1886-95). Translated by Count Charles Teleki Sr., and Vera Teleki. Unpublished manuscript. Michigan State University Library Special Collections.

Thomson, Joseph

1885 *Through Maasailand: A Journey of Exploration Among the Snowclad Volcanic Mountains and Strange Tribes of Eastern Equatorial Africa, Being the Narrative of the Royal Geographical Society's Expedition to Mount Kenia and Lake Victoria Nyanza, 1883-1884.* London: Sampson Low, Marston Searle and Rivington.

Timberlake, Jonathan

1994 "Vernacular Names and Uses of Plants in Northern Kenya". *Journal of East African Natural History* 83: 31-69.

Turpin, C. A.
  1948 "The Occupation of the Turkwel River Area by the Karamojong Tribe". *Uganda Journal* 12(2): 161-165.

Uganda Government
  1971 *Uganda 1969 Population Census, Provisional Results.* Entebbe: Ministry of Planning and Community Development, Statistics Division.

Usher-Wilson, L. C.
  1952 "Dini Ya Misambwa". *Uganda Journal* 16: 125-129.

Vries, Kim de
  2007 "Identity Strategies of the Agro-Pastoral Pokot. Analysing Ethnicity and Clanship within a Spatial Framework". M.A. Thesis. Faculty of Social and Behavioural Sciences, Department of Human Geography, Planning and International Development Studies, University of Amsterdam.

Wakefield, Thomas and Keith Johnson
  1870 "Routes of Native Caravans from the Coast to the Interior of Eastern Africa, Chiefly from Information Given by Sadi Bin Ahedi, a Native of a District near Gazi, in Udigo, a Little North of Zanzibar". *Journal of the Royal Geographical Society of London* XL: 303-339.

Weatherby, John M.
  1969 "A Preliminary Note on the Sorat (Tepeth)". *Uganda Journal* 33(1): 75-78.

Webster, David
  2007 *The Shimmering Heat: Memories of a Bush Doctor in East Africa.* Rushden, England: Stanley L. Hunt. Available from David Webster, The Grange, Longdon Hill End, Upton-Upon-Severn, Worchester WR8 0RN, England.

Whitehead, E. F.
  1950 "A Short History of Uganda Military Units formed during World War II". *Uganda Journal* 14(1): 1-14.

Williams, John G.
  1963 *A Field Guide to the Birds of East and Central Africa.* London: Collins.

Yadeta, Girma
  1985 "Dynamic Processes of Development in Marginal Areas: A Case Study from the Pokot of North West Kenya". PhD Dissertation. Lund: The Royal University of Lund, Sweden, Department of Geograpy.

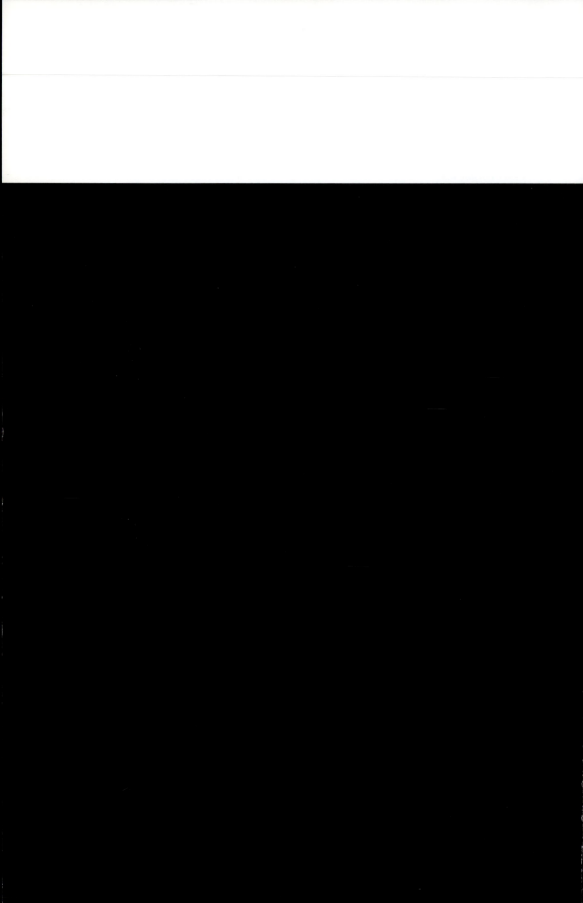

PHOTO

ESSAY

All photos were taken by Pat Robbins or at her request in 1970 and 1976, with the exception of the photos reproduced from Merwyn W.H. Beech's book, *The Suk: Their Language and Folklore* (1911)

Excavation, Kadam Mountain

Camp visitors

Domonguria sorts artifacts

Domonguria and friend by the campfire

Grinding grain

Author Robbins shows a photo to children

Big sister

Woman, children at home

Girls tend to young siblings

Domonguria, children

Moving in Turkana

Children's play village

Domonguria by storage hut in cave

Termite mound

Preparing for termite harvest

False entrance in termite hill

Large grain baskets in cave

The homestead

Students singing with Katabok school teacher at his house

Dance

Women singing at dance

Men's ox dance

The young woman on the right was circumcised during our stay at Katabok (note her shaved head and absence of wire necklaces). The metal jewelry and clothing worn by her friend (two views) shows that she is already circumcised and perhaps married.

The young man on the left is wearing a clay headdress, showing he has had *sapana*, but he has not yet applied the *atoro* on the top of his head. Note his finger ring knife, used for general cutting. His friend on the right sports a coiffure decorated in the back with bangles.

Pokot woman

Men with spears and bow

Pokot cattle

Domonguria, Katabok neighbors
(Chepuseipei is 4th from left. See her song and story on pp. 214-215.)

Women and children waiting to be blessed

Men wait together

COMET CEREMONY OF BLESSING

Neighbors watch as Robbins is anointed with chyme

Men's prayer circle

Man sleeping in front of Katabok school

Cattle returning from pasture

1976: Domonguria's family.
Men have removed their headdresses and women have removed their coiled metal jewelry.
Domonguria is dressed for town. Simon (far left) is a student.

Amumur dance (facing p. 22, Beech)

The *siolop* headdress (facing p. 36, Beech)

Lowalan, renowned warrior, wearing ostrich feather headdress (facing p. 6, Beech). See song and story on pp. 72-73, and endnote 47, this volume.

Man wearing *aparparat* (nose ornament) and fether headdress (facing p. 3, Beech)

Fixing a headdress (facing p. 31, Beech)

The *siolop* headdress, en face (facing p. 38, Beech)

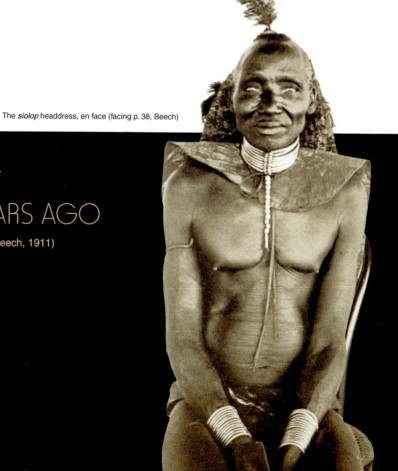

POKOT
100 YEARS AGO

(reprinted from Beech, 1911)